SEX, LOVE, AND LETTERS

Sex, Love, and Letters

Writing Simone de Beauvoir

Judith G. Coffin

Cornell University Press
Ithaca and London

First published 2020 by Cornell University Press

Printed in the United States of America

Library of Congress Cataloging-in-Publication Data

Names: Coffin, Judith G., 1952– author.
Title: Sex, love, and letters : writing Simone de Beauvoir / Judith G. Coffin.
Description: Ithaca [New York] : Cornell University Press, 2020. | Includes bibliographical references and index.
Identifiers: LCCN 2020005876 (print) | LCCN 2020005877 (ebook) | ISBN 9781501750540 (cloth) | ISBN 9781501750557 (epub) | ISBN 9781501750564 (pdf)
Subjects: LCSH: Beauvoir, Simone de, 1908–1986—Correspondence. | Authors, French—20th century—Correspondence. | Authors and readers—France—History—20th century.
Classification: LCC PQ2603.E362 Z48 2020 (print) | LCC PQ2603. E362 (ebook) | DDC 848/.91409—dc23
LC record available at https://lccn.loc.gov/2020005876
LC ebook record available at https://lccn.loc.gov/2020005877

To the memory of Vi and Ned Coffin, Margot
Coffin Lindsay, and Bill Coffin

CONTENTS

Acknowledgments

This book turned out to be harder to write than my first exhilarating encounter with the archive of readers' letters to Simone de Beauvoir suggested. It is a pleasure to thank the colleagues, friends, and institutions that have been helpful for so many years. My first debt of gratitude is to the Radcliffe Institute for Advanced Study, and especially the late, beloved Judith Vishniac, for getting this project launched. Ellen Fitzpatrick, Helen and Dan Horowitz, Susan Faludi, and Russ Rymer, my colleagues during that year at Radcliffe kept it going. I am grateful to Alan Tully and Jacqueline Jones, chairs of the history department at UT Austin, who allowed me to take leave when the chances arrived, and to the Institute of Historical Studies at UT, which provided an internal fellowship. Special thanks to Nancy Cott for her support, expert advice, warmth, and friendship for so many years.

Along the way, any number of friends and colleagues have provided a critique, comment, or insight that landed at just the right moment. Those include Darcy Vebber and Andy Romanoff; Hervé Picherit, Evan Carton, and Alex Wettlaufer; Leora Auslander and Thomas Holt; Tamara Chaplin, Herrick Chapman, Indrani Chatterjee, Carolyn Eastman, Seth Koven, Sheryl Kroen, Lisa Leff, Philippa Levine, John Merriman, Mark Meyers, Mark Micale, Lou Roberts, Marine Rouch, Joan Scott, Todd Shepard, Judith Surkis, and Jim Sidbury. They may not recognize their contributions, but I vividly remember each of them. Sandrine Sanos and Dan Sherman have endured sporadic barrages of questions from me, and they have responded with the kind of patience and humor one usually gets only from family. Thanks to them for being such good friends. I am especially grateful to the Friday afternoon writing group: Tracie Matysik, who has been its organizer, Ben Brower, Yoav Di-Capua, Sabine Hake, and Joan Neuberger. All are perceptive readers, ace editors, and excellent friends. Samantha Pinto was a font of energy and good ideas during the last year of writing.

I count myself lucky to have had gifted students, now colleagues, who helped with archival research and references, visual materials, computer glitches, or tricky concepts: Katie Anania, Matthew Bunn, Elizabeth Garver, Sarah Le Pichon, Mary Katherine Matalon, Michael Schmidt, and Evan Spritzer. It is hard to imagine the final stages of putting the book together without the blazingly efficient and indomitable Amy Vidor.

Thanks to Alice Kaplan, Emma Kuby, and Sharon Marcus, formerly anonymous, outside readers for Cornell University Press, who took time away from their lives and work to give such generous comments on the draft of the manuscript. Emily Andrew understood this project right away, perhaps because she is such a wonderful reader and appreciates what readers can bring to writers. It has been a pleasure to work with her and the whole team at Cornell University Press. A generous subvention grant from the Office of the President at the University of Texas at Austin has helped to defray the cost of publication.

It has become commonplace to photograph hundreds of documents in archives and work on them at home. The letters on which this book is based cannot be reproduced in any form. That has meant spending many summers working in Paris, which, as my fellow French historians know, is not always as glamorous as it sounds. I am grateful to the curators in the manuscripts division at the Bibliothèque Nationale, Mauricette Berne and Anne Mary, who helped with the archive, even as it was barely catalogued. Above all, I am very grateful for the time I have had with my long-standing friends and their families. Over many years, they have supplied nearly boundless camaraderie, festive meals, comfortable beds, historical information, and research clues. The late Dr. Cécile Goldet gave me an inside look at the life of an ob/gyn during the 1950s and 1960s, setting up clinics and smuggling contraceptives into France. Catherine Fermand, Jean-Philippe Pfertzel, and Julia Pfertzel, Martine Méjean and Pierre Goldet, Kattalin and Jean-Michel Gabriel, and Joel Dyon and Lydia Zerbib—thank you all for everything.

I am at a loss for words that will adequately thank Willy Forbath. He has read every part of this book, and some parts many times. Any phrase that seems well-turned or any particularly precise formulation probably bears his mark. His perceptiveness on so many subjects is matched only by his patience, enthusiasm for others' ideas, and wry wisdom in everyday matters. He has made this book better in every way, and the same goes for my life. Zoey and Aaron Forbath will attest to that, but they also deserve their own thanks for being such reliably good kids and, now, warm, funny, and smart adults. Thanks to Haley Perkins, Tom Langer, and, most recently, Henry Forbath Langer for bringing such joy to the family.

In the name of generational continuity, I dedicate this book to the memory of my parents, Ned and Vi Coffin, my aunt Margot Coffin Lindsay, and my uncle Bill Coffin. They had high standards, and they were good writers. They liked what they read of this book, and though it is too late to tell them, that meant the world to me.

A Note on Translations and Abbreviations

Translations of the letters are my own. So are the translations from the memoirs. The volumes are abbreviated as follows:

JFR: *Mémoires d'une jeune fille rangée* (Gallimard, 1958), in English, *Memoirs of a Dutiful Daughter*

FA: *La force de l'âge* (Gallimard, 1960), in English, *The Prime of Life*

FC: *La force des choses*, 2 vols. (Gallimard, 1963), in English, *The Force of Circumstance*

TCF: *Tout compte fait* (Gallimard, 1972), in English, *All Said and Done*

For *The Second Sex*, I have tacked between the 1953 translation by H. M. Parshley (Vintage edition, Random House, 1989) and the 2009 translation by Constance Borde and Sheila Malovany-Chevallier (Knopf, 2009), *TSS* 1953 and *TSS* 2009, respectively. I have provided page numbers for both translations and for the French editions *DS1* and *DS2*. Both English translations have been assailed, and the stakes of those debates are high, or at least bound up in the philosophical understanding of Beauvoir. Fortunately, the most important contributions to this debate have now been gathered up into one volume: Bonnie Mann and Martina Ferrari, eds., *On ne naît pas femme, on le devient: The Life of a Sentence* (New York: Oxford University Press, 2017). See especially section two and the articles by Margaret Simons, Toril Moi, Nancy Bauer, and Meryl Altman.

Thanks to *French Politics, Culture & Society* and the *American Historical Review* for allowing me to use some previously published material:

"Historicizing *The Second Sex*," *French Politics, Culture & Society* 25, no. 3 (Winter 2007): 123–48.
"Beauvoir, Kinsey, and Mid-Century Sex," *French Politics, Culture & Society* 28, no. 2 (Summer 2010): 18–37.
"Sex, Love, and Letters: Writing Simone de Beauvoir, 1949–1963," *American Historical Review* 115, no. 4 (October 2010): 1061–88.

Sex, Love, and Letters

INTRODUCTION

What I wanted was to penetrate so deeply into the lives of others that
when they heard my voice they would have the impression they were
speaking to themselves.

SIMONE DE BEAUVOIR, *The Prime of Life* (1960)

Nothing prepared me for the drama I found the first time I opened a
folder of readers' letters to Simone de Beauvoir. Perhaps it built from the
suspense leading up to that encounter: an uncatalogued archive, not yet
open to the public, a reputedly mercurial curator (who turned out to be
warm and extremely helpful), the flights of red-carpeted stone stairs and
the velvet-curtained glass door that leads to the manuscripts room in the
majestic Bibliothèque Nationale de France (BNF) on the rue de Richelieu,
the long ritual of swapping my library card for a *plaque* and the *plaque* for
a *fiche* and waiting in line to exchange the *fiche* for a folder of documents,
being issued a stubby yellow pencil and warned not to take any pictures.
It may have been my naïveté: I hadn't thought hard about what to expect.
I was reviewing new work on *The Second Sex* and was simply following
up on an intriguing article written by the curator of the collection she was
putting in order.[1] In any event, I was riveted to my chair for the rest of
day. What I found was an outpouring of projection, identification, expectation, disappointment, and passion. Men as well as women wanted to meet

Beauvoir, to share their memories or to share in hers.[2] They asked for advice on marriage, love, and birth control; they confessed secrets and sent sections of their diaries for her to read. The letter writers' tone was unexpected as well, alternately deferential and defiant, seductive, and wry.

What elicited this range of letters? Was it twentieth-century celebrity culture? Beauvoir's subject matter and the gripping combination of serious philosophical discussion and female testimony? Her "scandalous" persona as an independent woman? Was it who the *letter writers* were and what they were seeking: their ambitions or predicaments, the particular matters they needed to work through with her? Was it the historical moment: the search for personal and collective self-knowledge, the multiplying cultural "incitements to discourse" about the self and sexuality, the disconcerting transformation of gender roles and expectations in postwar France and beyond? Did Beauvoir herself ask for this kind of response? Those questions launched this book. *Sex, Love, and Letters* uses this virtually unexplored archive to examine the relationships that bind readers to authors and vice versa.[3] It is about both the lives of literature and theory and also the place of literature and theory in life. The letters put us in an unfamiliar vantage point; Beauvoir's work appears transformed as it becomes a way to see her readers and, through them, into the postwar world. Joan Scott puts it well: "The archive is a provocation; its contents offer an endless resource for thinking and rethinking."[4]

These letters disclose an exceptionally interesting author-reader intimacy, one that was consciously nurtured by the author as well as her readers. It was made intimate by the subjects discussed and the dense exchange of ideas, feelings, fantasies, and experiences. That this intimacy was largely imagined did not detract from its intensity. On the contrary: it was enabled by absence, distance, and the epistolary. The psychological processes of projection, recognition and misrecognition, inventing an interlocutor, styling oneself as a confidant, spinning out inner monologues—all the creative possibilities encouraged by reading and writing, writing letters in particular—account for much of the richness of this correspondence and the tenaciousness of the mutual attachment.

This intimacy was also an intellectual collaboration. Sylvie Le Bon, Beauvoir's adopted daughter and executor of her estate, helped transfer the correspondence to the Bibliothèque Nationale. In an article introducing the collection, Le Bon marveled at Beauvoir's fascination with her readers' letters: "How does a writer plunge herself into these existences that are unknown to her?"[5] Le Bon's self-conscious Beauvoirian wording—"existences"—signals that something philosophical is at stake. Beauvoir stashed these letters haphazardly in bags and boxes, but the fact that she saved them and created this archive is not random. It is a mark of what Beauvoir believed about writing, life, and philosophy. To reflect on the singularity of one's experience or situation, to describe and thereby unfold the meaning of what is given, and thus to come to consciousness of the world was, for her, the philosophical point of existentialism and phenomenology. That belief lay behind *The Second Sex*, which explored what it meant to say "I am a woman." It was one of the motivations for the long series of autobiographical volumes that set out her experience of creating a reality in the world. It also animated her interest in these readers. As Beauvoir repeatedly argued, readers' letters gave her work its truth and anchored it in the world. What is more, these ordinary people's attempts to describe themselves, to present their existences and situations, and to consider what it meant to be human were the stuff of philosophy.[6] For all these reasons, the readers' letters mattered to Beauvoir, they mattered to their authors, and they also matter to us. They are an archive of the existential condition of the postwar, co-produced by Beauvoir and her readers. They were generated by the cultural, intellectual, and political history of the distinctly tumultuous decades after World War II, which they also help us to reinterpret.

New histories of Europe have underscored just how long the "postwar" era lasted and how multifaceted and difficult it was.[7] The dawning horrors of that war—especially but not only the Holocaust—spurred urgent intellectual inquiry into the human condition. Stunningly rapid economic and social change upended gender relations and women's and men's expectations for their futures. The slow-rolling explosion of movements against colonialism, for civil rights, and for women's and gay liberation shook the structures of domestic as well as world politics. These changes had ramifications that fused the geopolitical and the personal, pressing people (whether intellectuals or not) to think and talk about their lives and selves. Readers' letters to Beauvoir highlight the postwar collision of tradition and rapid change. They capture thoughtful, ordinary people's efforts to fashion new selves as well the significant social, cultural, and psychological impediments to doing so. Mark Greif calls his history of mid-twentieth-century philosophical thought *The Age of the Crisis of Man* and rightly emphasizes the "tyrannizing uniformity and concealment of differences" in that discourse.[8] Readers' letters to Beauvoir reveal some of the existential turmoil of that age and of the struggle against the abstractions of Man—and Woman. The letters underscore the dense entangling of highbrow philosophizing, middlebrow literature, and popular introspection. They infuse thought with feeling and join historical developments to personal life.

Beauvoir sustained this remarkable rapport with the public over several generations, no small feat for an author. This book follows Beauvoir's relationship with her readers from 1949 to 1972, that is, from the publication of *The Second Sex* (1949) through *Memoirs of a Dutiful Daughter* (1958), *The Prime of Life* (1960), *The Force of Circumstance* (1963), and the retrospective autobiographical coda, *All Said and Done* (1972), which deepened and personalized the arguments of *The Second Sex* and sent new generations of readers back to it.[9] Beauvoir wrote much more than this, of course: novels, plays, short stories, and scores of essays on literature, ethics, politics, and philosophy. *Sex, Love, and Letters* centers on the exchanges with her readers and the writing that occasioned most of them, namely, *The Second Sex* and the volumes of memoir.

Beauvoir herself speculated about a book based on this correspondence. In her journal in June 1958 she confided:

> Letters. One from a Romanian woman, married, mother of two grown children, former militant against fascism and in the Communist Party, appalled by the execution of Nagy [Imre Nagy, leader of the failed Hungarian revolt against Soviet domination in 1956] and complaining about her life. She doesn't have anything to do, she has nothing she can act on. So many correspondents say the same thing: it is dreadful to be a woman. I was right when I wrote *The Second Sex*, even more so than I thought. If one pieced together passages from the letters I have gotten since that book, one would have a harrowing [*navrant*] document.[10]

The letters in this archive offer much more than this passage leads us to expect. They do provide perspectives on the condition of women in the 1950s and 1960s. They describe struggles with political powerlessness and low expectations, the confusing experiences of inhabiting a female body, the ignorance and fears surrounding sexuality, the gothic dramas of marriage, and so on. They also confront the many other issues that roiled the everyday lives of men as well as women in the postwar world, from the prosaic to the political: sickness, aging, housing and family, sexual and gender identities, Cold War tensions, colonial violence, and ethical commitments. They do not confirm that Beauvoir's analysis, whether in *The Second Sex* or elsewhere, was "right." The letter writers are as articulate about the limits of her concepts as they are revealing about their capaciousness. The readers show why Beauvoir remained such a magnetic figure for such a long time. They also reveal themselves as astute and provocative figures in their own right, however, and they show their epistolary relationship with Simone de Beauvoir to be a fascinating episode in the history of philosophy, feminism, culture, and politics.

Simone de Beauvoir probably needs little introduction. *The Second Sex* (1949) has been called "one of the most important cultural re-evaluations of all time."[11] In 1949, in a continent trying to repair a shredded culture and rebuild democracy, and in a nation that had only granted women the vote in 1944, she insisted that the question of women's equality and freedom had to be entirely rethought, as a particular form of the human condition. *The Second Sex* reconceived women's being as a "situation," "lived experience," or, perhaps most effectively, a dynamic process of becoming. "One is not born, but rather becomes, a woman." This terse and elegant sentence would become one of the canonical formulations of second-wave feminism. It remains one way to easily sum up the meaning of gender, though Beauvoir did not use the term and a distinction between sex and gender does not map well onto her thought.[12] *The Second Sex* took up the myths and structures in which "feminine" and "masculine" are embedded, casting a searchlight over Western culture: literature, family and kinship, economic systems, history, generations, psychological structures, experiences of growing up and growing old, and subjectivity. It laid bare the shortcomings of the reigning theories of gender inequality— liberalism, Marxism, and psychoanalytic theory—and set about constructing a systematic philosophical alternative. In this sense Beauvoir began to make feminist theory an enterprise in its own right.[13] *The Second Sex* defied mid-twentieth-century taboos on speaking of female sexuality. That a woman philosopher would write seriously and in detail about the female sexual experience prompted the distinguished conservative French writer François Mauriac to say to one of Beauvoir's colleagues at the journal *Les Temps Modernes* that "we all know now about the vagina and clitoris of your boss."[14] Mauriac's comment is now infamous, but as we will see in chapter 1, it only hints at the charged discussion of "decency" sparked by *The Second Sex* in 1949. Beauvoir did more than tread on territory that was taboo; she changed our understanding of how inequality and women's Otherness shaped sexuality as lived experience. In other words, she framed a new politics of sexuality. Second-wave feminism from the 1960s on would pursue the issues Beauvoir raised, examining first how sexuality and gender were intertwined, constructed, reproduced, and lived, and then, in more recent times, demonstrating the instability of sexuality and gender as categories. Even apart from their place in the history of later twentieth-century feminism, Beauvoir's rich theories of subjectivity, consciousness, embodiment, and feeling make her work a nearly inexhaustible subject of theoretical interest.

Beauvoir's life (1908–1986) was also extraordinary. She chronicled it herself, first in *The Mandarins*, a novel about intellectual and political life in postwar Paris, and then in three remarkable volumes of memoirs— *Memoirs of a Dutiful Daughter* (1958), *The Prime of Life* (1960), and *The Force of Circumstance* (1963)—followed by a coda, or reflective summary of her life, *All Said and Done* (1972). In 1918, the memoirs were republished in the prestigious series, the Bibliothèque de la Pléiade, the pantheon of French literature, a tribute to Beauvoir's ability to capture both the life of a writer and the centrality of *life* to literature and thought. The memoirs are a remarkable combination of autobiography, existential reflection, and historical chronicle. They were the works that established the dialogue and intimacy so clearly revealed in this archive. *Sex, Love, and Letters* is a historical study, but I hope it will encourage readers to look at the memoirs with a new sense of their literary dimensions and resonance.

Beauvoir's memoirs recounted in best-selling detail her childhood, youthful literary ambitions, frustrations, and then accomplishments. She took readers along with her around the world as she explored the Amazon and the Mississippi; hiked, skied, and drove through the Alps; hitchhiked across the Sahara; and traveled as a left intellectual to Cuba, China, and the Soviet Union, socialist countries on the other side of the Cold War, the Middle East, North Africa, and colonial or postcolonial countries on the other side of empire. She shared her political conversations and feelings. She did the same with the movements of her heart. Her lifelong nonmarriage with Jean-Paul Sartre made the existentialist twosome into one of the celebrity couples of the postwar world. But she also chronicled her love affairs with the American writer Nelson Algren, "poet of the Chicago slums," and Claude Lanzmann, journalist and director of films, most famously *Shoah* (1985).[15] Those relationships provided dramatically passionate—and sexual—counterpoints to her intellectual partnership with Sartre. Generations of admirers have seen in her life a seductive mix of glamour, literary fame, human possibility, political engagement, and female independence.[16]

Nearly every part of Beauvoir's self-fashioned image has been contested. Detractors have exposed the dark side of her life. Beauvoir compromised with the Vichy regime during the Nazi Occupation of France (1940–1944), taking an oath that she was neither Jewish nor a Freemason in order to keep her position with French state radio. She failed to stand by friends who were endangered by Vichy and the Nazis. Her political engagements were intermittent and often awkward. She may have seen herself as a rebel against "bourgeois" sentiment, conventional marriage, and romantic love, but her reputation has been thoroughly tarnished by details about her jealousies and above all the shabby exploitation of young protégés who became infatuated with her, Sartre, or both. Beauvoir swapped sexual partners with Sartre. She compared notes on those partners with him. For decades she refused to acknowledge her affairs with women and blithely denied that her silence on that score was consequential.[17]

Beauvoir's feminism sparks debate even when detached from these scandals. Critics have deemed her too liberal and individualistic, too Marxist, or unable to resolve the tension between the two, and therefore left without a coherent theory of history and change. Second-wave feminists bridled at her skepticism about feminism as a political movement, and her notorious assertion that "women do not say 'We'" inspired a generation of women's historians in the 1960s and 1970s to chart the accomplishments of women's activism and solidarity and lay out the infirmities of Beauvoir's theories of history.[18] Audre Lorde delivered her famous address "The Master's Tools Will Never Dismantle the Master's House" at a conference commemorating the thirtieth anniversary of *The Second Sex*. Since then, feminists marginalized by white European and American feminism have underscored how much Beauvoir's universalism casts as "Other" women of color, lesbian and queer women, poor women, and all those who do not fit white feminist categories.[19] Attentive readers find it hard to ignore Beauvoir's aloofness and diffidence concerning the women figures in her writings. Many have recoiled from Beauvoir's unwillingness to implicate herself in the female situation or condition. The French feminist Marie-Jo Bonnet's 2015 study is particularly biting about Beauvoir's deceptions and self-deceptions, starting with but not limited to her denial of her important lesbian relationships. She asks how Beauvoir has remained a trustworthy theorist of gender or sexuality, let alone an admired feminist icon.[20]

My question is not whether we should admire or distrust Beauvoir. The archive provides ample reasons to do both. I am concerned instead with how ordinary women and men came to cast her as an interlocutor in their everyday dramas, asking her questions more appropriate for an advice columnist than an intellectual and writer. While she saw herself as a writer and thinker whose topic was sex and women, countless readers saw her as a woman writer, writing for women. The paradox is plain: Beauvoir imagined herself floating above the predicaments of *The Second Sex*, but her own life provided endless examples of those predicaments, and readers pointed that out. To put it differently, Beauvoir situated herself within a French intellectual tradition of universalizing humanist inquiry, but her readers particularized her, placing her in a woman's body, or situation. That dynamic vexed her for much of her career. Yet she did eventually become what readers told her she already was: a writer for women, and not only a thinker about feminism but a feminist. Her distinctive weave of the personal, the political, and the philosophical was interpreted and shaped through the lives of others. In short, the "Simone de Beauvoir" that we know would not exist without her readers' formative role.

Introducing the letter writers is daunting because they were such a varied group of individuals—and because by French law, most of them must remain anonymous to protect their privacy. The letter writers were male as well as female, old and middle-aged as well as young, staid as well as rebellious. They wrote from all over the francophone world, including North and West Africa, from the Scandinavian countries, eastern Europe, Latin America, the United States, England, and from around the corner in Paris. Beauvoir was only one of the most prominent "engaged" writers on the international scene—not a French but a French-in-the-world figure. In the 1950s and 1960s, French existentialism stood at the height of its popular appeal, promising a world recovering from World War II a new humanism that could be translated into simple terms: radical freedom, self-invention, self-defining choices, responsibility, and engagement. Thus, earnest students of philosophy and literature wrote to Beauvoir, and so did consumers of magazines like *Paris Match*, *Elle*, and *Time*, which ran articles about her as the first lady of existentialism, or a "philosophical celebrity."[21] Beauvoir's work was read across the world, in French and in translation, bringing in new cohorts of readers and extending her long relationship with her public. "France is not the whole world," wrote a woman from Bogotá in 1970. "Overseas your work is devoured. I have friends who have only just started *The Second Sex*, and they are amazed at it."[22] Beauvoir's audience crossed boundaries of social class and educational capital as well as national borders: letters came from writers and writers in the making, teachers, university students, schoolgirls, social workers, factory workers, doctors, psychologists and psychoanalysts, and women at home. In light of the challenges of her work and the pluck required to write to an author, this is a remarkably wide spectrum of readers. Nearly a third of the letters came from men, a reminder about the range of Beauvoir's topics—and also that personal life, selfhood, and women's search for equality and freedom implicated and interested men.

These correspondents' motives for writing, their knowledge of the world, and their capacities for self-expression varied widely. Many were aspiring writers or intellectuals. "I too am in love with words and ideas," as one put it.[23] Some, however, had very little formal education. These differences in background are imprinted in the letters. Readers sent postcards, holiday greetings, professional business cards, clippings of reviews, and pictures (most of which have not been kept), as well as letters. Most correspondents wrote by hand, which was considered more formal and polite than typing. Some wrote fluidly and at great length, and others with obvious difficulty, crossing out words and phrases, and using notebook paper.

Readers wrestled with Beauvoir's radical ideas and her extraordinary life. They aired the strong feelings her work elicited. They raised a skeptical eyebrow at her studiously crafted self-presentation. They tried to reconcile their ambitions with her example and their situation They thought out loud about the classic existential question, the meaning of freedom, and equally about the relationship between sexual liberation, the emancipation of women, anticolonialism, and civil and human rights, movements that were intertwined, but not in predictable or necessarily harmonious ways. Readers reached for intellectual affinity, for the romance of sharing the adventures of a writer, and in several cases for erotic connection. That Beauvoir seemed to reveal so much of herself in all of her writing prompted readers to respond in kind: "This must happen to you often, doesn't it? That people write you and tell you about their lives?"[24]

With rare exceptions, Beauvoir's answers are gone. In many ways, this absence makes the archive *more* interesting; it certainly creates a fascinating methodological puzzle. To begin with, it decenters the author and her influence. It directs our attention instead toward the intimate publics in which authorship is situated—the imagined relationship between readers and author that is so central to the reception of ideas. That relationship is shaped by expectations, attachments, and fantasies on both sides. The letter writers reached for intimacy with the writer of their mind's eye and struck up a conversation with the person, or voice, that emerged from those writings. The archive asks us to imaginatively re-create those conversations. I have set out to reconstruct the back-and-forth between the letter writers on the one hand and Beauvoir (through her writing) on the other, emphasizing the dialogue the letter writers insisted on having. As one letter writer wrote, in the process of penning her letter she found herself "almost forgetting that this was a one-way conversation."[25]

Second, although we can read only one side of the story in the manuscripts room of the BNF, this was a decidedly two-way exchange. Scores of letter writers thanked Beauvoir for answering: "I can't believe you have written me back!"[26] Another gratefully wrote, "Twice in my life I have written to you, and twice you have replied, in your perception and compassion."[27] The most striking example of Beauvoir's engagement came to me a few years into my research. I read a long (ten handwritten pages) and self-dramatizing letter from a man who had been reading Beauvoir's autobiography. He reflected, enviously, on Beauvoir's "marvelous companionship with Sartre" as he dealt with his own turbulent love life. He had left his crumbling marriage and, after some hesitation, started a passionate affair with a younger woman. That relationship quickly grew complicated: each of them had affairs; he was jealous of his lover's young friends; she became angry about his possessiveness and his philandering. They fought and reconciled several times before finally breaking up. He copied out and included passages from her last letter calling off the affair. "I never thought that I could suffer so much from love at forty three years old," he wrote to Beauvoir, hoping that she would give him the key to this story that he "only half-understood."[28]

I reached the end of the letter and saw it was signed by the father of one of my close French friends. The letter writers must remain anonymous, so I kept this to myself. But I learned by roundabout means that Beauvoir answered, and I saw Beauvoir's reply, which was astonishing. Far from being too busy or aloof to respond to his story, she reviewed its details and commented on them, calling his possessiveness vis-à-vis his lover an example of "bad faith." She also took pains to correct his interpretation of her own life. His drama of jealousy and conflict, she wrote, did not have "anything in common with my pact with Sartre."[29] This remarkable letter was one of my first important clues about the unusual character of this relationship and how seriously Beauvoir took her readers. It moved the reader-author relationship to the center of this book.

Beauvoir's attachment to her readers jumps off the pages of her memoirs once one looks for it; it emerges in long passages on the power and pleasures of reading, in tributes to her readers, and in comments on how gratifying she found her connection with them.[30] As Beauvoir put it in an extraordinary passage from *The Prime of Life*, she wrote in order to be loved through her books but also to "penetrate" the worlds of others— to become a participant in her readers' inner dialogues and to merge her voice with theirs. Many letter writers wanted to tell her that she did exactly that. "You *communicate* with your readers," wrote one correspondent, who credited Beauvoir with a "hypersensitivity of the purest kind."[31] Wrote another: "It seems to me that there's a certain kind of communication between a writer and a reader that you have established—to perfection . . . [Y]ou are one of the few writers who is read—really read— by an enormous public."[32]

This relationship was neither a happy communion of hearts nor existential ventriloquism. Indeed, the aim of reaching "into the lives of others," in Beauvoir's intrusive phrase, was bound to foster misunderstanding and expectations that could not be met, and to encounter resistance and flashes of anger. Beauvoir's correspondents amply documented their *own* ambitions, desires, and ideas. They reinterpreted and re-appropriated Beauvoir's concepts and vocabulary. They obliged *her* to work through how they were using her writing and life—a process that questioned her politics, challenged her self-image as an Olympian philosopher, and pressed her to take up new subjects. As one letter writer put it, "When one publishes one's ideas on many things, doesn't one expect that they'll come back a little heavier, weighted by the presence of others?"[33] Indeed, Beauvoir's concepts, vocabulary, and life story did return to her "weighted by the presence of others," and very different Others at that.

The connection between author and readers had to bridge significant social and cultural differences. The exchange was often fraught with jealousy, resentment, anger, and thwarted desires on *both* sides. Beauvoir was particularly impatient, even cruel, with the many middle-aged married women who followed her eagerly but whom she deemed woefully conventional—distressingly willing to lower their expectations and narrow their horizons. They were remarkably undeterred. Their bond with Beauvoir was central to the process whereby they became philosophers of their own lives. The co-constitutive character of this bond ran deep.

Books, Readers, and Twentieth-Century Culture

The cultural history of the twentieth century has witnessed a burst of attention to audiences, the senses, and feeling. We have fascinating histories of spectators and, more recently, listeners. Books and reading, however, were as central to the dynamism of that century—and to people's lives, self-understanding, and political mobilization—as film, radio, and television. The iconic example of the twentieth-century "revolution of the book" is Penguin, founded in 1935, which showed publishers across the world the keen popular interest in affordably priced quality literature and nonfiction. American publishing, largely spared the disruptions of World War II, grew at a particularly marked clip through the 1940s. In the 1950s and 1960s, however, the revolution in publishing and reading swept across Europe and the decolonizing world.[34] The French *livre de poche*, or small-format paperback, which launched in 1953, made inexpensive, well-designed books among the goods of the revolution in consumption during the "thirty glorious years." The rapid expansion of education swelled the ranks of book-buying university students and democratized intellectual life. These developments went hand in hand with the emergence of new media; as the French say, the one did not exclude the other. French intellectuals not only enjoyed a storied tradition of prestige but also had a talent for performance and commentary that fared well on radio and television. Television shows like *Lectures pour tous*, which started broadcasting weekly in 1953, made the point that reading—and reading challenging philosophical work at that—was for everyone.[35]

The first volume of Beauvoir's autobiography, *Memoirs of a Dutiful Daughter* (1958), was published in *livre de poche* format in 1963. Beauvoir fretted that her reputation would suffer, and that she would be devalued as an author of "best-sellers." That was premature. Beauvoir's writing did not immediately become mass market fare: *The Mandarins* and *The Second Sex* were not published in paperback until 1968. Still, the appetite for challenging reading, for bold ideas, knowledge of the world, and knowledge of self, including sexual knowledge, was remarkable. Reading was no less revolutionary in the twentieth century than it had been in the eighteenth. That more democratic appetite for serious work drove the demand for literature and for a relationship and dialogue with Simone de Beauvoir.

The vitality of books and reading in the twentieth century is one side of the story. The powerfully gendered dynamics of the commerce and culture of print are another. As a woman philosopher and the author of autobiography, Beauvoir was bound to be pulled into the world of publishing aimed at women, the land of *Elle, Marie Claire,* and the magazines and books that specialized in romantic fiction, confession, and advice. Afternoon radio was part of this empire as well. In the decades after World War II, the commercial power of print, the political enfranchisement of women, and women's importance as consumers magnified the force of that cultural or literary field, and it multiplied the number of experts who claimed to speak to and for women. Beauvoir did not hesitate to add her voice to their number, though she assailed everything that "women's culture" stood for: sentimentality, mystified femininity, pandering to male vanity and entitlement, and women's narrow horizon of aspirations. In fact, sections of *The Second Sex* appeared as "The Femininity Trap" in American *Vogue* in 1947, well before they showed up in *Les Temps*

Modernes.[36] The power of Beauvoir's critique notwithstanding, the expectations and idioms of this commercial women's culture—an orientation toward emotional expertise and to confession or self-disclosure, the normalizing language of popular psychology—shaped readers' encounters with her. They knotted her relationship with ordinary women readers and powerfully shaped her work.

Following these exchanges between reader and author takes us to the heart of some of the most crucial debates and historical developments of the twentieth century. Four of those developments are especially important. The first is the prolonged and difficult aftermath of World War II. Nineteen forty-five marked the end of a catastrophic thirty-year conflict that opened with World War I and witnessed the collapse of economies and democracies, the rise of fascism, Nazism, Stalinism, and other forms of anti-liberal authoritarianism, *two* brutal total wars, and genocide. Reckoning with devastation on this scale could not have been simple. In 1945, as Tony Judt puts it in *Postwar*, "the grandest of all Europe's illusions—now discredited beyond recovery—was 'European civilization' itself." For another half century, Europe in particular would be "shadowed by history."[37] That context called French thinkers to a philosophical seriousness and responsibility that would redeem French culture in the eyes of the world. The popular diffusion of French existentialism, one of the many things these letters document, is one measure of their success.

The slow unfolding of the war's horrors shadowed Beauvoir and her readers. It troubled the first reviewers of *The Second Sex*, who charged Beauvoir and existentialism in general with an amorality that only confirmed the collapse of civilization. Critics accused Beauvoir's exploration of the female experience, the body, and sexuality of wallowing in the abject, of obscenity, of casting away the last restraints of decency. The war haunted the many correspondents who wrote to Beauvoir later, in the 1950s and 1960s, as they were using her volumes of memoir to work through their own painful memories of betrayal or complicity during those years. Hans Ulrich Gumbrecht writes of the "latency" of the Second World War: hidden, ill-defined, and unresolved, it repeatedly resurfaced in different cultural and political moments. Beauvoir's readers testify to that latency. The Cold War, with its polarized politics, denials, and amnesias, contributed mightily to the fact that, as Gumbrecht says, "the finish line of the postwar" kept being pushed back.[38]

The second development of the period, thoroughly entangled in the first, was the explosion of anticolonial revolt. In the space of two decades, the colonial empires of France, Great Britain, Holland, Belgium, Portugal, and Italy collapsed. The French war against Algerian independence from 1954 to 1962 was one of the most bitter and violent of these conflicts. We associate that war with French intellectual men like Frantz Fanon, Jean-Paul Sartre, and Albert Camus, whose alliances (or irreconcilable differences) polarized the international debate about the war. But *Sex, Love, and Letters* documents that it loomed large in Beauvoir's writing, how that writing was read, and the political emotions it stirred in the public. The struggles of decolonization reverberated across the world in the form of civil rights movements, an emerging discourse of human rights in the international legal and political arena, and a fight for the "decolonization of the soul" in the cultures of an emerging postcolonial world and the metropoles across Europe. Reading Beauvoir through the letters to her reveals some of decolonization's own "latency."

A third development of the century was the emergence of "sex" as a quintessentially modern topic: difficult but unavoidable, a test of individual and cultural courage, and privileged terrain of social and self-knowledge. "Midcentury sex," as I call it, was extraordinarily broad and ill-defined; it referred to what we would now call gender, gender roles, sexuality, sexual identity and subjectivity, desires, or drives. Midcentury sex had high stakes: it was understood to implicate selfhood, behavior, personality, social relations, culture, and politics. The subject was not new. Since the beginning of the twentieth century, European and American culture and thought had been forced to reckon with the growing intellectual impact of Freud, who remapped the place of sexuality in everything human, including cultural life.

The vehement and polarized responses to the publication of *The Second Sex* in 1949 owed much to the powerful associations stirred by that charged third word in its title. Beauvoir's work was thus pulled into a very wide range of discussions about what we would call sex; reviewers and readers alike grouped *The Second Sex* (1949), a philosophical treatment of women's otherness, together with the American Alfred Kinsey's *Sexual Behavior in the Human Male* (1948, translated into French in 1949), a statistical study of sexual drive and outlet. Scholars have found the Beauvoir-Kinsey association nearly comic, a misreading emblematic of contemporaries' inability to understand Beauvoir. I take it as a provocative recontextualization—a signal that we will have to travel back to an unfamiliar intellectual world to recover the question to which both books were an answer.

"Sex" was not simply an urgent matter for science and the social sciences; it was personal. Beauvoir's correspondents point us toward the existential dimensions of sexuality from the 1950s to the early 1970s. Sexuality was central to the Beauvoirian "experience of the world," shaped by freedoms, constraints, and lifelong confrontations with profound inequalities. Many readers who wrote to Beauvoir wanted to talk to her about this terrain of truth—sexuality and selfhood in all their dimensions. Their ability to do so was often limited by ignorance, isolation, and confusion. Readers who now might identify as lesbian, gay, trans, or queer struggled in the 1950s and 1960s to find language or categories that fit their misfit feelings. In France, hesitations about sexuality in general stemmed from the well-established tradition of *pudeur*—decency or discretion—which muffled expressions of sexual unhappiness or marital troubles, deeming those to be issues appropriately dealt with personally, or in the privacy of the family. "Decency" also patrolled the boundaries of the discourse on sexuality. It condemned public discussion of sexuality, especially female sexuality, unless it was subject to the civilizing influence of love or diluted in the solvent of romance that saturated popular culture in the 1950s. To speak of sexual violence was taboo. Equally important and less often noticed is that those taboos extended to matters of the body that were *not* necessarily sexual, namely, aging, illness, and dying. Beauvoir's "indecency" lay in placing not just sexuality but the body itself at the center of the human situation and for treating both as matters for open and serious reflection and discussion, not issues judged to be humiliating or merely personal.

Whether or not these letter writers' reckonings with themselves point toward the feminist horizon of the late 1960s and 1970s is an important question, and one not easily answered. The emergence of second-wave feminism is the fourth historical development traced in this book.[39] The passage from the personal to the political, in the famous shorthand, was halting, to say the least. Indeed, the relationship of the personal to the political, and the relationship of either to feminism, are moving targets. What is more, the fraught intimacy between Beauvoir and her readers will make it impossible to see her simply as an avant-garde political intellectual or feminist leader. As Canadian feminist filmmaker Bonnie Kreps observed, Beauvoir never sought to be the "Pied Piper of feminism."[40] Beauvoir's politics were interestingly complex. She was consistently and unflinchingly radical on the sources and ramifications of gender inequality, the sexualization of domination, and the ways in which intimacy and inequality warped each other. She emphasized the profound contradictions of female subjectivity. Her understanding of those contradictions undermined any confidence that women could act collectively as agents of political change. Beauvoir has been pilloried for her ambivalence about women's movements and for *The Second Sex*'s stance on feminism as, alternately, a movement whose time had passed ("perhaps we should say no more about it") and an impossibility ("women do not say 'We' ").[41] This ambivalence, however, is worth interrogating, and one of the feelings most commonly echoed by her readers.

Readers who wrote to Beauvoir often tried to account for themselves in her terms. They were thus especially explicit about the difficulties of explaining themselves, finding a voice, or establishing a presence. Describing oneself as a woman could provoke deeply mixed sentiments. Participating in politics in the name of "women" or "feminism" led to predicaments and impasses about which letter writers were exceptionally articulate. Lesbian and gay subjectivity and politics stirred similarly mixed emotions, questions, and puzzles. Letter writers spelled out not only their meaningful gestures of rebellion but also the powerful appeal of conventionality. Their accounts of their lives offer a micro-politics of rebellion and compromise. The letters offer a fresh look at the radical redefinition of feminism and sexual politics in the late 1960s and early 1970s.

Intimacy and the Intimate Public

In this reader-author dialogue, the categories of public and private, personal and political, interior and exterior make little sense. When I call this dialogue "intimate," I mean to blur those categories.[42] The historian Bruno Cabanes defines intimacy as "what lies at the core of a person: the inner space where self-image is formed, through the body and gestures . . . where relationships to others are shaped, through ties of blood and affection and . . . the memories with which we endow places and objects."[43] The role of body, gestures, and memories in the forging of self-image is particularly evident in these letters. The distinction between a personal core and an outer world, however, will be hard to sustain. For self-image is formed not in inner space but rather intersubjectively and discursively, by trying on and exchanging images, vocabulary, and concepts in just the way these letters illustrate. In this book I understand intimacy in terms of the nature of the bond that it forges, or its "density of communication," as the social theorist Niklas Luhmann puts it in *Love as Passion*. In an intimate relationship, no feeling or experience is insignificant or irrelevant, Luhmann argues, a point crucial to my approach here. Luhmann expresses it in a Beauvoirian way: intimacy invites one to share one's "experience of the world."[44] Both existentialism and phenomenology begin with the argument that humans are cast into the world or a "situation." The world unfolds its meaning, and subjectivity takes shape through language, cognition, and the body and senses. The process of becoming is ongoing. Beauvoir theorized this understanding of experience and tried to render it in her memoirs. For the women and men who wrote to her, intimacy meant discussing all these aspects of their situation or their experience of the world.

My understanding of intimacy also draws on Lauren Berlant's conception of "*public* intimacy." That term is meant to bring us up short, for it intentionally disrupts our familiar association of intimate with private. It provides an implicit critique of Jürgen Habermas's enormously influential history of the public sphere as a domain of reason and exchange of ideas. For Berlant, the public sphere itself is saturated with affect, fantasies, and desires to belong. She is writing especially about mass-mediated women's culture—women's magazines, sentimental fiction, radio and television talk shows, and the like—as spaces of "mediation in which the personal is refracted through the general."[45] That culture cultivates personal revelation and intimacy, or the illusion of intimacy, among people who may have little in common with one another. In the context of political disenfranchisement and enormous social and economic inequalities, the intimate public encourages a hopeful and reassuring fantasy of belonging. As Berlant writes carefully, those who are drawn into it "feel that their emotional lives are already shared and have been raised to a degree of general significance while remaining true to what's personal."[46]

Berlant's subjects are nineteenth- and twentieth-century American culture and politics, but her analysis zeroes in on the dynamics of the cultural field in which Beauvoir's writing landed. It describes the structure of expectations that many readers brought to Beauvoir's work. At several points in this book we will see the power of this kind of intimacy, its cruel illusions, and how both of those shaped the affective public political world created between Beauvoir and her readers. That power and these illusions have to be part of our reassessment of Beauvoir's legacy—and of our broader understanding of the dynamics of feminism and its history.

Situating the Archive

Beauvoir's correspondence tells us much about France at a moment when French culture needed to redeem itself in the eyes the world—in the face of the shame of World War II and the brutal repression of anticolonial insurgency. Partly for that reason, it is not just a French story. The new interconnectedness of the world in the postwar decades fostered a more international reading public. Beauvoir called this development "the emergence of oneworld" and remarked that it had transformed Sartre quite suddenly into a cosmopolitan author.[47] It did the same for her. "I have good eyes and good ears," reported one of Beauvoir's many attentive followers, from Michigan, who assiduously collected articles by and about Beauvoir from papers and magazines such as the *New York Times*, the *Saturday Review*, and *Le Nouvel Observateur*.[48] This letter writer understood herself to be implicated in the political and existential issues she discussed with Beauvoir, and she believed that these issues "knew no borders."[49] European intellectuals soon ran up against the borders of their thinking. The categories of Self and Other which Beauvoir, Sartre, and others applied so broadly to thinking about colonialism, race relations, anti-Semitism, and gender elided and obscured many of the differences they were trying to theorize. The universalism that would soon mark them as outdated, however, made them gripping thinkers in the 1950s and 1960s. Moreover, many of the key historical developments traced in this book, such as the midcentury literature on sex, the rising discontent with traditional marriage in the 1950s, and antiwar and anticolonial protests were international, but they had specific national or regional inflections. The social movements of the late 1960s made the sense of global connection particularly acute. A historian is pulled toward the most relevant contexts, social developments, or cultural frameworks. In this book, those frameworks are sometimes distinctly French and sometimes transnational.[50] Adjusting the lens is part of the historian's task.

A few more words of introduction to this archive. It is not complete. Almost all the letters from the late 1940s and early 1950s were lost or inadvertently destroyed.[51] Beauvoir reported in her memoirs that *The Second Sex* elicited a spate of ugly and insulting letters; only a few such letters are in this archive. We have a few more letters from the time of *The Mandarins* in 1954, when the Goncourt prize won her many followers. The wave of correspondence swelled dramatically with each volume of Beauvoir's memoirs and the publicity that attended them. In the aftermath of *The Force of Circumstance* (1963), the mail brought her a thousand letters a year. Some came directly to her apartment; some arrived via her publisher. Beauvoir did not classify them in any way, and she discarded the envelopes, which has complicated the ongoing process of dating and cataloguing the archive at the BNF since 1995.[52] She did not save copies of her responses.

The archive is at once very large and inhospitable to statistical analysis, at least at this writing: it is still being catalogued. The letters cannot be duplicated in any form, and with a few exceptions, the writers must remain anonymous. The letters may be too idiosyncratic or singular to substantiate a broad-gauged social history of reading. As Gérard Mauger points out, a true case study of reading practices and experience requires evidence about readers' lives, their circles of friends and family, their education, and the other books on their shelves. That evidence is not here.[53] I do not claim that these correspondents are representative of Beauvoir's readers as a whole, or the reading public. They nonetheless offer us glimpses of the *processes* of reading, writing, and introspection and let us follow the British historian Carolyn Steedman's argument that "past forms of cognition and affect are to some extent retrievable, and it is one of our jobs to interrogate them."[54]

The history of reception begins with the point that the history of any work of literature is "inconceivable without the active participation of those for whom it is destined."[55] From that starting point has burst an enormous multidisciplinary scholarship, too vast to summarize here. I am not primarily concerned with documenting the agency of readers, for Beauvoir's correspondents provide persuasive countervailing testimony about the power of reading, writing, and identifying to *construct* experience. This author-reader relationship was reciprocal but rife with all kinds of inequalities: Beauvoir had many more resources, discursive and other, than most of those who wrote to her. Still, even those correspondents who seemed content to bask in the pleasures of Beauvoir's prose, try on her concepts, or marshal vocabulary to which they otherwise had little access cannot be described as passive. As one reader put it very well, she might be more a "receiver than a giver." She nonetheless presented herself as particularly attentive, responsive, and immersed in a multisensory experience:

> I have always considered myself a receiver rather than a giver; I read, I think, I listen a great deal, but I do not create. I am very sensitive—a sort of instrument played by the world: I vibrate, I choose and reproduce the sounds that I love, I accept the ideas and the impressions that suit, and that seem strong [*bonnes et valides*].[56]

Beauvoir wrote that "a book is a collective object: readers contribute as much as the author to its creation."[57] These letters make us take that point seriously. They do not simply provide the context in which to better understand Beauvoir's ideas.[58] Intellectuals are not the only people who think, and the letters are themselves documents of intellectual history, how ideas are produced and transformed, and how networks of followers take shape. Beauvoir's autobiographical project was ongoing, and accompanied by regular essays and interviews. Readers' letters came in as she was writing and revising. This was an actual dialogue, in real time.

The letter to the author is a cultural practice that is part of the history of literature, thought, and politics.[59] Some of the most perceptive comments on that practice come from Belgian writer Amélie Nothomb (1966-). Nothomb confesses she is compulsively attentive to letters from her readers. Her short novel, *Life Form* (2010), starts with an invented correspondence between herself and one of her readers, an American soldier stationed in Iraq. There will be no spoilers here, but as their epistolary exchange becomes increasingly fraught, riddled with power plays and deceptions, the novel becomes a reflection on Nothomb's actual

correspondence with readers. Her observations on the reader-author relationship are wry and wonderful; we see that the dynamics in Beauvoir's
correspondence a half century earlier are very much still in force. Nothomb's readers boldly conjure up the excitement of discovered connection.
Reader meets author "like Robinson Crusoe and Friday on the beach on
the island!" Readers insist on recognizing themselves or their opposites in
the author: "[T]hat's just like me! That's just the opposite of me!" Nothomb muses on the perils of becoming enthralled by this apparent communion of souls. As an author, she writes, "you are so intoxicated that
you cannot see the danger that lies just ahead. Suddenly the other is there,
at your door. Others [the readers] have so many ways of moving in and
imposing themselves." Beauvoir's readers moved into her work with some
of the same unexpected and novelistic richness.[60]

Finally, the pleasures and perils of working with letters in general are
legion, and a historian cannot avoid what the cultural theorist Margaretta
Jolly calls letter writing's "*oddness* compared to other ways of relating."[61]
Letters are purposefully direct and seductive. They are theatrical, and
doubly so when addressed to an iconic figure. Countless writers in this
archive described their letters as a "message in a bottle." One dramatically
likened writing Beauvoir to "looking at a strange door. You are approach-
ing it, you are hesitating . . . you are stepping into a new world."[62] Small
wonder I was riveted to my chair at the BNF. Letters do not simply escort
us into some otherwise inaccessible inner world, however; they are thoroughly mediated by the epistolary genre and letter-writing practices, and
those are historical, changing, and interesting in their own right.[63]

The book opens with two chapters that place *The Second Sex* in a broad
historical setting. The letters Beauvoir received from this period are gone,
either discarded or destroyed. Thus for the first readings of *The Second
Sex*, critics and reviewers have to be at center stage. Experts perhaps, the
critics proved no less interestingly unpredictable than more ordinary readers a decade later. What is more, their reactions stuck to the text and Beauvoir's public image. From chapter 3 on, *Sex, Love, and Letters* takes the
letter writers as its guides. Starting with the correspondence unleashed by
Memoirs of a Dutiful Daughter, I follow the currents that deepened but
also roiled this author-reader relationship: interactive remembering and
often passionate identification; sharing political distress and shame; and

confessing sexual confusions, conjugal unhappiness, and gendered anger. The explosion of feminism in the early 1970s prompted Beauvoir to declare in *All Said and Done* that she was willing to call herself a feminist. This conversion would not resolve her ambivalence about women as a collectivity. Nor would it end her readers' many conflicts with Beauvoir, feminism, or their other political commitments and identities. The conclusion reflects on the political and affective dynamics in this author-reader bond and on the archive of letters as a cultural artifact of the twentieth century.

Early in her career, when Simone de Beauvoir was writing *The Second Sex* and beginning her memoirs, she could not have known what an extraordinary impact these books would have. The intense epistolary bond with her readers took her by surprise, and it shaped her legacy. It has also left us a remarkable archival world of its own to explore, a world that offers historians an opportunity to study the intertwined practices of reading and writing, the cultural phenomenon of letters that shadows the history of books, and the twentieth-century discussions of sex, love, and politics.

1

THE INTIMATE LIFE OF THE NATION

Reading The Second Sex *in 1949*

The human condition is one thing; the condition of women is
another—worse. Everyone agrees on this, more or less.
DOMINIQUE AURY, review of *The Second Sex*, 1950.

Almost all of readers' letters from the time when *The Second Sex* was first
published have been lost. It is important nonetheless to reconstruct how
the public was introduced to what is now Beauvoir's most famous work.
This chapter and the one that follows do so by reconsidering the critical
reception of *The Second Sex* in that first moment. Reviewers and critics
saw themselves as custodians of literary standards and public taste as well
as those who set the agenda for national discussion. They held very firm,
and often contrasting, views concerning the broader reading public. Those
views provide new ways to understand Beauvoir's arguments and the expectations that took shape around her.[1]

The matter of the reception in 1949 has been distorted by our view
of Beauvoir as a pioneer ahead of her time. That assessment is meant to
be appreciative, underscoring Beauvoir's boldness and acknowledging the
difficulty of such an ambitious text. *The Second Sex* was what French students colloquially call a *pavé* (cobblestone, or massive text): eight hundred
pages of challenging philosophical argument, literary criticism, history,

social science, and startlingly detailed description of sexual and bodily experience. It offered, first, an agenda-setting topic: a philosophical reconsideration of the female condition, or situation; second, an argument, that woman was defined as the Other of man, particular, and subordinate; and third a genre of writing that was at once authoritative, Olympian, and interior. *The Second Sex* was a lot to contend with. The ahead-of-its-time narrative, however, fast-forwards to the 1970s, when *The Second Sex* became a feminist classic, as if Beauvoir addressed only one subject and one yet-to-emerge constituency. That story ignores the many ramifications of Beauvoir's work and obscures how *The Second Sex* actually landed when it came out.[2] The controversies, debates, and preoccupations of the moment shaped the dialogue around the book and Beauvoir's image.

In France, women's suffrage had been granted in 1944, late by nearly any standard, and only after an excruciatingly long impasse on the subject was broken by a decree, issued by General Charles de Gaulle's French government in exile under pressure from its allies. Women's suffrage was more of an anticlimax than a turning point or cause for celebration. The sting of France's defeat in 1940 and Nazi Occupation, and above all the humiliation of the Vichy government's collaboration with Hitler's regime (1940–1944), were very fresh. France's geopolitical position had plummeted. Tensions of empire, created by anticolonial revolt and colonial repression, were readily apparent. Within France, acute material shortages, trafficking in counterfeit food-rationing tickets, and the terms of economic and political reconstruction were urgent matters. Shortages and strikes fractured governing coalitions at home. The escalating Cold War polarized international and domestic politics. In the face of this crisis and an acrimonious debate over a painful past, postwar intellectuals in France sought to project forward—"to recover the future," as Sartre declared.[3]

Beauvoir's tone captured that determination. In the first paragraph of *The Second Sex*, Beauvoir writes as if she is pushing aside the clutter of books and papers on her desk to clear her mind and start over:

For a long time, I hesitated to write a book on the woman. The subject is irritating, especially to women; and it is not new. Enough ink has been spilled on the quarrel of feminism, and it is now practically over. We should say no more about it. It is still talked about, however. And the voluminous nonsense uttered during the last century seems to have done little to illuminate the problem. After all, is there a problem? And if so, what is it? Are there women, really?[4]

Beauvoir's intellectual clearing of the decks called for rethinking the very starting point: "woman" or "femininity." She conceived womanhood in existential and phenomenological terms—as a "condition," "lived experience," or, perhaps most effectively, a dynamic process of becoming. "One is not born, but rather becomes, a woman."[5]

Beauvoir positioned herself as a woman in a new generation of intellectuals, impatient with past discussions. She bridled at the "voluminous nonsense" written *about* women. She sharply distanced herself from models of political actions *by* women. "We are no longer like our partisan elders," she writes a few pages into the introduction. "By and large we have won the game . . . Many problems appear to us to be more pressing than those which concern us in particular." She believed that feminism offered only a narrow and reformist politics, which paled by comparison with the other movements that were changing the postwar world: "Women do not say 'We,' except at some congress of feminist or similar formal demonstration . . . The proletarians have accomplished the revolution in Russia, the blacks in Haiti, the Indo-Chinese are battling for it in Indo-China; but the women's effort has never been anything more than a symbolic agitation. They have gained only what men have been willing to grant; they have taken nothing, they have only received."[6] In its urgency, its disavowal of bourgeois feminism, its attentiveness to civil rights and anticolonialism, and its insistence on recasting a humanism for the future while also reconceiving the humanity of women, *The Second Sex* was very much a book of postwar France.

The Second Sex did not meet with silence. The historian Sylvie Chaperon has detailed the scandal and mud-slinging the book and its author encountered. Some of the furor arose from the deep political divides in the French cultural world. Beauvoir and Sartre's radicalism provoked conservative rage, but their determination to remain nonaligned in what was becoming a cold war of the intellectuals made them targets of communist scorn. *The Second Sex* became a proxy war in this conflict.[7] Parts of the book were also shocking, opaque, or both. The issues that critics raised in 1949, especially the boundaries of public discussion and the conceptions of decency and modesty that mapped those boundaries, would resurface repeatedly in the decades that followed. Those conceptions did not apply only to matters of sex; they reached broadly into what we might call the intimate history of the nation.[8] The feelings roused in these discussions would also infuse letters from readers.

Critics often wrote remarkably personally. They claimed to imagine vividly the public's conversations about *The Second Sex*. Depending on their position in the landscape of postwar journalism and critical thought, they offered very different conceptions of what that public would—or should—accept.[9] I examine three different and important sites on that postwar landscape. First up is the newly founded (1949) *Paris Match*, a magazine that resembled the American *Life*. *Paris Match* published long excerpts from *The Second Sex* in some of its first issues. Its editors expressed confidence their readers would welcome Beauvoir's bold provocations. The second is *Les Temps Modernes*, also newly founded, with Sartre and Beauvoir at the editorial helm. A small, radical, and intellectual journal, it had a far edgier notion of what provocative meant. The third site is the literary supplement of the oldest daily newspaper *Le Figaro*. There, the distinguished Catholic writer François Mauriac, casting himself as the defender of French literature and the nation's reputation, mobilized an all-out attack on existentialism and associated enemies. Mauriac spoke on behalf of a public that he believed to be dismayed by the book's obscenity, self-revelation, and prurience. Over the next two years, first in a forum organized by Mauriac and then individually in different journals, scores of critics from different positions in the cultural world would try to summarize and assess *The Second Sex*, bringing Beauvoir's arguments into conversations they believed the nation and their readers needed to have. The way these reviewers presented *The Second Sex*, wove Beauvoir's arguments into their intellectual agendas, and wrestled with the powerful feelings she aroused dispels the generalization that Catholic France was shocked. It provides a much fuller sense of the culture and politics of this postwar moment. It outlines the public's expectations of intellectuals—and intellectuals' expectations of their followers.

Paris Match

The Second Sex came out in stages.[10] When the first volume was published in June 1949, *Paris Match* took notice. On August 6, 1949, the magazine published an issue with long excerpts from that volume. A red banner across the magazine's cover announced simply, "*La femme, cette incon-nue.*" "The Woman, This Unknown" is less dramatic than the wording in French, where the "this" conjures up a figure or region that is unexplored or mysterious, playing with the clichés of the enigma of the feminine or Freud's reference to the "dark continent" of women's sexuality. Accord-ing to *Paris Match*, Beauvoir herself had chosen this heading, perhaps to pique interest in her critique of these myths. "What is woman?" *The Sec-ond Sex* asks. The answer leads the reader from a discussion of "the data of biology" and the meanings attached to sexual difference to a critique of psychological, social, and literary portraits of the feminine. Along the way, knowledge that is scientific, verified, or common sense is shown to be socially constructed and mystified. There is no essence of femininity, Beau-voir argues in volume one. Instead there is only the rich facticity of the fe-male body and an equally rich constellation of myths that cast the woman as Other, shaping experience and female consciousness and subjectivity.

Right below the banner announcing Beauvoir's book, *Paris Match* placed a cover photograph of the French screen idol Henri Vidal posed, Rock Hudson–like—his chest, chest hair, and nipples showing through a fishnet T-shirt.[11] Vidal was an icon of male sexiness, a former body-builder and star of six films, almost all of which featured his athletic torso. In the just released film *Fabiola* (1949), Vidal played a young, handsome, secretly Christian gladiator in a drama about the crumbling Roman Empire, whose rulers blame Christian minorities for its decline. He is denounced and sentenced to die, but fights back against his persecutors in the gladiators' arena. The analogy to Nazi persecutions and heroic resistance was obvi-ous. It was also politically palatable: cheering for a persecuted Christian minority required no hard thinking or self-scrutiny about anti-Semitism. Vidal's photo and the film are reminders of the lurking presence of World War II in the background of discussions of *The Second Sex* in 1949.

Paris Match was a landmark in the new world of the postwar French press. It had launched just a few months earlier, in March 1949. Its owner, Jean Prouvost, already a well-known press magnate in the inter-war period, was tainted by charges of working too closely with the col-laborationist Vichy government. As part of getting a new authorization to publish, Prouvost overhauled *Match,* the sporting magazine he already owned, and turned it into something modeled on the American magazine *Life*.[12] At *Paris Match*, "the image ruled." But the magazine also cared about words and often featured writers in its pages. It aimed to cover "current events" (*actualités*) and provide its readers with "eyes and ears on the world."[13] A bracing modernity was thus part of its pitch to readers, and its August 6, 1949, cover is a good indication of how it imagined the readers it sought to reach. Pairing the writing of Simone de Beauvoir, whom *Paris Match* called "the first female philosopher in history,"[14] with Vidal's visible and sexy male body, the magazine addressed its audience as curious, intelligent readers who were ready, after the war's horrors and in the face of a painful and slow recovery, to be awakened.

Inside that August issue, *Paris Match* introduced Beauvoir and published excerpts from volume one of *The Second Sex*. The introduction (unsigned) said what one might expect from a magazine that covered current events and cultural and political celebrities. Beauvoir was beautiful, with an "austere and serene face"—"a rest for weary eyes." She spurned high fashion, bought inexpensive dresses in Portugal, and owned one coat, which she had brought back from her recent trip to the United States. She had "learned to read in a private school on the Left Bank of Paris" and "learned to think at the Sorbonne." And learned she had, for she passed the *agrégation,* or doctoral degree, in philosophy in 1929, when she was twenty-one, "the youngest woman ever to have passed any *agrégation.*" Now "the first woman philosopher in the history of man," she "had just written eight hundred revolutionary pages on a table at the Café de Flore" in Saint-Germain-des-Prés, then the center of Paris's existentialist scene.

The magazine's editors did not seem to doubt that their readers could handle Beauvoir's arguments. *Paris Match* had opened its pages to her so that she could lay out for its "female and male readers" all the "issues that troubled modern womanhood," namely, "abortion, prostitution, the equality of the sexes, marriage, and divorce." Since French women had only very recently achieved political equality, the time was ripe for a woman thinker to rethink the "eternal woman question" in "lucid" philosophical terms. Simone de Beauvoir had taken up an immense and original task: "extricating from the great human adventure a philosophy of her sex." *Paris Match* summarized its understanding of Beauvoir's argument: "Women need to escape from the condition of inferiority that men have imposed on them and that the majority of women have accepted—until now."[15]

Paris Match had a circulation of about 250,000. Its presentation of *The Second Sex* thus gives us some idea how hundreds of thousands of readers first encountered the book. The magazine offered its public plenty of framing and guidance. Each excerpt came with a paragraph-long headnote. While the excerpts were abridged, each was still six to nine paragraphs long and often contained some of Beauvoir's pointed and startling language. The excerpt quaintly titled "The Monthly Curse," which presented parts of Beauvoir's discussion of biological femaleness, is a case in point. In it, Beauvoir moves from asking "What is woman?" to laying out the bundle of images "femaleness" brought to mind. She shifts quickly from the difficult-to-define to the unsettling and even grotesque:

> The Woman? That is simple, for those who like simple formulas, she is a womb, an ovary; she is a female—this word is sufficient to define her. From the mouth of a man, "female" sounds like an epithet or insult. The man is not afraid of his animal nature; on the contrary, if someone says of him "that's a male!" he is proud. But the term "female" is pejorative . . . The man looks to biology to justify this feeling. The word "female" conjures up a saraband of images: the monstrous and swollen termite queen ruling over the enslaved males; the female praying mantis and the spider, satiated with love, crushing and devouring their partners; the bitch in heat roaming the alleys, trailing odors behind her . . . sluggish, eager, artful, stupid, callous, lustful, ferocious, debased—the man projects onto the woman all females at the same time.[16]

The selections that followed minced no words about childbearing and the family: "The woman giving birth . . . feels as if she is a passive toy in the hands of obscure forces . . . [G]iving birth and nursing are not *activities*; they are natural functions: the woman passively submits to her biological destiny."[17] *Paris Match* included a long excerpt from Beauvoir's discussion of Friedrich Engels's *The Origin of the Family, Private Property, and the State* (1884) and Claude Lévi-Strauss's *The Elementary Structures of Kinship* (1949). Beauvoir read Lévi-Strauss's study in manuscript, and his now famous structuralist analysis of marriage and kinship as relations *between men* informs the philosophical and historical argument in her book. Women had "never composed a separate group set up *on its own account* over against the male grouping. They have never entered into a direct and autonomous relation with men."[18] Beauvoir traces the development of economic formations, legal codes, and social institutions that established woman as Other. The nineteenth-century bourgeois family sealed the woman's dependent status; nineteenth-century bourgeois notions of female purity redefined her character. The expansion of prostitution to provide sexual services to bourgeois men was an inevitable consequence of this process. The excerpt reviewed the legacy of the Revolution of 1789, from Olympe de Gouges's "Declaration of the Rights of Woman"—and de Gouge's death on the guillotine—to the patriarchal reformulation of laws of marriage under the Napoleonic Code in 1804.

Paris Match did not flinch from "The Enormous Problem of 'Birth Control.' " That excerpt compared "Anglo-Saxon countries," which legalized birth control, to France, which not only banned contraception but also prohibited disseminating any information about contraceptive techniques. The French state aimed to give the medical profession a monopoly on sexual knowledge. That effort had not prevented women from learning about contraception—or terminating their pregnancies. "Despite religious and legal prohibition, abortion plays a significant role in all countries. In France, there are between 800,000 and 1 million abortions a year—as many as live births—and two thirds of women who have abortions are married women who already have one or two children," Beauvoir wrote.[19]

The following week, *Paris Match* readers would find Beauvoir's critique of the mystification of femininity in literature. Fears of the flesh, temptation, or women's magical powers; taboos surrounding menstruation; the cult of motherhood or virginity—all those were projections, compensations, or ways of working out ambivalence toward nature or fear of mortality. The first selection concerned Henry de Montherlant, whose 1930s series *Les jeunes filles* was "bedside reading" for many French women. The choice was pointed. Montherlant had flirted with the far right and Vichy, and at the Liberation he had been banned from publishing for a year. Beauvoir made clear that his collaborationist sympathies were matched by his contempt for women and his inability to create even remotely interesting female characters. "Montherlant and the Woman as Slug" was the title of that section.[20] Beauvoir wrote that D. H. Lawrence, the author of *Lady Chatterley's Lover*, was "worlds away" from Montherlant, but no less attached to a "passionate belief in male supremacy." Two short excerpts made equally quick work of the "slightly modernized Catholic" Paul Claudel and the surrealist André Breton.[21] Beauvoir concluded with a warm appreciation of Stendhal. His women were "of flesh and blood," she wrote: passionate, ambitious, boxed in by social expectations and prohibitions—they were "generous hearts" trying to "find their way in the shadows."[22]

I summarize the issues of *Paris Match* to introduce Beauvoir as she was presented to hundreds of thousands of readers, and to capture the magazine's tone, which was more matter-of-fact than scandalized. The new magazine was seeking to make a mark. Open-mindedness and fresh subjects went with a certain *liberté de ton,* and all three were features of the *Paris Match* brand. As far as *Paris Match* was concerned, Beauvoir's irreverence was perfectly compatible with the cover shot of Henri Vidal and splashy photos of women getting away to the beach at Deauville in August.

Elle, another noteworthy newcomer to the postwar magazine world, exuded a similar enthusiasm for new freedoms and a belief that its women readers were ready to shed inhibitions and confront what its editors saw as the demands of a postwar world. That meant participation in politics, the hard work of postwar recovery, cultural open-mindedness, and self-knowledge, including sexual self-knowledge. A columnist at *Elle* writing about the newly popular topic of "female frigidity" exhorted readers to "lift the veil of false modesty" (*fausse pudeur*), to shed the image of women as fragile and ignorant tender flowers.[23] Like *Paris Match, Elle* deemed this image ill-suited to the difficulties of postwar recovery and rebuilding a modern nation.

Pudeur is an important term, a nodal point of the emotionally charged French discourse on the body, sexuality, and gender—and essential to the broad questions at issue here and in the chapters to come. A single equivalent in modern English is difficult to find; depending on the context, it means "modesty," "restraint," "discretion," or "decency." The *Littré,* the nineteenth-century French dictionary of usage, explained that *pudeur* derived from the Latin (*pudor*) for shame (and *pudere,* to be ashamed) and defined it as a "delicacy or discretion that prevents one from *saying, hearing, understanding,* or *doing* certain things without being embarrassed by them."[24] In *Studies in the Psychology of Sex* (1897), the British writer Havelock Ellis spelled out its gender dimensions quite bluntly: modesty, and its closely allied and overlapping emotion shame, constituted a complex of fears that could "almost be regarded as the chief secondary sexual character of women on the psychical side."[25] Modesty preserved the delicate emotional equilibrium of both sexes; it protected and sheltered. Put differently, it disciplined female sexuality, which, while necessary to the female desire that affirmed men, also threatened to run amok, undoing male rationality and unsettling the differences between the sexes. Thus, while an excess of *pudeur* might be out of date, as *Elle* claimed, how far one could set aside its rules was very far from settled. What is more, *pudeur* in the sense of "restraint" extended beyond the sexual to matters deemed personal or "too close to the intimate life of someone or to the essence of something."[26] The French rules of *pudeur* were closely entwined in feelings about the intimate life of the nation and its uncomfortably close recent history, around which many would have liked to build protective walls of privacy.

Les Temps Modernes

At another pole of the French world of letters, Beauvoir herself and the journal she was associated with, *Les Temps Modernes*, were pressing much harder against the limits of the acceptable. *Les Temps Modernes* had already published selections from the first volume of *The Second Sex* as Beauvoir was writing it, in 1948. Now, in the spring of 1949, it offered an advance look at edgier sections of the second volume. *Les Temps Modernes* published "The Sexual Initiation of the Woman" in May 1949, followed by "The Lesbian" and "Maternity" in June and July. "Maternity" sounds anodyne enough. To begin with, however, the article (like the chapter in *The Second Sex*) opened with a long analysis of abortion and the institutionalized hypocrisy and immorality of laws that outlawed it. Abortion "haunted" the sexual life of a woman, wrote Beauvoir. It was often the experience that transformed her understanding of the world and brought her up against the full social meaning of femininity. The world was not made in her image; her experience of sexuality was radically different from a man's; at the most crucial moments, her body and choices were not hers. "Maternity" included page-long graphic descriptions of women hemorrhaging in city clinics from self-induced miscarriages. The *Paris Match* excerpts on birth control, however audacious they may have seemed in a mass circulation magazine, looked extremely tame by comparison.

It was no less daring for Beauvoir to insist on female desire and sensuality, from infant and girlhood pleasures to the eroticism of lesbian

relationships. Publishing "Maternity" and "The Lesbian" virtually alongside each other deliberately presented the two as different female situations, with overlapping sensual pleasures, and Beauvoir lingered on
those pleasures.[27] She chastised psychoanalysts for their "moralizing con-
formism" about homosexuality and their inability to understand it as an
"authentic" attitude. Any individual's history, or sexual development, was
not a "fatal progression," she wrote, but a series of choices, and the "normality of the choice did not confer on it any privileged value."[28]

"The Sexual Initiation of the Woman" was the riskiest of these three
articles, and it was the lead in the May issue of *Les Temps Modernes*. Neither Beauvoir nor the editors introduced the article or the larger project.
The article itself simply plunged in: "In a sense, the woman's sexual initiation begins at infancy, like the man's. There is a theoretical and practical
apprenticeship that follows continuously from the oral, anal, and genital
stages though adulthood. But the young girl's erotic experiences are not
a simple extension of her previous sexual activities; they are very often
unexpected and brutal."[29] Today, if we know Beauvoir's work, we readily discern her purpose. The "theoretical and practical apprenticeship"
of sexuality was part of the process of becoming a woman, the process
traced in volume two of *The Second Sex*. Beauvoir's helpful sentence that
framed the volume, "One is not born but becomes a woman," however,
was not in the article to explain the author's purpose. Moreover, by the
second paragraph Beauvoir has swept the reader into discussion of clitoral
orgasms and the tenuous relationship between women's sexual pleasure
and reproductive heterosexuality:

> The clitoral system does not change with adulthood, and the woman pre-
> serves this erotic autonomy her whole life; like the male orgasm, the clito-
> ral spasm is a kind of detumescence that comes quasi-mechanically, but it is
> only indirectly linked to normal coitus. It plays no role whatsoever in pro-
> creation. The woman is penetrated and impregnated through the vagina; it
> becomes an erotic center uniquely through the intervention of the male, and
> this always constitutes a kind of rape.[30]

The matter of vaginal sensation embodied the erotic complexities of
female sexuality: "Pleasure is reached by the contractions of the inside surface of the vagina; do these contractions result in a precise and

definitive orgasm? This point is still being debated. The anatomical data are vague."[31] Beauvoir was summarizing what were then obscure debates about female sexuality. She was drawing particularly on Helene Deutsch's theories of "doubled sexual organs" and the tensions between clitoral and "mature" or vaginal orgasms. These theories were produced by Deutsch's efforts to square her ideas with Freud's; here they map onto the existential tension between being for itself and being for others.[32] As a standalone piece, "The Sexual Initiation of the Woman" could be a slightly opaque and startling introduction to Beauvoir's existential phenomenology of the woman's body.[33]

By Beauvoir's own account, the 1949 articles in *Les Temps Modernes* were the ones in which she put most on the line, for they placed sexuality at the center of the lived experience of a woman.[34] Sexuality was a high-stakes venture for all human beings, Beauvoir argued, and inextricable from the process of coming to terms with one's desires, identity, and future. It was integral to the search for being. If one's body was the "instrument of one's purchase on the world," sexuality was one of the principal ways in which one found a foothold—or tried to. For women, sexuality involved navigating a minefield of social prohibitions and expectations, alienating experiences, and pleasures renounced, denied, or, as in the case of orgasm, simply hard to achieve. Beauvoir wrote unabashedly, in the language of scientific frankness, and joined that language to a philosophy of female being.

Paris Match did not publish excerpts like these. *Les Temps Modernes*, obviously, stood worlds away from even a bold mass market magazine. It had a very different notion of what it meant to be provocative and no use for any form of *pudeur*. *Les Temps Modernes* insisted on responsibility and *radical* freedom rather than the cheerful celebration of life and liberty of the postwar, and on ruthless truth-telling and self-scrutiny in the place in eye-catching photographs and popular psychology.[35] It was one of many small intellectual journals to appear on the landscape of the postwar French press. That landscape had been transformed by the massive shuttering of newspapers and journals that had collaborated with the Nazis during the Occupation.[36] *Les Temps Modernes* did not simply step into that new space; it proposed a new agenda for postwar culture. Writers could not escape their historical moment; they had to engage it. As Sartre wrote in his presentation of the journal, "We do not want to

miss anything of our time." Sartre set out the journal's philosophical position: there was no human nature but rather a human condition. Humans
were finite: they were born and died, and they existed in the world. Every
human was *situated*, and a situation was given. Human freedom and ethical responsibility were nonetheless starting points. "It is not difficult to
understand that a man, although totally conditioned by his situation, can
be a center of irreducible indeterminacy . . . One does not do whatever
one wants, and yet one is responsible for what one is: such are the facts."[37]
Against the bleakness of France's dark years and the stunning shattering
of norms over the course of two world wars, this philosophical stance
was enormously attractive. Engagement's exalted view of the importance
of writing and the writer's power to grasp human reality and change the
world appealed as well, for it built on the prestige of literature and intellectuals even as it recast that prestige in postwar terms. Sartre's "theo-
rization of engagement was a true symbolic coup de force," writes the
historian Gisèle Sapiro.[38] While *Les Temps Modernes* was at "the pole
of small-scale literary production," it attracted much attention in radical
intellectual circles in France and abroad.

What were the readers of *Les Temps Modernes* to think of "The Sexual
Initiation of the Woman"? How did Beauvoir's article, or *The Second Sex*
in its entirety, reflect the journal's project? The difficulty of answering
those questions was part of the scandal, so the journal's aims are worth a
brief discussion. *Les Temps Modernes* set out to redefine the subjects that
needed to be investigated, encouraging critical inquiry in a wide range of
topics and genres. It would publish poetry, literature and literary criticism,
philosophy, and cultural criticism of cinema and music, notably jazz. As
Beauvoir emphasized in her retrospective account, *Les Temps Modernes*
embraced essays, life writing, philosophy, and "every form of cultural
product, every social expression, however low or insignificant."[39] It would
reach across the Atlantic, Europe, and the colonial world. It would also
try to get close to the ground, covering daily life as well as politics, petty
theft as well as war crimes, psychological and psychiatric studies as well
as the philosophy of ethics. Every issue would feature a document, or testimony, accompanied by investigations and reporting.

The journal's philosophical stance joined the existentialist insistence
on the creation of meaning to phenomenological investigation of perception, or how the world comes to be known by oneself. The key phrase

of phenomenology is *lived experience*. The psychology and experience of colonial racism and white supremacy were excellent examples of the project and its political aims. *Les Temps Modernes* published literature and poetry by the negritude writers. It translated the work of African American writer Richard Wright, notably *Black Boy*. The project of bringing new voices into a global conversation on race and the excruciating everyday experience of racism was especially important to Beauvoir. An analysis of racism figured prominently in her *America Day by Day*, published in five installments in *Les Temps Modernes* just before the excerpts from *The Second Sex*. She drew inspiration and concepts from the African American existentialists like Wright and the theorists of negritude—Léopold Sédar Senghor (from Senegal), Aimé Césaire (from Martinique), and Léon Damas (from Guiana)—who had written on the experiences of colonialism and being black under the rule of French culture, with its universalist pretentions and racist premises.[40] On gender as on race, Beauvoir aimed to strip away myths of natural difference that rationalized inequality and oppression.[41]

The purpose of *The Second Sex*, then, lined up with other *Les Temps Modernes* projects, though the fit was hardly obvious. In the spirit of *Les Temps Modernes*, Beauvoir's study was interdisciplinary.[42] It swept across an international theoretical and social scientific literature that pertained to the condition of woman broadly understood: psychoanalysis, research on sexuality, the history of capitalist property and the family, the anthropological study of kinship. Beauvoir aimed to uncover overarching social structures as well as capture perception and experience. Finally, as one of the editors of *Les Temps Modernes*, Beauvoir relished plunging into controversy; this was a period of rebirth, bubbling with experiments and debate. In her words, there were "so many challenges, errors to correct, misunderstandings to dissipate, critics to push back against."[43]

If the journal courted controversy, it got it. Even radical intellectuals could find "The Sexual Initiation of the Woman" disconcerting. When *The Second Sex* came out, Beauvoir's fellow intellectual (and sometime ally) Albert Camus reportedly said Beauvoir had made French men look ridiculous. She quoted the distinguished French writer Julien Benda's remark that "the generative act consists of the occupation of one being by another" as one example of the grandiose imagery of male sexuality in French literature, where the man was glorious, penetrating, and conquering.[44] Camus may have balked at Beauvoir's page-long descriptions of how men and women experience sexual desire. The man proudly gets an erection, she wrote, while the woman passively becomes "moist." Those passages included one of Beauvoir's more arresting formulations: "Female heat is the soft throbbing of a mollusk."[45]

Le Figaro Littéraire and the Scandal of Decency

Camus may have been embarrassed at such talk, but the distinguished writer and critic François Mauriac was outraged. "Does the subject studied by Simone de Beauvoir, 'The Sexual Initiation of the Woman,' belong on the table of contents of a serious philosophical and literary journal?" Mauriac asked indignantly on the front page of the literary supplement of *Le Figaro*, France's solidly bourgeois newspaper.[46] Mauriac had not reacted to the first volume of *The Second Sex*. But "The Sexual Initiation of Women" in *Les Temps Modernes* was another matter, and it set him in motion immediately. From his post at *Le Figaro* he issued a cultural call to arms, producing what turned into a three-month-long inquiry on the lamentable state of contemporary French letters. Nearly every biography of Beauvoir or history of *The Second Sex* mentions Mauriac's angry public denunciation of the book, and especially his private note to Beauvoir's colleague at the journal Roger Stéphane that he had learned a lot about the vagina and clitoris of Stéphane's boss in the latest issue of *Les Temps Modernes*. Mauriac would later say that such language was beneath him. It was not. A year later Mauriac again fumed privately in a letter about women writers with doctorates in philosophy who criticized his work. He could no longer bear "these educated idiots in high heels, these screeching and pedantic cunts," he wrote.[47]

In 1949 Mauriac was an immensely prestigious figure, "the prototype of the Catholic intellectual," member of the French Academy (Académie Française) since 1933, veteran of the intellectual resistance to Vichy and the Nazis, and a Catholic known for courageously defying right-wing dogma.[48] He supported the Republicans in the Spanish civil war. (The Republicans defended the Spanish government against Catholic conservatives and against the military, which was in armed revolt against it.) Come Vichy and the Occupation, Mauriac helped to keep the French Academy from giving itself over wholesale to collaboration. Though a conservative Gaullist, he made common cause with communist literary figures in writing for the Resistance newspaper *Les Lettres Françaises*, and was briefly honorary president of the National Committee of Writers. At the Liberation in 1944, he emerged as the most important literary voice of the Gaullist Resistance. That Mauriac was also a crude misogynist, however, is neither surprising nor the most interesting point to be gleaned from considering his response to Beauvoir's articles. Much more important was his mobilization of other readers, writers, and representatives of French letters to debate Beauvoir's subject. In the context of understanding the discourse of *pudeur*, it is also revealing to consider what Mauriac believed was at stake in writing about sex.

On May 30, immediately after spotting "The Sexual Initiation of the Woman" in *Les Temps Modernes*, Mauriac denounced it in a front-page editorial, warning that it represented a dangerous cultural turn. France should stand at the center of a postwar revival of humanism. It could not betray its international followers. "Too often we are shamed by comparing what certain peoples expect of us with what we offer them . . . But I nonetheless believe that what radiates out from Paris across the ruins of Europe is more important and more serious than in any other era," he argued. "What do we give to the youth of the world that reads our journals and books?" Mauriac asked. What was "the youth of the world" gleaning from Saint-Germain-des-Prés, the current center of the so-called avant-garde? Jabbing at Jean-Paul Sartre, who had been Mauriac's nemesis for a decade, he said the answer made him "nauseated." (*Nausea* was Sartre's first novel, published to some fanfare in 1938.) "We have literally reached the limits of the abject."[49] Simone de Beauvoir's article was only the logical and unbearable conclusion of broader literary and theoretical tendencies. The turn to the "abject" and the obscene had to be repudiated:

> This is not a question of taking up arms against audacious, great work or the [kind of poetry that] transfigures and purifies. Man has to be known, and we must carry our torchlights into the abyss. But the abject is never beautiful. Are [the Marquis de] Sade and his emulators a matter for psychiatry or literature? Does the subject studied by Simone de Beauvoir, "the sexual initiation of the woman," belong in the table of contents of a serious philosophical and literary journal?[50]

Over the following issues of *Le Figaro* and its weekly literary supplement, Mauriac painted a panorama of literary and philosophical amorality, immorality, and abnormality. That tableau placed existentialists alongside surrealists, who were subversively fascinated by dreams and the unconscious, and Freud, who had transformed culture's understanding of the human. He associated all of those with the revived literary interest in the Marquis de Sade and erotic literature and the baneful influence of André Gide, Mauriac's shorthand for homosexuality.[51] The erotic had been loosened from any moorings in morality, which not only offended Catholic sensibilities but also constituted a danger to the literature and culture in which all had a stake. Mauriac issued a special invitation to "young intellectuals," who represented France's future, to share their views on the subject with *Le Figaro Littéraire*. His question was bluntly accusatory and political: "Do you believe that the systematic recourse to the forces of instinct and to madness in literature today [in the humanities] and the cultivation of eroticism that this has encouraged constitutes a danger for the individual, the nation, and for literature itself? Are some men, some doctrines responsible for this?"[52]

Forums on the responsibility of literature were a tradition at *Le Figaro* and reflect French cultural preoccupations. The newspaper (and Mauriac) had organized a similar discussion in 1940, just after the fall of France to the Nazis.[53] The 1949 inquiry sparked a great deal of interest. *Le Figaro Littéraire* published more than thirty responses, and the newspaper received even more than that. The particularly painful aftermath of the war intensified the moralism of the literary field in France, and that moralism, or sense of writerly responsibility, fueled both Beauvoir's project and Mauriac's anger.

Not surprisingly, many of the writers who responded had less to say about Beauvoir's arguments than about her subject as symptom of the war's aftermath. "The cataclysm that we have suffered will sow its seeds of death for decades" and has encouraged the "doctrine" of existentialism, wrote one young intellectual, who defined existentialism as the "morbid attraction of despair." Wrote another, warming to Mauriac's theme, "A world is ending, worn out and rotting, and it leaves behind a nauseating stench that turns one's stomach." The "collapse of Christianity and of the institutions of the state" had sown "chaos." How could a culture survive when subject to "uncontrolled desires," in an "atmosphere of cynicism, and without any moral norms"? Those who "stood with the nation, and had risked their lives for their country," knew that moral codes had to be clear.[54]

Conservatives and communists alike called for a literature that would restore the country. French literature needed to be "constructive, ardent, and generous"—to end the mourning for France's lost grandeur and redeem the nation in the eyes of the world.[55] Pierre Boisdeffre, perhaps the most prominent young conservative to join in the conversation, impatiently called on his colleagues to "leave the imposters and masochists to their nausea" ("nausea" was code for Sartre) and to rediscover "a literature founded on the grandeur of humanity."[56] Several communists specifically endorsed Boisdeffre's language and his thirst "to construct a new world."[57]

Few respondents, however, could summon Boisdeffre's apparent confidence. Accusation and denunciation mixed with self-laceration, and it was often hard to discern whether Beauvoir, Sartre, Gide, Freud, and the Marquis de Sade were being charged with peddling lies or revealing painful truths. Many who responded agreed with Mauriac; they called the present a "swamp," a time of "chaos" and the debasement of conscience, and an era characterized by a "deep contempt for man."[58] Some of the contributors lacerated philosophical doctrines that in the name of "realism" and "honesty" had banished meaning from the world and reduced the human to the sexual. Others argued that the times called for serious self-scrutiny. Why would we want to "distort the image in the mirror"? Literature reflected society, and French society was bereft of hope and heroes. "We will get the literature we deserve" was a common sentiment.[59]

Mauriac touched many raw nerves: not just sexuality but also collaboration, shame, humiliation, repression, and sin. In this anguished swirl of recriminations and self-accusation, Beauvoir's *arguments* counted for very little. But her *subject* sparked a charged series of reactions and associations. To speak of the "sexual," or to insist that it was important to do so, was to reduce and debase the human; it represented the surrender of civilization or the individual will to the dark forces of sex and the "stench of instinct."[60] It is perhaps not surprising that in the war's aftermath, a discourse of wounded and anxiously recuperating humanism would assimilate "Freud," a shorthand for all psychoanalytic schools and any attention to sexuality or the unconscious, to capitulation and defeatism. But it is remarkable to see how often it did so. Powerful images of a recent past, of betrayal, dishonesty, compromise, open collaboration, or indifference—the whole range of wartime wrongs—made those associations particularly painful.

World War II loomed over this forum. Several contributors said as much: Mauriac had turned a debate about French literature and thought into a question of guilt.[61] Another contributor spelled out the issues as he saw them: Mauriac's fear of sin, of succumbing to temptation, and of committing crimes had much broader resonance; he was channeling a culture trying to escape its own demons.[62] The writing throughout the long Mauriac forum on Beauvoir's book was laden with similar metaphors of sin, fear, shame, and repression, of *pudeur* and denial.[63] Whatever the writers' position on *The Second Sex*, the subject of sex raised the specter of exploring hidden secrets and confessions. Beauvoir's champions defended her work in those very terms, hailing her as an advocate for individual and collective self-scrutiny, for "the will to face up to the present" or the book's "unpitying analysis."[64] *The Second Sex* was a sign of "a literature that was moral, healthy, and alive."[65]

François Mauriac's own position was deeply Catholic. When other contributors to his debate pointed out that Mauriac's novels from the 1930s teemed with the very "eroticism" he now deplored, he responded that they misunderstood the term. He cited the *Littré* and the dictionary of the French Academy: the erotic comprised everything having to do with love. Eros was the cry of human desire and all that entailed; it was the battle of the spirit against the desires of the flesh or the "drama of man, divided against himself," a conflict transcended only by discovering the love of God. The drama of man dealt in the erotic; Beauvoir's article on female sexuality dealt in the abject.

Virtually none of those who took up their pens in *Le Figaro Littéraire* or in other reviews adopted religious language. As one young contributor pointed out, the Catholic right had been so discredited by Vichy's "moral order" that "the Catholics do not dare say anything on this matter." Several responses mocked Mauriac: "You want us to define ourselves with reference to a few ideas. Evil and Purity . . . God's grace and vile flesh . . . [T]hese ideas have gone to people's heads too . . . Is evil beautiful? Does sexual initiation belong in a philosophical journal? *We don't care.*" One contributor reported: "Our time no longer has the theological

fear of the flesh . . . [T]he sexual has been emptied of the notion of sin."
Yet the female body, sexuality, and the language in which they could be
discussed remained encircled by taboos that layered religious with more
secular prohibitions. Reviewers lamented Beauvoir's "remorselessly precise language," which spared "no horrible detail" and depicted "the woman's body as a haunted house." Her medical-philosophical language made
what should be "natural and beautiful" instead "sickening." Her view
of sexuality was "vulgar," "obscene and pedantic," "an inventory of the
amoral drives of the individual," and "a display of the unavowed"—or
unavowable (*étalage de l'inavoué*).[66]

As he ended his forum, Mauriac apologized to the readers of *Le Figaro*:
he was profoundly disappointed by the relative *absence* of indignation. He
rued the hardened sensibilities of a young generation of writers and readers who had grown up not with children's songs and fairy tales but instead
with the "stories of the camps of terror" (*récits des camps d'épouvante*).
He did not hesitate to raise what he felt to be the stakes: "Decency [*La
Pudeur*], too, was deported; Decency, too, has returned from Auschwitz.
Erotic literature testifies against us, the older generation, in the sense that
we are responsible for the crimes among which our sons had to grow
up."[67] It was one of the most striking comments in the whole three months
of debate, a jarring (and confusing) combination of accusation and self-
accusation. It registers the shock and ongoing horror at the wave of
devastating testimony from survivors about their experiences in the concentration camps. This wave included David Rousset's *L'univers concen-
trationnaire* (1946) and *Les jours de notre mort* (1947); Robert Antelme's
L'espèce humaine (1947); Germaine Tillion's first collection of her fellow déportees' testimony on the women's camp at Ravensbrück (1946),
a project to which Tillion would return; and Louis Martin-Chauffier's
L'homme et la bête (1948), which expressed the same Catholic anguish
as Mauriac's work.[68] Mauriac's gesture was very much of the moment;
like many of his contemporaries, he reached for the meaning of the crimes
that had been witnessed. For Mauriac that meaning lay in the destruction of humanity itself and the sacredness of life. In this writing, those
themes blur with the moral crimes of the French state and nation, anguish
at having to forge ahead in a world of shattered values, Mauriac's sense
of being accused or testified against, and his misogynist rage at Beauvoir's defiant irreverence. There is anguish, too, in Mauriac's harrowing

image of "Decency" returning from Auschwitz, a traumatized witness to the bankruptcy of his generation's values. If "Decency" had any claim to value or moral traction, it surely lay not simply in concealing humanity's darker impulses but in keeping them at bay. Its brittleness exposed, decency devolved into hypocrisy and self-delusion. The new defenses and gestures of self-protection make sense in this historical context. So does the anger these writers turned against a woman who dared to write not about the affirming love of women for men or their families but rather about women's sexual desires and nightmares.

Silences

Across all of the contemporary French reviews of *The Second Sex*, a few subjects received almost no notice. The enfranchisement of French women got scarcely a nod, as if the vote had mooted "the old suffragette dream."[69] Only a few French reviewers seemed to think Beauvoir represented a larger stirring of women's discontent.[70] Many referred, however, to dismal gender relations across the Atlantic or American "matriarchy," an allusion to women's political influence.[71]

Reviewers rarely mentioned contraception or abortion outright, though several obliquely lamented Beauvoir's "sexual egoism" or "selfishness." Sympathetic reviewers tiptoed around the issue, writing of the difficulties women faced at a historical moment when they were assuming new burdens in the workplace without being freed from "long-standing servitude" and "wrenching questions that are biological and social." One noteworthy review by a Protestant woman underscored women's everyday dilemmas, and their isolation when faced with unwanted pregnancies; women grappled with their responsibilities with no aid or understanding from a silent and distant Catholic Church. When Beauvoir's 1949 article "Maternity" came out in *Les Temps Modernes*, women and men began to furtively visit the journal's editorial offices and her apartment to ask for addresses of doctors who would provide abortions.[72] The willingness of *Paris Match* to broach the topics of contraception and abortion suggests that the mass circulation magazine had taken an accurate measure of the widespread public desire for sexual knowledge and for controlling childbearing—Catholicism notwithstanding.

The critics, or expert readers, were also nearly silent on the relationship of racial and colonial to gender subjugation. The specific character of women's Otherness and women's failure to "contest the sovereignty of men" were central concerns of *The Second Sex*. Beauvoir analogized myths of feminine inferiority to anti-Semitism and to the racism of the Jim Crow South, drawing from Gunnar Myrdal's analysis of prejudice in *An American Dilemma* (1944).[73] In her conclusion, she likened the position of men of goodwill to that of colonial administrators who cannot avoid complicity in structures of subjugation. Beauvoir's analysis of women's tangled confrontation with contempt and prejudice were deeply indebted to the contemporary literature on racism and the experience of it. Richard Wright's influence loomed large in *America Day by Day* (1948) and *The Second Sex*.[74] How the subjugation of women resembled or differed from that of others joined Beauvoir's concerns to those of her most important interlocutors and friends, to internationally influential studies like Myrdal's *American Dilemma*, and to the emerging concern with anticolonialism on the French left and at *Les Temps Modernes*. In the words of the one reviewer who even mentioned this part of Beauvoir's argument, it "gave the book an accent of truth" and "justified" the attention paid to it.[75] Yet the obvious parallels between American racism and French colonialism received not a word, although racism, carefully circumscribed as "American," was a very common topic on the French left. No one was prepared or willing to consider the subjugation of women on the same plane. The analogies between racial and gender subordination would be disconcerting to left and right alike, and thinking them through would lead toward matters that were genuinely explosive: the role of violence, of sexuality, and of the policing of sexual relations in both systems, miscegenation, lynching, and rape.

Dominique Aury

To emphasize the silences and scandal that greeted *The Second Sex* in 1949 risks underestimating the serious and sustained discussions it provoked. As historian Sandrine Sanos rightly points out, Beauvoir was not the only woman willing to tackle the subjects of women's condition, including sexuality. Françoise d'Eaubonne, one of the few bold feminist writers of the period, defended Beauvoir and ridiculed Mauriac's inquisitorial style. The writer and psychoanalyst Maryse Choisy applauded Beauvoir's willingness to bring psychoanalysis into conversation with hoary clichés about women.[76] The most noteworthy review, however, came from writer Dominique Aury. Aury (a pen name; she was born Anne Desclos) was a fascinating figure: translator, editor, voracious reader, cultural and literary critic affiliated first with the right and then with the Resistance, and well known and connected in the French literary scene.[77] By 1950, when she reviewed *The Second Sex* for a small journal of culture, she was on the editorial committee of Gallimard and was editorial secretary of *La Nouvelle Revue Française*, where she worked alongside its director, Jean Paulhan. She was involved in quasi-secretive relationships with both Paulhan and the radical and feminist writer Edith Thomas.[78] Aury praised Beauvoir for her moral clarity, her patience, her courage, and her wide knowledge. She chided anyone who was surprised by either Beauvoir's arguments or her explicitness. The language in Beauvoir's analysis of female sexuality was commonplace in the international literature on psychoanalysis, sexology, and social science, and her arguments about the history of the family had been laid out by Marxists in the nineteenth century. If anyone was shocked by Beauvoir's approach, Aury wrote, that was because "it seemed understood, once and for all, that there are reserved domains, doubly taboo, forbidden, first, to the general public and, second, to women." To discuss sexual acts was a privilege reserved for doctors and priests. *The Second Sex* had violated "the rules of *pudeur* and a good upbringing." Such frank talk from a woman was a "usurpation," the more so since Beauvoir spoke without feigning embarrassment or modesty.[79]

Aury's review illustrates a radical contemporary's assessment of *The Second Sex*. She admired Beauvoir for wrestling fearlessly with the important questions about the condition of women. She endorsed Beauvoir's analysis of woman's infuriating dependence and her position as the Other of man. Above all, Aury applauded Beauvoir's detailed and graphic rendering of the lived experience of the female body. She spent several pages recapitulating Beauvoir's account of becoming a woman: a girl's disgust and humiliation at her first menstrual period, a young woman's first experience with intercourse, a woman's ongoing fears of becoming pregnant, and her profound ambivalence about motherhood. Beauvoir had captured especially well a young woman's powerlessness and shock in the face of "the processes that take hold of a young body and don't let go." As she put it, Beauvoir "delves into the psychoanalytic literature on infant sexuality, adolescence, and the emotional lives of women, and she comes out as if she were emerging from a descent into hell."[80]

Aury's review is remarkable. It is even more so because under deeper cover and a different pen name, Pauline Réage, she was the author of *The Story of O*, which went on to become one the most popular erotic novels of the 1950s. *O* is told in a woman's voice; it is an erotic fantasy of willing and absolute submission to all the sexual desires of the man with whom she in love, however cruel they may be, including passing her on to serve other men sexually. *O* abandons herself to grotesque exposure, humiliation, and torture, and revels in sadomasochistic pleasure. The French Commission of the Book, trying to shut down the publication of *The Story of O*, described it as "violently and knowingly immoral, with scenes of debauchery with two or several characters alternating with scenes of sexual cruelty . . . an assault on moral standards." Aury herself later described it as a "the story of a love so pure that it survives all kinds of debauchery." She asserted that she wrote it as a series of letters to seduce Paulhan, who admired de Sade and had challenged her to write something in that vein. *O*'s fantasies had emerged from her own erotic imagination, Aury said: she wanted her character's voice and behavior to make plain that the erotic world of a woman was as "wild [*fou*] as that of a man, and as obsessive." Aury was writing her review of *The Second Sex* while at work on *The Story of O*, although her novel would not come out until 1954.[81]

At the end of her review, Aury expressed skepticism about what she considered Beauvoir's Enlightenment-style faith in the power of reason to change her readers' minds. She pushed back against the optimistic conclusion of *The Second Sex*, where Beauvoir envisioned women and men joining hands in "fraternity" to forge a new world. Change would not come so easily, Aury wrote, and Beauvoir had not reckoned with how much women themselves contributed to their condition. That charge was not quite fair. Beauvoir took woman's "unusual complicity with her oppressor" and the appeal of "capitulation" very seriously; she called on women to "abdicate the privileges" that came with agreeing to be man's subordinate and Other.[82] Woman's position as Other distorted her subjectivity, twisted her character, and stifled resistance. But Beauvoir's psychological existentialism apparently did not convince Aury. In fact, against this backdrop *The Story of O* reads as an implicit counter to *The Second Sex*. For Beauvoir, the intimate politics of capitulation played out as a failure of will. For Aury, O's fantasy represented a woman's more intractable and opaque psychic investments in her condition. Beauvoir emphasized ethical choices; Aury laid bare the perverse dimensions of pleasure (male and female) and the power of errant or inadmissible fantasies.[83]

Finally, and this is central to the subject of readers, Aury went on in her review to imagine herself as both the author of *The Second Sex* and a woman reader. Beauvoir's long and explicit discussion of female sexuality, which detailed painful sexual experiences *and* lingered over sexual pleasures, was risky for the author, Aury remarked perceptively.[84] Beauvoir had revealed more of herself than she perhaps recognized, creating an uncomfortable intimacy with her readers: "Exposing herself in this way implicates herself and implicates other women along with her. They will not be least among those who resent her."[85] Aury, who wrote under *two* pseudonyms, plainly knew something about self-protection, the dangers of self-revelation, and the codes of *pudeur*. False *pudeur*, as *Elle* magazine had scornfully called it, might be thoroughly dated, but the female body and female sexual feeling remained sites of vulnerability, humiliation, and shame. To lay out in detail women's sexual desires and sensual pleasures, as both Beauvoir and Aury did, might suggest that women lacked the self-control and dignity that were essential features of womanliness. To intimate that they were also afflicted with chronic sexual unhappiness seemed a crowning indignity.

How ordinary women would read *The Second Sex* occasioned much critical speculation. Would they find themselves understood, explained, and defended? Or exposed and accused? One reviewer of *The Second Sex* in 1949 called the book "a detached and cold manual." He believed that women readers would never recognize themselves "in the windows of Mme. de Beauvoir's museum of natural history," declaring, "I am persuaded that a woman can only move men and, especially, women if, when discussing women, she writes as a woman."[86] Reviewers like Aury argued just the opposite: Beauvoir put herself at center stage; this *was* a woman's voice.[87]

That a woman would write about sex as a woman, with an emphasis on "lived experience," proved one of the most disconcerting features of all of Beauvoir's work. It was a challenge to the discursive rules or emotional balance of decency. It was a striking example of the difficulties of finding a language of sexuality that was not reflexively considered erotic or pornographic, and the dangers of a tone that implicated and threatened the reader. The intimate, detailed, and personal character of Beauvoir's work was not incidental but deliberate and philosophical. Beauvoir's theoretical stance was much like her friend and fellow phenomenologist Maurice Merleau-Ponty's: "Whatever is metaphysical in man cannot be credited to something outside his empirical being—to God, to Consciousness. Man is metaphysical in his very being, in his loves, in his hates, in his individual and collective history. And metaphysics is no longer the occupation of a few hours per month, as Descartes said; it is present, as Pascal thought, in the heart's slightest movement."[88] In *The Second Sex*, few movements of the heart or yearnings of the body went unexplored. That exploration was and would remain an important but difficult-to-manage element of Beauvoir's bond with her readers.

The Second Sex was written in an astonishingly short year and a half. It reflected Beauvoir's many ambitions as an engaged postwar intellectual: to advance existentialism as a philosophical tradition; to theorize the body and bodily experience as suggested by phenomenology, which meant reading the research and literary testimony on sexuality with an eye to lived experience; to confront the major literary figures of her culture; and to understand the experience of Otherness and racial prejudice in some of its forms. An intellectual culture so adamant about responsibility and the power of the written word shaped Beauvoir's sense of purpose. *The Second Sex* was pulled in different directions by its author's intense and radical engagement with the many issues of her time—by her determination not to "miss anything." Inevitably readers ricocheted off the different parts of the argument. *The Second Sex* was an enormous and difficult book, and this was a painful and uncertain moment. The critics, and the journals and magazines they represented, seized on points that preoccupied them: the basis for cultural renewal, the traumas of the war, the boundaries of the erotic and the obscene, and writers' responsibility to speak truth while respecting the disciplines of decency and privacy. As Beauvoir herself noted, this was "an era that wanted to know itself."[89] The demand for self-scrutiny and self-knowledge, however, sat uneasily alongside postwar protectiveness about the intimate political life of the nation and the enduring image of the female body as a particular danger zone.

2

BEAUVOIR, KINSEY, AND
MIDCENTURY SEX

The frenzy with which a whole section of the public, and not only
Anglo-Saxons, devours anything on this subject . . . [is] worth a
study in itself.

JULIEN BENDA, "Social Life and Female Sexuality"

Of the many baneful cultural trends that François Mauriac associated
with *The Second Sex*, the most prominent was a new wave of research on
sexuality exemplified by Alfred C. Kinsey's 1948 report, *Sexual Behavior
in the Human Male*. In nearly one thousand pages documented with co-
pious statistics, Kinsey and his team of American scientists scrutinized an
extraordinary variety of sexual acts, practices, inclinations, and tastes that
they had discovered among their fellow citizens. Mauriac considered the
genre, the findings, and the public interest in them appalling. Writers no
longer treated love and eros; they had turned toward "sexuality as an object of study, as a problem." At a time when culture and philosophy might
provide armor for the human soul, they had only exposed humanity's vulnerability and "torn away all veils."[1] Mauriac's indictment swept together
Beauvoir, Kinsey, Sartre, and Freud, and a remarkable number of critics who either answered Mauriac's call in the *Figaro Literary Supplement*
or reviewed *The Second Sex* elsewhere named the same names.[2] Critics,

deeply invested in the role of literature and the responsibility of the writer, warned that *The Second Sex* and the Kinsey report debased the public. They likened the two studies to the "erotic jungle" of American popular culture and fashion magazines, a world of commerce, sensationalism, and prurience. When they sought to situate *The Second Sex* in the larger history of contemporary culture, they fastened onto the scholarly study of sexuality and the public's apparent fixation on the subject.

Alfred C. Kinsey received a Ph.D. in biology from Harvard in 1920. As a professor at Indiana University, he taught entomology and zoology and studied variations in gall wasps. Kinsey turned to the varieties of *human* sexual behavior in 1938, researching sexual histories, beginning with those of students in his classes and then branching out into the region and the nation. Funding from the Rockefeller Foundation and National Research Council enabled him to found the Institute of Sex Research and to compile data on an impressive variety of sexual practices. Six thousand aggregated cases served as the basis for *Sexual Behavior in the Human Male*. The report was published in the United States in January 1948. It hit the bookstores of Paris in December of the same year, six months before the first volume of *Le deuxième sexe* came out in the spring of 1949. Remarkably enough, the entanglement continued, for *The Second Sex* was published in the United States by Alfred A. Knopf in 1953, just ahead of Kinsey's second report, *Sexual Behavior in the Human Female*. Beauvoir and Kinsey, then, were read and reviewed together on both sides of the Atlantic—a fact that has received little serious comment in the many recent studies of either thinker.[3] Scholars have often noted how Beauvoir's work was entangled in contemporary American research and writing—especially, but not only, on race—and the formative role of her experiences in the United States.[4] But the relationship between *The Second Sex* and the Kinsey report is harder to grasp.

It sometimes appears as if readers in the early 1950s, even those more than capable of understanding Beauvoir's philosophical arguments, found it impossible to read her *without* reference to Kinsey. Consider, for example, one eminently ideal reader: a brilliant and learned philosopher, a European woman, a refugee from Nazism living in the United States and included on Alfred Knopf's "ladies' list" for in-house reviews of *The Second Sex*. The marketing department at Alfred A. Knopf sent her the

galleys, asking her for comments to use in their advertising and promo-
tion. Hannah Arendt replied:

> I thank you for your kindness in sending me Simone de Beauvoir's *The Sec-
> ond Sex*, and I sincerely regret that my answer will disappoint you. The
> truth is that I did not like the book, but think that it will have a considerable
> success. In a way, it fills a public demand for the never published Kinsley
> [*sic*] report on the Female and I feel that its lack of Kinsley's scientific ap-
> paratus and its (limited) accuracy will not diminish its value in this respect.

Arendt may not have read Kinsey (she didn't get his name right), but she
plainly knew of "Kinsley" as a cultural phenomenon: a widely discussed
demonstration of the broad appeal of the "apparatus" of science and of
the American public's appetite for sexual knowledge. Arendt had little use
for Kinsey's brand of science, and none for Beauvoir's philosophy either:

> I at least would not have been disturbed by the lack of this kind of "scien-
> tific" standards. But I have been irritated by Miss Beauvoir's historical gen-
> eralizations which, I think are due to her one-sided and poor selection of
> sources. The omission of almost all great love-stories in literature, the com-
> plete oblivion of Shakespeare, Homer, Sophocles and the preference for a
> very dubious kind of confession literature lowers the level of discussion to
> a point where almost every opinion becomes more or less arbitrary. The in-
> troduction of philosophical categories into the discussion (no matter which
> intrinsic value these categories may have) does not help; they are and func-
> tion like preconceived notions which exclude both historical evidence and
> tangible experience.

Sex was not insignificant, but Arendt would have preferred an analysis
akin to Freud's *Civilization and Its Discontents* (1929), which focused on
the tension between the social, or binding, aspects of the matter and its an-
tisocial, disruptive, and unconscious ones. She wrote:

> The objective problem of the book is to treat sex as a social phenomenon.
> The problem itself is, of course, entirely legitimate. But it so happens that sex
> as a procreative force is the fundament of society while, in another sense, it
> always has been an anti-social power. The two saving graces in a discussion

of sex as a social phenomenon would be a sense of humour and a reveren-
tial awe for love. Discussions which move beyond love and humour have a
certain tendency to become plain ridiculous because of the special nature of
the subject matter. I have the impression that this book does not always succeed in avoiding this danger and that its author is curiously unaware of it.[5]

Arendt studiously ignored Beauvoir's arguments about women's subjugation. She declined to acknowledge any affinity between Beauvoir's
subject and her own concerns with sources of authoritarian rule, anti-
Semitism, colonialism, and racial inequality. If any lineage connected the
existential phenomenology of Martin Heidegger, the philosopher who was
Arendt's mentor (and more), to Sartre, Beauvoir, and their brand of philosophy, Arendt would have none of it. Rather, she classified Beauvoir's
work under the distant and emphatically lesser rubric of Kinsey-ish studies of sexual behavior, in which humans were only updated biological
animals.

To juxtapose the Hegel-and-Stendhal-citing French existentialist
and the zealous zoologist from Indiana is commonly considered simply
another instance of how contemporaries misunderstood and misread *The
Second Sex*.[6] In fact, the Beauvoir-Kinsey pairing offers a fuller intertextual appreciation of Beauvoir's work. Both books represented what I call
"midcentury sex": a historical moment with a distinctively expansive conception of the meanings and salience of sexuality. The French sociologist
Michel Bozon has pointed to the "variable geometry" of the term "sexuality": the crisscrossing lines and circles that connect the overlapping
domains of body, psyche, emotions, identity, motives, desires, social relations, and culture. As Bozon argues, this geometry has tended to become
more variable with time.[7] From the late nineteenth century on, theorizing
and retheorizing sex and sexuality multiplied those variations, and by the
middle of the twentieth century, they were crowded under the one rubric
of sex: a compelling, important, and nearly incoherent subject.[8]

The midcentury moment in the intellectual history of sexuality was
produced by a conjuncture of trends ongoing since the late nineteenth century. Those included the emergence of sexual science, the psychoanalytic
reinterpretation of sexuality, feminist and gay reform movements that
connected sexual to social reform, and anthropology's fascination with
kinship and culture. In the aftermath of two world wars, those longer-
term trends crossed paths with both somber reflections on human cruelty,

Hannah Arendt   130 Morningside Drive   New York 27 , N.Y.

December 16, 1952.

Mr. William Cole
Alfred A. Knopf, Inc.
501 Madison Avenue
New York 22, N.Y.

Dear Mr. Cole:

I thank you for your kindness in sending me Simone
de Beauvoir's book The Second Sex and I sincerely regret that
my answer will disappoint you. The truth is that I did not like
the book, but think that it will have a considerable success.
In a way, it fills a public demand for the never published Kinsley
report on the Female and I feel that its lack of Kinsley's scientific apparatus and (limited) accuracy will not diminish its value
in this respect.

I at least would not have been disturbed by this
kind of "scientific" standards. But I have been irritated by Miss
Beauvoir's historical generalizations which, I think, are due to
her one-sided and poor selection of sources. The omission of almost all great love-stories in literature, the complete oblivion
of Shakespeare, Homer, Sophocles and the preference for a very
dubious kind of confession literature lower the level of discussion
to a point where almost every opinion becomes more or less arbitra-
ry. The introduction of philosophical categories into the discussion
(no matter which intrinsic value these categories may have) does
not help; they are and function like preconceived notions which exclude both historical evidence and tangible experience.

The objective problem of the book is to treat sex
as a social phenomenon. The problem itself is, of course, entirely
legitimate. But it so happens that sex as procreative force is
the fundament of society while, in an other sense, it always has been
an anti-social power. The two saving graces in a discussion of
sex as a social phenomenon would be a sense of humour and a reveren-
tial awe for love. Discussions which move beyond love a nd humour
have a certain tendency to become plain ridiculous because of the
special nature of the subject matter. I have the impression that
this book does not always succeed in avoiding this danger and that
its author is curiously unaware of it.

Very sincerely yours,

Figure 1. Hannah Arendt's reader's report on *The Second Sex*, December 16, 1952.

violence, domination, and submission and the ambient eroticism of mass culture and consumerism. One of the reasons Beauvoir became such a rich and polarizing figure was that by the late 1940s, "sex" brought together so many high-stakes questions. Was it primarily anatomical, psychological, or emotional, conscious or not; an instinct to reproduction or an outlet of pleasure; an expression of love or contempt? How did one discover anything about it, and what needed to be discovered? What was the right scale of inquiry: the individual, society, or the species? Any discussion of the topic was bound to disturb philosophical convictions, ethical stances, social visions, or scientific methodologies, and to conjure up utopias or nightmares. Looking at this larger context thus helps us understand better the world of Beauvoir's readers. While most readers' letters from this period have been lost, Kinsey looms large in the few that remain, and the fact that critics were also riveted on the Beauvoir-Kinsey connection underscores the stakes of the association.[9]

Kinsey in France, Beauvoir in the United States

For critics and readers in postwar France, "Kinsey," quickly came to stand for many things: American social science's infatuation with aggregates; the quantification of everyday life; a conception of sex that was severed from reproduction, population, family, love, marriage, children, or sociality; and the media's prurient fascination with sex. What is more, Kinsey's catalogue of actual sexual practices (from homosexuality and masturbation to bestiality) proposed what most considered hair-raising claims about the ordinary repertoire of "the American male."[10] That Beauvoir placed the married woman and the mother alongside the lesbian and the prostitute suggested to reviewers that she shared Kinsey's outlook about the boundaries of the normal. Defenders as well as detractors made that point. Jean-Marie Domenach, left-wing Catholic intellectual, editorial secretary (and later editor) of the left anticommunist Catholic journal *Esprit,* and champion of *The Second Sex*, read Beauvoir's work as a confirmation of Kinsey's most important insights. He applauded her chapter on lesbian sexuality by invoking Kinsey's decisive "revision" of classic conceptions of normality. Critics found this association alarming. The "amoral and the abnormal" were fast becoming "not the exception, but the rule," warned Pierre Boisdeffre, the young conservative in Mauriac's forum in the *Figaro Literary Supplement*, a confusion all the more vile for coming on the heels of the horrors of the war.[11]

"Kinsey" also stood for American national culture and character, and to associate *The Second Sex* with the Kinsey report was to raise the specter of America's rising cultural sway. Worries about the American troops at the end of World War II contained strong currents of sexualized and racialized fear, and American capitalism's appetite for European markets had raised warnings of seduction and subjugation. Thus Kinsey's findings confirmed Europeans' long-standing view that the United States was "a cauldron of individual energy and appetites under a surface of puritan morality." Only a country so overwrought would be "obsessed" with sexuality.[12] Only a country that was so naïve could be gulled by statistics, and then persuaded by pseudo-science to pursue the "false and imaginary problems" associated with sexuality. Beauvoir might profess concern for women's emancipation, her critics warned, but the winds blowing from the United States encouraged only the marketing of thinly disguised pornography to the masses. As one particularly hostile French critic put it, "I would not worry about Mme. de Beauvoir's 'frustrations' if they did not belong to this crusade . . . if they did not come after the sorry stupidities [*pauvretés*] of the Kinsey report . . . if they were not echoed by a whole series of publications adapted to different readerships, at the bottom of which is the base pornography of *Amour Digest* and *Sexual Digest.*"[13]

"Kinsey" as a broad cultural phenomenon helped to popularize *The Second Sex* even as it shaped possible interpretations. Being associated with the best-seller and media sensation magnified the importance of Beauvoir's study as a symptom of broader changes in mass culture. Critics pointed to the rising popularity of women's magazines such as *Elle* and *Marie Claire* that promoted sexual self-knowledge (or salaciousness); the politically enervating effects of psychology; and consumerism disguised as eroticism, or " 'sexuality' lightly perfumed."[14] Jean-Marie Domenach believed in the serious study of sexuality as a window onto the human person, society, and intersubjectivity. He insisted that subject was far removed from what he labeled "Hollywood-style para-sexuality," sponsored by the media and commerce and aimed at stoking public appetites and fantasies. Consumer culture's rage for goods, fashion, and film stars was "polygamous" and "perverse"; the works of Beauvoir and Kinsey were not.[15] Other thinkers discerned no such distinction.

When *The Second Sex* was introduced to American readers four years later, the Kinsey report was used to frame it. Newspapers from cities in the American Northeast concurred on *The Second Sex*: "There is little doubt that this book will be popular, widely read, and perhaps as thoroughly

discussed as the Kinsey Report" (the *Hartford Courant*);[16] *The Second Sex*
"should please every Kinsey fan. And like the Kinsey classic . . . it deserves
study rather than snickers" (the *Boston Traveler*);[17] "A French Gauntlet
Tossed to Dr. Kinsey" (the *Herald Tribune*).[18] On the front page of the
New York Times Book Review, Harvard anthropologist Clyde Kluckhohn
declared that *The Second Sex* "should be a required companion volume
to all who read the forthcoming report of Kinsey and his associates. For
Mlle. de Beauvoir says much about sexuality that is important which we
are not likely to get from the Indiana group."[19] Kluckhohn's high-profile
endorsement prompted one of Beauvoir's friends in the United States to
write her a letter of congratulations: "If the public takes the review seriously, you may have an extraordinary economic success . . . Let's hope you
get rich!"[20] Other reviewers echoed Kluckhohn, billing *The Second Sex*
as "a companion volume to the forthcoming Kinsey report on the sexual
behavior of the second sex."[21]

American reviewers cast Kinsey and Beauvoir as contrasting types:
American Male and European Female; scientist and humanist; and
youthful American optimism and decadent European radicalism. Like
their French counterparts, they trafficked in generalities about national
character and used them to keep troublesome ideas at a distance. Beauvoir's "exact sensory imagery" was French.[22] Her philosophy—what one
reviewer called "the repulsive lingo of Existentialism"—was French.[23]
Beauvoir's feminism was deemed French: women might be second-class
citizens on the old continent, but not in the United States; Beauvoir
"painted a world that had vanished from the American scene."[24] That *The
Second Sex*, with its "nihilism," "defeatism," "negative sensationalism,"
and "distorted imagery," issued from a bleak European mood was a common theme in American reviews, and one that echoed François Mauriac's
lament about postwar culture.[25] In a hostile review of *Sexual Behavior in
the Human Male*, the Harvard sociologist Carle C. Zimmerman managed
to assimilate the Kinsey report to the "dubious philosophy" of existentialism, which had evacuated meaning and value from civilization.[26]

"National character" was well ingrained in the discourse of 1940s and
1950s social science and Cold War thinking. The postwar years thickened
networks of intellectual and cultural exchange between the United States
and Europe; in fact, Beauvoir's travels to the United States while she was
writing *The Second Sex* illustrate these new networks. As Judith Surkis has

pointed out, "the very articulation of national sexual difference depended on a measure of contact and exchange with—as well as denial and refutation of—other models."[27] The many references to national character were thus both cosmopolitan and defensive. They also exemplified the new status of sexuality as a key to personality, psychological formation, and selfhood, a view encouraged by a popularized Freudianism. If culture was "a new form of selfhood bestowed on society," as neo-Freudian anthropologists in the Culture and Personality school argued it was, the organization of sexuality, kinship, and sex roles was revelatory in ways previously unimagined.[28] Reading Beauvoir and Kinsey as representatives of "French" or "American" sexual behaviors or sexual cultures was a ready-to-hand interpretive scaffolding. The struggle to categorize the two books, sometimes assimilating them to each other, sometimes casting them as caricatures of different and alien national characters, points to a larger confusion about their subject. It was also a reaction to the peculiar genre-breaking nature of the books, which made them at once sensational and puzzling.

Sexual Behavior in the Human Male packed "more dynamite than anything since Darwin," in the words of an American journalist.[29] Beauvoir's friend Françoise d'Eaubonne likened the presentation of evidence and argument in *The Second Sex* to the "tranquil advance of a tank," calmly flattening everything in its path.[30] Both of these ground-leveling studies stood on land that had been leveled several times already. By the middle of the twentieth century, at least two generations of thinkers had been rethinking sex and reckoning with the consequences—scientific, psychological, moral, or legal—of their redefinitions.

This history was international; research was carried out in freestanding scientific and increasingly professional institutes, and published in journals that circulated across the globe. It also mobilized thinkers, including women writers and researchers, who did not enjoy access to the main corridors of scientific power. Studying sex was an interdisciplinary project, launched at the border of medicine and psychology, but drawing in culture and anthropology. To summarize quickly the developments between 1880 and World War II, an "all-encompassing rubric of sex," which placed biological elements of male and female at the source of masculine and feminine social roles, temperaments, and emotions, proved increasingly untenable.[31] By the middle of the twentieth century, the term "sex" remained standing, but several generations of theorizing, retheorizing, and claim-staking had so compounded its ramifications that the term finally collapsed under its own weight. After the middle of the century, it would be superseded by a plurality of terms: gender, gender roles, sex, and sexuality. The multiplication and redefinitions of terms continues to this day, with little chance of stabilizing the volatility of "sex" and its implications.

Sexual science as a distinct and reputable body of knowledge emerged in the last decades of the nineteenth century. Most of this landmark early work took the form of clinical studies like the intimidatingly titled *Psychopathia Sexualis* (*Sexual Psychopathy: A Clinical-Forensic Study*, 1886) by the German psychiatrist Richard Krafft-Ebing (1840–1902). Krafft-Ebing wrote in German, but the Latin title was a warning sign about the appropriate audience for such work: judges, criminologists, and fellow doctors, not the lay public. *Psychopathia Sexualis* presented hundreds of detailed cases of sexual "perversions," the term for all sexual acts that were not procreative. With each subsequent edition, Krafft-Ebing elaborated on these "perversions," finding new cases and inventing new terms. *Psychopathia Sexualis* became a compilation of psychiatric knowledge about sexual diversity. More fundamentally, however, Krafft-Ebing, along with other psychiatrists of the late nineteenth century, started to shift away from understanding deviant sexualities as exterior and "more or less singular" symptoms of a mental disorder. They cast them instead as integral to a "more general, autonomous and continuous sexual instinct"—a person's sexuality.[32]

Krafft-Ebing showed a certain sympathetic understanding of the perversions he catalogued, intimating that they were not necessarily *immoral*. Albert Moll, who introduced Krafft-Ebing in France, also insisted that perversions of nature did not create dangerous human "perverts," and his findings elicited a steady stream of testimony from those who now felt better understood.[33] Other researchers were more emphatically political and reformist. The British physician and intellectual Havelock Ellis (1859–1939), for one, minced no words denouncing the censoriousness of medicine and law regarding "pathological" sexualities. His 1896 study of homosexuality, *Sexual Inversion*, at first could be published only in German. Booksellers who carried the clandestine English version were prosecuted, and the presiding judge described the study as filth masquerading as science. "In this particular field the evil of ignorance is magnified by our efforts to suppress that which never can be suppressed, though in the effort of suppression it may become perverted," wrote Ellis in the 1897 preface to *Studies in the Psychology of Sex*.[34] Between 1897 and 1928, Ellis went on to set out seven volumes' worth of sexual impulses, needs, desires, and behaviors—autoeroticism, narcissism, sexual inversion, and homosexuality—arguing that all were common manifestations of the sexual instinct. (*Sexual Inversion* became the second volume in that series.) More work on inversion, homosexuality, and transsexualism came from Magnus Hirschfeld, founder of the Institute for Sexual Science in Berlin in 1919, who theorized "intermediate sexualities" and performed the first genital sex change operation in the 1920s. Other research along the same lines chipped away at the understanding of masculine and feminine as anchored in biology and expressed, "naturally," in the necessarily different and complementary emotions, temperaments, and social roles of men and women. Unsettling that paradigm created new puzzles: Was sexual inversion to be understood in terms of gendered behavior or not? In men? In women? It did so within relatively narrow medical and psychiatric circles, however. Until 1935, *Studies in the Psychology of Sex* was available only to the medical profession.[35] Female sexuality, including female inversion, often figured as an afterthought in much of this work.[36]

Freeing same-sex relations and female sexuality from stigma, fear, and their destructive consequences could be very much part of this project. Hirschfeld publicly campaigned for the decriminalization of homosexuality in Germany and elsewhere. In Germany he made common cause with the feminist Helene Stöcker, the leading figure of the German League for the Protection of Motherhood and Sexual Reform. The League championed reforms that would break the lockgrip of marriage on relations between and among men and women, decriminalize homosexuality, liberalize divorce, recognize illegitimate children, and allow contraception and abortion. Reformers and sexologists alike asked about the purpose of "sex," about the human search for intimacy as well as pleasure, about the compatibility of pleasure and reproduction or desire and love. They probed the broader implications of sexual emancipation. How would freedom from sexual domination, conjugal misery, or prohibited desires expand the human self, enlarge social and individual potential, and enable humans to act more ethically toward one another? How would it change the female condition?[37]

The German and British representatives of sexology may be the most familiar, but these kinds of questions and research were initiated in different countries, and new knowledge circulated across the world, though unevenly. Provocative findings in key texts traveled quickly, even if the texts were not translated.[38] Scholars of sexuality plunged into comparative research. That research often shored up colonial and racist hierarchies, but it also found similarities, and universals of human sexuality, that troubled convictions about European superiority.[39] Sexology was broad-ranging and varied. Different schools of thought assessed the relative significance of the biological, the psychological, and the cultural very differently. They converged, however, on a new understanding that one could speak about sexuality "without invoking, in any essential way, anatomical facts."[40]

The vastness of the terrain of "midcentury sex" owed most to the revolutionary impact of psychoanalysis in ever wider circuits of scientific and cultural knowledge. Freud did far more than galvanize developments under way in the sexual sciences; he resituated sexuality in a new theory of personhood, at the juncture of body and mind. Sexuality was *the* primary link between biological and psychic structures.[41] Its formation was complicated. Infant sexuality was a "polymorphously perverse" domain of feelings and desires; as an individual matured, the web in which both mind and body were enmeshed only got knottier and more layered. Individuals only slowly became male- and female-sexed beings, and the process of psychosexual development was not a happy reunion with destiny but instead a scarring and necessarily indecisive battle with desires, prohibitions, and internalized repressions. How that process produced masculinity and femininity, and how femininity in particular—the famous "dark continent" of psychology—should be understood were among the most contentious issues in interwar psychoanalysis.[42] Karen Horney, Melanie Klein, Ernest Jones, and Helene Deutsch debated whether Freud's understanding of a masculine libido could yield any coherent theory of female sexual development. They argued about the respective contributions of society, culture, and biology to the "specific characteristics of the sexuality known as female."[43] Outside of psychoanalytic circles, these debates seemed dauntingly technical. In France, neither psychoanalysis nor the literature on sexual science made many inroads until the 1950s; notions of sexual diversity were held at arm's length, labeled "American" or "Hirschfeldian." No one reviewing Beauvoir (or Beauvoir alongside Kinsey) on either side of the Atlantic attempted to situate her in the psychoanalytic debates about femininity.

Psychoanalysis, however, vastly multiplied the meanings of sexuality. As Philip Rieff writes, Freud used the term "sexuality" for "concrete sensual acts as well as the feeling of parent for child (parental narcissism), and child for parent (incest wishes), and even the bond between leader and follower ('identification'), teacher and student (the analytic 'transference')."[44] This reconceptualization reverberated through the sciences, psychology, and medicine but also anthropology and social and political theory. The Culture and Personality thinkers made sexuality integral to the study of anthropology and comparative cultures.[45] In interwar high culture, "Freud" became part of the language of modernism, speaking to modernism's interest in the communication, interiority, and complexities of the self and consciousness. By the early 1950s, popularized Freudianism (with the accompanying concept of sex as central to personhood) was thoroughly embedded in popular culture, commerce, and media.[46]

Two world wars sharpened the awful urgency of rethinking the human. Sexuality was implicated in an enormous range of issues that haunted postwar culture and intellectuals, from restoring the population to shoring up the family and marriage, putting civil society on a new footing, and the grim challenge (often approached in a Freudian manner) of understanding aggression, violence, submission, and prejudice. It figured in the discourse of radicals, who counseled frank talk, and in that of conservatives, who were more convinced than ever of the valuable disciplines of "civilization," the division of labor, strong fathers, and devoted mothers.[47] Exactly *how* sexuality mattered in the analysis of postwar questions was not always clear. Dagmar Herzog captures particularly well the extraordinary resonance of psychoanalysis and the concepts that tumbled around sexuality as it had been reconceived by Freud and a generation of followers, bowdlerizers, and critics:

> Like the many schools of thought which borrowed from it, [psychoanalysis] did not only theorize sex per se, but continually wrestled with the riddle of the relationships between sexual desire and other aspects of human motivation—from anaclitic, nonsexual longings for interpersonal connection to anxiety, aggression, and ambition. For some psychoanalytic

commentators, sex—desires or troubles—explained just about everything. For others, the causation was completely reversed: sex was about everything but itself; nonsexual issues—including, precisely, ambition, aggression, and anxiety—were continually being worked through in the realm of sex.[48]

To return to Bozon's metaphor, if sexuality had a "variable geometry," midcentury sex was like a Möbius strip, turning on itself in an endless loop.

Beauvoir and Kinsey

Beauvoir and Kinsey swept this long history aside, rejecting the premises of everything that had come before. Both were strikingly uninterested in acknowledging forerunners or affiliating themselves with positions taken in past debates. Both were anti-Freudian, though in very different ways. Both scorned the conservatism of their time—the postwar paeans to motherhood, the family and authority, and heterosexual fulfillment. Reading them with and against each other and in light of contemporary preoccupations brings out their very different conceptions of sex itself, and the two texts illustrate two of the many very different routes that led through this midcentury moment of retheorizing the sexual, the human, and the political and on down to the later twentieth century.

Kinsey's subject was the sexual behavior of the human species, and he approached it with a militant naturalism. *Sexual Behavior in the Human Male* was "a taxonomic study of the frequencies and sources of sexual outlet among American males."[49] Sexuality was an impulse that sought "outlet," or release; counting the frequency of outlet (orgasm) "was the only measure [of sexual experience] distinct enough to allow of statistical treatment."[50] Kinsey was not indifferent to the psychological; indeed, his arguments with psychologists and his skepticism about commonsense psychology mattered enormously to the book's high profile. He believed that focusing on measurable behaviors would provide ammunition against both professional and popular dogma, mystification, and moralizing. To know sexuality was to quantify and recognize the actual extent of sexual variation in humans.

In the introductory chapters of *Sexual Behavior in the Human Male*, Kinsey detailed the mushrooming number of sciences, academic disciplines, and cultural institutions that claimed interest in or expertise on sexuality: medicine, ethics, religion, philosophy, radio programs, psychiatry and psychoanalysis, law and government, criminology, specialists in youth and juvenile delinquency, and, more broadly, the entire educational establishment. The list ran for two columns over two pages of the report. These institutions and therapeutic practices, Kinsey showed, held—and upheld—firm convictions about what constituted normal and desirable sexual behavior. Here, Kinsey came out swinging: these beliefs had no serious foundation. "Man's absorbing interest" in sexuality was matched only by his "astounding ignorance." Kinsey wrote of Ellis and Freud, sexology and psychoanalysis, that "none of the authors of the older studies, in spite of their keen insight into the meanings of certain things, ever had any precise or even an approximate knowledge of what average people do sexually." Basic psychoanalytic concepts were "dogmatic and without supporting data." Social scientists in general proceeded on the basis of "hunches" and "impressions," "barbershop techniques," "hobnobbing as tourists in some social milieu"—producing "obvious confusions of moral values, philosophic theory, and the scientific fact."[51]

Kinsey boldly claimed that natural science was well suited to understanding the complexity and sheer scale of modern life: "It has not always been realized that problems in social fields involve the understanding of a *whole species*." Kinsey aggregated and calculated averages. He did more than that, however. Among the striking features of his report are his ambitious breadth of description, his insistence on the vast range of commonplace sexual behaviors, and his militant inclusion of what he called "sexually extreme individuals" in the "ordinary" human community. He was not interested in the case study, and in that respect he stood quite far from the tradition of European sexology. Sex, in Kinsey's scheme, had no goal other than outlet. It thus could not be "perverted." Kinsey mapped what he called "the order of the variation which may occur between two individuals who live in the same town and who are neighbors, meeting in the same place of business, and coming together in common social activities." Not only could such sexual variation pass undetected, but also, Kinsey wryly observed, it seemed not to disturb the functioning and neighborliness of small-town America. Understanding this "order of variation" required his researchers to shed their preconceptions concerning normal and abnormal when they conducted interviews for the project. In fact, Kinsey instructed his investigators not to theorize but rather to become acquainted with the range of sexual practices about which they were asking: "It is difficult to explore effectively unless one has some understanding of the sort of thing that he is likely to find."[52]

It is easy to see why Beauvoir might have found such irreverence bracing. She was reading Kinsey's report on men in December 1948 as she composed the introduction to *The Second Sex* and began to write the second volume. "There are some very interesting things in it," she wrote to her American lover Nelson Algren, "and other rather funny ones! I should be pleased if the same work was already done for women; it would help me for my book."[53] Kinsey's assault on denial and ignorance appealed, as did his disdain for the mystification of heterosexual romance and his blunt description of pleasures and outlets, which managed to shock without sounding indignant. Reading Kinsey may have encouraged Beauvoir to introduce *The Second Sex* with the dismissal of the "voluminous nonsense uttered about women in the last century"—an intertextual gesture of grand revisionism.[54]

Yet Beauvoir's starting point could hardly have been more different. The humanity of humans could not be bracketed out: "The human being is a historical idea, not a natural species."[55] To be human was to develop all of one's possibilities, to "open" or "project toward" the future, to be self-creating, to seek to be able to transform oneself and one's world. These were the "fundamental aspirations of every subject." The drama of femininity and female sexuality lay in the effort to realize these aspirations in a world that cast woman as inessential and the Other. How, in her situation, a woman could become *human*, navigating a maze of external and internalized obstacles—this was the core of Beauvoir's study.

For Beauvoir, sexuality mattered as one dimension of "the body as lived by the subject."[56] She took from Freud the emphasis on the psychological *appropriation* of anatomical givens. She argued, however, that his theory of sexuality was based on a male model, with only an impoverished concept of female desire and sensuality. She also argued that Freud's view of the human psyche did not "open toward the world." The theory of the unconscious was fundamentally at odds with phenomenology as a philosophy of consciousness and flatly incompatible with Beauvoir's vision of individual ethical choices and freedom. Psychoanalysis offered only an "ersatz moral system" centered on psychological normality.[57] Beauvoir knew relatively little of Freud's work, and what she did know came secondhand. Beauvoir drew heavily on the case studies collected by the Austrian (Polish) doctor and psychoanalyst Wilhelm Stekel, for whom Freud had no use. Ironically, her account of female sexuality was taken almost directly from Helene Deutsch, who was defending Freud against feminists like Karen Horney and casting motherhood as the woman's rendezvous with destiny and well-being. [58] Beauvoir's critique of Freud was respectful, and in 1949 France, her attention to psychoanalysis was enough to brand her as vaguely Freudian.[59]

In the larger context of midcentury sex, Beauvoir's rebellion *against* Freud and the Freudians in the name of freedom is more striking. So is her rereading of female sexual development through the voice of a woman, reckoning with the body's desires, constraints, and meaning as consciousness and experience. She made virtually no reference to earlier feminist reformers, although her work was also concerned with sexual ethics, woman as a moral subject, and the asymmetry of women and men. Repression did not take the form of stifling social conventions or norms announced by the kinds of overconfident experts whom Kinsey assailed; instead it cohered around the axes of gender and difference. Because sex was hopelessly entangled in love, it offered powerful invitations to complicity, self-deception, and settling for less. Masculine domination was inscribed into and naturalized by the sexual act itself, reaffirmed in the pervasively gendered language and imagery of desire. Beauvoir's project was neither to reconcile an imperious drive with the necessary demands of civilization nor to advocate greater sexual toleration, but to claim for woman freedom and the position of the desiring subject. As she wrote in 1959 (appropriately enough in *Esquire* magazine), to refuse to be a "remote idol" was "to assert that one is man's fellow and equal, to recognize that between the woman and him there is mutual desire and pleasure."[60]

The detailed treatment of the little girl's desires, puberty, menstruation, sexual initiation, and eroticism, both lesbian and heterosexual, in volume two of *The Second Sex* laid out the body as lived by the subject. Those chapters aimed to render concrete and recognizable the many experiences of living in and being a woman's body: woman as materiality and consciousness, circumscribed by a limited horizon of possibility. Those chapters demonstrated the "dramatic character of sexuality," which for Beauvoir meant not only pregnancy, childbearing, and the essential values that those involved, but also fear, vulnerability, pain, desire, and pleasure.[61] One did not have to read very much or very carefully to come upon startling images either of sexual violence and alienation or of women's wants and pleasures. American reviewers, like their French counterparts, wondered whether ordinary readers would be "aroused" or "repulsed."[62]

"It's about sex, and she simply goes all out," said one reviewer.[63] The rebellious, angry, or pleasure-seeking moments in Beauvoir's account of sexuality unsettled readers like Clyde Kluckhohn, who worried that "perhaps there is too much about sexuality in *The Second Sex*" and deemed anthropologist Margaret Mead's work "wiser." He would have preferred more emphasis on the social and cultural determinants of what Mead and others called sex roles and less on the drama of the body.[64] By contrast, Brendan Gill at *The New Yorker* applauded Beauvoir's study, particularly its "salt of recklessness."[65]

Beauvoir's radicalism vis-à-vis sexuality differed starkly from Kinsey's. Kinsey's radical move lay in detaching sex from love, behavior from relationships; Beauvoir considered the intersubjective and social dimensions of the sexual encounter essential. Just as Fanon, Richard Wright, and the African American existentialists were concerned with the lived experience of racial domination and Otherness, she described the lived experience and what we might now call the micro-politics of sexual encounters, in which questions of consent and mutuality, power and domination were always in play. Kinsey studiously sidelined what Beauvoir put center stage. The frightening, high-stakes, predatory, or violent aspects of existentialist sexuality—as well as those that are ecstatic and life transforming—did not figure in *Sexual Behavior*. If *The Second Sex* occasionally verged on melodrama, Kinsey's "scientific equanimity" and neutral language of observation, which deliberately bracketed the role of culture and feeling in what he called "securing coitus," was deadpan.

Kinsey had little to say, for instance, about rape. He criticized his contemporaries' moralizing disapproval of nonmarital coitus. He situated criminalized sexual acts like adultery and sodomy on a broad continuum of sexual behaviors. In the process, sexual violence almost vanished from sight. Rape figured only once, alongside venereal disease and illegitimacy, as an actual social problem associated with sexuality. Kinsey reserved most of his attention for showing that masturbation, oral sex, and homosexuality did not deserve social reprobation and legal repression. Contraception and abortion, important topics for Beauvoir, earned virtually no discussion in *either* of Kinsey's reports. Again, that exclusion was deliberate; Kinsey focused on "sexual outlet" precisely to correct what he termed "the confusion of sexual behavior and reproductive function." Kinsey became almost comically obtuse on the issues of pregnancy and women's fear of it, where sex and reproduction necessarily came together. "The probability that a pregnancy may result from any particular act of coitus is actually low," he claimed unhelpfully.[66]

The common ground between Kinsey and Beauvoir is equally evident. Kinsey insisted that women experienced pleasure and desire. Indeed, he was clearer on this score than Beauvoir. Concerning the hypothetical and much-debated transition from clitoral to vaginal pleasures, Kinsey wrote, "There are no anatomic data to indicate that such a physical transformation has ever been observed or is possible."[67] Both authors aspired to describe vast, semi-hidden worlds of *experience* in concrete terms, to shatter myths, and to break new moral and intellectual ground, partly through sheer detail. There is an odd affinity between Kinsey's taxonomy—his hundreds of categories of sexual behavior and desires and statistics tallying of thousands of Americans' sex lives—and Beauvoir's no less ambitious gathering up and description of all the widely divergent myths, practices, and desires that shaped the range of female sexual experiences. Her phenomenology aimed "not to explain but to formulate an experience of the world."[68]

An epistemological gulf lay between the two thinkers' approaches—between the path of neutral observation, taxonomic induction, and the dream of scientific verifiability on the one hand and phenomenology and the dream of authenticity on the other. There is a philosophical and political gulf, too, between the kinds of freedom that Kinsey and Beauvoir, respectively, hoped to promote. For Kinsey, freedom meant the overcoming of inhuman, illiberal restrictions and restraints. For Beauvoir, it entailed the realization of a more authentic, more mutual human intersubjectivity. A striking affinity remained: both aimed to clear away "voluminous nonsense," destructive myths, moralizing, and dogma accumulated over centuries through the force of honest description. As Beauvoir put it, in a line that defined what the two studies shared in 1949, "The debunking of love and eroticism is an undertaking that has wider implications than one might think."[69] The entire edifice of social and psychological thought around sex needed to be razed in order to clear space for the two writers' new stores of knowledge, though they had been gathered very differently. As one critic observed of *The Second Sex,* "The net effect of the book, even for those who disagree with most of it, is that an unexpected amount of truth has been presented."[70]

The status of *The Second Sex* as "companion volume" to Kinsey was relatively short-lived. *The Mandarins* in 1954 and Beauvoir's memoirs, beginning in 1958, became more relevant intertexts. Interestingly, however, those who continued to link her to Kinsey were predominately gay critics and spokespersons who credited Beauvoir and Kinsey with torpedoing normative concepts of "natural" sex, defending gay and lesbian desire, and offering a more expansive notion of sexual possibilities.[71] Returning to the Beauvoir-Kinsey connection underscores the centrality of embodiment, sexual experience, and the articulation of desire to the process of becoming fully human. It recovers some of the radicalism of *The Second Sex.*

Midcentury Survey Research

In terms of ordinary readers, one last feature of midcentury sex deserves notice, namely, its links to new forms of survey research. In the postwar world of commerce and advertising, "sex," now less tethered to ideas of vice or pathology, could be figured as a variation of a more general consumer desire. Advertising research firms and corporations thus would pay for studies that promised to discern the hidden desires of the public. So would politicians and newspapers. Magazines found surveys of wants and desires enormously popular among readers.[72] While survey research and the market for it developed more slowly in France, by the 1950s, Kinsey-like surveys multiplied in many forms. For women's magazines in particular, quasi-statistical and lighthearted reader questionnaires or polls made it possible to push at the boundaries of *pudeur*, or acceptable discussion of sexuality. It also appealed to their readers' curiosity, daring, and modern desire for self-knowledge. *Elle* magazine reported enthusiastically on Kinsey's report on women: the anonymity of statistics enabled individual women to confess without personal fear or collective scandal. Learning how to "measure yourself in relation to the norm" or "to know oneself and to know others," as *Elle* regularly asked its readers to do, familiarity with the language of statistics, and understanding the rudiments of social psychology were all part of living in the modern world.[73]

In 1958, *Elle* commissioned a survey on sex and love. The upshot of that project, *The French Woman and Love* (*La Française et l'amour*) is a brilliant hybrid of Beauvoir and Kinsey, produced out of a network that wove together social science and mass culture. The study appeared in nine serial issues of *Elle* in 1959, in an austere statistical form in the French Institute for Public Opinion journal *Sondages*, as a made-for-television film, and, finally, as a mass-market paperback, with essays by well-known journalists and writers.[74] *The French Woman and Love* was partly a statistical survey, based on a sixty-question form distributed to one thousand women from different regions of urban and rural France. It was partly a "socio-psychological study," based on long interviews conducted with ninety women concerning their "life as a woman." To that testimony the survey added interviews with experts: psychiatrists, gynecologists, directors of girls' schools, authors of advice columns in the women's press, and a nun in charge of a birthing center for unwed mothers. The authors kept their distance from Kinsey—this was a study of psychology, not physiology—but they affirmed the appeal of survey research. "To apply scientific methods to the analysis of our interior world" was to keep up with the times, the introduction announced.[75] The survey's directors proudly reported that the intimacy of the subject and the indiscretion of the questions had not proved an obstacle to their research. Women who were interviewed answered all the questions carefully and in detail. *Sondages* reported, "The practice [of] polling and interviews has modified the public's feelings not only about the problems of love but also, in general, about cooperating in all sorts of psycho-social studies."[76] Françoise Giroud, who helped launch the study, commented that it might be odd to speak of love in the language of statistics, but she believed that language was preferable to the squeamish euphemisms of mother-daughter conversations or the speculations of half-ignorant teenagers.[77] The ubiquity of studies like these helped to make sex more speakable.

The study's structure virtually followed the template of *The Second Sex*. It moved through different stages of a woman's life: childhood, adolescence, virginity, first sexual experience, marriage, adultery, divorce, and the woman alone, tame versions of what Beauvoir had called women's "situations," notably omitting prostitution or lesbianism. "Can a MODERN woman still incarnate the eternal feminine?" *Elle* asked. The section on childhood ran with a banner headline that asked how a woman was "initiated into the mystery of her own destiny."[78] Maintaining mystery while debunking myths was a tricky business, but it was *Elle*'s specialty, and the magazine was one of the central routes for the popularization of Simone de Beauvoir.

From *Elle* magazine to Hannah Arendt, the association of Beauvoir with Kinsey was riveting. That association has struck Beauvoir's biographers as a sign of incomprehension and a trivializing reduction of the European philosopher's text. For some intellectual historians, taking the pairing seriously might illustrate the dangers of letting "the armies of 'the context'" overwhelm a serious philosophical study.[79] The issue here has been what the two texts show about "sex" at midcentury, namely its dense entangling of what would later unspool as separate strands of theorizing sexuality and its ramifications— Freudian, Marxist, liberal, liberationist, feminist, and so on. Kinsey and Beauvoir had different political projects. His was sexual liberation, which spoke powerfully to both hetero- and homosexual unhappiness and yearning in his time, and which became increasingly important for gay liberation. Beauvoir's argument was for women's freedom, though she refused to call herself a feminist. Over the following fifty years those political projects would intersect at some points and collide, painfully, at others.

The pairing shaped readers' encounter with Beauvoir's ideas and the circulation of her text.[80] The Kinsey phenomenon stunningly confirmed the appeal of midcentury social and sexual knowledge and self-knowledge. It contributed to making the practices of survey-type questions part of the infrastructure of secular discussions of sexuality. The Kinsey report carried *The Second Sex* along with it into the circuits of the commercial women's press and the "intimate public" of women's culture, with that culture's expectations of interaction with and among readers. Those circuits of women's culture reoriented Beauvoir in the popular imagination, familiarizing her, and setting the stage for the conversations and confidences to come. By the time "The French Woman and Love" was published in 1959, Beauvoir's connection with an intimate public had also been forged by her fiction—*The Mandarins*, in 1954—but more important, the venture into memoir.

3

READERS AND WRITERS

Madame de Beauvoir, I have the pleasure of being among the most
ardent admirers of your work and personality!!
September 13, 1958

For some reason I can't explain, after reading this book I suddenly
feel very close to you and feel the need to tell you that.
January 4, 1960

I place great hope in you, and you will cruelly disappoint me if you
don't give me the confidence or the support that I expect.
April 19, 1960

In the 1950s, Beauvoir burst into the world of literary stardom. *The Manda-rins* (1954), Beauvoir's novel about postwar French intellectuals' political, literary, and ethical debates—and their steamy love lives—won many readers and a blizzard of publicity even before it was tapped for the prestigious Goncourt prize in 1954.[1] Beauvoir was already an accomplished writer. She had written novels, plays, and philosophical essays on justice, ethics, and morality (on subjects from the trial of Robert Brasillach for literary collaboration during World War II to the uproar surrounding new publications of the Marquis de Sade). She had published her reflections on her travels through the United States (*America Day by Day*, dedicated to Richard and Ellen Wright). She had written her "book on women." *The Mandarins* followed five years later. The novel offered a panorama of the whole range of issues that engaged postwar Parisian intellectuals: the dark history of collaboration and the death camps, arguments about the Soviet Union's camps, efforts to create a nonaligned left, and in general, the burdens of the past and the uncertainties of the future.[2] Beauvoir denied it was a roman à clef, but it was hard to mistake how clearly it was based on the arguments, dilemmas, alliances, friendships, and affairs of Beauvoir's circle. That surely made writing a balancing act; Sartre, for instance, insisted it be revised from top to bottom, and Nelson Algren, with whom Beauvoir started a long affair when she was in the United States, was furious to find himself barely disguised in the novel's pages. The upshot of her hard work was an epic of postwar existentialism and all of its attendant anguish—the kind of readable, serious fare that fueled the mid-twentieth-century expansion of book publishing. It won over readers who might never have read Beauvoir otherwise. Gallimard, the publisher, inserted postcard questionnaires in *The Mandarins* asking if readers had liked the book and if they intended to read more. "Yes, but I wasn't able to read *The Second Sex*," answered one.[3]

The success of *The Mandarins* paved the way for the even more popular *Memoirs of a Dutiful Daughter* (*Mémoires d'une jeune fille rangée*, 1958), *The Prime of Life* (*La force de l'âge*, 1960), and *The Force of Circumstance* (*La force des choses*, 1963). Beauvoir's success was international: a publisher in Yugoslavia wanted to translate *Memoirs of a Dutiful Daughter* right away and so did an Israeli publishing house, although it turned down *The Second Sex*. Beauvoir was a celebrity in what was then a global metropolis; readers wrote to her from Warsaw, Zagreb, Aleppo, Durban, and Montreal as well as the former (and soon to be former) colonies of France in North and West Africa. Indira Gandhi wrote to say how much she enjoyed *The Mandarins*.[4]

By the end of the decade, the memoirs sent readers back to the earlier volumes. This is the point at which the collection of letters begins to expand. "I have just finished your book *Memoirs of a Dutiful Daughter*, and I want to tell you how it has overwhelmed me," wrote a reader from Hussein Dey in Algeria. Like many others, this reader was "devouring" Beauvoir, working backwards from *Memoirs of a Dutiful Daughter* through *The Mandarins* and *The Second Sex*. Readers now spelled out how they understood the connections between Beauvoir's different works: *The Mandarins* was "a victory of your ideas" and "a delightful and warm complement to the sweeping objective and scientific overview of the woman in *The Second Sex*." They interpreted the love affair between Anne, the French psychoanalyst, and Lewis, her American lover, in *The Mandarins* as a continuation of *America Day by Day*: a tale of "two cultures, two different sensibilities, and two different sexualities." Readers could now see many more links between Beauvoir's life and the arguments she had made earlier in *The Second Sex*: "It is good that this book was written by you, a person who embodies the very qualities one refuses to ascribe to a woman."[5] The long relationship that took such firm hold with the memoirs was built on a cumulative Beauvoir effect: a series of arguments, the life of a writer and the writing of a life.

Literary Celebrity

Readers skipped from one of Beauvoir's books to another; they read articles about her, interviews with her, and excerpts from her work in *Elle* magazine, and excerpts and reviews in *Le Figaro*, *France-Soir*, and *L'Express*; they saw her profiled in *Match*, interviewed in *L'Humanité*, and photographed in *Jours de France* and *Time*. She appeared on the radio and on the television show *Lectures pour tous*.[6] Reading Beauvoir, then, often meant reading *about* her, and even that needs to be understood in the largest sense: the public read about her ideas and the reactions they provoked, about her memoirs and fiction, or about her scandalously public "private" life. Subscribers to *Elle* could reconstruct Beauvoir's ideas concerning the "servitude of marriage" from the pages of the magazine. One letter writer cheerfully acknowledged that she had read nothing more than Beauvoir's horoscope![7]

The literary culture of Paris in the 1950s burnished intellectual prestige with a combination of political importance, moral seriousness, and glamour. The 1950s marks the high point of French investment in the literary field. As Judith Lyon-Caen and Dinah Ribard point out, the notion of engagement that we associate with the French existentialists—the conviction that intellectuals had a responsibility to take positions and speak to the issues of their time—rested on a countervailing view of the literary enterprise as "a terrain of creative activity that is both autonomous and disinterested." Engagement seemed bold because it claimed to bring politics into what was considered the separate, hallowed ground of the literary.[8] Nationally, postwar French literature and philosophy were invested with outsized hopes that they would redeem the country's standing in the world. State-assisted radio and TV programs promoted French letters.[9] As an international movement, popularized existentialism offered a very large public an accessible philosophy of the human condition, self-invention, and transformation. It offered readers across the French imperial world connections to the metropole. To a burgeoning anticolonial movement it could provide a philosophy of possibility, and psychological and political freedom.

This French literary culture was thoroughly embedded in new media and commercial mass culture. Writers' images and arguments were refracted through the kaleidoscope of magazines, journals, radio, and TV, with their faster pace, greater commercial pressures, and larger audiences. Beauvoir and Sartre were among those who peopled the pages of glossy postwar weeklies featuring personalities, fashion, world events, sports, and splashy visuals. The press representative at Gallimard, Beauvoir's publisher, pleaded for pictures and quotations she might provide to reporters—and campaigned hard to get her the Goncourt prize. Nescafé, perhaps hoping to use the famous cafés of Saint-Germain-des-Prés in an advertising campaign, asked Beauvoir to endorse their coffee. Letter writers requested autographs and photographs, the better to visualize Beauvoir and her life. "I have often seen your name, and I see excerpts and photos of you in the papers. That is why, I think, that I am writing to you," wrote one for whom names, books and photos apparently did not suffice. "There aren't any records with your voice, are there?"[10]

For some—usually men—Beauvoir's visibility made her familiar and more approachable. "In a recent photo, you seemed less distant and I dared to write to you," wrote one.[11] "A one martini girl!" joked an enthusiastic follower in Mexico City, alluding to *Time* magazine's coverage of Beauvoir's memoir *The Prime of Life.* "I do not hold the cafés against you, you know," he added, "This is why one can write to you easily, as one would to an ordinary person."[12] Wrote another, "Simone de Beauvoir, you belong to all of us, that is why I do not call you Madame."[13] The words of this last letter writer encapsulated the new expectations of a mass culture that was at once more democratic and more commercial. The possessiveness in these missives generally is striking: intellectuals like Beauvoir were cultural properties, icons to be argued over, and, most arrestingly, personal intimates who could deserve your loyalty or betray your trust. When a woman, even a philosopher, was the cultural property or imagined personal intimate, the sexism was blunt: "I'm sure men must look at your legs as well as read your books."[14]

Some of the letters to Beauvoir plainly recall letters to movie stars, with their overidentification and "fetishistic" search for information. "Every news item whispers a little secret, one that allows the reader to possess a little intimacy with a star," as the great French sociologist Edgar Morin wrote à propos the new dimensions of the expansion of mass commercial culture of the 1950s. Celebrity and fandom were powerful elements of the cultural field in which the letters in this archive took shape. So were advice columns, psychological questionnaires, and romantic fiction. Correspondents did long to "possess a little intimacy" with Beauvoir. At the same time, many specifically refused to be pigeonholed and disparaged as "fans." "I have never even as a teenager, indulged in 'fan mail,'" wrote a thirty-four-year-old woman from Durban in South Africa in English. It was "therefore with a tentative reserve and positive difficulty" that she took up her pen. A woman from London (also writing in English) put it in almost exactly the same terms:

> Over the last ten years, having read a fair amount of books, this is the very first time I have ever had the incentive to write to the authoress and thank her. In fact, I am a little scared for I am not sure if one can write in such a manner as this. Despite a few off-putting vague comments from my fiancé (who seldom reads) that I'm like a fan writing to Elvis Presley for his photo and autograph I'm unconcerned and refuse to be put off.[15]

That the letter writers felt they had to repudiate the label of "fan" signals the powerful pull of celebrity culture; it does not mean that Beauvoir's correspondents escaped it. This ongoing relationship with Beauvoir, which deepened with every volume of memoir, had many features of what Sharon Marcus calls "the suspenseful, interactive, serial drama of celebrity."[16] The bond and connection between author and letter writers was thoroughly mediated by celebrity culture, attachment, intimacy, emulation, imitation, and mis- and overidentification. It had many other dimensions as well. It was subtended by older cultural practices, like letter writing and diary keeping, and emerging ones, like psychoanalysis. Its discourse was existential sincerity and popular psychology. The nearly identical phrases and formulations that recur across a wide variety of letters to Beauvoir are striking. The letter writers are to a very important extent interpolated into the vocabulary and discourse of the mid-twentieth century. They are creatures as much as creators of this cultural and intellectual moment, even as they experience that moment as fresh and their reactions as specific to them. The intimacy that emerges from the letters is very much a mid-twentieth-century phenomenon—psychological, cultural and political.

The Epistolary as Genre

"One martini girl" aside, few correspondents believed they could write to Beauvoir as if she were "just anyone." On the contrary, they were acutely self-conscious of the distance between them, of the dangers of sounding stupid, naïve, or ignorant. They apologized for their inability to write, for being too "lyrical" or, very often, "childish" (*puerile*). They were ashamed to be seeking advice and intimacy from a powerful person as if she were a parent and unable to recognize, as an adult surely would, the gulf that separated them from a philosopher-writer. As one of many correspondents told Beauvoir, she so loved *Memoirs of a Dutiful Daughter* that she could not "resist the slightly childish desire to respond to you." She allowed herself to imagine that Beauvoir had written, first, to her. (On this score she was both representative and correct, as we will see.) Another reader was particularly articulate about the difficulty of striking the right tone and about the self-expressive traps into which one could easily tumble. She had started her letter to Beauvoir three times: "To reduce the distance between the 'woman of letters'—the famous writer who I imagine—and the anonymous student, all too aware of my limits and my unpromising future, I have put on the grand style and rhetoric—so much so that my starchy prose has kept me from getting to the point for several pages."[17] Her evocation of the perceived distance between the woman of letters and the anonymous student, however stylized, nonetheless highlights the challenge of this kind of letter and the courage of many of these ordinary readers.

The intensity of feeling and self-dramatization throughout these letters is striking. Correspondents opened by evoking contradictory feelings they could neither contain nor understand, the tension between their admiration for Beauvoir and their timidity, or their uncertainty that the subjects they wanted to raise were appropriate. Many said that they had not wanted to write, or that they had resisted the impulse to do so, but that they had been unable to help themselves. The gesture was partly a tribute to the author, whose work had touched them powerfully enough to sweep away their resistance and hesitation. In the process, they had become characters Beauvoir might admire, taking risks and putting "honesty ahead of pride."[18] In other words, they were also paying tribute to their best selves. Their suspense-building openings partly imitated Beauvoir's own writing. "I have long hesitated to write a book on women," starts *The Second Sex*; remarks about the "imprudent adventure" of writing about oneself preface *The Prime of Life*. (Words like "starchy" and "puerile" also came from Beauvoir.)[19] Whatever the different motives and meanings, the effect is one of inner turmoil, or an excess of feeling that needs to be released. *Épancher*, to pour out, recurs throughout the letters.

That effect, so enormously seductive, belongs to the epistolary genre. Letters are carefully scripted. Writing them is "a social practice with its own set of codes, and its rules are well known."[20] The modern culture of writing in Europe and the United States has long included epistolary manuals: collections of model letters with examples of elegant or polite phrases for expressing feelings or making requests. The number of these manuals soared with the expansion of literacy; each major publishing house offered different versions, some providing practical templates, others cultivating epistolary grace, and all reinforcing codes of social hierarchy, power, and politeness. These conventions were well established by the turn of the twentieth century; they were taught to students in the schools of the Third Republic (1870–1940) and beyond. To practice letter writing stimulated students' ideas, gave them practice in expressing them, and inculcated conventions of courtesy; it was an important piece of French pedagogy. As Martha Hanna remarks, we can see the effects of the Republic's letter-writing curriculum on soldiers' letters during World War I, and that long war, with its excruciating periods of isolation in the trenches, sadly provided ample time for further practice.[21] The spread of literacy and this kind of practice made letter writing a much more common part of everyday life than in the previous century. Through the 1950s, manuals continued to tutor those who had difficulty writing certain letters.[22]

Beauvoir's correspondents evoked the rules or explained why they were bending them: "Dear Madame, I would have liked to write Dear Simone de Beauvoir, but my husband tells me that is not done." Or "Madame, or rather Dear Madame, if you will allow me, because you have counted too much for us for too long not to erase the distance."[23] The many I'm-not-sure-what-to-call-yous register the changing protocols of letter writing in the twentieth century and a less formal culture of communication. So does the paper on which the letters were written. A few correspondents scribbled on informal notebook paper, usually in a sign of emotional disarray. But the letter writers' hesitations were also specific to this particular reader-author relationship. Beauvoir was vividly present in her writing. This may have invited familiarity and identification, but anticipating how a learned intellectual—a *Grande Écrivaine!!* as one letter writer put it— would judge one's prose as well as one's story was intimidating.

The epistolary craft also emphasized striking a direct and conversational tone. As the *Grande encyclopédie du XIXe siècle* had aptly summarized it: "A letter is a conversation with a person who is absent. To succeed, imagine that you are in the presence of the person who will read you, that he can hear the sound of your voice, and that he has his eyes fixed on yours." In other words, the letter was a theater and aimed to create what the historian Cécile Dauphin calls the "illusion of orality." The oral culture of conversation and self-presentation, of course, had its own elaborate etiquette that had to be followed. The tension between the direct, conversational tone and deference made the letter something of a tightrope act. And once a letter was sent, there was no pulling it back. The stakes were high.[24]

On the one hand, then, the letter is hardly a spontaneous outpouring of feeling. On the other hand, the very distance a letter has to traverse makes it an excellent "theater for the construction and performance of self," in Liz Stanley's words. The distinctive absence of context or background in a letter to a stranger requires the correspondent to fill in everything she or he considers important and relevant. "Everything that needs to be known is presented within such exchanges . . . [T]extuality is all," as Stanley puts it.[25] In that sense, many of these correspondents did "pour out" themselves, struggling to be articulate and complete, borrowing phrases and characters from Beauvoir's work or the writings of others to help in the process. One correspondent opened his letter with a passage from the French philosopher Louis Lavelle's *Adventure of Narcissus* (1939), describing the tentative steps and half steps that made self-reflection so difficult: "Then begins a series of maneuvers, of feints and passes; he steps back from himself to see himself, and then reaches forward to grasp himself."[26] The passage reminded him of his own way of thinking, and of Beauvoir's *Memoirs of a Dutiful Daughter*, which he had just finished and found breathtaking.[27]

To see letter writers setting out their ideas, feelings, desires or fantasies, memories, identifications, and attachments—however tentatively or provisionally—is also to see them constructing scene sets for the "theater of the self." A man from Belgium, writing in English, described the aesthetic and existential pleasures of composing a letter *to* an unknown person *as* an unknown person, which permitted one to dart in and out of a self: "In a letter, the writer declares outright that he is addressing the unknown. In a letter, the one who writes may also be the one who is unknown. It is an artifice, but an artifice not without its delights . . . it is an artifice in which the writer detaches himself from his self, and does not suffer to be a victim of it."[28]

Building sets for this theater took many forms, first of all a vividly imagined intimacy. Correspondents wrote as if they had lived (and often slept) with Beauvoir's characters and books: "I have just spent two days in bed with, as a wonderful companion, your latest book." Or "I want to thank you for this passion that I could feel while reading this book [*The Mandarins*]. For an entire night, I *lived* among the Dubreuilhs." While Beauvoir asserted that the Parisian intellectuals in *The Mandarins* were not her actual circle of friends, this only encouraged guessing games: "I feel as if I've known you for two years, and all thanks to a book. Could you tell me how much of yourself you have put in *The Mandarins*?"; "I think you are Anne: 'intelligent, understanding, feminine and, above all, human'"; "I think you must resemble Anne: How I would like to meet you!!" Not only was Beauvoir down-to-earth, with a "wide angle of vision," but she was able to understand everything as well. "Your intelligence intimidates me but at the same time it inspires trust, because you are very understanding," wrote one of her correspondents. They wanted to move from text to author, as another revealingly put it, "to know the real face of the person onto whom I have projected myself so entirely in the imagination and to listen to her voice."[29]

Projection, identification, and longing for attachment escalated sharply after the publication of *Memoirs of a Dutiful Daughter* in 1958. "I didn't have to read your memoirs to admire you, but they permitted me to love you." A (male) doctor was smitten: "Madame, Would it be possible to meet you?" Professions of recognition and self-recognition poured into her mailbox. Correspondents were eager to say that they were born in the same year, to the same kind of family, that they had also broken with the church, that they had literary ambitions or, on many occasions, that they were stunned to find on Beauvoir's pages exactly what they had written in their own diaries. Discussions of ideas passed through the medium of identification. One reader wrote to assure the philosopher (and, seemingly, herself) that she had not stolen Beauvoir's ideas: "I simply realized that your ideas fit with mine, which made me happy. This is why I took the liberty of writing to you."[30]

As letter writers themselves remarked, Beauvoir offered them a flattering mirror. If so many rushed to recognize themselves in her, it was with a swell of pride, or because she offered them a better version of themselves. "Everything you say in your memoirs I have felt; I would have liked to have been able to say it, but I explain myself very poorly," wrote one reader. "Never had I read in a female autobiography . . . lines that were so clear, so courageous, and so free from any camouflage." Wrote another: "I was a girl like you, a young woman like you! This is what thousands of women surely think—proudly—when they read you."[31]

Memory

Intimacy was also forged through what the literary scholar Nancy K. Miller calls the "interactive remembering" that is so much a part of reading memoir. "The path of identification provides one of the major byways along which interactive remembering moves. You follow the threads that take you back, even if then there was no story, just the loose threads you see now woven into a readable fabric, material for another story: your own," writes Miller. "The screen [of memoir] prompts the construction of memory itself."[32] Flattering or self-affirming identification was one such byway; exchange or reciprocity was another. Beauvoir had taken the risk of offering herself up to a public that was not necessarily understanding, observed many of her correspondents. One described Beauvoir's memoir as "a long confidential letter" directed to those who admired and wanted to know more about her. A woman from Berlin spelled out her understanding of the autobiographical exchange: "When I read memoirs or autobiographical works, I also want to tell something of myself; I have the feeling that I should reimburse you for your confidences."[33]

Memoirs of a Dutiful Daughter brought in scores of effusive and grateful interactive memories of childhood, almost all of them from women and a great many of them nearly identical in their phrasing, a suggestion that we are opening a window on a regular feature of this reading. "All of the memories that you evoke, I had lived them; many of the feelings that you describe, I have felt them: fear, boldness, unhappiness in a family, loneliness (moral and physical); I have known all that," wrote one woman. Another confided: "Everything you say in your memoirs I have felt . . . I would have liked to be able to say it." Women who were older than Beauvoir especially warmed to her account of a stifling bourgeois upbringing and a suffocatingly strict Catholic education. Young people in the late 1950s or early 1960s, these older women wrote, could barely imagine a girl's childhood and adolescence before World War I, let alone understand the battles that they (the letter writers) had had with *their* parents, who came from an even older, entirely pre–World War I generation. "The divorce between the present generation and the one of the last century is fascinating to me," observed one. That remark interestingly blurred any differences between her generation and Beauvoir's. The letter writer was twenty when World War I began; Beauvoir was ten when it ended; a world of difference lay between the two. She nonetheless used Beauvoir's memoirs to frame her own story, as if inhabiting a *common* past or an already existing story fortified her emergent sense of self or subjectivity. Adolescent turmoil was a common and, again, affirmative theme. While "being young was awful," they knew now that they were "not crazy" or alone. "I thought that losing my mother at 11, or being half Dutch and half French caused my unhappiness," but even "with a very different heredity you went through the same trials." Narrowly escaping a conventional marriage proved another experience with which readers identified. (Beauvoir presented not marrying her charming but needy cousin Jacques as just that kind of narrow escape in *Memoirs of a Dutiful Daughter*.) The shared experience became a *discovered* turning point in a life story that made sense if it were plotted around such a moment.[34]

The Prime of Life (1960), which ended with the liberation of France in 1944, offered some of the same scaffolding for memories of World War II. Here the interweaving of memory and identification was more complex. A Jewish man wrote a long letter to Beauvoir in which his appreciation for *The Prime of Life* was tinged with resentment at how sheltered and privileged she had been. His father had gone into the Resistance as soon as the Nazis arrived in 1940 and spent the war on the other side of the line of demarcation, taking on nearly suicidal missions until he was captured and shot on the eve of the Liberation. He was based in Lyon, which was in Vichy France, unoccupied until November 1942. The city was first a stronghold of the French Resistance and then a headquarters for Gestapo repression of it. In the bloody "springtime of fear" in 1944, as the war in western Europe turned against Hitler, the Nazis and their Vichy collaborators rounded up and murdered hundreds in the region—members of the

Figure 2. Plaque memorializing seven Jewish men who were executed by Vichy France's Milice at the cemetery of Rillieux, outside Lyon, on June 29, 1944. The plaque was vandalized in the 1990s, then restored, and is now in the Center for the History of the Resistance and Deportation in Lyon.

Credit: Benoît Prieur—CC-BY-SA.

Resistance as well as Jews who may have been in the Resistance or not. The letter writer did not say this, but his father was among the organizers of the Comité Amelot, a Jewish resistance committee that helped Jewish families hide and escape. We know he was shot on June 29, 1944, with six other Jewish men by Vichy's Milice, in the cemetery of Rillieux just north of Lyon.

This correspondent gently observed the ways in which Beauvoir's memoir distorted her past, making her wartime activities seem more political than they had been. For instance, Beauvoir described a bicycle ride with Sartre in the country as if they had crossed the line of demarcation between occupied and unoccupied France with the purpose of meeting Sartre's friends in the Resistance. The correspondent knew something of the Resistance, and he was skeptical. As he put it tactfully, Beauvoir had painted this pastoral scene in a faintly radical or patriotic light. He did not think she did so consciously or that she had betrayed her readers' trust. He wrote pointedly, that as far as World War II was concerned, Beauvoir had "managed to get through the war pretty easily." But "even if in the same circumstances I would have acted differently," he continued, "at no point from the first line to the last, did I ever feel you were a stranger." He considered her a kindred spirit and was willing to embrace her version of how the war fit into one's life: even if one had only muddled through the Occupation, one could nonetheless turn the war into a formative experience and a basis for moral clarity and engagement in its aftermath. Indeed, he worked to weave his memories with her account, as if he were a coauthor, summoning up his own recollections as well as correcting hers. "Your notes on the exodus from Paris reminded me of crossing the city just before the Germans arrived. Paris, in the middle of the day, absolutely empty; I am surprised that you didn't write about that," he wrote. "Your 'descriptions' fit with my 'memories.'" Nancy K. Miller puts it well: memoir is "the record of an experience in search of a community, of a collective framework."[35] One of the products of this back-and-forth between reader and author was a community of memory, one not spontaneously formed but painstakingly constructed.[36]

This archive of letters dramatizes the feelings that such interactive remembering could stir, from painful to nostalgic, and the forms that remembering could take: passive or energetic, self-affirming or self-effacing. A young woman in Germany who had never read a word Beauvoir had written had learned about *Memoirs of a Dutiful Daughter* in a Catholic newspaper. "Would you like to write the history of MY life?" she asked.[37] This was perhaps the most lopsided engagement with the book, but a revealing extreme: the reader-author bond ranged from recognition (I know you!) to affinity and resemblance (I am like you!) to more passive and trusting (tell my story!). Most of the letter writers believed Beauvoir uniquely well qualified to interpret their feelings, understand their families, bring them out of their isolation, and give public significance to their lives. The German letter writer simply turned over her biography; others used Beauvoir's life to reconsider and to rewrite their own.

Autobiography

Readers were surprisingly confident that Beauvoir wanted to hear from them and to hear about themselves. While they routinely apologized for intruding in her life, many remarked that, in the words of one, she had "opened the door to an exchange." Another wrote, "After all, you attract correspondence by telling us how many letters you received at the time of your earlier books—and how interesting they are." In her first books, said a third, "you revealed me to myself. In the later one . . . you are the one who reveals herself, you are the one who confides. You listen to me, I listen to you, isn't that a dialogue?" Another, capturing the distance that this dialogue had to bridge, wrote that he felt "trapped in the character of a subprefect"—a rigid minor bureaucrat from the provinces. He was not sure he had the intellectual resources to talk to Beauvoir about her work, but he had noticed Beauvoir's "constant concern to build bridges between you and your reader."[38] Writing to her and relating his own history was one way of expanding the sense of the world he inhabited, breaking out of isolation.

It may not be surprising to find enthusiastic readers of Beauvoir's memoirs wanting to write about themselves. But their investment in the autobiographical is remarkable, and so is the role they give her (and that they believe she covets) in the enterprise: "I need to tell you my life and I need to write it." Or "I am writing a long autobiographical novel. Would you read it?" And "Would you be willing to read one or two of my diaries [*cahiers intimes*] and tell me what you think?" They felt called on to write about themselves, as a "deliverance," or a way to bring order to themselves, or an "affirmation" of their ideas and a way to become authors of their own lives. As one put it: "I hope you'll excuse me for sending you a sketch of a 'biography,' where I wrote down, all in a jumble [*pêle-mêle*], some impressions of childhood. Those impressions, even if totally disorderly, bring images of those who we have loved. Doing that makes the meaning of life easier to understand." This reader believed her project had been prompted by a new, more democratic culture of biography:

> The word "biography" only applies to great men, or great writers like you. "Biography" seems pretentious—ridiculous, even—when it moves outside of that frame and focuses on only one individual among the multitude. But what's wonderful about our time is that it permits those who feel the need to do on a very small scale what those who are important [*les grands*] do on a large one.
>
> Couldn't this word, biography, become "popular" . . . and affirm the personalities that are nearly smothered by the routines of everyday life?[39]

There are scores of letters in this vein. Some of the most telling come from people who believe their words have failed them or—interestingly—that their experiences would not bear either the weight of what they wanted to say. "I have tried to write. I have things to say, and that I want to say," wrote a thirty-one-year-old hospital intern. "But I feel very poor: I have no past. I have only one experience, the hospital, and that is not very interesting." Another, a middle-aged Jewish woman, had written hesitantly to Beauvoir, and Beauvoir had responded, asking her to tell her more. She replied: "I said that I wanted to tell you my life. It's not a biography; mine would have so little value . . . I am 35, French, bourgeois, Jewish. My parents disappeared in Auschwitz in 1943. Fifteen other members of the family are gone—deported or disappeared." She quickly moved on, as if she knew no one wanted to hear about it. She shrugged herself off: "I had not been 'engaged' in any way during the war . . . I did nothing worthwhile [*pas d'action valable*]."[40] To tell her story would lead to accusing others, acknowledging her own powerlessness and shame, or both. In any event, unlike the correspondent whose father had been shot for resistance, she didn't measure up to the high standards of self-creation demanded by existentialist thought. Nor would her story of passivity and loss be welcome in the broader culture of memory in 1950s France. That culture not only lionized the Resistance; it also cast ordinary French citizens as having endured the Occupation stoic and grim-faced behind closed doors, and emerging whole, ready to undertake reconstruction. That was not this correspondent's story.

Those who *refused* the implicit summons to autobiography also tell us much about potential pain, embarrassment, or even betrayal that lurked in the genre. One wrote that while she might speak of her childhood freely, she had "no desire to speak of it in writing, and no impression that doing so would either 'do me good' or help me to see clearly." Why had Beauvoir written her memoirs: to "relive" part of her life or to "exorcize" it? she asked, adding, "I apologize for my indiscreet question; I assure you that I had not the slightest intention of asking it when I began this letter." But "I can't write about myself. I don't think I am alone in this." Other letter writers castigated Beauvoir for violating the privacy of her friends, family, and teachers by using their real names—in some cases damaging their reputations for no reason whatsoever.[41] Autobiography not only risked self exposure, it could trench on the intimate circle of family and friends.

In the backdrop to this incitement to autobiography lies the longer history of private self-writing: the journal and the diary, the *cahier intime*, or intimate notebook. A journal was not necessarily private or intimate: men and women kept journals of their calendars and travels, their expenses and business decisions, births, deaths, and marriages in their families, all with an eye to keeping records and helping memory. They were often overwhelmingly practical and routine. Middle-class women's enthusiastic journal-keeping of their travels helps to explain why Beauvoir's very long and detailed passages on hiking, driving, or bicycling in the Alps, the Dolomites, or the Atlas, hitchhiking across the Sahara, or taking a boat down the Mississippi were so popular. These were adventures, the more remarkable for testifying to Beauvoir's determined freedom as a woman. They inspired readers' daydreams and jogged their own memories. Reading had also long been a subject for diaries: people recorded the books they read and the thoughts those provoked. In Protestant cultures, spiritual self-accounting had been a common everyday ritual for men as well as women and by the late nineteenth century became a popular form of self-expression and increasingly female. In France, however, the *cahier intime* was more specific: kept by a girl as part of her ongoing religious education and conceived of as a project of setting out one's goals, practicing devotion, and cultivating virtue and humility, preferably on a daily basis.[42] It appealed to those who were shy about their writing or ideas. As one correspondent put it, "I like to write, but only letters (or in a journal) where I speak to someone I love."[43]

The practice of the *cahier intime* changed and broadened as it worked its way into literature in the late nineteenth century. The diary of Marie Bashkirtseff was a milestone in this regard. Bashkirtseff was born in Russia but moved with her mother to France when she was eleven; there she educated herself in the humanities, studied painting at the only Parisian academy that admitted women, and had some brief success before she died very young—at twenty-five—of tuberculosis. Her journals, published posthumously in 1887, became a publishing sensation. Bashkirtseff started keeping a diary when she was thirteen, and even as a young girl made no bones about her ambitions ("I want fame") or how they were frustrated. Bashkirtseff offered a new model of self-writing, but a controversial one. Was her unabashed self-absorption appropriate in a young woman? By most accounts French critics and readers were very reluctant to indulge such preoccupations. The deferential confessional model still held sway, especially in families and among Catholic educators, who were on guard against too much self-expression. One should confide secrets to God in humility, with God in mind, avoid pride and complacency, and "above all efface the self" (*á tout prix il faut en chasser le moi*).[44] The late nineteenth century did bring an explosion of girls' journal writing—at home and as part of the expanding public education of girls. But the schools of the French Republic were less enthusiastic about this pedagogy than their British counterparts. Whether or not this reticence was Catholic, it does seem to have been French.

Perhaps most important for our subject here, mothers supervised their daughters' diary writing, and in Catholic schools, young women handed in their diaries to the nuns and had them returned with comments. In the secular classroom, a *cahier* was an exercise book, and a standard exercise involved copying out passages from texts read to commit them to memory, with attention not only to proper spelling but also to handwriting and the *mise en page,* or presentation on the page.[45] Mastery and even appropriation of a text was part of the exercise, but self-expression was not. The correspondence with Beauvoir bears the imprint of these secular as well as older Catholic cultural traditions.[46] The weight of a hierarchical educational culture is pronounced.

Readers read Beauvoir as a summons to write, to autobiography, to a coherent and purposeful life story. A long tradition of cultural theory underscores how emboldening and significant that was. For the cultural critic Raymond Williams, the ability to have and to describe "experiences" was central to remaking oneself, communicating with others, and building bonds of community.[47] Feminist Kate Millett put it this way: "For a subject class taught to hide, to be ashamed even of our thoughts— autobiography is a terrifying, exhilarating vertigo to women."[48] To encourage women in particular to write their lives was generous, and a thrilling challenge, correspondents would say: "You were interested. You told me to tell you about myself . . . I have tried to do it, and spell out [*concrétiser*] on paper what I thought would be easy to tell you. What an adventure!"[49] Beauvoir's bridge building to her readers and her supportive words to would-be writers offered them the kind of sympathetic and intelligent interlocutor they had always wanted but never felt they deserved. Identifying with Beauvoir, and especially writing to her about that identification, was a way to construct a different self: rebellious, independent, curious, and composed.

At the same time, however, much in this reader-author relationship replicated the pattern of handing in your journal to have it graded. Many of the letter writers sound very much like earnest students offering to send Beauvoir their diaries or their "reading notes"; they copied out passages from her texts as if they were performing a classroom exercise and waiting for her commentary.[50] They strike us as dutiful daughters rather than rebellious ones. This is not to disparage the correspondents but rather to underscore that the development of the self that went on in these exchanges was an intersubjective process; the theater of the self requires an audience. To find words for their feelings as reading Beauvoir challenged them to do, to be able to narrate chaotic, half-remembered, or chance events of one's life as "experiences," did confer significance and authority. But doing so also followed scripts and prompts, or discursive rules.[51] One exciting dimension of these letters is that their seemingly spontaneous outpouring of the soul provides a remarkably vivid example of the discursive formation of experience.

Sexual Knowledge

Readers pulled Beauvoir into "conversations" about many subjects: the war in Algeria, marriage and romance, and the seemingly impossible politics of feminism. But from the beginning, the intimacy of this correspondence derived from the subject matter of sexuality, which modesty (*pudeur*) made impossible to discuss with others, even family members and friends. We do not usually think of Simone de Beauvoir dispensing advice or serving as a confidant on sexual matters. But readers had good reason to see her that way. *The Second Sex* could seem an encyclopedia of sexual knowledge. *The Mandarins* advertised her psychological expertise. (Anne, the transparently autobiographical central character, is a psychoanalyst.) In *Memoirs of a Dutiful Daughter*, Beauvoir cast herself as a precocious observer of shades of feeling: "I learned to distinguish between distress and melancholy, lack of emotion and serenity; I learned to recognize the hesitations of the heart, its deliriums, the splendour of great renunciations and the subterranean murmurings of hope."[52] Remarks like this brought a rush of confidences. "Please excuse me, I did not want to write my confession or trouble you, but you seem to understand the unhappiness of women of all conditions. Tell me honestly," began one. Wrote another, "since your first books, then *The Second Sex*, then the memoirs, I have wanted to 'talk' to you."[53]

Talking required words, however, and sexual desire, pleasure, and unhappiness were shrouded in taboo. A middle school teacher from Belgium began her letter as follows, trying to ask a question about sexual arousal and orgasm without using any of those terms:

> I have redone this letter so many times that I must make up my mind to send it as it is. I wanted it to be short so as not to bother you, and I did not want to give in to a need to pour out my heart. On the other hand, when I explain myself you will be able to judge how much I need your help.
>
> The wisdom of your observations, the courage and the generosity of your intellectual position show that you clearly can recognize the importance of the subject of my letter (I cannot yet make up my mind to just set it out) . . .
>
> I hope that you will not consider it inappropriate if I turn to you for information on hygiene.[54]

Only on the second page did this letter writer reach the subject: she had never felt either "love or voluptuous excitement," and no one had ever made her "quiver with desire." A combination of reticence and confusion made it impossible for her to say more than that on paper; she asked Beauvoir to meet with her in person. Beauvoir could write about the specifics of "women's eroticism," masturbation, and vaginal pleasure, using terms quite acceptable in scientific and medical discourse; few of the readers could bring themselves to use remotely the same language.[55]

Sexual knowledge for girls had been promoted since the turn of the century by feminists and a few progressive doctors. A handful of manuals, like *Mothers of Tomorrow* (*Mères de demain*, 1902) and *How I Taught My Daughters* (*Comment j'ai instruit mes filles*, 1907), explained what mothers needed to tell their daughters and how they should do so. By all accounts, however, girls gleaned almost nothing from their mothers before they got their first menstrual period, and even after that, they were offered as little information as possible.[56] In 1949, when *Elle* magazine polled readers on whether they supported "sexual education," the majority did. The number one priority of the state and medical profession, however, was population growth; French law accordingly had banned contraception *and* discussion of it since 1921. After World War II, France was the most pro-natalist state in Europe. Family allowances, baby bonuses, and single-salary supplements helped reduce class inequalities by allocating resources to working-class families with children. The state was uninterested in the distribution of sexual knowledge and unlikely to promote anything other than a narrowly defined "sexual hygiene" and care for women during pregnancy and childbirth. By "sexual hygiene" the state meant curbing venereal disease, which after World War II could no longer happen through the system of state-tolerated brothels with required medical examinations for prostitutes—and not their clients. That system, which had flourished in the nineteenth century and was revived by the Vichy government between 1940 and 1944, was shut down at the Liberation. Brothels that served the American troops were allowed to quietly continue. Condoms were legal, but the anti–venereal disease educational efforts had so closely associated condoms with prostitution that they were disreputable in other contexts—an ironic measure of educational "success." Other initiatives for sexual education, even the tamest, went nowhere.[57]

A new attention to "sex" was a hallmark of the 1950s, Sarah Fishman has argued: "Sex was seen as a motivating force in behaviors beyond sex itself and as a defining feature of personality."[58] But this understanding of "sex," which we considered in the previous chapter, was so sweeping and abstract that it sometimes had little bearing on bodies, practices, and pleasures—behaviors that were actually sexual. Bits of information were gleaned from erotic literature and knowing midwives, or passed through families and friends in shorthand and shrouded with euphemism. As with pleasures, so with precautions, prophylactics, and abortions. "The secrets of sex were put together like a jigsaw puzzle," writes historian Sally Alexander.[59]

Many women and men hoped Beauvoir could give them "an address," shorthand for a doctor who would discuss or provide birth control or abortion. *Reliable* sexual knowledge was a valuable commodity.

A remarkable letter from 1957 underlines the point. It was written by a man, married for six years, already the father of four, and intent on learning what Beauvoir knew about birth control. The letter is matter-of-fact: "Madame, what I want to ask you is very simple: you speak on several occasions of a 'blocked woman' or a plug that seems to protect the woman. Here is my question: where can I obtain such protection?" He was referring to a diaphragm, which was available only in England, Switzerland, and the United States. Legally, it could not be sold or even brought into France.

> Perhaps I should explain myself. Married in [19]51, I'm expecting my fourth child next January. The first one was from our marriage, the second was from carelessness, but the third one was conceived two days after the end of [my wife's] period, and the fourth when the flow had not yet ended. As you can imagine, my wife is now more afraid than ever of this biological fact that she does not entirely understand but the effects of which she has to suffer.
>
> If we want to continue to have some natural relations, my only option is to find a reliable protection; the Ogino method certainly does not offer that.
>
> I would like you to give me the address where I could obtain such an instrument if, of course, my request does not seem rude or tiresome.
>
> p.s. If possible, give me the exact name of this device.

He enclosed a picture of his children.[60]

He is an intriguing character, unabashed and quietly angry that despite their best efforts, he and his wife cannot rely on the information they have managed to get. Ogino-Knaus calendars, which were developed by a Japanese doctor and an Austrian sexologist, explained how to calculate the "safe" periods in one's menstrual cycle; they fit into an acceptable Catholic model of abstinence but had very limited usefulness. He makes his own sexual needs and interest in contraception clear, but he knows that his wife "suffers the consequences" in a starkly different way. It is an excellent picture of *both* the common and the asymmetrical stakes in conjugal sexuality. The letter writer's tone and straightforwardness were unusual, but the couple's situation was not. In this period illegal abortion rates soared among married as well as unmarried women.[61]

Letter writers breached taboos surrounding homosexuality, though with very different degrees of self-confidence or certainty. The same young man who teased Beauvoir about being a café-going "one martini girl" thanked her for answering his letter. We do not know what Beauvoir had written, but he replied: "The world is so oppressive and indifferent. Your understanding towards homosexuals is particularly valuable. I wish you would write about them." He was Canadian, though he lived in Mexico City, where he worked at a radio station. Young, male, cosmopolitan, and confident (at least in this relationship with Beauvoir), he was able to wield a twentieth-century vocabulary of homosexuality without being overwhelmed by fear and confusion. By contrast, an older woman from Neuilly, lonely in the bourgeois outskirts of Paris, seems to struggle for words:

> I am so cold among males and females. I am looking for a rare bird who, before feeling male or female, is conscious of being human. It seems that this rare bird is found often enough among men, but to approach it one has to be of the same sex. Finding such a bird among women would only be possible for persons of the opposite sex. If this is the case, what can be done? I know that you are one. Could I talk to you?

She may have used this carefully coded language in other contexts, for she is cautiously confident that she will be intelligible to Beauvoir. She appears to have been right. Beauvoir must have answered, for the woman wrote again, sounding much less disoriented: "While I am absolutely normal I do not fit into any category."[62] The contrast between the tone and the images of sexual feeling and identity in the two letters is striking: the man from Mexico City is able to write "homosexuals"; the woman resorted to formal "allusion and metaphor" to describe her sexuality. As

Michel Foucault pointed out long ago, the issue is not silence but "the different ways of not saying such things, how those who can and those who cannot speak of them are distributed, which type of discourse is authorized, or which form of discretion is required in either case."[63] The relative invisibility of lesbians, the sparse number of safe gathering places, the vulnerability of women and the codes of *pudeur* surrounding female desire, and her own shyness meant that this woman also lived her sexuality very differently. Sexuality was so hedged by legal prohibitions, taboos, inhibitions, and ignorance that, more than in most other realms, knowledge and experience were built on any number of factors of a social situation: gender and age, social class, a particular family, professional circles, and milieu. Those elements combined in any number of ways; one project or experience led to another in a manner that could produce entirely different trajectories and possibilities. And those possibilities quite overflowed the expressive limits of the available language.

"Textuality is all" in a letter; many letter writers highlighted their painful search for words: "If I could only have you before me, I know you would find the words to make me speak, but on this poor piece of paper . . ." The writer's father was an alcoholic, her family a wreck, and she could not imagine any path out from her provincial loneliness. Even love was "destroyed in a milieu like [hers]" by a combination of social class and provincial culture:

> I go out on Sunday, like everyone I go to a boring dance on Saturday—what sadness [*tristesse*]; I flirt—but never would I let myself be seduced. I am twenty years old and I guard this thing in me pure—maybe sometimes I have the desire to—but I am bourgeois . . .
>
> You could never understand me, you with your wonderful and free life—ah! Everything seems so easy when I read you and yet I can't express to you everything that I feel.[64]

A woman who described herself as a factory worker without a high school diploma had nonetheless read *The Second Sex* and *The Mandarins* several times and had, she said, lent it to her friends:

> I have behind me a wretched past, a childhood without a father, and some abominable adventures [*aventure* = adventure, but also sexual experiences] which I find difficult to write about or describe.

What I would like is your personal address, to be able to confide in you,
to talk about things that one usually reserves for friends.[65]

As one last example makes clear, sexual violence and humiliation, especially within the family, were nearly unspeakable: "Maybe my nightmare
is just something ordinary, but I hate my father, he is . . . oh, you can imagine. Prostitution is nothing . . . Saint Mary Magdalene, I was 12, that's really nothing. But that . . . I want to die [ellipses in the original]."[66]

Readers used the language of confession; they told their stories using
nineteenth-century tropes of fallen women who had been led astray by
their "passions." The discourse of moral failure combined with that of
psychological despair: "Youth, which people find so wonderful, was for
me a dreadful period when the passions drag you into a ghastly abyss
from which there is no escape."[67] They were torn between their urgent
need to break out of their isolation and their shame, a shame that was
heightened by powerlessness, ignorance, and a lack of words to express
themselves. They hoped that Beauvoir would understand.

Courrier du Cœur and the Intimate Public

Readers with no "head for metaphysics" trusted that Beauvoir would take
their confidences seriously: "Reading you, I felt the warmth of a friend's
voice."[68] The French historian Mona Ozouf proposes one way of inter-
preting this remarkable bond, saying that Beauvoir's work reads as if it
were "an immense *courrier du cœur*," or "letters from the heart," the
French term for the confessional, advice-seeking forum in a women's magazine.[69] One might find the analogy irritating: Does a woman writing for
women immediately conjure up Dear Abby? Beauvoir confronted subjects, from homosexuality to abortion to sexual violence, well beyond the
pale of that genre. Her themes were not women's recurrent romantic disappointments but their self-deceptions, traps, and failures. For her, sexuality was an existential minefield or high-stakes adventure. The women's
press, by contrast, almost never spoke of "sex" or "sexuality"; "love," a
sentiment that cultivated virtue, selflessness, and happiness in the everyday, was the term of choice.[70]

Yet the analogy to advice columns is not so far-fetched. Sharing confidences, breaking out of one's isolation, finding that one's confusions,

wounds, anxieties, and desires were not singular, the expectation of psychological savvy, worldly knowledge, and emotional attentiveness, and the promise of an interlocutor who considers your situation familiar and significant—these *were* features of the *courrier du cœur*.[71] More broadly, these are features of what Lauren Berlant calls the "intimate public" of women's culture—the affective community surrounding sentimental novels, Dear Abby letters, dime store romances, and radio and television programs, especially daytime participatory ones. Several letter writers apologized for addressing Beauvoir as if the *philosophe* were an advice columnist. Here is one among many:

> Please excuse me for the liberty I take in writing you. I have read your excellent book *The Second Sex*, and I think that you are the only person who can give me advice. I am facing a difficult problem, one that is conjugal and familial. I sometimes feel quite alone and very discouraged. I cannot bring myself to write to some Courrier du Cœur. I think that you can give me advice that would be useful and wise, because you have a very general, very understanding view on all these problems. If it would not be too much trouble, would you be able to meet with me?[72]

"Letters from the heart" provided a point of reference on the communicative terrain of mass culture and the public discourse about private feelings. Even as letter writers like these distanced themselves from the tone of magazine talk, scorned by the high-minded and well educated, the intimate public proved a surprisingly powerful force field for readers' work with Beauvoir's writing. We will see the weight of this "intimate public" much more clearly later on, especially in the chapter about letter writers wrestling with their romantic disappointments and marriage. For now I simply want to underscore its features as an aspect of the intimacy in Beauvoir's correspondence.

Much was going on in this author-reader correspondence. Its intimacy was overdetermined: it was an effect of the epistolary genre; it was nurtured by the sense of breaking taboos surrounding subjects that letter writers dared to broach with Beauvoir, especially sexual feeling; it was confessional; and it was also a feature of this mass-mediated women's culture.

Psychoanalysis

It is time to emphasize that a vividly imagined intimacy and desire for connection emphatically ran both ways.[73] Consider the full passage from *The Prime of Life* that set out her goal as a writer. Beauvoir imagines her voice reaching readers almost unmediated, entering their lives and thoughts, and in the process attaining literary (and not only literary) immortality: "What I wanted was to penetrate so deeply into the lives of others that when they heard my voice they would have the impression they were speaking to themselves. If my voice were multiplied through thousands of human hearts, it seemed to me that my existence, reshaped and transfigured, would still, in a manner of speaking, be saved."[74] This is strong stuff. Her very language bespeaks a willful entry into intimate connection. It is not surprising to find scores of readers citing the phrase back to her—or to see the desired response getting out of hand. As one reader explained, she now felt *entitled* to know her. Beauvoir had fostered her expectations and demands, and if the reader's feelings were running amok, the author was to blame:

> I would like to retreat behind a dignified reserve . . . But I do not know how to wait: I never knew how . . . I have participated in so many moments of your life, this book [*The Prime of Life*] has clarified so many things that have been blurry to me that I am even more disappointed to be without news from you.
>
> You speak of "penetrating into the lives of others." You have reached this goal, and it gives you responsibilities, and speaking for myself, I can no longer consider you a stranger . . .
>
> There: reactions like these are probably unpleasant, and you had not envisioned them. But I do not feel responsible.[75]

Eliciting love and becoming a love object, jealousy, possessiveness: these cannot help but evoke the dynamics of psychoanalytic transference—the dynamic between analyst and analysand and the ghosts, fantasies, and desires that both bring to the psychoanalytic dialogue. The intellectual historian Tracie Matysik puts it well: "For Freud, transference was at once the mechanism that facilitated the analysis, because it enabled intensities of desires, anxieties, and repressions to reveal themselves and, at the same time, that which inhibited the analysis, as it operated through misrecognitions and misidentifications."[76] This formulation is very apt for the exchanges between Beauvoir's readers and the author, rife with both intensifications of desire and misrecognitions. Of course, Beauvoir was not interested in being a good analyst, a silent figure behind the sofa encouraging the free flow of her readers' imaginations or asking what they were projecting onto her and what it meant. She *wanted* to influence their imagined renderings of, identifications with, and investments in her, and even to instruct and correct them. She pressed them toward a version of themselves that made sense within her framework: coherent, responsible, in charge of themselves. This would often misfire spectacularly.

The parallel to psychoanalysis certainly suggested itself to many of Beauvoir's correspondents, who believed that she was vaguely Freudian or that she was casting herself as a lay analyst. In this regard, Beauvoir's quarrels with Freud in *The Second Sex* made less of an impression on the reading public than the star role of psychoanalysis in *The Mandarins*. Anne, the transparently autobiographical heroine, is a psychoanalyst through whom we see and interpret the other characters, even as she struggles to master her own disruptive passions and a tumultuous affair with an American writer. Several readers imagined their letters to Beauvoir as conversations with Anne, conversations that obliged them to talk about themselves in new and uncomfortable ways, pushing beyond cliché and commonplace. "It is incredibly uncomfortable to write to a woman as amazingly intelligent as you," wrote a reader from Switzerland. "It's worse than finding oneself face to face with a psychoanalyst like Anne." She had never been in analysis, but she believed that writing her letter gave her a taste of what it would be like.[77] "It is difficult to speak about oneself, you can only manage to do it by answering questions," wrote one of the many who wanted to meet Beauvoir, eager for not only a sympathetic ear but also a demanding interlocutor and a clarifying conversation.[78] Several wrote that Beauvoir's memoirs had modeled for them a new kind of probing self-scrutiny. Said one: "Your close and faithful personal analysis is valuable for all women. No one has done this before. (And I say that as a Freudian.)" Another correspondent who described himself as "a little bit psy" admired what he found the "courage and the controlled sincerity" in *The Prime of Life*.[79] Here, as in other letters, letter writers conflated "psy" with existential sincerity, although those were very different projects. The existentialist insisted on the value of "sincerity" or honesty in self-knowledge and the ongoing struggle against bad faith, or denying one's freedom. The psychoanalyst was much less confident on this score, and psychoanalytic denial could not be willed out of existence. If readers blurred psychoanalysis and existential sincerity, that reflected the historical moment and Beauvoir's own sense of herself and the purpose of writing.

Psychoanalysis stood for a radical intellectual agenda as well as an emergent cultural practice or technique for excavating the self. A letter from one of Beauvoir's American admirers makes that point. Like many correspondents, she asked to meet Beauvoir. Unlike many others, she got to do so.[80] It sounds as if their conversation was intense and wide ranging; it included the young woman's aims for her university education, her religious and spiritual beliefs, and political action. She wrote Beauvoir immediately afterwards: "Thank you so much for meeting with me! Now I am sure I will do psychoanalysis. I really want to study religious faith, and especially sexual questions, women in particular."[81] The most important contribution of psychoanalysis to midcentury sex had been to ask provocative questions about sexual difference and identity and to insist that the answers to those questions were difficult and counterintuitive.[82] By the early 1960s, it was increasingly *the* discipline for doing so. Looking back on their conversation, this young woman understood that rigorous self-reflection would lead outward as well as inward, that both her own self-understanding and the sexuality of women were bound up in social and cultural taboos, prohibitions, and myth—and that they might require political action. Her new fascination with psychoanalysis ran alongside a keen but wary interest in feminism: "For the moment, I have many concerns with feminism. But that is still abstract, on the level of discourse. Two of my student friends . . . have decided to tackle *The Second Sex* as soon as the fall semester begins. I am very pleased."[83] In the next decade or two this kind of project, taken up by this woman and others like her, would transform both psychoanalysis and feminism.

The year 1960 (after *The Mandarins* and *Memoirs of a Dutiful Daughter* and at the time of *The Prime of Life*) represents the high-water mark of Beauvoir's relationship with her public. This archive of readers' letters testifies to how thrilling it was to read Beauvoir's work and the many reasons *why* it was so thrilling: the exhilarating identifications, the summons to a new self, the challenge to write or rewrite one's own personal history, the presentation of intellectual work as emotional drama. Her memoirs provided a scaffolding around which readers could consolidate or reinterpret their own memories, anchoring them in a shared story—at once historical and existential—of breaking away from a family or a religion, muddling through a war, and fighting for personal independence, political meaning, and integrity in war's aftermath.

Here is how one reader described how she felt after reading Beauvoir: "I'm simply deeply engrossed in each and every book you have written; afterwards I am reflective and extremely contented; and it is a gratifying warm feeling to be able to think, day-dream, re-live, put-to-use even, the sentences, and experiences one has digested from another person's novel or memoires."[84] She is eloquent on fantasy, memory, the pleasures of reading, and also on practicing the vocabulary or trying to learn the grammar of "experience" and the meaning and authority that confers. It is a remarkable tribute to reading and how it can shape a subjectivity.

Since the eighteenth century, readers have written to authors to intensify the reading experience and to prolong its pleasures, to pay tribute to what the Romantics heard as the powerful beckoning voice of the artist-author, or to stake one's own claim to being a thinker or writer, however modest. The letters to Beauvoir echo those to Jean-Jacques Rousseau or George Sand; readers identified with characters, asked if they were real, and commented on them as a way of making them their own: "Does Julie live?" (to Rousseau); "With you, I became a little girl again" (to Sand, about *Histoire de ma vie*).[85] These were all powerful reading experiences: intensely interactive, and eliciting memories, identifications, connection, and community. The word Beauvoir's correspondents used very frequently was *bouleverser*, which means to overwhelm and unsettle, and implies transformation. They underscored the powerful sensations of reading. Even when competing with the new media of the twentieth century, reading remained not only intellectual but affective and even physical. A book could overwhelm or stir readers in some of the same ways that film, radio, or television stirred spectators. This archive's particular testimony on reading, of course, was shaped by reading memoir and—even more important—by corresponding with the author, which vastly heightened what Philippe Lejeune has called "the thrill of live connection" (*le frisson du direct*).[86] The general point remains: these readers' letters reinsert books into the cultural dynamism of the twentieth century. Books have both fueled and responded to readers' expectations for sensation. The soaring popularity of memoir in the second half of the twentieth century and into the twenty-first may owe something to this interactive promise.

Beauvoir set herself in the older autobiographical tradition of Rousseau and Samuel Pepys (though not George Sand), and her correspondence will remind French cultural historians of Robert Darnton's famous analysis of letters to Rousseau.[87] But more than a century and a half stood between Rousseau's *Confessions* and the kind of autobiography that Beauvoir began to popularize. So did a century and a half of rethinking feelings and the self, most obviously the female self. Any of Rousseau's women characters—Julie, the virtuous mother-martyr in *Julie; or, The New Heloise* (1761), or Sophie, cast as Émile's helpmate in *Émile or On Education* (1762)—could exemplify the target of Beauvoir's critique: woman as the inessential Other around whom the myths, culture, and psychosocial formations of modern Europe had taken shape. Beauvoir proposed a version of the female self who could speak—and to whom she spoke—frankly, with the lines of communication cleared of self-annihilating sentiment. Her mode of connecting with her readers was not the Rousseauian communion of hearts but existential argument and psychological introspection. Her currency was emphatically neither confession, tribute to a higher authority, nor sentiment. She called on women to lay claim to a consciousness and win possession of themselves.

By the middle of the twentieth century, autobiography and memoir were beginning their rapid ascent into the "genre of choice" for authors and the public, and "a structure for enunciating the self and also a mode of cognition" that was encouraged in larger cultural contexts, not just the writing of books.[88] The struggles of Beauvoir's readers to write about themselves, on which many were so articulate, register this larger cultural incitement to autobiography as well as her specific summons not to waste their lives: "There are many times when I should comment or voice an opinion. I haven't, however, the right moment passes and eventually you wind up at the end of your life with nothing stated, being uncommitted and full of nice rosy thoughts *inside*. This time I don't want that to happen."[89] Readers open a window on the real difficulties that discourse posed for women in particular; that they took up the challenge points toward profound cultural transformation and a rethinking of the personal. "I would not call myself your disciple," wrote one, "for the word implies docility; I am one of your distant companions in this struggle to find oneself (all of oneself), which is so difficult for women in particular."[90]

This image of companions in struggle easily lends itself to seeing this moment as a dress rehearsal for second-wave feminism. But there is no easy way to chart the political implications of this changing consciousness of self. There is indeed an emancipatory politics of struggling to find a voice, and thus in these readers' seemingly modest but moving efforts to break out of their loneliness, to glean valuable bits of knowledge, and to bridge the distance between themselves and the kinds of freedom that Beauvoir represented. There is a politics to the way in which Beauvoir provided resources, discursive and other, to those who were hemmed in by isolation, by ignorance, and by a sense of themselves as unworthy of interest. This relationship, however, could be trusting without being egalitarian.

The illusion of intimacy could vanish abruptly. In some cases, the bubble burst in comic fashion: "I am a little vexed. In your letters, you write 'Dear Madame,' but I am a man. Does that mean that all the good things I have been able to decipher [Beauvoir's handwriting was notoriously difficult to read] do not apply to me?"[91] In other cases, the illusion was banished by protest and a coming of age. One particularly outgoing and engaged correspondent, who exchanged long, warm, and reflective letters with Beauvoir for years, and even asked Beauvoir to comment on her diary, wrote one day that despite all the ideas they shared and their common vision of the world, there were things she had not told her and could not tell her. She did not want to shock or hurt Beauvoir, but wrote "we are not real friends."[92]

Beauvoir's preface to *The Prime of Life* (1960) also showed a new self-consciousness on her part about her readers and their expectations. "Sincerity" would be her guidepost, but she warned her public that there were limits to self -disclosure. The warnings continued in the first chapter of *The Prime of Life*, which included a long discussion of how she negotiated intimacy and sincerity in her relations with Sartre. Would they tell each other everything? What would that mean? What would that kind of truth telling do to their trust in each other?[93] She laid out the ethics of intimacy in a way that problematized her relationship with her readers as well as with her partner. Sharp-eyed readers took note. "Sincerity is not weighed and measured; it is total . . . Think about that," wrote one.[94] Even in this halcyon moment in the love affair between Beauvoir and her readers, currents of doubt, mistrust, and ambivalence ran through the relationship. The politics of this correspondence were open-ended, and pointed in different directions.

4

The Algerian War and the Scandal of Torture

You have lived History, the history of our country . . . [Y]ou made
me *feel* truthfully [*sentir avec verité*] the intensity of these last
twenty-five years.
January 1964, Nogent-sur-Marne

We do not usually associate Simone de Beauvoir with the Algerian war.
Yet her memoirs were thoroughly intertwined with that conflict and with
some of the most dramatic years of the French Republic—indeed of European history since World War II.[1] Her writing about those years, 1954
to 1962, brought a tidal wave of correspondence. That correspondence
shows her relationship with her readers deepening and becoming more
difficult. It was one thing to identify with and admire the author of *Memoirs of a Dutiful Daughter*, as so many readers did, and to use Beauvoir's life to reconstruct their own childhoods or to rekindle their youthful
dreams and ambitions. It was quite another thing to ride with Beauvoir on a roller-coaster of political feelings elicited by the French state's
war against Algerian nationalism, the revelations of torture in that war,
and, inevitably, historical memories of Nazi imperialism and brutality in
which the French state and society had been complicit during World War
II. Sharing these experiences, as Beauvoir insisted her readers should—
"living the intensity of the twenty-five years" since the Second World War

began—was bound to have mixed results. It elicited confessions of similar memories and nightmares, testimony about war crimes and applause, but also anger at her stances, and often contemptuous political repudiation. It brought in letters from both ordinary bystanders to the conflict and well-known participants, including Djamila Boupacha, the young Algerian militant arrested, tortured, and raped by the French military in 1960. Letters came from soldiers, some conscience-stricken about their role in the war and others fiercely unapologetic, from social workers and schoolteachers who felt implicated in the French state's actions, from antiwar activists, and from European settlers in France's colonies. This does not constitute a microcosm of the French public, but it provides a close-up of the dynamics of public response and the war's place in the intimate life of the nation.

The Algerian war was the crucible of the French Republic, writes Herrick Chapman. It was also the crucible of Beauvoir's autobiographical project. Beauvoir came into her own as a writer, winning the Goncourt prize for *The Mandarins* in 1954, the very year that the Algerian nationalist movement broke out into armed conflict.[2] The French military effort to crush that movement became brutal, long, and polarizing, lasting from 1954 to 1962. Along the way, it destroyed the French Fourth Republic. In fact, *Memoirs of a Dutiful Daughter* was finished in the spring of 1958, just as the government began to collapse, brought down by a putsch engineered by armed right-wing European settlers in Algiers and the powerful supporters of French Algeria who were at the head of the French military. Threatening a coup d'état enabled the defiant military to muscle General Charles de Gaulle back into power. De Gaulle had withdrawn from politics in 1946 in protest against the Fourth Republic's constitution; now, in the spring of 1958, he agreed to return, vowing to rescue the nation from the brink of civil war by taking on emergency powers, end parliamentary dysfunction by revising the constitution to expand the power of the executive, and resolve the crisis of empire, though he did not specify how.[3] *Memoirs of a Dutiful Daughter* arrived in the bookstores a few days after the referendum of September 28, 1958, in which French voters ratified those constitutional rearrangements despite the left's adamant opposition, and amid charges that the unholy alliance of the military and conservative politics smacked of Vichy and fascism. The crisis of 1958 ended the Fourth Republic and created the Fifth. De Gaulle was elected president in 1959. He stepped down in 1969.[4]

Beauvoir wrote *The Prime of Life* during the next two years (1958–1960), against the backdrop of furious left protest against de Gaulle's authoritarianism, his refusal to negotiate with the Algerian FLN (the Front de Libération Nationale, or National Liberation Front, was the leading nationalist movement in Algeria), and the French military's ongoing use of torture, killing, deportations, and camps in Algeria.[5] *The Prime of Life* covered the period from 1920 to 1944, including the fall of France to Hitler in 1940, the Nazi Occupation, the Vichy regime, and the Liberation. Its writing, however, was infused with the crisis of the Algerian war.

The Prime of Life was published in 1960, a year of escalating political conflict, fierce and increasingly ineffective repression, and more resistance from different quarters: the FLN and its supporters on the one side and the partisans of "French Algeria" on the other. It witnessed one of the most publicized cases in a series of scandals of torture, that of Djamila Boupacha. Later that year the government put on trial the so-called Jeanson network of antiwar activists, led by the anticolonial radical Francis Jeanson, who had been giving underground aid (funds and arms) to the Algerian FLN as well as supporting French soldiers who refused military service in Algeria. In the "Manifesto of 121" (September 1960), prominent writers and public intellectuals endorsed the moral duty of "insubordination" and draft resistance.[6] Beauvoir had a hand in all of these headlines. She was brought into the Boupacha case by Boupacha's lawyer, Gisèle Halimi. Already well known as a defense advocate for Algerian nationalists, Halimi was a naturalized French citizen, born in Tunisia and educated in law and philosophy in Paris. Shortly after being admitted to the French bar in 1956, she began to lend her skills to the anticolonial cause. She took on some of the most difficult and well-publicized capital cases (including those of several women), and over the course of those trials developed a legal strategy for publicizing and confronting torture. Halimi made Beauvoir head of the committee to defend Boupacha and got her to write about the case in *Le Monde*. With Halimi, Beauvoir put together a collection of essays and documents about Boupacha and torture cases in Algeria, *Djamila Boupacha*, published in 1962.[7]

"Never have I heard so much about you, never have I tried so passionately to follow you . . . to share your ways of seeing, of living." So wrote one of the many correspondents who were watching closely—and feeling vicariously—from afar.[8] Beauvoir's political activities in 1960 helped to make *The Prime of Life* a best-seller. Gallimard received orders for forty thousand copies of the book before it was published. Remembering the Nazi Occupation and Vichy during the scandals and violence of the Algerian crisis, living the two wars as one, gave *The Prime of Life* enormous resonance, as a great many letter writers told Beauvoir.

In the midst of the political whirlwind of 1960, she plunged immediately into the third volume of her memoir, *The Force of Circumstance*. Beauvoir wrote nearly nine hundred pages during the violent last years of the Algerian war, finishing the first draft by the time the Évian accords between France and the provisional government of the Republic of Algeria ended the conflict. *The Force of Circumstance* was published a year later, in 1963.[9] Almost half of the second volume concerned the domestic politics of the war, so Beauvoir was chronicling many of the events more or less as they happened. *The Force of Circumstance* tacked between diary, chronicle, and memoir, highlighting the dizzying experience of those years. Beauvoir summoned her readers to share her political feelings and historical memories—and to understand the Algerian war and the French military's brutality as a return of France's complicity in the repression of resistance under Vichy and during the Occupation.

"I lived the Algerian war as a personal drama," Beauvoir wrote.[10] That drama was unhappy. She might have ended the volume with the triumph of Algerian independence and the defeat of French imperialism, or with its global dimensions, namely, the waning of colonialism across the world: the Cuban revolution of 1959 and the decolonization of much of Africa between 1957 and 1960. That was not the tone. Instead, *The Force of Circumstance* concluded with a portrait of the author as exhausted, demoralized, and defeated.[11]

She started to write *The Force of Circumstance* at the peak of her literary career, at the moment she had accomplished what she had dreamed of at twenty: as she put it, "to make myself loved by my books."[12] The acclaim for *Memoirs of a Dutiful Daughter* and *The Prime of Life* and the torrent of readers' enthusiasm encouraged her to risk herself, to pour out hundreds of pages of experience and feeling. She was more explicit in her dialogue with her readers than ever before. Their questions had spurred her to continue her autobiography. She now considered them participants in her project. "This book asks the reader to be my collaborator," she wrote, by which she meant that the reader was going to have to work, to trust her and to follow her until the very end.[13] Many readers did—or tried to. But the author-reader drama also ended unhappily. *The Force of Circumstance* irritated reviewers and, more important, left many in Beauvoir's long-loyal public disappointed, fretful, and largely silent on issues she cared about most. Beauvoir later grumbled that the public not only disliked the book but also disliked it for all the wrong reasons.[14]

This is a complicated story, involving a many-sided colonial war and revolution, Beauvoir's writings in different genres, and various responses. Her activities as a public intellectual elicited one set of reactions from correspondents, and her often difficult-to-decipher memoir another. Beauvoir's "personal drama," as she called it, had several dimensions: political activism, historical memories, political feelings, and bodily weariness. Those need to be disentangled to be understood. This chapter concerns Beauvoir's very public political intervention in the 1960 case of Djamila Boupacha, first in an article in *Le Monde* and next in an edited collection of documents on Boupacha's trial. Beauvoir plunged into the scandal created by the dirty secrets of a "dirty war" (*sale guerre*), searching, like many who opposed the war, for a way to communicate in a polarized political climate, to speak of atrocities, and to move a public numbed by revelations. The article in *Le Monde* especially occasioned further demands for loyalty from her allies and correspondents (including Boupacha herself) and furious accusations from her adversaries that she was ignorant, a traitor, smearing her country's reputation, or peddling obscenity. The Boupacha scandal made Beauvoir a public figure associated with the intersection of colonial violence, torture, and sexuality.

"Pour Djamila Boupacha"

By Beauvoir's account, the affair of Djamila Boupacha and the scandal of torture in the Algerian war marked a long-overdue break from her apolitical past. *Memoirs of a Dutiful Daughter* and *The Prime of Life* underscored Beauvoir's youthful naïveté. She enjoyed a privileged and sheltered childhood, and she repaid the security her bourgeois parents provided by being a dutiful daughter. As a student, she shrugged off politics, lulled into indifference by her comfortable situation.[15] Looking back on the 1920s, she ruefully emphasized that her politics involved nothing more than personal rebellion. "People would shake off their sclerosis, they would freely invent their lives: that was our aspiration," Beauvoir wrote.[16] Her politics had been not just heedlessly petty-bourgeois but royally ignorant; she had been as obtuse at the beginning of World War II as King Louis XVI on the eve of the French Revolution.[17] World War II had "marked" her profoundly (a theme to which she would return), but she had not resisted in any way. In her autobiography she presents herself as a writer, a woman of letters, who only belatedly becomes political. Her account emphasizes the drama of engagement and assuming responsibility for the world around oneself; it is slightly misleading about her political naïveté.

Beauvoir was hardly shut off from postwar politics. Quite apart from her philosophical essays and *The Second Sex*, she wrote about political ethics and the trial and execution of the writer Robert Brasillach for collaboration.[18] What is more, from her editorial post at *Les Temps Modernes* she had worked on and certainly thought about any number of issues in world politics. Whether she coveted the limelight or not, she and Sartre were public figures: "Every French writer was a flag."[19] She had gone with Sartre to meetings of the African Democratic Assembly (Rassemblement Démocratique Africain, or RDA), with representatives from French West and Equatorial Africa; she went to the 1955 Bandung conference of Asian and African states, and from Bandung to China for a five-week visit. Inspired by Bandung and decolonization, and encouraged by the Goncourt prize for *The Mandarins*, she took on the subject of the ongoing Chinese revolution and its transformation of women's condition, published as *The Long March* (1957). She knew virtually nothing of China, spoke no Chinese, and cared too much about presenting China as an alternative form of socialism and the emancipation of women. The book was not a success. Meanwhile, she had barely registered the 1945 killings at Sétif, when Victory in Europe demonstrations in several towns in eastern Algeria turned violent, bringing massive French retaliation. She only started paying attention to French-controlled Algeria when deteriorating conditions, repression, and rising anticolonial militancy led to open war in 1954.[20]

By the mid 1950s, few politically sentient French persons could ignore Algeria. The FLN opened its offensive in the fall of 1954 (October 31) with the so-called Toussaint Rouge, a well-coordinated series of attacks in thirty areas. Prime Minister Pierre Mendès-France responded with his famous statement that Algeria was unlike France's other colonies. Comparisons with Tunisia and Morocco, colonies from which France would soon withdraw, were irrelevant—and dangerous: "No government, no Parliament, no matter what its political leaning would cede on this fundamental principle." François Mitterrand, the minister of interior, put the matter bluntly: "Algeria is France."[21] Socialists downplayed the extent of the uprising and professed confidence that basic reforms would maintain and even revitalize the "association" of France and Algeria. Conservatives blamed the Republic's decadence—its political divisions and weak executive—for emboldening Algerian nationalists and failing to support the military. By 1956–1958, the petroleum reserves of the Sahara had entered the situation as part of the economic rationale for French interests. Both right and left resented the United Nations' eagerness to take up discussion of Algeria as an international matter, interfering in French affairs.[22] In 1956, the same year that Tunisia and Morocco officially won independence from France, the legislature granted the government sweeping special administrative powers in Algeria and organized a new draft, calling up even men who had already completed a tour of military service. The number of soldiers deployed in "pacification" rose from 200,000 to nearly half a million. The French state never acknowledged the conflict as a war, preferring euphemisms like "operations" or "events."

The war grew more complex and violent every year. Like most anticolonial and revolutionary conflicts, it set off wars within wars and polarized along many lines. The Algerian FLN fought not only the French military but also rival nationalist groups in Algeria and in mainland France.[23] A militant right-wing movement emerged among European settlers, or *pieds-noirs,* determined to prevent the French government from "betraying" the settler community in Algeria by negotiating with the nationalists. The French military leadership on the ground in Algeria often shared this distrust of the civilian government in the metropole, warning that talk of reforms undermined morale. The fighting was brutal; each side killed and intimidated soldiers and civilians accused of collaborating with the enemy. Tactics that were cruel as well as ineffective turned international opinion against the French effort and—more slowly—whittled away support at home. In 1957, Raymond Aron in *The Algerian Tragedy (La tragédie algérienne*) declared that French colonialism had neither conscience nor economics on its side. His was a minority voice. Still, the French government's arguments that an "Algerian" nationality was a fiction, for Algeria was French; that France owed the European settlers in Algeria protection; and that without its empire France would become a third-rate former European power all increasingly rang hollow.[24]

The French military used an arsenal of repressive military and police tactics: in the countryside, deportations or population transfers, detention camps, land mines through swaths of desert that might be crossed during FLN offensives, and cross-border bombing raids; in the cities, curfews and military *quadrillage* (cordoning off) of urban quarters, executions, and torture. As the French military turned from trying to hold territory to breaking networks of revolutionaries, it turned to "new formulas" of fighting, including torture.[25] "We weren't fighting for houses or neighborhoods, we were fighting to take men, to detect the rebellion. We were looking for those responsible," one of the special operatives explained. He used a chilling and very French metaphor for the task. It was like using a snail fork (*une fourchette d'escargot*): "You had to make it come out—tear the one who was responsible out of its shell."[26]

By 1957, the facts of torture were "known by some, suspected by many, and surrounded by a discreet, embarrassed silence [*silence pudique*]."[27] After 1957, silence alternated with revelation and scandal. In 1957 two young women, Djamila Bouhired (twenty-three) and Djamila Bouazza (nineteen), both members of the FLN, were tried for their participation in the FLN offensive of the Battle of Algiers, which included the bombing of the Milk Bar, a café frequented by Europeans. Both were condemned to death. Bouhired's case in particular brought a squall of publicity, produced by the defense lawyer Jacques Vergès, who made her case into a political trial, refusing to deny Bouhired's commitment to the nationalist cause, defying court protocol, and accusing the French government and military of deploying the terror tactics for which they were trying his client. After Bouhired was convicted, Vergès undertook a successful campaign to spare her from the guillotine, emphasizing her innocence and the military's brutality. Vergès wrote an account of the case, *Pour Djamila Bouhired* (1957), and FLN pamphlets publicized the sacrifices and brutal treatment of the two young women. In 1958 an Egyptian director made a film called *Jamila the Algerian*. Vergès himself acknowledged, "My defense strategy caused many of my clients to be sentenced to death, but it prevented their execution, due to the media coverage of these impossible trials."[28] Zorah Drif, one of the other women associated with the bombing of the Milk Bar, was also captured, tortured, tried, and sentenced to hard labor.[29]

Testimony about torture accumulated in French journals, pamphlets, and short books. The most famous firsthand account was Henri Alleg's *The Question*. Alleg was born to Polish Jewish parents in London who moved to Paris. He left Paris in 1939 for Algeria, where he became a member of the Communist Party and editor of the newspaper *Republican Algiers (Alger Républicain)*. In 1957 Alleg was arrested along with his friend the mathematics professor Maurice Audin; both were accused of undermining the French state and interrogated—tortured—to uncover Algerian nationalist and communist networks. Audin was killed in prison. Alleg survived to write *The Question,* which was published, prefaced by Sartre, in 1958. It sold 65,000 copies in the first five weeks, but when the publisher, emboldened to sell even more, ran posters advertising *The Question*, the government seized the book. That launched a torrent of intellectual protest about freedom of speech and torture.[30] With Alleg's book the public lost "the right not to know," as one of Beauvoir's correspondents wrote.[31] Beauvoir received many letters from people who wanted their stories about brutality in Algeria heard, and she also reported that for every eyewitness account accepted by the editors of *Les Temps Modernes*, they turned away ten other accounts.

It was one thing to denounce torture and another to support or even contemplate Algerian independence; in between lay stalemate. While broad sections of the left publicized the tactics of the "dirty war," militant partisans of "French Algeria" pounded at the shame and danger of abandoning Algeria, shame doubled by the dishonor of the defeat in Indochina. Disgust at France's increasingly brutal tactics was matched by the outrage with which right-wing settlers and their military allies declared that negotiating with the FLN would constitute betrayal and desertion. In the center, well-respected survivors of the Nazis' camps like Germaine Tillion condemned torture in the strongest terms and denounced old-style colonial rule, but Tillion for one did so as an advocate of France's continued presence in Algeria.[32] On the left, by 1960 the real issue was no longer one's stance on colonialism, torture, or the terms of negotiations but rather how to effectively support the FLN's struggle for independence. That included calling for young men to refuse military service, which crossed the line drawn by government censors. The "Manifesto of 121," which proclaimed support for both Algerian independence and draft resistance, had to circulate by mail. (*Les Temps Modernes* published the Manifesto as blank pages followed by the signatures.)[33] On the military front, the army was plainly unable to repress the Algerian revolution. The government could not effectively muzzle dissent, but neither could it change course or objectives. It is as if the impasse created by these contradictions could *only* produce a slowly unfolding string of revelations about the war's grotesque violence before a numbed public. Frantz Fanon's acerbic diagnosis in 1959 was apt: "The entrenchment of the war had all the earmarks of a morbid infatuation."[34]

Torture was already a familiar scandal when the affair of Djamila Boupacha began.[35] The night of February 10, 1960, a posse of fifty policemen, soldiers, and agents of state security (*gardes mobiles*) stormed Boupacha's family home, arresting Djamila, then twenty-two, her father, sister, and brother-in-law. The immediate matter was her suspected role in a bombing at a brasserie at the University of Algiers in November 1959, which had been discovered by the police before the bomb could go off and kill anyone. She was held for thirty-three days before being charged. The waiters at the brasserie did not recognize her; there were no other witnesses or pieces of evidence. The military was also after Boupacha's links to networks of Algerian nationalists. She was interrogated first at El Biar, the same gruesome detention center where Maurice Audin had died and Henri Alleg had been tortured, then at a barracks in Hussein Dey on the outskirts of Algiers, and again at El Biar. She admitted to being a liaison for the FLN but she had to be tortured into signing the account of the bombing that the police constructed from circumstantial evidence. At the first preliminary hearing, where this confession was used, she said she wanted to be examined by a doctor, and that she had been tortured.

Little was exceptional about Boupacha's arrest, torture, or rape except her response.[36] Her brother contacted Gisèle Halimi, who managed to meet with Djamila just before her trial was scheduled to begin.[37] Halimi got her to retract her confession and got the trial postponed and moved to France. Djamila agreed to let Halimi talk about her rape, which other clients had refused. Halimi then brought a civil suit against the French government for illegal detention and torture, and launched a campaign to ensure that the case made headlines. Halimi asked Beauvoir to head that committee and publicize the case. Beauvoir's column in *Le Monde*, "Pour Djamila Boupacha," was published June 2, 1960, before the trial was scheduled to start on June 17.[38]

Beauvoir's article described how the military had made Boupacha talk. "They taped electrodes to her breasts, then they put them on her legs, her anus, her genitals, and on her face. Beatings and cigarette burns alternated with electric shock torture." Boupacha was water-boarded. The guards told her, "We are not going to rape you; you would enjoy that too much." She was raped with a bottle. Here Beauvoir quoted Boupacha's own words: "They tortured me with a bottle, which is the most atrocious of torments. They tied me down in a special position, then they shoved the neck of a bottle into my vagina." A witness "whose name and address we know," Beauvoir continued, "had seen Boupacha dragged, unconscious and bleeding, by jail-keepers through the halls of Hussein Dey. (Djamila was a virgin.)"[39] The parenthetical comment at the end appeared exactly that way in *Le Monde*.

Le Monde's editors tried to tone down the article's explicitness. They changed "vagina" to "belly." They asked Beauvoir to rephrase "Boupacha was a virgin." It is not clear what wording they would have preferred, but in any case, Beauvoir refused. She had quoted the prison guard's response when Boupacha's father protested that "de Gaulle has forbidden torture!"—namely, "What happens here is none of de Gaulle's fucking business." *Le Monde* made her tidy up that language.[40] *Le Monde*'s editors also notified the colonial authorities of their intent to publish the article, and in Algiers, though not in mainland France, that day's issue was seized before it reached the stands.

Beauvoir's description of Boupacha's torture was shocking but in fact less graphic than most accounts of torture. She was pointedly terse and unsentimental. She used Boupacha's words without elaborating on them. She did not make Boupacha into a martyr, a vulnerable, young, and pitiable virgin. Unlike other commentators, Beauvoir made neither Islam nor virginity an issue; Boupacha was simply an "Algerian" national. Beauvoir steered clear of the kind of quasi-pornographic descriptions of the victim, the rape, or her rapists that scholars have shown to have been so common in public discussions of torture; those description were a ready-to-hand way to condemn the abnormal "perversion" of the perpetrators.

Unlike other writers, Beauvoir did not speculate about the erotic charge (*jouissance*) or pleasure of humiliating; she did not speak of "delirium" or "depravity"; she did not equate political evil with sexual sadism or perversity.[41] In her account, torture and rape did demonstrate the power to expose, control, and humiliate; this was plainly existential rather than instrumental violence. The issues were the travesty of justice, the military and government cover-up, and above all, the French public's disheartening numbness. "The worst thing about scandal is that one gets used to it," she wrote.[42]

Letters responding to the column in *Le Monde* came immediately, and reactions were divided. Beauvoir's admirers called the essay a model of engaged literature. "If ever literature has been useful, that was the day!" one wrote.[43] Supporters applauded her for reminding France of its erstwhile position as champion of humanism and its values. But furious letters poured in from readers in France and, especially, France's colonial holdings. They accused Beauvoir of being ignorant about the conflict, an armchair intellectual or a moralizing hypocrite who shrugged off atrocities committed by the FLN in Algeria or Paris. "Torture exists in Algeria," wrote one correspondent. "Everyone knows it, and it is revolting. But you cannot denounce only the crimes committed by 'our' soldiers and remain silent about the horrors committed by 'theirs'; their victims are friends of France who also have the right to be defended." Did Beauvoir not know about atrocities committed by "Jamila's [*sic*] friends," or Algerians tortured by the FLN in Paris, about concentration camps and political murders in Guinea? (In 1958, Guinea under Ahmed Sékou Touré had become independent from France, dependent on Soviet economic aid, and fiercely repressive of political dissent. Camp Boiro was a notorious political prison.) Was Beauvoir not "moved" by any of this? "Permit us to shrug our shoulders at the indignation of our country's intellectuals . . . They are passive, silent, and accepting about the suffering of anyone who doesn't think as they do. That's the scandal, and trust me, no one is getting used to it."[44]

Beauvoir's relatively terse discussion of Boupacha's rape did not blunt accusations that she was peddling obscenity. Torture was shameful, to speak of it more so, and to bring out the sexual dimensions of torture was obscene. Readers wrote *Le Monde* directly to denounce the article as a "disgrace," a "collection of details so horrifying and unhealthy that you would think you were reading the Marquis de Sade," as one put it.[45] "Let me tell you something," wrote another reader to *Le Monde*. "An author who takes this kind of sadistic pleasure in laying out all the most sordid aspects of the human beast, and a journal that publishes them are much closer to the torturers than they think."[46] Beauvoir's high-minded humanism was fatally undermined by detailing human depravity. These letter writers assailed *Le Monde* for debasing itself and its readers by contemplating such horrors. Boupacha might well be innocent, one reader admitted, but it should be possible to defend her "without descending to the level of the prison guards." An author who considered herself ethical and a respectable newspaper would leave this "nauseating task to others," scolded this reader. "The real scandal is that you have you have no idea of the scandal to which you are exposing yourselves and your readers. By giving this kind of publicity to such vile ugliness, you have branded yourselves with the red iron of shame."[47]

From this point of view, the scandal was not rape and torture but instead the fact of speaking of it in such blunt language, in public, in a reputable newspaper, and as a woman. The taboos Beauvoir had defied in *The Second Sex* a decade earlier resurfaced here with a vengeance, in the context of colonial war, and sexualized and racialized violence. It is worth noting how the angry letter writer indulges his sadistic (and misogynist) fantasy of punishing Beauvoir and *Le Monde* for what he believed they had done, namely, arousing feelings of excitement and cruelty in himself. Private conversations at dinner tables gave rise to similar reactions, as this more personal letter to Beauvoir reported: "When I talked about what was happening, I was told that this need to constantly talk about torture was unhealthy [*malsain*, which means corrupting as well as unhealthy]— it showed that there was something disturbing about me—something sadistic!"[48]

François Mauriac, who had led the charge against *The Second Sex* in 1949, was one of the first of the public to accept increasingly credible reports about torture in Algeria. Mauriac wrote about those reports in *L'Express*, the French equivalent of *Time* magazine, in 1955, and described angrily the wall of public denial that he ran up against. The public might accept that "all civilizations rest on some hidden horror: prostitution, traffic in women, prisons, insane asylums, torture. These were necessary evils. But woe to anyone who openly talks about them!"[49]

In 1949 Mauriac had assailed whole sections of *The Second Sex* as an affront to decency that reached "the limits of the abject." Torture, however, was a subject he considered self-evidently important and public, one that implicated the dignity and the honor of the state and nation; the rules of "discretion" did not apply.[50] Mauriac's polemic against denying torture did not quite capture the tensions in the public discussions: the dialectic of abashed silence and salacious revelation, or the fascination with humanity's cruelty. It was not that the public was unable to look, but that it worried it would not be able to look away, that to speak of a taboo subject was to revel in it. One reaction to this kind of shameful and frightening fascination with cruelty (whether or not it was sexual) was to attack the messenger—Beauvoir, in this case, or the letter writer being warned about her "sadism." The tensions were apparent, though, in Mauriac's marked reluctance to raise his voice about Boupacha's rape. "We've heard it all so often before," he wrote in *L'Express*, "and there is no need to believe what we hear. The plaintiff in this case wants to call a gynecologist as expert witness. I hope no reader expects me to say why."[51] Like the editors at *Le Monde* who crossed out "vagina" and even "virgin" in Beauvoir's column, Mauriac drew the line at subjects he deemed beneath him and the public. If the female body was a particularly dark site of vulnerability and fear, talk of sexualized violence would arouse as much fascination as the moral indignation a writer might be looking for.[52]

Against this backdrop, Beauvoir's column about Boupacha in *Le Monde* showed a good deal of ethical self-consciousness. She tried to avoid all the conventional traps of sexualizing and sentimentalizing the victim, reenacting the torture or turning it into a spectacle, or insisting that the perpetrators were perverse or exceptional. Beauvoir insisted fiercely on the "scandalous banality" of the episode. Yet to judge by these letters, none of her writerly effort succeeded. The episode drives home the more general difficulty of writing about atrocities, a difficulty not limited to France in the Algerian war. It was virtually impossible to write about torture without being attacked for being prurient, salacious, and immoral, even as the writer was trying to call for a moral reckoning with the grim facts of the crimes.

Beauvoir's political intervention in the Boupacha case spooked other readers and some of her political interlocutors. One of these was Dr. Marie-Andrée Lagroua Weill-Hallé, an obstetrician-gynecologist and head of Le

Planning Familial (Family Planning), at that point the principal champions of overturning France's laws banning contraception. Beauvoir had just written the preface to Weill-Hallé's volume *The Great Fear of Loving*, a collection of case studies, based on Weill-Hallé's own patients, of women facing unwanted pregnancies. The case studies laid bare the grisly consequences of banning contraception, driving women to dangerous and criminalized abortion. Gisèle Halimi, Boupacha's lawyer, had recruited Weill-Hallé to the committee for Boupacha's defense, and had asked her to be one of the gynecologists to examine Boupacha and confirm that she had been raped. Alarmed at this overture, the doctor wrote to Beauvoir. Her colleagues at Family Planning were "appalled" that she had agreed to examine Boupacha; to have Weill-Hallé's name associated with Boupacha would have "very unfortunate repercussions" for the organization's reputation. Her colleagues had warned Weill-Hallé that she was making a disastrous political mistake. "Of course I know how to take charge, but their unanimity worries me."[53]

In Beauvoir's presentation of Weill-Hallé's book, the "scandal" of illegal abortion took on many of the features of the "scandal" of torture. In both cases the public was shocked to be confronted with what were utterly common practices. Illegal abortion was the dirty secret of women's bodily unfreedom and legal, social, and intimate inequality; torture, including sexualized torture, was the dirty secret of colonial rule and war. In both cases, the serial revelations of scandal only numbed the public. The laws that drove women, isolated and humiliated, to induce miscarriages themselves—*those* laws were "sadistic," Beauvoir had written in *The Second Sex*. This sort of association made Family Planning skittish. The organization's literature and public pronouncements emphasized that many women seeking abortions were dutiful mothers who had had several children before deciding they could bear no more.[54] Those mothers were white. Their cause was not to be tainted by association with political prisoners, the self-assertions of Algerian nationalists, and the sexual humiliation of a woman of color.[55]

Other people who wrote to Beauvoir were despondent and torn. While they were bystanders, they felt implicated. A twenty-three-year-old Algerian woman who lived in Paris with her fiancé (also Algerian) wrote of the pain of exile and the shame of relative safety. She had lost both her parents and an uncle to the war, and she wanted only to go home and begin the work of rebuilding. She was horribly ashamed (*honteuse*) to be in the metropole while her "brothers and sisters were being tortured" and shamed, too, by her inability to make any meaningful contribution to her community: "I want with all my heart to be useful, to do something . . . Believe me, these are not just words to soothe my conscience." She was not a radical militant; she had simply tried to organize relief for Muslim women in France, but Catholic philanthropies would not support such activities. "I know you are on the Committee for Boupacha. If you see or write to her," she asked, "please tell that that young Muslim women are proud of her and admire her." A social worker employed in services for North Africans similarly found that the Algerian war had made it impossible to believe in good faith that her work was useful: "For a long time, I believed that devoting myself to the cases I was given and finding solutions to those problems would give me a good conscience. Now I have no illusions on that score . . . I am literally dying of shame. I can't bear it."[56]

Djamila Boupacha's legal advocates and political champions successfully got jurisdiction in the case transferred to France. They also prepared a complaint to discover and prosecute those who had tortured her.[57] The examining magistrate, who is responsible in the French legal system for gathering evidence, pressed the army for pictures of those who had questioned Boupacha (in fact, to spare them from having to appear in court).[58] The military refused in the name of protecting the "esprit and morale" of the services involved. The Committee for Boupacha upped the ante, despite dissent from some of its members, and brought a complaint against the French minister of war and the commander in chief of Algeria for harboring malefactors and criminal breach of public liberties.[59] Halimi and Beauvoir assembled a book that included much of the testimony contained in Boupacha's *dossier d'instruction*, or legal file. Doing so flouted the rules that barred lawyers from divulging such information while a case was under way, and Beauvoir coauthored the book in order to share the legal liability with Halimi.

The archive of Beauvoir's correspondence holds a single letter from Djamila Boupacha herself, written in November 1961, while she was on a hunger strike as she was being held in the Fresnes prison in the southern outskirts of Paris. (During World War II, members of the French Resistance were held prisoner at Fresnes before being shot by the Nazis.) By late 1961, peace negotiations between the FLN and the French state had opened and then broken down. What is more, metropolitan France was shaken by uncertainty, bitter division, and violence. The right-wing paramilitary defenders of "*French* Algeria," now mobilized as the OAS, (Organization of the Secret Army), set out to fight the FLN, intimidate opponents of the war in the metropole (who included writers, journalists, professors and teachers, and politicians), and sabotage any further negotiation between the French government and the Algerian nationalists. They bombed targets in Paris.[60] The Algerian FLN, determined to establish itself as the force to be negotiated with, stepped up its attacks on rival nationalists and mobilized its forces in metropolitan France. On October 17, 1961, tens of thousands of Algerians demonstrated in Paris to support the FLN and protest harassment by the Paris police. The police struck back, and in the repression, well over one hundred Algerians were killed—beaten to death or drowned by being thrown in the river.[61]

Boupacha's letter to Beauvoir was written against this backdrop. For her, the accumulating atrocities made it even more important for the committee to press its suit against the military higher-ups. She had never expected the army to allow her or her advocates to discover the names of the men who tortured her, she wrote. Nor did she expect the suit to succeed. "There have been too many crimes and too much wrongdoing [*malheur*]." If the military condemned the perpetrators, they would have to condemn the army; there would be no soldiers left to fight the war. She vowed, however, to "keep going to the end," and she wanted to be assured of unequivocal support. This was a moment for testing allegiances. While she thanked Beauvoir and "all of the French" who had supported her cause, she warned about the grim legacy of the conflict. That the war would end with Algerian independence was beyond doubt. Score settling would follow. All of France would be implicated in the military's crimes:

> I am afraid that afterwards, the people of my country [*les gens de chez nous*] will say that all the French were our enemies and that they all tortured us.
>
> If the Algerians and the French are to become sincere friends, it would be better if the patriots were clearly ["clearly" inserted here for emphasis] separated from the torturers.
>
> It seems as if the generals do not want to separate the patriots from the torturers.
>
> That would be bad for Algeria, but it would be especially bad for France.

I know that Algeria has friends in France, and many Algerians know that as well.

I am only a girl of 23, but this war has taught me many things.

I am happy to have been able to write you this. I am afraid nonetheless.

I embrace you very warmly [*Je vous embrasse très fort*].[62]

Boupacha was at once warm and full of warning, resolute and understandably afraid, and her letter captured from one side the polarization as the conflict came to an end, with recriminations to come.

Halimi and Beauvoir's book on the Boupacha case appeared at the end of January 1962, in the midst of ongoing terror and violence in metropolitan France. In a single week between January 15 and January 21, 1962, the OAS bombed twenty-five targets in Paris and its suburbs, and the bombings continued for another two weeks.[63] Françoise Giroud, coeditor of *L'Express*, whose own apartment had been targeted by OAS bombs,

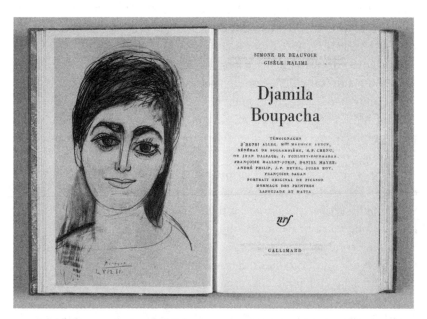

Figure 3. Title page of *Djamila Boupacha*, edited by Gisèle Halimi and Simone de Beauvoir, published by Gallimard in 1962.
Drawing by Pablo Picasso, © 2019 Estate of Pablo Picasso/Artists Rights Society (ARS), NY.
Photo by Adrien Didierjean, © RMN-Grand Palais/Art Resource, NY.

reviewed *Djamila Boupacha*. Sickened by the combination of the grim details of torture and domestic political chaos, she wrote as if she were addressing Boupacha herself: "We are burning of humiliation. While your nation is being made, ours is coming apart."[64] That same day, February 8, 1962, saw an enormous demonstration against the OAS, reviving themes from the 1930s of antifascism and Republican defense. The demonstration defied a ban imposed by the government (and the police), who were determined to quell civil unrest in metropolitan France and round up supporters of the FLN, especially communists and Algerians. Police repression again turned deadly, killing nine demonstrators, including three women and one sixteen-year-old boy, all militants in the communist-led Confédération Générale de Travail (General Confederation of Labor), at the Charonne Métro station, northeast of the Bastille.[65] A horrified reader from Stockholm wrote to Beauvoir of watching France being "torn apart" and of the "horrible events that keep the whole world in suspense." An Italian newspaper telegraphed: "WANT TO REPORT EXTENSIVELY ON YOUR BOOK ABOUT DJAMILA BUPASCIA [*sic*] PLEASE SEND YOUR INTRODUCTION ASAP IN LIGHT OF NEW EVENTS ABOUT ALGERIA STOP."[66] In *L'Express*, advertisements for *Djamila Boupacha* with a cover drawing of the young woman by Pablo Picasso—a cover with some cultural clout—ran alongside maps of Paris showing where OAS bombs had exploded the night before, editorials warning of the government's "impotence and complacency about the rise of fascism," and photographs of the massive funeral processions mourning the victims of Charonne.[67]

Djamila Boupacha was a clarion call: the book offered not only the details of the trial but testimony on other cases of torture as well. It was widely publicized in the European press and translated immediately into English, one mark of the international public's increasingly dim view of French intervention. The book was fully in the style of the French intellectual. Halimi's long account of the case highlighted her close relationship with Boupacha and her family; it had the personalizing tone of Voltaire's intervention in the case of the torture and execution of Jean Calas, a French Huguenot accused of murdering his son to prevent him from converting to Catholicism. Beauvoir echoed Émile Zola's famous denunciation of the military's framing of Alfred Dreyfus, *J'Accuse!*: "Since 1954, we have all been complicit in a genocide that in the name of repression and pacification has claimed more than a million victims: men and women, young and old, children, machine-gunned during *ratissages* and burned alive in their villages . . . Over the last few months, even the most cautious newspapers have poured out horrors: assassinations, hangings . . . scores of corpses, hands crushed, skulls split open." Nor did she leave it at that. Her accusation was blunt. The public professed to be heartsick and appalled by the evils of Nazism. Now that public had a simple choice: either "you line up on the side of the executioners" or "you refuse this war that dares not speak its name, the army that feeds on it, and the government that does the army's bidding."[68]

Letters poured in. *Djamila Boupacha* and correspondents' letters about it are one summary of the Algerian war's desperate endgame. The terms on which the war ended changed feelings, heightening both shame and vitriol. Young men who refused to serve in the military confessed their moral crises to Beauvoir and asked her to give them moral and political guidance: "I have decided to offer my services to another country, preferably an African one, or to Cuba . . . Believe me, I only want to construct my life according to my conscience." Young soldiers who were humiliated by defeat, their complicity in war crimes, or both wrote particularly wrenching letters. Many wanted to add their own testimony to the accounts that Beauvoir and Halimi had gathered in *Djamila Boupacha*. One soldier, who wrote several letters to Beauvoir, passed on reports circulating in the army about "cleansing" villages and killing civilians, including children. He had seen photos of atrocities: "I know about shocking crimes committed in Algeria by the French, by soldiers—crimes that should make all the French turn red with shame . . . [T]he army is rotten to the core . . . [H]ow can one not be ashamed; I am ashamed." He hastened to add, however, that the army's officers did not share his views; nine out of ten officers were partisans of "French Algeria." "You can't imagine how the men in the army talk about you," he wrote regarding Beauvoir's position in the Boupacha case.[69]

In fact, Beauvoir could imagine very well. A few days after the Évian accords were signed, ending the war, a lieutenant wrote her a letter.[70] He spelled out all the good he had done as a soldier stationed in a Kablye village in the mountains above the city of Tizi Ouzou, in north-central Algeria. He had served as a doctor, teacher, and organizer. Several times villagers had reciprocated by warning him of ambushes. He had never tortured or threatened anyone. He emphasized that he was a young person, and not cruel or cynical. He wrote that he hoped his youth would "lend weight" to his letter. Over two long handwritten pages, he laid out his youthful idealism and good intentions. The process of summoning and describing his feelings—his vulnerability, and his anxieties about how his service and work in the military would be judged by history—slowly overwhelmed him. At the end of the letter he exploded in rage at Beauvoir, her book on Djamila Boupacha, and the left's opposition to the war:

> The mud you sling at your country and your Army, the venom you spit, the hate you sow—these are not a matter of ignorance, they are a public disgrace and defamation . . .
>
> When the day comes in France to divide the good from the evil, those who served the Country from those who betrayed it—on that day, if people like you aren't lucky enough to be judged legally incompetent, you will be put up against the wall.[71]

Like Djamila Boupacha, but from another position on the political spectrum, he saw this as a moment for drawing lines, and for reprisals.

These letters came from the "inner circle" of the Algerian war: people with enormous stakes in how the war would be remembered and in history's verdict on their participation. They were a minority, but a mobilized minority. By 1962, mainstream opinion had belatedly coalesced around the conclusion that France could consign this episode to the past. World opinion had turned decisively against the French intervention in Algeria; the vast majority of French voters favored Algerian "autodetermination"; and the Évian accords were ratified by 90 percent of French voters.[72] That the Algerian war had been forgotten—consigned to a repudiated past—became a staple of French political commentary. It has remained a staple of histories of postwar and postcolonial France. These letters to Beauvoir about *Djamila Boupacha* amply document ideas and emotions that ran counter to any such consensus. The letters came from very different parties to the conflict, from Algerian nationalist fighters and shattered soldiers, as well as officers in the military and European settlers, or *pieds-noirs,* who felt betrayed by the war's outcome and by metropolitan opinion.

Within this inner circle of the Algerian conflict, hatreds hardly ceased with the cease-fire. Witness the postcard Beauvoir received in June 1964.

Her affair with Claude Lanzmann had ended in 1958, but Lanzmann's Jewishness provided the pretext for a tirade calling Beauvoir a whore and accusing Jews who supported Algerian nationalism of betraying the *pied-noir* Jewish community, France, Israel, or themselves: "When your Jewish pimp supports the FLN, he betrays his brothers who have taken refuge in Algeria. He betrays his country Israel . . . The Jews around you would do better to help with the construction of their country rather than to work for the destruction of a France that has protected them."[73]

This kind of vitriol, like the OAS's public campaign of terror protesting the historical *fait accompli* of Algerian independence (including an attempt to assassinate de Gaulle in August 1962), helped drive many in the French public far to the sidelines, retreating from the conflict and all that it represented: "I am sick of these assassinations and the killing of innocent people, of this long Algerian war—what French person doesn't share these feelings? And I don't belong to any political party."[74]

The desire to move on from the war did not bring either silence or forgetting. It did mean that none of the bitter feelings aired in the letters in this archive would receive much attention until later on, and that they would continue to unsettle the body politic. Djamila Boupacha was released from prison as part of the end-of-the-war agreements in 1962. The same agreements granted the military immunity from charges of torture—again, with an eye to moving on from the conflict. As the historian Raphaëlle Branche astutely notes, the amnesty (which was expanded in 1966, 1968, and 1982) aimed to calm the legal and political waters, but over the longer run, it has done just the opposite. If questions about individual responsibility and accountability went unanswered, that only assured they would be repeatedly raised.[75] These letters to Beauvoir about Boupacha, then, are a prelude to that later chapter in the history of France.

5

Shame as Political Feeling

You asked the reader to be your collaborator. I was one, fully. I was
even more, a friend. Today . . . we are separating.

June 1964, Cahors, France

Djamila Boupacha was a political intervention from a public intellectual.
The book not only reported on Boupacha's trial but also gathered testimony on other cases of torture. It helped confirm international disapproval of what seemed to be the last gasp of French colonialism. The
sections of Beauvoir's *Force of Circumstance* (1963) that dealt with the
Algerian war were written in a very different way, excavating several layers of memory, feeling, and experience. *The Force of Circumstance* was
not simply more personal but more deliberately philosophical, and it addressed both Beauvoir's intimate public and her fellow intellectuals.

Her previous volume of memoir, *The Prime of Life,* had come out in
the fall of 1960, on the heels of the Boupacha scandal. It recounted the
years between 1920 and 1944. *Elle* magazine published excerpts from
The Prime of Life to whet the public appetite, and Gallimard sold tens
of thousands of advance copies. Critics called it her best work. So did
many readers. Characteristically, Beauvoir transformed the acclaim into
exigency. She had to earn the praise she was reaping and to prove that

she was not simply producing books in the dreaded and debased genre of commercial "best-sellers."[1] In *The Force of Circumstance*, she took risks. In the preface, Beauvoir called on her readers to be her "collaborators." She wrote in deliberate philosophical detail about her antiwar politics and political feelings. She foregrounded her shame at French governments past and present and her emotional and bodily weariness as she grew older. (Beauvoir was preoccupied with aging; she was fifty-five when the book was published.) *The Force of Circumstance* reflected on antiwar politics phenomenologically, in other words, as lived experience. That project took some unexpected turns, bringing readers into Beauvoir's conversations with Sartre and Frantz Fanon about shame as a political emotion. Readers found it thoroughly disconcerting and responded with confusion, anxiety, and anger.

The Force of Circumstance was a difficult book. It layered different historical moments, bringing together Beauvoir's shame at the revelations about torture in Algeria with the remembered humiliations of defeat and occupation in World War II. Beauvoir wrote in detail about her political powerlessness and emotional distress in the face of events. What is more, she insisted, as a good phenomenologist, on her shame as a lived *experience*, and a bodily experience at that. *The Force of Circumstance* was about Beauvoir's shame, and it was shaming. It knotted the personal with the political in ways that were bound to confound readers.[2]

The Force of Circumstance was also a painfully self-conscious account. Readers and critics at the time—and since—have found it maddeningly self-absorbed and overly dramatic. After all, Beauvoir was a metropolitan intellectual who stood very far from the center of the real suffering in the Algerian conflict. The self-consciousness and performance were deliberate, however. The volume was not only a phenomenology of emotion—in this case, shame—but also a study of what Beauvoir considered to be an *appropriate* political feeling.

From One War to Another

The Force of Circumstance takes on a long sweep of time, from the liberation of Paris from the Nazis in 1944 to the end of the Algerian war in 1962. The first half of the book, like her Goncourt-winning novel *The*

Mandarins, is concerned with intellectual debates after World War II—
with the aftermath of Nazism and fascism, Cold War tensions, writers'
lives, and Beauvoir's struggles to remain an independent woman. This is
straightforward enough, as is the opening of the second half of the book,
when Beauvoir wins the Goncourt prize and begins her rejuvenating love
affair with the much younger Claude Lanzmann, a journalist and member
of the editorial board at *Les Temps Modernes* who would go on to make
films, the most famous of which was *Shoah* (1985).

The Algerian war occupies four out of five chapters in the second part,
and there the pace shifts abruptly. Especially at the end, Beauvoir scram-
bles to catch up with herself, pressed for time and overwhelmed by the
rush of events around her. She switches from memoir to diary and past to
present, from looking back to not being able to see ahead. In *The Prime
of Life*, she had included long excerpts from her diary in 1939, at the out-
break of World War II, and in 1940, during the fall of France. *The Force
of Circumstance* has many more such passages. They come at moments
that her memory could not "resuscitate" or at times when she feels that,
in her words, "the world crashed into her life, shattering it."[3] They aim
to recreate both the feelings of the moment the diary describes and her
experience of trying to *write* about that moment. Nearly a third of the
account of Algeria is in diary form. Beauvoir concludes *The Force of Circumstance* a year after the war ends with a brooding, dark self-reflective
epilogue on the passage of time, aging, her accomplishments, failures, and
disillusionments.

Beauvoir finds it disorienting to return to earlier moments and discover herself "ahead of events that are now in the past." Time plays tricks on her.
During long hours of research at the Bibliothèque Nationale, reading newspapers from years earlier, she writes: "I found myself in a present weighted
with an uncertain future and which has now become a long-gone past:
it was disconcerting . . . I no longer knew in which year I had landed."[4]
In *The Force of Circumstance*, time feels something like an accordion:
drawn-out passages (on travels to Brazil and Cuba, for instance) give way
to very compressed ones, which pack together layers of history and feeling. As a formal matter, the interlacing of memoir and diary and the different authorial voices (one in the present, the other as present in the past)
draw out the suspended simultaneity of the different historical moments
and the way that the past weighs on the present and vice versa. This would

become a common trope of postmodern French writing.[5] This style invites the reader to feel Beauvoir's disorienting political alienation.

Letters to Beauvoir about *The Prime of Life* and the Boupacha affair from readers in 1960 had already demonstrated to her that they found the connections between the Algerian war and World War II resonant, especially concerning torture. The reports of torture would have been appalling by any standard and in any time, but they were particularly painful in late 1950s and 1960s France. Vichy, with the support of a great many French citizens, had collaborated with the Nazis during the war; now the French were beginning to sound like the Nazis themselves. Many of Beauvoir's French readers felt this issue to be utterly personal: "I had always believed the German people were guilty, for they tolerated the death camps of Germany and torture . . . It is unthinkable that the masses would be apathetic about these practices in FRANCE." A man who had endured "the Gestapo's jails and concentration camps" was heartsick and ashamed at the thought that the French "were no better than the Nazis in 1940." How could the public not see "the comparison between today and this period twenty years ago"? How could his fellow citizens remain passive in a "society that is sinking into the depths of corruption"? A young woman who was a leader of her local trade union remembered feeling distressed and powerless in the face of her union's reluctance to take a stand against the Algerian war. Her conscience struggled with that history. She had been only fourteen years old when World War II ended, but she still regretted having "missed the Resistance." Like many in the 1960s, she was swept up in the cultural current of "resistentialism," which cast the Resistance as a heroic, redemptive episode. That moment had passed her by. She now had two children, and no time to engage in politics. Her thinking about present politics was haunted by the past. Could she in good conscience plead the excuse of her "family responsibilities"? "I find this heart-wrenching," she wrote, "and I wonder if many of us aren't asking ourselves the same anguished questions."[6]

Beauvoir made these anguished questions about history repeating itself central to her account of the Algerian war in *The Force of Circumstance*. She returned repeatedly to the failure of the Republic in 1940, the Occupation, Vichy, and collaboration. She cast the left's inability to block the military's near coup d'état of 1958 that brought de Gaulle to power and swept aside the Fourth Republic as a reprise of France's "bitter defeat" at the hands of the Germans in 1940. She recounts overhearing conversations in which her compatriots tried to reassure one another on the collapse of the Fourth Republic in 1958 that it "can't be as bad as 1940." When the elite paratroopers, the shock troops of the Algerian conflict, march through Paris, they remind her of the SS, and she feels the same "impotent and furious disgust," the same "shudder" that she experienced at seeing swastikas unfurled over the French capital. Writing of the calm with which her fellow citizens assented to de Gaulle's authoritarianism—and the disturbing comfort of well-dressed men and women walking through the evening streets on the eve of the general's investiture—she says that "something hideous was being unmasked."[7] In her telling, 1958 was the return of 1940. De Gaulle, the man of June 18, who had summoned France to resistance against the Nazis, now appears as the specter of Philippe Pétain, the military hero of World War I who headed the Vichy government after France's defeat. France was disgraced, and a craven desire for authority raised its head again. Many of these passages were written in the form of excerpts from her diary.

Shame

Shame at history, past collaboration, complicity in torture, or passivity fills *The Force of Circumstance*. It appears as classic survivor's guilt at the beginning of the volume, as Beauvoir realizes that the liberation of Paris in August 1944 did not mean the end of the war; although the Nazis had lost Paris, they razed Warsaw, crushed a rising of the Resistance (*maquis*) in Vercors, and continued to execute, deport, and murder. As prisoners returned from the camps, "the joy of being alive gave way to shame at surviving." The trial of Adolf Eichmann in 1961 revived shameful memories of deportations. As the book continues, shame becomes something of a chain reaction: incidents in the present activate both shame and shameful memories of the past, and the combination leaves her paralyzed. Beauvoir describes her reaction to reading accounts of torture (Algerian prisoners hung by their feet until their bodies were swollen and black, or buried half-alive) as a kind of "tetanus of the imagination." She writes, "The depths of a nation's moral degradation lay perhaps in this: we got used to these things," repeating the theme of the essay on Boupacha, and similarly implicating her audience in her sense of responsibility and conscience.[8]

She is ashamed of her fellow French citizens. When she goes out to cafés with Sartre and Lanzmann, the three huddle around a table in a far corner so that they do not have to hear the racist terms being thrown around in others' conversations, and in order to block out the vitriol directed against French "traitors" like themselves who support the Algerians. At a nightclub, actors in a comedy sketch are unfolding newspapers, and she can't help but pick out headlines about "Rivet" (a small town southeast of Algiers and target of a French military "pacification" operation) and Oradour (the site of Nazi atrocities in June 1944). One set of atrocities summons memories of another. She finds the audience's obliviousness and laughter appalling: "I used to love crowds: now even the streets seem hostile; I feel as dispossessed as I did during the first days of the Occupation."[9] Emphasizing her isolation, of course, underscores her (and her friends') political virtue; for those skeptical about Beauvoir or French intellectuals, or those more directly involved in the conflict, this self-righteousness is not the most attractive feature of the volume.

Her philosophical preoccupations, however, become clearer as the book unfolds. The shame of seeing herself through others' eyes is classically existentialist: "I need *estime* to live, and I see myself through the eyes of women who had been raped twenty times, men whose bones have been shattered, and children driven insane."[10] Sartre writes of shame in *Being and Nothingness* that it "is by nature *recognition*. I recognize that I am as the other sees me . . . [S]hame is an immediate shudder which runs through me from head to foot without any discursive preparation."[11] As a phenomenologist, Beauvoir underscores her shame as an experience that involves body as well as consciousness. She finds her awareness of her complicity in France's crimes *physically* unbearable. "I am French: these words burn my throat," she writes. "I felt as if I had one of those illnesses where the most serious symptom is the absence of pain." Her hands "sweat with shame."[12]

With every page of *The Force of Circumstance*, the humiliation and pain of complicity in France's present crimes and remembered complicity in World War II become more inextricable from exhaustion and age, both her own and Sartre's. She gives readers a ghoulish portrait of Sartre furiously at work on *Critique of Dialectical Reason* and drained by the effort, slurring and confusing his words and drinking too much. When she tries to stop him, they fight; she smashes a glass on the kitchen tiles. In fact, she learns, Sartre had almost had a heart attack, his second major health scare after his unexplained collapse while visiting the USSR in 1954. Beauvoir has nightmares. She and Sartre talk about sleeping pills and tranquillizers; their friend Michel Leiris nearly overdoses on barbiturates. Then 1958 brings de Gaulle to power, a victory for the army, and the "defeat of everything [we] want France to stand for." Beauvoir's love affair with Lanzmann unravels. She calls 1958 the "excruciating year" (*l'année accablante*).[13]

Still, Beauvoir remains very much at the center of things, involved with the antiwar movement, working with Halimi and for Boupacha, and increasingly prominent in international circles. She and Sartre became unofficial spokespersons for the French left and self-appointed counter-ministers of culture. (Minister of Culture André Malraux was closely associated with de Gaulle and Algeria.) She and Sartre travel to Brazil and go from there to Cuba, to meet Fidel Castro and honor the revolution. As tensions and violence rise at home, their notoriety brings them into the crosshairs of the right-wing paramilitary OAS, which twice targets Sartre's apartment with a bomb.[14] Beauvoir did not live in that apartment with him, but she worked there every afternoon. She is afraid and vilified. "This is what happens when you piss people off with your politics," an angry neighbor at 42 rue Bonaparte shouts after her across the rubble left by the second explosion.[15]

The high point of the volume, a remarkable event, remarkably told, and revealing about the intellectual and political concerns to which Beauvoir was speaking, comes in July 1961, when Beauvoir, Sartre, and Lanzmann meet in Rome with Frantz Fanon. While she and Sartre were at the height of their political notoriety, Fanon was perhaps *the* central intellectual figure of the global revolutionary politics of 1960–61 and certainly "one of the most remarkable personalities of his time."[16] Fanon was French, from a middle-class family in Martinique. His revolutionary peregrinations began in 1943, when he left Martinique to fight with the Resistance; after the war he stayed to train in psychiatry and medicine in Lyon. He took a position in the psychiatric ward of the Blida-Joinville hospital in Algeria (several hundred miles southwest of Algiers), where he was working when the Algerian war broke out. That position required him to treat

French soldiers as well as Algerian nationalists; in 1956 he left to work with the FLN, or National Liberation Front, training fighters in Tunisia, doing research across Algeria, and representing the FLN to Kwame Nkrumah, the socialist and Pan-Africanist president of Ghana. Fanon's concerns reached well beyond Algeria, to the psychology of racism and colonial rule, African politics, and global decolonization. His intellectual trajectory dramatized the increasingly broad reach of thought that combined negritude with Marxism, existentialism, and anticolonial revolt.

In 1952 Fanon had authored *Black Skin, White Masks*, which was published with a preface by Francis Jeanson, Sartre's student and an anticolonial activist. A collection of Fanon's essays came out in 1959 as *Year V of the Algerian Revolution*. ("Year I" of the French Revolutionary calendar was 1792, the overthrow of the monarchy and the beginning of the Republic. Year I of the Algerian revolution was 1954, and Year V, 1959.) At the time he met with Sartre, Beauvoir, and Lanzmann (who arranged the meeting) in Rome, Fanon had just sent Sartre the completed *Wretched of the Earth*. Sartre found the text astonishing—"incendiary, but also complex and subtle"—and agreed to write the preface. Fanon was also dying of leukemia, though he refused to speak of it. He recounted the history of his psychiatric work at Blida in Algeria. He told them, Beauvoir says, that he had coached revolutionaries on how to calm their nerves and keep their hands from trembling when they planted a bomb or threw a hand grenade. He gave revolutionaries psychological and physiological strategies for resisting torture. Sometimes on the same day, he said, he would also be summoned to treat French officers on the verge of nervous collapse after interrogating suspects.[17] Whether or not this account is exaggerated, it is a remarkable and classically Fanonian portrait of the internalized tensions of colonialism, racism, and the fight against them, and it is written by Beauvoir as such. She describes Fanon as deeply ambivalent about violence and spooked by his own "catastrophism": "The aftermath of the Algerian conflict would be terrifying: The villages will rise. There will be half a million deaths. A million." She also understood that Fanon knew much more than he would say about murderous divisions within Algerian nationalism. This subject, too, was off limits, but "these dark secrets, combined perhaps with personal hesitations, gave his words a tone that was enigmatic, obscurely prophetic, and disturbed." Fanon told Beauvoir and Sartre that an Italian hotel worker had asked him whether it was true that he hated whites, and that he had replied, "The core of the problem is that you other whites have a physiological horror of Blacks."[18] Beauvoir's account doesn't hide how troubling she found their encounter. On the contrary, in good existentialist fashion, she relates the experience of herself as seen by others and blurs with it Fanon's account of living under racism; in her mind she is identifying with Fanon's experience as a racial Other.

The meeting becomes an occasion for yet more shame, shameful weariness, and a rattling exchange about French intellectuals' loyalties and commitments. Beauvoir underscores both Fanon's impatient, stakes-raising demands and her and Sartre's inability to respond. Fanon reproaches Sartre for not making some significant political gesture, such as refusing to write or withdrawing from public life: "You owe us. How can you continue to live and write as if nothing were going on?" Fanon speaks glowingly of Fernand Iveton, the union leader and communist from Algiers who had joined the FLN and taken up arms; just before being executed by French authorities, Iveton declared that he was now "Algerian." Sartre assures Fanon of his full solidarity with the Algerian revolution but says he remains "French."[19] They talk late into the night, and when Beauvoir interrupts, observing "as politely as possible" that Sartre needs to get some sleep, Fanon is scornful: "I don't like people who hold back" (*Je n'aime pas les gens qui s'économisent*)." Fanon reported to a friend that he wished he had been able to talk one-on-one with Sartre, and that he found Beauvoir's presence irritating. His disdain did not escape Beauvoir.[20] After this meeting, Sartre went on to write his now famous preface to Fanon's *Wretched of the Earth* (published in 1961), summoning his fellow Europeans to "look at ourselves, if we can bear to" and to "face that unexpected revelation, the strip-tease of our humanism." ("Striptease" is in English in the original.)[21] And in *The Force of Circumstance*, the conversation with Fanon comes shortly before a somber epilogue in which Beauvoir feels depleted, haggard, and betrayed by humanism and bourgeois culture.

Beauvoir had asked her readers to be her "collaborators." How did they respond? "It's very rare to find a book that you don't want to or can't put down—I think this is your best book," wrote one of the many correspondents who had relived a crucial moment of history with her. Wrote another: "It leaves you with such a strange impression to read your own story told by someone else, finding the same events and the same reactions . . . What you lived in the spotlight I lived as an unknown, in the shadows." She had shared Beauvoir's soaring hopes as well as her crushing defeats:

> The immense hope of the Liberation, then our disappointments, our efforts to create a unified left and to encourage women to become aware of their responsibilities. The Front Républicain, the socialist betrayal, and especially the Algerian war. This disgust, this stupor when we discover the reality of torture and at the same time that the French had accepted being torturers. I see myself after rereading *The Question* [Alleg's book on torture] knocked flat, powerless . . . The bitterness at the tidal wave of the "yes" vote for the referendum, the demonstrations [in protest].

She had wanted to sign the Manifesto of 121, but doing so would have meant losing her government clearance as a "prison visitor," who watched over and testified about conditions under which prisoners were held, which she considered her most important political role.[22]

The Force of Circumstance, like the other autobiographical volumes, mobilized memories; letter writers recalled futile political discussions in trade union or communist meetings in provincial cities, or the insults and silent disdain in the bourgeois neighborhoods of Paris. Readers reported, revealingly, the wariness with which their neighbors met newspaper accounts of war atrocities, especially torture. As a woman from Besançon had noted at the time of the Boupacha affair, no one in her neighborhood trusted either the communist *L'Humanité*, which they assumed simply exaggerated all the crimes of colonialism, or the left-wing Christian press, which they dismissed as edited by dreamy airheads: "If more detailed proof is forthcoming, the man on the street simply concludes, as I've heard any number of times: those are former SS who do that—or Germans who have signed up for the [Foreign] Legion."[23]

Other opponents of the war wanted to testify to the terrible feelings of isolation and fear during the years of the Algerian war; they were overwhelmed to learn theirs was a shared experience. The hostility of their fellow citizens had upended their world in a way that reminded them, too, of an earlier war. "My husband learned he was Jewish when he was nine years old, when the Germans arrived in Paris," wrote one woman. "He says he has known the capacity of the French for collective cowardice since the Occupation. But for me, it was the Algerian war, the voluntary blindness, the refusal to know. We felt like foreigners in our own land. Language lost all meaning." This couple had been under surveillance by the state's domestic intelligence services. By chance they were lucky enough to have moved before they could be detained: "Virtually no one understood, let alone helped." Unlike Beauvoir, this woman and her husband had not been able to "bask in the reassuring complicity of shared indignation . . . No one here cares about philosophers' ideas and politics." They were nonetheless gratified to have their memories validated. A woman who was probably Algerian wrote with similar generosity: "I lived this long war moment . . . [her ellipses] in the same way that everybody of my race did, with the obsession that I was a hunted criminal. This fear and this obsession were natural for us. But I appreciate that they found an echo in you, and that you were able to willingly endure what we had imposed on us by the force of circumstance."[24]

Shame had been a nearly constant theme in readers' letters to Beauvoir during the Boupacha affair. The letters that came in response to *The Force of Circumstance* are soaked in shame, the readers' feelings commingled with Beauvoir's: "I felt the same shame that you did at being French." Readers redeployed existentialist vocabulary: "Like you, I was ashamed to the point of nausea at being French."[25] They echoed the doubled shame of two wars that Beauvoir had put at the center of the memoir.

The most interesting letter in this regard came from a thirty-eight-year-old woman who, like many readers, was torn between her desire to write and her fear of intruding on Beauvoir or appearing "ridiculous." She was "bourgeoise," with a law degree—"Just the average, typical Frenchwoman. Still, I have a small particularity: I come from a Jewish family, atheist to be sure, but nonetheless I was profoundly marked by the war." No one in her family had been deported, but "those were the four years that counted the most in my life, and it is probably impossible for me to tackle any problem without my old complexes reappearing." The most poignant part of the letter comes in what follows, where she excuses herself for dwelling on or making too much of *her* past: "I won't go on about 'my war,' don't worry. I am only noting that the fact is there."[26] It is a strikingly personal instance of Jewish memory, and a revealing example of how that memory did not find a home in Beauvoir's universalizing framework.

This reader had just finished *The Force of Circumstance*. She admired Beauvoir's politics. She and her husband, both on the left and lonely among their more conservative friends, felt the Algerian war "like a thorn in our side." That "thorn" takes her suddenly, in the next sentence, to World War II:

> For thirty years I've hated the Germans. (And this is not a figure of speech: in '34 my father's cousin, a Jewish Frenchman living in Berlin and married to a German woman, had to flee Germany; another managed to get out of Dachau in '39, so I heard talk of persecutions from the time I was very young.)
>
> . . . [S]ince I have known about the events in Algeria, I've heard about camps and torture, and I haven't done anything, I'm sick and ashamed . . . The fact that I've voted no in all the referendums and been to many demonstrations doesn't change anything.

She apologizes for everything: for intruding on Beauvoir, for her bourgeois family *and* her inability to break free of it; for her (secular) Jewishness, which has marked her, *and* her need to talk about that; for her self-involvement; and for her political powerlessness. Reading Beauvoir's account of the Algerian war brings to the surface her long-held and tightly coiled feelings of inadequacy, rage, and hurt. At the same time, it prevents her from untangling those feelings. It is as if her complicity as a French citizen in crimes in Algeria rules her testimony about World War II out of court; shame shuts down what was already a very muffled emerging discussion of the Holocaust. The chorus of comments from readers to the effect that the French in Algeria had proved no better than the Nazis, or that Beauvoir had shown them that "the present situation is worse than what happened under the Germans," illustrates the impossibility of reflecting on one war without the other. It also strikingly illustrates the confining, even repressive aspects of this discourse of recurrence, of twice-told historical guilt and shame.[27]

Jean-Marie Domenach, the editor of *Esprit* and often an adversary of Sartre and Beauvoir, strenuously objected to this aspect of *The Force of Circumstance* when he reviewed it. It was profoundly wrongheaded to insist, as Beauvoir did, on framing the events of the present as the return of the past. Domenach believed doing so muddied the analysis of political events as they were happening and made it impossible to think clearly about how a political person or party might effectively respond to those events on their own terms. Beauvoir's account meshed with Sartre's and *Les Temps Modernes'* increasingly militant positions after the crisis of the Republic in 1958. They gave up trying to stay nonaligned and made common cause with the communists, calling not just for draft resistance but for a revolutionary confrontation with a resurgent fascism. That meant rejecting calls for peace and instead taking up arms with the FLN against de Gaulle as well as the OAS. Domenach found this stance preposterous: the OAS and de Gaulle did not represent the same political phenomenon, and the FLN could not be an "instrument of regeneration, and the future of the French left."[28]

Historians have interpreted Beauvoir's layering of past and present as an example of the broader cultural problem of the work and politics of memory. Jean-Louis Jeannelle, a leading literary historian and Beauvoir expert, reads *The Force of Circumstance* as a classic instance of the "Vichy syndrome." For Jeannelle, Beauvoir's overblown anguish and physical revulsion over her complicity in French crimes in Algeria represent the return of repressed memories of the Occupation and the dubious choices she made at the time. Taking an oath that she was neither Jewish nor a Freemason in order to hold on to her job on a Vichy radio station is one example. Beauvoir rationalized those choices in her memoir, contending that "there was no way to do differently."[29] Jeannelle contends those uncomfortable memories magnify her shame about the nation's dirty war in Algeria. Michael Rothberg's concept of "multi-directional memory" suggests a less pathological diagnosis. Memory is not a zero-sum matter, Rothberg argues, and memories, like historical or political analogies, need not inevitably distort and crowd one another out. Thus, Beauvoir's anguish about Algeria was not necessarily the return of some repressed Other, nor were her readers trapped in their unmastered past.[30] The matter of historical memory in postwar France is enormous, and these are only two approaches. Both have been contentious, though each captures a dimension of Beauvoir's writing and her many-sided conversation with her readers.[31] More than memory is involved here, however. If, like Beauvoir's readers, we stick with her through the end of *The Force of Circumstance*, we see much more of both her world and theirs, the conversations into which she was pulling them, and the preoccupations and anxieties that *they* wanted *her* to share.

"I Have Been Duped"

The correspondence responding to *The Force of Circumstance* is overwhelming and fills two large cartons for 1964 alone. Its center of gravity is the book's epilogue, Beauvoir's twenty-page stocktaking of her career, politics, and life as she reckons with mortality and what she considered old age. The epilogue grabbed readers' attention because it was melodramatic, because it put Beauvoir's relations with readers at stake, and because the issues she raised became the locus of the shame that she had summoned in them.

Beauvoir opens by calling her relationship with Sartre the one "certain success" of her life. She admits she is proud of her literary accomplishments and her role as an intellectual, however unforgiving the spotlight of celebrity and demands of political prominence. Her modest contributions to political battles (which she does not exaggerate) have made her feel part of history. The epilogue strikes different notes—defensive, defiant, and self-critical or self-pitying—but as it unfolds, pessimism and weariness get the upper hand. She reprises the themes of defeat, age, and failing health, Sartre's even more dramatically than her own. She evokes the loves she has lost (Algren and Lanzmann), the prominence of younger and more energetic women writers, and her narrowed horizons: "I've hit the wall of age . . . For years, I thought that my life's work was in front of me, and now, suddenly, I find it is behind." She is alienated from her aging body: "It is strange to no longer be a body . . . to no longer find new desires in myself."[32] A reviewer in *L'Express* summarized it this way: "The hatred of the mirror is described with a disconcerting cruelty."[33]

The last pages of Beauvoir's epilogue are also an existential protest against the absurdity of death and the extinction of experience: books read, places visited, knowledge accumulated over a lifetime; all this will vanish—"this unique ensemble, my own experience, with its logic and contingencies . . . No part of all this can be resuscitated."[34] She closes with a famously enigmatic effort to rekindle her adolescent optimism and passion for the boundless possibilities of life. The promises that she made herself and that stirred her heart have been kept, she says. But "as I look back with incredulity at that credulous adolescent, I am astounded to see how I have been duped."[35] She ends the book on that sentence.

Many of the book's official reviewers went straight for the epilogue's melancholy self-assessment. Beauvoir's critics did not hesitate to pass their own judgments on the life of a left and feminist intellectual or to wield clichés about aging women.[36] *Le Monde* asked Pierre-Henri Simon to review the volume, perhaps because he had weighed in against brutal and cynical violence in Algeria, which left the French power "debased and humiliated." Simon, however, said virtually nothing about the history Beauvoir recounted and in which he, too, had been involved: nothing about the torture cases and their consequences, de Gaulle, Gaullism, or the meaning of the Algerian war for Algeria, France, or the world. He deemed *The Force of Circumstance* badly written and distressingly preoccupied with the existentialists' (sexual) affairs. He claimed *not* to be gloating about "the aging woman who turns around to assess her life." But he wrote that if Beauvoir had been "duped," finding, as she looked back, deceptions rather than the riches of a life well lived, such were the wages of the philosophy of nothingness (existentialism) and its "unrestrained egotism," of rejecting "traditions," "the laws of society," and, jabbing at Beauvoir's refusal to have children, "the natural responsibilities of a human couple."[37]

Similar high-profile nastiness came from the journalist Maria Craipeau in *France Observateur*. Craipeau cast Beauvoir as an intellectual hanger-on, desperate to participate in the events of her time and frustrated by "her life on the margins." Craipeau scoffed that every historical period got the heroine it deserved: Vera Zasulich (the Russian populist) and Rosa Luxemburg (the revolutionary Polish German socialist) lived "*real* lives" in "*real* times," but Beauvoir suited the "sterility of the present." The admiring references to Zasulich and Luxemburg harked back to Craipeau's earlier Trotskyism, before she signed on with *France Observateur* as a middle-brow sentimentalist. Many of Beauvoir's readers were irate at these reviews. Craipeau specialized in "melodrama, tremolo, and commonplace," observed one.[38]

Still, Beauvoir's phrase "I have been duped" flummoxed even sympathetic critics, and it upset countless readers. This reader chastised Beauvoir for her self-absorption and political pessimism, and for abandoning her political allies:

> I read little and write even less. I do not imagine that my reactions will bring you anything new. If you have often heard the same thing, let me simply say that I'm adding my name to the petition from your readers.

I loved *The Force of Circumstance*: what it is about, and the fact that it is a chronicle, a chronicle lived through you. I don't mean you the writer, but you as a human who deserves a rare Respect among writers (with a capital R)!

How could I let you end on this "duped" without wanting to scold you?

What do you expect [from aging] other than a healthy fatigue and a communion with simple people?

It is true that very few workers still read you, but you help them, and in a way that would be difficult to replace, given where you are situated.

In any event, thank you. With affection, if you will permit me, from an unknown friend.

He acknowledged that writing one's memoirs always led one to put oneself in the past tense: "I was." Still, Beauvoir had a present and a future! As for what she had lost, why did she want to see it as "stolen"? Why not consider her life and idealism to have been a "gift"?[39]

Many letter writers, also otherwise appreciative, considered the epilogue an *adieu* to her readers and her relationship with them: "I am not able to respond—and you probably don't expect anyone to respond—to your cry of indignation and bitterness as you reflect on your life and its significance. But I know that you crush the joy of the person who is reading you." This reader considered the declaration of bitter defeat a "low blow," especially since it was delivered at the end of the book. Some readers wrote more gently: "Your epilogue is so sad. But at 50 something you are <u>hardly Dead</u>!" Or "I haven't yet read your latest book, but I've heard that it ends with regret and bitterness. Why?" An admiring and puzzled reader mused, "I learned so much that had been hidden from me about Algeria from your book. Why is the conclusion all about growing old and dying?" Or, with rising feeling, "I won't let you say 'never anymore.' Melancholy and sadness looking back at what you have done? No!" Or from another reader: "Dear Madame, I am sick at heart, and a little paralyzed by your pain. I can so imagine your anxiety, your fear, your regrets, your pain."[40]

There are scores of memorable letters in this genre, and their self-dramatization easily matches Beauvoir's. One came from a loyal reader from Switzerland who bought *The Force of Circumstance* as soon as it came out, and after a quick glance concluded it was Beauvoir's last book. She described her reaction: "I sat there immobile, frozen, as if someone had just told me something terrible had happened. I didn't dare open the book, I didn't want to believe that I was going to read 'Simone de Beauvoir's last book.' I suddenly felt a large emptiness inside myself and in the world."[41]

Like many, she expressed a mixture of disappointment and anger, for Beauvoir had invited her, the reader, to a dialogue. A man who wrote Beauvoir described his distress as that of someone who has been "torn away from a very long dialogue." The separation was made more wrenching by the uniquely intense relationship between a reader and an author of memoir: the "silent and intimate isolation" of their "communion." Apart from readers' predictable efforts to be reassuring—doctors told her that her depression would pass, the devout suggested she reconsider religion, and men wrote to say she would surely find love again—the most striking feature of the correspondence about *Force of Circumstance* is the distress of so many readers.[42] That was partly a response to Beauvoir's dramatic good-byes to all that, but no less telling about these readers' felt intimacy with the author, the intensity with which they relived the century through her memoir, and the enormity of their expectations.

Her correspondents' distress and reassurances irritated Beauvoir. As she replied to one well-meaning correspondent who had misinterpreted the volume, he was not alone: no one understood the epilogue. In fact, she had not given up on life or her work.[43] She was repelled not by what she saw in the mirror but rather by what history had revealed to her: the hollow promises of bourgeois culture, the fragility of humanist values, the bad faith of her fellow citizens, and especially her own inescapable complicity in her nation's crimes.[44] Over a series of interviews she explained that she had fully expected the book to "displease," but because of what she said about the war and her politics. She had sensed that the pages on Algeria were "anachronistic" as soon as she wrote them, she groused, exasperated by her public's refusal to fully engage them; by 1963 the shameful end of a shameful war was shrouded in sullen silence.[45]

By 1963, forgetting was already a rich theme of commentary, set out in films like Edgar Morin's *Chronique d'un été* (1961) or Chris Marker's *Le joli mai*, filmed in 1962 and released at the same time as *The Force of Circumstance*.[46] Like Beauvoir, Marker and his co-director were confounded to discover how little the events of the war and the peace resonated, how few of their fellow citizens shared their concerns, and how quickly the end of French colonialism became *dépassé*. The book reviewer at *L'Express*,

Otto Hahn, was from a Hungarian Jewish family; he had survived the war in hiding in France and worked at *Les Temps Modernes* from 1960 to 1965, so he had lived these years with Beauvoir and her colleagues. He noted in his review that *The Force of Circumstance* makes us "notice everything that we have already forgotten."[47]

Some letter writers wanted to explain why they would not talk about the war. The stakes were too high, wrote a *pied-noir* who disagreed with Beauvoir's political stance but did not want to argue; hardly anyone could step outside "the madness of Algeria" (*bain de folie de l'Algérie*) and offer any "sound judgment." While Beauvoir might rue her aging, he welcomed the "aging of history," for he hoped it would soothe the bitterness and horror of both the Algerian war and World War II. A letter writer who shared Beauvoir's politics said that the book left an "odd and bitter after-taste." Beauvoir had certainly been right to tell all. But for this reader, the end of the Algerian war was still unbearably close. A university professor wrote to say that he shared Beauvoir's emotions. Indeed, he found them impossible to shake off: "I felt the same things myself at that time—shame at the violence and the passivity of people, and anger too. I rediscovered these feelings while going through your book, I realize they haven't left me, they keep coming back, despite myself, in what I write today." He had never shown anyone the poetry he had written during the war: "I don't know why, I was ashamed." He had not hesitated to speak out openly against the war while it was going on, but he was now ashamed of his vulnerability, of how much he took politics to heart, and of his inadequate powers of expression. He could not share his work with even a sympathetic audience.[48] Beauvoir became a lightning rod for these readers' own emotional responses to the debates around them, for their helplessness, or for their political passivity.

Shame is the inescapable presence in the readers' writing as well as Beauvoir's, and it has meanings that overflow the themes of "forgetting" and the "Vichy syndrome." Beauvoir did not use "shame" casually. Her deliberate emphasis on emotion followed from the existentialist tenet that humanity should be understood intersubjectively, the self in relation to the other. As Sartre had written in 1948, emotion opens onto the "indispensable structure of consciousness"; it is one of the principal ways in which "consciousness *understands* its being-in-the-world."[49] More specifically, *Being and Nothingness* says of shame that it is "by nature *recognitio*n.

I recognize that I am as the other sees me."[50] The shame that floods Beauvoir in *The Force of Circumstance* is that of the self which is living in the awareness of Other, whether that Other is Djamila Boupacha, demanding that her allies stand by her; the many victims of colonial wars; Frantz Fanon, scornful of the French *philosophes'* inability to keep pace with him; or international opinion turning against the French tactics in Algeria. That emotion takes corporeal form is also a tenet of existentialism and phenomenology. *The Force of Circumstance* was Beauvoir's own contribution to the phenomenology of emotion.

What is more, Beauvoir's philosophical concerns connected her memoir to anticolonial writing in the francophone world, where shame as painful self-recognition was a central theme and trope. The disturbing gaze of the colonized Other loomed large in Sartre's preface to Léopold Senghor's *Anthologie de la nouvelle poésie nègre et malgache* (1948). "Négritude" reversed the white regard: "For three thousand years, the white man has enjoyed the privilege of seeing without being seen . . . Today black men look at us, and our gaze comes back to our own eyes."[51] Shame is no less fundamental to Fanon's 1951 essay on the lived experience of blackness under colonialism and racism: "I cast an objective eye at myself, discovered my blackness, my ethnic characteristics—and my eardrums were bursting with cannibalism, mental retardation, fetishism, racial taints, slave trades." Alienated self-awareness takes on emotional dimensions: "My long antennae pick up the catchphrases strewn over the surface of things . . . Shame. Shame and self-contempt. Nausea." In Fanon's account, unlike Beauvoir's, shame and self-contempt are transformed into a revolutionary subjectivity: "I resolved to assert myself as BLACK. Given that the other was reluctant to recognize me [*me connaître*] there was only one solution left: to make myself known [*de me faire connaître*]."[52]

The web of cross-references thickens. Sartre emphasizes the shaming gaze of the colonized in his preface to Fanon's *Wretched of the Earth*, written just after the conversations in Rome that Beauvoir had described so strikingly. In a surprising, and even baffling, passage in that preface, Sartre summons Europeans to study Fanon's book, be ashamed, and thus become revolutionary: "Have the courage to read this book, for in the first place it will make you ashamed, and shame, as Marx said, is a revolutionary sentiment."[53] Marx's assertion comes from an 1843 letter to Arnold Ruge, his coeditor at the *Deutsch-Französische Jahrbücher*.

Its subject, fittingly, was the dimming international reputation of a great power, namely, the Prussian autocracy of the 1840s, as Prussia jettisoned reformist promises and cracked down on liberal and radical movements. "Germany has ridden deeply into the mire," Marx wrote:

> The glorious robes of liberalism have fallen away and the most repulsive despotism stands revealed for all the world to see. Germans will learn the hollowness of our patriotism and the perverted nature of our state, and hide our faces in shame. I can see you smile and ask what good that will do; revolutions are not made by shame. And my answer is that shame is a revolution in itself . . . Shame is a kind of anger turned in on itself. And if a whole nation were to feel ashamed it would be like a lion recoiling in order to spring.[54]

Tracking down the passage that Sartre was citing hardly solves the puzzle of how shame becomes "revolutionary." It demonstrates instead that shame describes a very wide range of easily elided states.[55] What Marx and Sartre call shame is a wound to honor or self-esteem; it summons those humiliated to redeem themselves by living up to their moral code. It seems rooted in a decidedly nineteenth-century economy of emotion and gendered as well. It seems especially inapposite in the case of Beauvoir or most of the letters about *The Force of Circumstance*, so hobbled by self-criticism, weariness, and insecurity.

On the one hand, Beauvoir wrote *The Force of Circumstance* as a full participant in this conversation with Sartre and Fanon; all three were reading the same texts and reaching for the same references.[56] *The Force of Circumstance* rendered the lived experience on the colonizer side of the dialectical divide; it was a belated response to the conversation with Fanon in Rome; it makes sense as part of a dialogue with Fanon's essay "The Lived Experience of the Black Man" or *The Wretched of the Earth*. She was bringing readers into those important conversations. On the other hand, Beauvoir's shame seems to be in a different register. While Sartre insisted on the purposefulness of emotion, Beauvoir confessed her emotional exhaustion, asking whether one couldn't be "present in the world without wearing oneself out in emotions that do nothing for anyone."[57] Beauvoir's shame did indeed "coil back on itself," but in a spiral of self-incrimination and laceration. She seems in the throes of shame-induced weariness or paralysis rather than any version of the shame that Marx, Fanon, or Sartre had in mind, and the same applies to her readers' interpretation of her experience and their own.

Gender matters here. As Toril Moi points out, Beauvoir's understanding of women's "situation," however philosophically close to Fanon's analysis of the lived experience of blackness, doesn't allow her to imagine anything like the political subjectivity that Fanon theorized and championed.[58] Shame's gendered dimensions were strikingly on display in Sartre's preface to Henri Alleg's *La question* written in 1958, two years before Beauvoir's essay on Djamila Boupacha. Sartre had been preoccupied since World War II with whether he himself could have withstood torture; he wrote that Alleg "saved us from despair and shame because he is the victim himself and because he has conquered torture . . . We have gained a little of our pride: we are proud that he is French."[59] Sartre turns standing up to torture into the litmus test of manly political courage. The masculinist bravado of this passage did not escape one of Beauvoir's observant women correspondents, who offered a different perspective. What did Alleg's ability to bear suffering prove? The reader continued: "Everyone knows that there are limits to what a human body can endure . . . He [Alleg] could have kept quiet until dying and he would have died all the same. He could have been driven mad and talked; would that have meant he 'lost the right to remain a man among men?' I don't think so: man is equally human in his moments of weakness and greatness [*grandeur*]."[60] Beauvoir's essay on Boupacha did not make the young woman's confession an issue as a revelation of youthful or pitiable feminine weakness. Boupacha's full humanity did not need to be demonstrated; her honor did not need to be rescued by her allies and protectors.

Gender is not necessarily the master key to the meanings of shame. Men on the French left in the late 1950s and 1960s sounded similar themes of humiliation, frustration, powerlessness, and passivity as their parties reeled from their inability to end the Algerian conflict and their sense that history was being made without them.[61] Francis Jeanson, the radical anticolonialist who was tried for setting up clandestine networks to aid the FLN, found his conversations with Fanon no less disconcerting than Beauvoir did, and he also described his discomfort in corporeal terms.[62]

The men and women who wrote Beauvoir were hardly alone in running together political and personal or corporeal shame, or being riveted by her "deterioration." Beauvoir lamented her readers' inability to differentiate her political disgust at the French in Algeria from her distress about an aging body. The force field of gender and sexualized imagery made it particularly difficult *not* to read her work in this way.[63] Yet it was (and is) in fact *not* so easy to distinguish feelings of self-diminishment, defeat, dismay, and emotional exhaustion about politics from personal bodily shame, anxiety, and weariness.

The specific character of shame as affect and emotion is also in play here, and worth attending to for its larger cultural and political ramifications. As Eve Kosofsky Sedgwick astutely points out, shame is at once isolating and contagious: "Bad treatment of someone else, bad treatment *by* someone else, someone else's embarrassment, stigma . . . seemingly having nothing to do with me, can so readily flood me."[64] Sedgwick's description captures well the feeling that overflows so many of these letters, and helps us to understand how that feeling commingles with Beauvoir's while simultaneously evoking deep loneliness and despair. In shame, the moral and political are entangled in the psychological. Shame involves conscience, seen as an interior of moral sentiments that can be aroused, as well as consciousness, understood as the workings of the mind, imaginative identifications, subjectivity and intersubjectivity. Beauvoir and the letter writers were writing about both. They were also writing about the bodily aspects of emotion, in this case shame's physical sensations. They were writing about feelings that wore one out, with nothing to show for it, which is central to Beauvoir's account. These emotional dynamics may be more relevant to understanding Beauvoir and her correspondents than the "Vichy syndrome," and they are less abstract than that interpretation.

The Taboo of Age

Correspondents in 1963 and 1964 wanted to write about mortality and aging. These subjects were profoundly frightening and difficult in their own right, surrounded by unspoken fears, denial, shame (at one's own decline or others'), centuries of accreted prohibitions and myths, codes of decency and proper behavior. Mortality and death were rarely understood as what Beauvoir would call "situations," the experience of which were shaped by wealth, class, the allocation of public resources, debates about the relationship between public and private responsibility, gender division of labor, changes in family structures, and so on. The grim details of old age were taboo, and for a great many of Beauvoir's readers closer to home than the subject of torture. Beauvoir's mother died as *The Force of Circumstance* was appearing in 1963, and Beauvoir published an unsparing account of her mother's passing, *A Very Easy Death,* in the spring of 1964. By that time, readers' concerns with death and age in response to *The Force of Circumstance* were overdetermined.[65] They had been manifest, however, from the outset. "I won't read *The Force of Circumstance* if it is about decrepitude, ugliness, and death," wrote one correspondent after reading a review in *L'Express* when the book first appeared. "It will make me feel too sad for you."[66]

Many readers agreed that "the first signs of aging are awful." Others rebuked her with their own experiences, underscoring Beauvoir's privilege as a middle-class intellectual. Their letters are quite telling about how class hierarchies *felt* or were embodied: "I don't believe that getting old is a degradation [*décheance* in French, which means both moral and physical degradation or deterioration]. Anyway, I have deteriorated much more than you, and surely because I work as an intern in a hospital—my arms, legs, and back are going—and I am only 31."[67]

A particularly thoughtful reader, a communist, wrote a three-page-long letter in a small, careful hand. He opened by evoking his political fraternity with Beauvoir, calling her "battles" his own. He went on to underline their differences. He cited her memoir's passage on the awful sight of the deportees and prisoners returning from the camps after World War II, a moment that had revealed the depths of the public's ignorance about atrocities, or the widespread denial of what it should have known.[68] "I was among those you saw returning from the camps," he wrote:

> I'm about the same age as you—I'm 52, but I feel like the deportation cancels out that small difference. Like you, I've felt age do its work on my arms and legs, my eyes, my brain, and my heart. Over the last year in particular, I've often thought about death—as someone implicated. Not the kind of death you dream of sometimes when you are in good health: a sudden death, heroic if possible, and in any case abstract and far away, but real death, that which comes at the end of a long "natural" decline.[69]

The letters responding to Beauvoir's accounts of age and death are some of the most moving in the archive. A ninety-one-year-old doctor wrote with a shaky hand to thank her for her sensitivity. He had just lost his wife, at eighty-three, to a degenerative disease:

> Madame,
> I've been through a terrible, bitter experience. My 83-year-old wife passed away on November 3, 1963. She suffered atrociously—for 8 days she had not one moment of respite. She had atherosclerosis, an obscure illness of unknown etiology. I did receive both your books—and I thank you for your kindness.[70]

Another wrote about the death of a fifty-nine-year-old friend, the victim like Beauvoir's mother of a metastasized cancer. The letter writer was stricken with grief from witnessing her friend's pain, and from the horror of seeing a human deteriorate: "Her ordeal lasted two years and a month . . . I didn't leave her for one day. So I saw everything. I saw the same thing that you saw—the wretched side of a human being falling apart, losing its beauty (she was beautiful) and suffering so. She had passionately loved art and life."[71]

One last example: a letter from a woman who had first sent Beauvoir a harsh letter when *The Force of Circumstance* came out. She wrote again in June 1964, ashamed of her previous letter and moved by *A Very Easy Death*. Her own mother had also died a few months earlier, but under very different conditions. For reasons that it "sickened" her to recall—several elementary misdiagnoses, an overcrowded clinic, an absent doctor, and medications that could not be procured—her mother's death, like Beauvoir's mother's, had not been "gentle" (*douce*). She blamed herself for being too "cowardly" to write about her mother's suffering: "You could never entirely relieve me from feeling like a coward because I am incapable of testifying to the death of my mother. Unable to express anything with truth; every word that I write seems to me a betrayal. To some extent, you atone for this betrayal."[72] Whether she meant exhausted, afraid, sickened, inhibited, or all of those is difficult to tell, for her letter is very terse. She was echoing what she had read, however. Cowardice, like betrayal, looms large in *A Very Easy Death*, for Beauvoir cannot rescue her mother from either the clutches of the doctors or the comforting lie that she will recover from her cancer.

Many correspondents pleaded with Beauvoir to write more on the pain of aging and to help them face the obstacles it presented. One even said (with no apparent irony) that Beauvoir could counsel or minister to them "a little like your friend taught FLN partisans to endure torture."[73] Odd associations like this may have exasperated the author, but they suggest how much the personal and the political were, in the telling, imbued with some of the same feelings.

In his appreciative but measured review of *The Force of Circumstance* in 1964, Jean-Marie Domenach wrote that the book took one back to the past and "reminds us what we all too willingly forget in the euphoria of today." Before Gaullists and right-minded opinion makers (*les bien pensants*) "discovered decolonization" as historically inevitable, they had vilified antiwar protesters and accused them of treason.[74] The Algerian war may have been shrouded in euphemisms, and talk of torture was distorted by taboos. The war did not unfold in silence, however; nearly all parties to the conflict clamored to witness and testify to the rightness of their cause.[75] *The Force of Circumstance* was one such witnessing.

Beauvoir's writing during and about this historical moment did a great deal of cultural work. It collected testimony, it provided a scaffolding for collective memory, and it was a magnet for feeling. The memoir gave readers who had been active in the movement against the Algerian war an occasion to discover they had not been alone, though the relief of retrospectively discovered solidarity and reassurance of a place in history mingled with remembered bitterness at what they had suffered. Her writing roused fury on the other side of the political spectrum, among partisans of "French Algeria" or defenders of the French army's honor. The letters protesting Beauvoir's article on Boupacha or reporting on the mood inside the military capture the venom between opposing sides of the conflict. Even within the circle of admiring readers there was no happy community of feeling.

In the history of Beauvoir's long and volatile relationship with her readers, *The Force of Circumstance* represents one of the low points. Beauvoir spoke about and to her readers in the preface and throughout the volume; her public had rescued her from isolation and kept her self-doubt at bay.[76] She invited readers to share ever more of her experience and feeling, and she was disappointed and angry when readers did not respond appropriately. She was disillusioned by their neediness and their apparent inability to make a productive politics out of reading her—to embrace her political emotions in a productive manner. Her confidence as a writer took a blow. "I was paralyzed," she wrote, "by the misunderstanding that greeted *The Force of Circumstance*: words had betrayed me, I no longer trusted them."[77]

Beauvoir declared herself to be more comfortable writing for and speaking to the young people who understood her politics (or so she believed) than to the more staid and middle-aged members of her public. But the persona she offered in *The Force of Circumstance,* buffeted by history, losing lovers, trying to keep pace with events, confessing fatigue and failures, did not necessarily appeal to that younger audience. Several younger letter writers thanked her for reconstructing the history of the Algerian war for their generation, but as one bluntly put it, "In *The Prime of Life* you were an ideal woman, in *The Force of Circumstance* you are weakness—you disappoint us."[78] Some of the most appreciative readers were those who could warm to the themes of loss and age. Beauvoir chafed at these readings of the book, but on this subject, as on the matter of accepting being a writer for woman, she took her readers' insights and testimony seriously. In 1968 she embarked on a full-length sociological study of old age, *La vieillesse.*

Beauvoir considered her intervention in the politics of anticolonialism and this volume of her memoir a failure. *The Force of Circumstance* and the dialogue about it amply document the paralysis of French thinkers as they struggled to be relevant to a movement that was passing them by. It illustrates Beauvoir's self-absorption and the limits of the framework of Self and Other, if the Other is always other and one is only writing about oneself. Beauvoir's discussion of shame as consciousness is interesting, but shaming was not an effective call to conscience.

The Force of Circumstance was an impressively complex text, a historical chronicle and a contribution to a phenomenology of politics as embodied experience. If the text was misread, as for Beauvoir it was, that was because it was swamped by her literary and philosophical ambitions and political emotions, and by the letter writers' own worlds, lives, and preoccupations—their illnesses, deteriorating bodies, and grief. What is more, in the letter writers' imaginations, Beauvoir represented possibility and becoming, the responsibilities of freedom and democracy after

World War II, and the hope that French intellectuals could champion opposition to global colonialism. Given the readers' expectations and their deep attachments, Beauvoir's confession that she was weary and disillusioned was bound to produce anger. If *The Force of Circumstance* was a failure, it was as revealing about politics and culture as success might have been.

6

SECOND TAKES ON *THE SECOND SEX*

> I vaguely sensed, in a confused way, everything that was coming
> in my life, all that I was going to want to do but not be able to,
> *everything that was unfair and ridiculous in the life of women.*
> November 17, 1963

In 1960, the same year that Beauvoir wrote about Djamila Boupacha, she reluctantly agreed to be interviewed by the magazine *France Observateur* on the future of women and feminism in France. The interviewer, Marie Craipeau, had just written an article on the subject, and she plainly considered that future dim. French women, Craipeau intoned, had proved disappointingly traditional, slow to "adapt" to a rapidly changing world, and ill-at-ease with modernity: "Woman has become a hybrid being, uncomfortable in her skin. Woman's new strength is not gentle; her new voice has a grating tone." The journalistic clichés and shopworn argument rankled Beauvoir. So too did the middle-class women Craipeau surveyed for her article and Craipeau's smug conclusion that Beauvoir's arguments, or feminism generally, seemed to have had little effect.[1] Indeed, Beauvoir retorted rapid-fire to Craipeau, her irritation plain to see: perhaps she should rewrite *The Second Sex*, as so little progress had been made.

Women were easily dissuaded from taking on ambitious projects, readily diverted from assuming self-sovereignty or facing their freedom,

Beauvoir contended. They all too quickly lost the "taste for risk" (*goût du risque*) they had savored as young girls. The women surveyed in the article showed how quickly they had "settled into mediocrity . . . They were satisfied with so little." Beauvoir used "women" as sweepingly as the journalist had. She went on to throw a few unkind darts at the middle-class women who tried to "reach beyond" or "transcend" their condition (*dépasser leur condition*) by writing. Frustrated and self-conscious amateur women writers produced small-minded literature, narrowly focused on themselves and their problems: "*Que ce 'moi' des femmes est encombrant!*" (The "me" of women is such an encumbrance!)[2] As we have seen, and as Beauvoir knew by 1960, many of her readers and correspondents fit just this profile. Her vexed relationship with these members of her public was a recurring theme of her career as a writer, an engaged intellectual, and a feminist.

The 1960 *France Observateur* interview reiterated Beauvoir's earlier diagnosis in *The Second Sex* of the contradictions of femininity and their political repercussions. The "encumbrances" of the female self were among the reasons why "women do not say 'We.'"[3] The "baffling contradictions of the female subject" distorted women's voices and muddled their politics. In *The Second Sex,* the problems that beset an individual woman's effort to assume her personhood also plague the collective politics of feminism; in Beauvoir's view those included an obliviousness to class or individual privilege; the hollowness of theoretical and formal equality; the constant and hard-to-avoid invitations to complicity and collaboration with partners of the other sex; the temptation to jockey for personal advantage; and the proclivity to be shrill, manipulative, and resentful. (This was Beauvoir's view in 1949, reiterated on several occasions through the 1970s.) One of *France Observateur*'s women readers wrote in after the interview to say Beauvoir was right: the problem lay with women themselves and their timid conservativism. The proletariat would fight. So too would "blacks," the reader wrote. "But woman will not change UNTIL MEN WANT HER TO BE CHANGED."[4]

Simone de Beauvoir's feminism was double-edged. She was unflinchingly radical on the sources and ramifications of gender and sexual inequality. For some of the same reasons, she was also thoroughly skeptical about women as agents of political change and the reach of feminism as a cause. Her doubts were anchored in her theory of the deep contradictions of woman as a subject.[5] They were bolstered by a reflexive Marxism. "The condition of woman . . . depends on the future of work in the world," she asserted, and therefore would change only with a transformation of relations of production. "That is why I have made a point not to close myself into [*m'enfermer dans*] what is called 'feminism,'" she wrote in 1963.[6] Her political commitments lay with what she considered the broader causes of civil rights, socialism, and movements like Algerian anticolonialism and the Cuban revolution. As the phrase "close myself off" also suggests, she had a visceral, nearly claustrophobic reaction to cozy assumptions of female belonging as well as to the narrow class politics of feminism. As Beauvoir herself noted, she sometimes wrote about femininity like a war correspondent from the sidelines of a battle, a stance that disoriented critics, reviewers, and ordinary readers alike.[7] Readers often voiced confusion about her political positions and the way she tacked between socialism on the one hand and calls to individual engagement on the other. They were stung by her criticisms. Yet many shared her mixed feelings.

In the 1960s, "feminism" became a new set topic, a matter for debate and discussion on which cultural and political figures as well as the informed public were expected to have opinions. It did not emerge directly from women's suffrage in 1944; global political movements that made analogies between civil rights, women's rights, and decolonization plausible and exciting contributed as much as suffrage to the emergence of feminism; they enabled the vote to matter. So did new discourses of political power that resulted from transformations in French politics and elections. Women as citizens and consumers made their presence felt in a changed media world. Combined, these new elements of the historical conjuncture gave *The Second Sex* a second life. The book could hardly be described as a movement statement, for Beauvoir's stance was too skeptical, but the moment would recodify the meaning of the text. Correspondents of the 1960s, unlike the critics in the late 1940s and 1950s, understood the book as speaking to feminism. They wanted to engage Beauvoir on the subject. Writing to her became an occasion to express their enthusiasm or to rehearse ambivalence, to sort through the new expectations they were encountering, their puzzles, disappointments, and impasses.

The Politics of Decolonization and the Condition of Women

In the mid-1960s it seemed that a "feminist wave had crested." An enthusiastic young sociologist from Ferney, the town that had been Voltaire's home in the eighteenth century, conveys a sense of the new intellectual climate. She was researching "the couple and sexuality," an issue that had displaced "the family" as a center of interest and debate across Europe and the United States. She had just finished *La majorité sexuelle de la femme*, the newly translated book by Drs. Phyllis and Eberhard Kronhausen (*Sexual Response in Women*), with a preface by Beauvoir that applauded the Kronhausens' "frankness, courage, scientific rigor," as well as their blunt challenge to received wisdom about women's "physiological destiny."[8] The young sociologist, however, had also rediscovered the Kinsey reports on sexuality and wanted to revive interest in them. She found Kinsey's claims significantly broader and more subversive than the Kronhausens'; they involved "average people" rather than just "emancipated elites." Shouldn't it be possible, she asked, to popularize Kinsey's arguments without sensationalizing his findings or sacrificing sociological rigor? It was important to reach a "large public" on a subject that, despite changing norms, remained "sensitive" (*délicat*).[9]

The correspondent from Ferney, like many other readers, had also been impressed by the new, hard-hitting study by Andrée Michel and Geneviève Texier, *La condition de la Française d'aujourd'hui* (The Condition of the French Woman Today), published in 1964. That study borrowed from the structure of *The Second Sex*: the first part offered a critical analysis of myths; the second turned to experience, in this case a sociology of the family, sexuality, and labor. It spoke "to the here and now."[10] Andrée Michel, a veteran of resistance to the Algerian war and a sociologist at the Centre National de la Recherche Scientifique, became enormously influential in French left intellectual circles. Her book's mainstream popularity would nonetheless be dwarfed by that of Betty Friedan's *The Feminine Mystique*, which was translated into French that same year, in 1964. Beauvoir's text now took a place on shelves alongside new books about and by women—including, notably, the rediscovered *Room of One's Own* by Virginia Woolf, which had been written in 1929. In short, the young sociologist from Voltaire's hometown was describing an international current of thought that, like the Enlightenment, was often about

rediscovery: translating, circulating, republishing, and explicating important texts for an increasingly eager and educated elite. As we know, the
Enlightenment was subtended by a sociocultural infrastructure of coffee-
houses, corresponding societies, essay contests, and literary salons. The
1960s rush of interest in women's politics and character likewise involved
cultural institutions: new publishing houses, new journals and magazines—and new programs for radio and television, for since the 1950s,
print had been forced to share the field with new media.[11]

In 1949, *The Second Sex*, with its leveling of old arguments, topos of
a new beginning, and rekindled humanism, had been very much a "postwar" book. In 1949, Beauvoir's core concepts and vision of the world were
already inextricable from writing about racism, colonialism, and global
struggles for the sovereignty and dignity of Europe's Others. *The Second
Sex*'s second life, in the 1960s, was very much framed by the end of the
war in Algeria, which I traced in the last chapter. The view of decolonization as a process with a historical logic *and* as a development infused with
a revolutionary non-European subjectivity played a key role in transforming metropolitan politics. The new discussion of women's condition drew
heavily on the discourse and personnel of antiwar and anticolonial groups
and individuals. "Now that the Algerian war is over," a student who had
headed what she called the "anti-fascist" committee in her lycée wrote to
Beauvoir, an organized and politically informed student movement was
ready to refocus. The National Union of Students had become "beneficia-
ries of this feeling that something must be done."[12] Beauvoir was peppered
with queries from others who saw continuities between anticolonialism in
France, the Women's Strike for Peace in the United States, and the British
women's left, or between the mobilization of Catholic critics of the Algerian war and Catholic women organizing against clericalism and male
authority in the church. "Every Catholic woman has some kind of revolt
to articulate," wrote a woman who described herself as a socialist and a
Catholic. Many who had been active in the resistance to the Algerian war,
like Andrée Michel, Gisèle Halimi, or Évelyne Sullerot, poured their energies into feminist causes. Sullerot, who had lived in Algeria and worked
with the FLN, herself became a one-woman publishing house, writing on
women's work, lives, futures, the women's press, and myths of love in
culture.[13] Andrée Michel had been affiliated with the Jeanson network of
the *porteurs de valise*, the "baggage handlers" who supplied funds and

identity papers to members of the Algerian FLN.[14] Michel and many of these women became the leading figures of what they called the Mouvement Démocratique Féminin (Women's Democrat Movement), or MDF, founded the year the war ended, in 1962.

The crisis of the Algerian war, the collapse of the Fourth Republic, and the birth of the Fifth Republic changed the playing field of French politics. The presidency now counted for more, and so did women as an electoral bloc. As soon as the Évian accords ending the war were signed, de Gaulle campaigned to modify the French constitution, proposing in a referendum in October 1962 that the president be chosen in direct nationwide elections rather than by Parliament. His campaign appealed specifically to women voters, who—political experts and de Gaulle's advisers firmly believed—appreciated the general's confidence-inspiring authority, his peacemaking in Algeria, and above all his role in passing woman suffrage in 1945. The MDF bristled at this call to women as conservative voters and riposted with a counter-appeal that tried to rekindle the anticolonial left's opposition to de Gaulle's flouting of constitutional procedures and executive overreaching.[15] To no avail: the constitutional revision of 1962 passed easily. De Gaulle's success in remaking the institutions of the Republic prompted much talk in the aftermath about the "personalization of power"; political observers presented this personalization as of a piece with a new, mass-mediated politics in which charisma and authority were marketed to passive citizen consumer-spectators. When these same experts polled women and discerned that many had voted for the constitutional revision, they found it impossible to resist casting women as central actors in the new politics: women's alleged "super-Gaullism" flowed from their political immaturity, irrationality, susceptibility to advertising, attraction to "stars," and consumerist passivity.

The year 1965 brought the first national election of a French president since 1848 and the first since women had received the vote. The election campaign, which set de Gaulle against socialist François Mitterrand, encouraged yet more theorizing of "women's political character": efforts to imagine how the guardians of family and tradition would contend with their new electoral responsibilities. The tone of the discussion and the campaign in general exasperated feminists like Andrée Michel, who pointed out that a booming economy called upon female labor without providing child care. France had 3.9 million children under four and 33,000 places in child care centers (*crèches* and *garderies*). Women's jobs were segregated, their wages were lower than men's, and they were promoted less often. They were overrepresented in poorly paid professions and underrepresented in the universities. They were assailed, daily, by the mystifying insistence on "discretion" about sexuality, propaganda against contraception and abortion, and odes to virtuous motherhood.[16] It was true that Mitterand as candidate vowed to repeal the laws banning contraception, but a single campaign could not erase a long tradition of condescension and neglect on the left as well as the right. Why was the female voter being imagined as an odd outcropping on the political landscape, Michel asked, when women might be addressed simply as *citizens* with multiple interests and facing specific obstacles?[17]

Michel and Texier's book on the condition of women drew material from well beyond the borders of France. The authors invoked the lesson of racial subjugation in the United States, namely, that one could not expect "new situations of equality" to arrive automatically; they had to be produced by social movements and "firm administrative measures and laws."[18] Such measures included court-ordered desegregation; sending U.S. marshals to escort James Meredith to register at the University of Mississippi over the governor's protest (1962); and the Civil Rights Act of 1964, banning discrimination in education, employment, and public accommodations. In France as elsewhere in Europe, American racism loomed large as a negative model, and the battle against racial inequality—whether in the form of legislation and executive orders or as the civil rights movement—was a powerful positive example. The Algerian war had been part of a global rebellion against colonialism and racial domination. That war was over, but the struggles had now come home.

By the mid-1960s, the term "decolonization" was everywhere as a shorthand for the necessary and progressive liberation from subjugation in all forms. Some historians argue that the term had lost its radical edge. In much popular parlance, decolonization had acquired the air of an inexorable modernizing process with "irresistible momentum";[19] like technological change, new forms of communication, the exodus from rural areas, women voting, or *Elle* magazine, decolonization was part of the process of moving forward. A 1965 law reforming marriage so that women could open their own bank accounts was touted as the "decolonization of married women."[20] According to totalizing and determinist social-scientific theories fashionable in the 1960s, modernization inevitably created new roles for women; actually existing women needed only to adapt to the times. This common mode of thinking about history did significant cultural work: it sharpened a sense of generational difference and highlighted what now seemed the archaism of traditional femininity. In the 1950s, the analogy one of Beauvoir's letter writers had drawn between "undertaking the liberation of women" and decolonization seemed far-fetched; now it was becoming everyday.[21]

But the term "decolonization" had a radical edge as well. While it did not evoke armed uprising and revolution, it did stand for the enormous and difficult task of digging out from under deep and encrusted layers of cultural as well as political domination. It had existential resonance.[22] A Tunisian exile, describing to Beauvoir his alienating experience in France, said, "What I have seen and felt in Paris in 1962 has completed my radical 'decolonization.'" Another correspondent introduced himself as "a man of the Third World . . . since last year intellectually decolonized."[23] Edgar Morin opened his 1962 *L'esprit du temps,* an analysis of mass culture and its ramifications, by calling the global spread of movies, magazines, and television a "second colonization," one that was "not horizontal, but vertical, penetrating the great reserve that is the human soul. The soul is the new Africa . . . [W]ords and images swarm from teleprompters, rolls of film, tapes, the radio and television, anything that rolls, flies, or navigates carries newspapers and magazines. There is not a molecule of air that does not vibrate with messages that some machine or gesture makes audible and visible."[24] To "decolonize" was to reclaim the soul, and to write as Morin did was to harness the power and significance of anticolonialism as critique. It was also to refer to Henri Lefebvre's radical theorizing of the capitalist "colonization of the everyday." Lefebvre's *Critique of Everyday Life* came out in 1947. He followed with a second volume in 1961, and by that time, his concept had taken hold. Capitalism's power to conquer the everyday, and everyday resistance to that conquest, would go on to be central to radical left thought later in the 1960s. In 1968 Beauvoir would explain that what feminists were demanding was *not* just formal equality or a "superficial emancipation" but rather a "decolonization," or an end to "the colonization of the interior."[25] Decolonization implied more than a blandly modernizing politics; the term had inherited radical as well as liberal meanings.

The decolonizers of the "soul" or the "interior" took aim squarely at the women's press, an enormous commercial enterprise with the cultural clout to match. Evelyn Sullerot, who wrote about women's magazines among many other subjects, estimated that nearly all of France's women read at least one of those magazines every month—to her dismay, for that reading was "the pathological and therapeutic expression" of the narcissism and insecurity nurtured by women's culture.[26] Two of Beauvoir's British correspondents considered it urgent to expose the "false concepts spread by the mass media."[27] For Andrée Michel, contemporary women's magazines were saturated with sexist myths: "Whether they debase or elevate the woman, the myths of femininity surround a metaphysics of sexuality which is deeply rooted in the cultures of virility and the phallus."[28] The passage captures Michel's anger and her radicalism.

This was the cultural terrain that proved so hospitable to Betty Friedan's liberal intervention *The Feminine Mystique,* translated by one of the founders of the MDF, Yvette Roudy. Friedan argued that popular and middlebrow culture alike were dedicated to the dubious proposition that "femininity" should be women's highest calling, and that the narrowing of women's horizons and ambitions created a pervasive cultural malaise that Friedan dubbed "the problem that has no name." It is hard not to read *The Feminine Mystique* as *The Second Sex* lite; its rudimentary existentialism called on women to break free from alienating myths of femininity. Those myths (or the "mystique," in Friedan's variation) were peddled by mass circulation women's magazines, college courses, advertising, and, broadly, Freudian thought, which Friedan called both deterministic and a "Victorian mixture of chivalry and condescension." American culture promoted a "smiling empty passivity," which left American housewives starving for fulfillment.

What Friedan borrowed from Beauvoir was evident, but the contrasts are striking. While Friedan argued that the "problem that has no name" was "far more important than anyone recognizes," her version of that problem was less complicated than it sounded.[29] Women had the resources in themselves to break free of the malaise; they needed to leave their houses, continue their educations, and work as either volunteers or waged laborers. By contrast, Beauvoir's "What is woman?" intentionally opened onto a maze of ontological uncertainty and offered no simple blueprint for action. American historian Daniel Horowitz underscores how much Friedan's labor union activism counted in her life. But Horowitz also shows that Friedan stoutly refused to acknowledge her radical past. *The Feminine Mystique* had little that compares with the materialism, let alone the Marxism, of *The Second Sex*.[30] Friedan's discussion of sexuality provides a particularly revealing foil to Beauvoir's. Friedan had virtually no interest in the experience of the body, desire, or the weight of culture in either; the sexualized dimensions of gender inequality were non-issues. She stuck to the psychological, making a point of her disagreements with Freud. The alleged "sex hunger" of American women, which in Friedan's words were documented "*ad nauseam* by Kinsey" and laid bare in the "salacious details" of magazines and popular fiction, really reflected women's *other* dissatisfactions: "They seek in sex something that sex cannot give."[31]

Unlike Beauvoir, but like Andrée Michel in *La condition de la Française*, Friedan addressed the present. Unlike either Beauvoir or Michel, Friedan wrote in lively journalistic form and made her points in one short volume. Most important, Friedan also set her analysis of women's existential unhappiness in the mushrooming literature about "organization man," the hollowness of American society and mass culture in general— David Riesman, *The Lonely Crowd: A Study of the Changing American Character* (1950); William Whyte, *The Organization Man* (1956); and Vance Packard, *The Hidden Persuaders* (1957), among others. In Daniel Horowitz's words, "[Friedan] took from other writers an analysis that blamed the problems of diminished masculine identity on life in the suburbs, jobs in large organizations, and consumer culture; she then turned this explanation into an argument for women's liberation." Those references mattered enormously to *The Feminine Mystique*'s impact in the United States and in Europe, where they meshed well with preexisting convictions about the emptiness and materialism of American culture.[32]

Friedan read Beauvoir carefully, but she wrote about her as if the French writer came from a distant European past. "When a Frenchwoman named Simone de Beauvoir wrote a book called *The Second Sex*" sounds like the opening to the tale of a land far away.[33] Nonetheless, *The Feminine Mystique* became an important part of the feedback loop for the 1960s re-readings of *The Second Sex*. As the Kinsey reports had magnified the transatlantic interest of *The Second Sex* in 1949 and coded it as a book about "sex," so *The Feminine Mystique* burnished Beauvoir's reputation as the European radical who had first systematically studied the issues of "myth" and "mystification"—and who had launched feminism as theory and cultural criticism.

Friedan would later acknowledge her intellectual debt to Beauvoir, but reluctantly. In 1973 she wrote to Ellen Wright (Richard Wright's wife and Beauvoir's friend as well as her literary agent) to try to set up an interview with her French rival.

> Simone de Beauvoir's thinking had a profound influence on mine even before I became consciously interested in the problem of women and began writing my own Feminine Mystique. I suppose, in a way, it was Simone de Beauvoir herself who made me recognize my own existentialism . . . I do not know if Simone de Beauvoir has been aware of this, but I have been trying each time I've been to Europe over the past seven years, to meet her.

What she wanted to discuss with the French thinker was the future of "this great movement for whose original ideology we *both* seem to share some responsibility."[34] Friedan refused to stand in Beauvoir's shadow.

Finally, in 1975, Friedan got the interview she wanted, but it was a catastrophe. The two women disagreed on virtually everything, and Friedan sounded like a centrist caricature. She promoted her "Economic Think Tank," insisted on the promise of social mobility, and rejected socialism. She called lesbianism a "distraction" for the feminist movement and opined that the student movement (in France and the United States) had been destroyed by its indifference to effective leadership. In a column published alongside the interview with Beauvoir in the *Saturday Review*, Friedan did not hold back her opinions: "The authority with which she [Beauvoir] spoke about women seemed sterile, cold, an abstraction that had too little relationship to the real lives of all the women struggling now in France and in America for new directions. I felt almost like a fool, struggling with those mundane questions that real women have to confront in their personal lives and in movement strategy. Those questions did not seem to interest her at all."[35] The American feminist Ti-Grace Atkinson, who had corresponded with Beauvoir since 1965, was aghast at Friedan's hostility. "I should have warned you about Betty," she wrote in a letter.[36]

To return to the mid-1960s, however, it is striking how readily the liberal critique of mass culture's colonizing of the soul was taken on board by the cultural outlets it targeted, as if those who worked in, wrote for, and read this press were particularly sensitive to criticism directed their way. The Italian newspaper *La Stampa* (with a circulation of half a million) asked Beauvoir to write for its new women's page in June 1963. "This page, with its new conception and ideas, is a great victory, and not only in Italy," an editor of the paper assured her. *La Stampa* wanted to distinguish itself from run-of-the-mill papers, whose columns for women were "idiotic," she explained. "For the first time, we are going to speak to women as adults; we are not shutting them up in the kitchen or with the children." The editor proposed that Beauvoir write on topics such as "lies women tell—and tell themselves" or "the woman alone," and she remarked how much she had liked Beauvoir and Halimi's book on Djamila Boupacha.[37] Of course, it was perfectly possible to expose mystifications of femininity on one page and peddle them on another. *Elle* proved especially adept on this score. Still, the letter from *La Stampa*'s editor was one of many signs of European-wide ferment and debate among those who presumed to address female readers.

All of these changes—the end of empire, global movements for civil rights, the reorganization of the Republic and women's new prominence in the nation's electorate, the expansion of consumption and the imagery of consumer culture—transformed the political and social world. Combined, they constituted what the economist Jean Fourastié would later call the "invisible revolution" of the postwar decades. Fourastié, like so many others, found the "condition of woman" a particularly compelling aspect of this revolution and its ramifications. In 1963 he wrote Beauvoir to say he had formed a research group on women's work and the female condition, and that he was rediscovering *The Second Sex*.[38] As the contours of a new France were coming into focus, Beauvoir's rigor and range, along with her ability to connect structural inequalities with everyday experience and stirrings of unrest, put her on many reading lists. "The public now associates your name with the broad movement for the liberation of women that characterizes our time," an editor at Gallimard wrote to Beauvoir in 1963.[39] This was the moment in which many readers went back to *The Second Sex*; this was the historical conjuncture that changed the book's conditions of intelligibility. No longer was woman's emancipation solely a "revolutionary tactic" or a phrase associated with the left intelligentsia. It had been transformed into a project embraced by a broad group of modernizers—and, to a certain extent, by the intimate public.

New Readers

The Second Sex was now framed by scores of other books on women and "femininity," by studies of Beauvoir, and by Beauvoir's own memoirs, which detailed her gradual discovery of the female condition and its significance, stressing the importance of the book that few had actually read. Enthusiasts of the memoir now turned back to *The Second Sex*.[40] These "second takes" on *The Second Sex* convey a sense of heady excitement and change. "I don't think anything like this kind of feminism has ever been written before," wrote an animated young man from the United States. "You have put the whole question of feminism on a new plane of understanding—and . . . even explained feminism and enabled us to understand what was wrong with it before." He felt no need to elaborate on feminism's shortcomings, for Beauvoir had done that effectively in the text: "feminism" was narrow, bourgeois, a quarrel, and associated with formal rights. He plainly appreciated Beauvoir's "fraternal" mode of address, her commitment to broadly humanist causes, her ability to articulate the existential dimensions of the struggle, and her warnings about the reverberations of women's discontent. He was grateful to her for spelling out the relationship between his domestic unhappiness and structures of inequality. He put the insight he had gained in comically self-referential terms: "I am suffering because my wife resents my domination."[41]

A male student from Brussels wrote that he "had always been for the emancipation of women, but only as a revolutionary tactic. Now, your personal experience had definitively convinced me of your conclusions in *The Second Sex*."[42] Readers praised the book as broad, or encyclopedic: "I am dazzled [*émerveillé*] by the synthesis of the social and the sexual." They repeatedly referred to Beauvoir's "lucidity," which was both sociological and psychological, and which they set against the muddy chaos of their own thoughts and feelings. They admired the striking combination of Olympian overview and "personal analysis" that was so "close up and true to life." Indeed, "no one had done that this way before you."[43]

Feminist activists thanked her for helping them find a new footing in a perplexing political world. Two British women wrote:

> For some time now we have been discussing the idea of bringing together, in book form, the thoughts of some of our outstanding English women of left wing opinion, on the position of women in present day society. We have, however, been confused as to a unifying theme, and have been so much inspired by your work which has helped to clarify our thoughts . . . about the socialist approach to woman and her role in society.[44]

A French woman, a former member of the Communist Party, wrote to Beauvoir, "No one before you" had been able to apply Marx's notion of alienation to women. Though she was "no longer quite a Marxist," she thanked Beauvoir for restoring her "moral and intellectual bearings."[45] The communist press was not about to endorse Beauvoir's existential Marxism, but the new interest in *The Second Sex* did provide an occasion to reconsider the book. The reviewer for the Communist Party's *Nouvelle Critique* grudgingly praised Beauvoir for not writing in a "women's genre"—and for avoiding the "narcissism of most women's writing" and looking at the wider world.[46]

Beauvoir's life became the book's preface and her memoirs the paratextual support for reading *The Second Sex* in the 1960s. Her bold personal example was a favorite theme; different readers found her "disdain for taboos," her freedom from "out-of-date traditions" and "academic and bourgeois prejudice" to be a "call to liberation." "I know of no one else who can give young people a sense of the need to live intensely if not always wisely or well."[47] One such young person, whose parents had warned her that the siren call of existentialism would pull her away from her family and distort her view of the world, wrote, "You made me understand that it wasn't the *literature* that was upsetting me." She knew now, she wrote, that her unhappiness came instead from wanting the kind of independence that Beauvoir had achieved. "My father made fun of me, saying that I worshipped you, and that your life was an exception because you were an unusual woman, strong enough to live that kind of life."[48] Wrote a twenty-nine-year-old woman with a doctorate (*agrégation*) in English, divorced with two children, "You show what a woman can accomplish, and what women today could be if only they were more lucid and courageous." She called Beauvoir's life "an example, a lesson, and a revelation"; it was "dazzling." Only recently had the combination of her personal experience and reflecting on Beauvoir's books "finally opened my eyes to my own condition and that of the women around me." That passage virtually quoted Beauvoir's own account of her dawning awareness of the condition of women in *The Prime of Life*, though the reader used Friedan's term "malaise." At the same time, she was puzzled by the historical moment and troubled by her feelings. She could see the world changing before her. As a result, women seemed to be suspended between "two worlds, one not quite born and the other not quite dead." She felt "sometimes bitter, often indignant, and above all filled with desire to do something for women. But what? And how?"[49]

This reader was not alone. *The Second Sex* was now understood to be about feminism, and many letters aired confusions and hesitations on that subject. Beauvoir's books might have converted many who read them, opening their eyes to broad issues, wrote one reader. But what would become of these "scattered convictions"? Better to stick to traditionally defined women's issues such as moral and sexual education for young people, or food allowances for divorced women with children. Another reader sighed about "women's total ignorance concerning important social and economic issues"—and copied out a passage from *The Prime of Life* where Beauvoir wrote of women's inability to think systematically.[50] A male doctor, head of a cardiology unit, wrote cheerfully that *The Second Sex* had finally enabled him to "convert my wife to feminism." For "like you," he continued, "I have been struck that the worst obstacle to feminism comes from women. Men are vastly less responsible for the inferiority of the feminine condition than are women themselves."[51] The argument and condescending tone were common, often tinged with the certainty that women were in the thrall of the Catholic Church or, in the words of one Catholic feminist, "the mortal danger of clericalism and women's responsibility for it."[52]

Correspondents puzzled about how they were supposed to *feel* and what they were expected to *do*. "Everything you write in that study is at once good [*beau*] and difficult. I think all of that will make me more conscious of my being [*consciente de mon être*] and will do me good in the end," wrote a Canadian woman. Still, *The Second Sex* left her "vacillating between depression and exaltation." How Beauvoir imagined they should balance self-reflection, or being true to themselves with looking outwards and engaging the world, puzzled many. One of them copied out a passage in which Beauvoir characteristically waxed impatient with the "encumbrances of the self" and summoned women to engage the world: "To do great things, today's woman needs above all to forget herself: but to forget oneself one must first be sure that one has already been found. A woman is a new arrival in the world of men, poorly supported by them; she is still much too busy looking for herself." So "how," the reader queried, "were you supposed to find yourself without spending all your time looking?" or without falling into "either narcissism or self-disgust?" She had concluded that "to have already found oneself is a gift. A gift, however, is always a little mysterious. Where does it come from? Do you consider it a 'gift'? Or is it the result of a search?"[53] Wrote another, "I don't know if 'the gospel according to Simone de Beauvoir' to which I refer almost daily keeps me in a state of agitation in my personal and professional (lecturer) life or helps me on." She was American, and in good American 1960s fashion, she added, "The answer is blowing in the wind."[54]

The articulate anticolonial militant from Besançon whom we met in the chapter on Algeria wrote a remarkable letter about the conundrums of political activism. She told Beauvoir that she had read *The Second Sex* when she was eighteen, before she had any depth of experience: "It brought into focus and justified my demands for autonomy. But mine was still only the protest of a good student who wanted the right to intelligence. Now I can see that my liberation was only formal." She reflected on the many years she had spent in politics since, working in unions and political groups opposed to the Algerian war. She was frank about how haphazardly she had made important choices, relating the details in a way that makes them concrete and utterly plausible. She married young and immediately became pregnant because she "disliked traditional French methods of birth control." Besides, she thought, since there weren't enough openings that year for her to take the *agrégation*, "one might as well have a child." She had a second baby thirteen months later, so at the time she wrote she was caring for two children alone while her husband was away at military service. Like many of the married women who wrote letters to Beauvoir, she found it impossible to fathom Beauvoir's boundless energy and her appetite for political engagement, and she wondered if Beauvoir was able to imagine the exhaustion of working-class women's everyday lives. She and her fellow workers were "so used to being tired that they considered it normal." She spelled out the many obstacles to mobilizing her fellow women workers: their families' demands on their time, the low expectations they had internalized, the absence of alternative models, and rampant discrimination in unions and political parties, a subject she plainly knew firsthand. What made her letter remarkable, however, was the way she laid out the political dilemmas, in terms that very much paralleled Beauvoir's: "So one doesn't know what to do. Wave the banner of feminism? What would that accomplish? Take on activities only for women? You run the risk of falling back into complicity and collectively abdicating responsibility. Stand up—not as a woman, but as a human being? They are always looking for 'feminine' motivations and use them to refuse you any importance . . . to devalue anything you do."[55] She is offering an eloquently everyday restatement of what Beauvoir considered the impossible condition of the female subject. How could one act responsibly as a "woman"? The dilemmas are ethical, existential, discursive, and strategic: to act in the name of "women" is to bow to convention, to be complicit in narrowing one's interests and ambitions, or to compromise one's full humanity. The letter writer finds the label "woman" as tired as she feels. The phrase "they are always looking for 'feminine' motivations" beautifully captures her fear that she is being stalked by a gendered identification, or indeed sabotaged from within by what was termed a "feminine complex." The letters from the mid-1960s are especially emphatic about the flickering character of gendered self-consciousness and the anxiety, irritation, and rejection that often accompany it—about gender trouble. They encapsulate both the era in which feminism was taking shape as a social movement and the enduring problems of grounding it in any notion of woman.[56]

To be sure, some letter writers *did* strike the defiant "founding" notes we might expect to hear as a feminist movement took shape across Europe and the United States. Here, for instance, is a twenty-nine-year-old Dutch woman who wrote Beauvoir in 1967. She was very happily married with two young children, she wrote, but after fourteen years of studies (she had a diploma in art history), she found that being a housewife left "a kind of emptiness" inside her. "All of my friends were in the same situation, and no one could help me," she said. She had grown up in the company of boys, she was used to talking to men as her equals, and she had always preferred their company. Beauvoir had captured her attention: "You showed me that women are like men, but different. I became a feminist. I started reading books by women. I found Mary McCarthy and Margaret Mead more interesting than I ever would have thought was possible." The history and structure of the family and sexuality were suddenly compelling; so was "woman's" intriguingly complex relationship to "humanity." This letter writer also wanted Beauvoir to know that her new interests had helped her reknit her relationship with her mother. She had copied out long passages from *The Second Sex* for her mother, who went on to read more on her own. Like the letter writer, the mother had "fallen under [Beauvoir's] influence . . . [N]ow, for the first time, we understand each other."[57] The happy embrace of "woman" and "feminist," the discovery that women's lives were intellectually interesting, and generational reconciliation to boot: it is a cheery picture and rather rare, at least in the mid-1960s.

It was more common to join self-discovery to generational rage. An energetic and rebellious sixteen-year-old from Paris wrote Beauvoir a wonderful letter, all the more striking since it was well before Beauvoir's integration into the canon of French literature and thought. *The Second Sex*, she said, was the only book besides Descartes's *Discourse on Method* that had "not only given me knowledge but also illuminated my process of thinking."[58] The comparison is startling: disembodied Cartesian doubt is a very different thing from the phenomenologist's practice of bracketing assumptions and trying to understand being and perception in the world. But what counted for this letter writer was Beauvoir's starting point in the introduction, namely, her radical doubt. The letter writer also made it easy to imagine how exhilarated she was by her reading: she thought and therefore she was!

She described herself as projecting into the future and recoiling from what she saw there, namely the narrow horizons and the daily absurdities of adult womanhood. She was outraged by her mother's indifference to Beauvoir's critique.

> My mother didn't stop me from reading the book, but she told me it wasn't interesting. Not interesting???!!! I devoured it. I took notes. I made it into my weapon of choice, my bedside reading [*livre de chevet*—perhaps the most common phrase for describing The Second Sex]. I admire you . . . I love you.

The Second Sex had become her "weapon," the more powerful because it was addressed specifically to the women of her generation:

> I ask myself whom you wrote it for . . . for those fat ladies who are ashamed to read you because you tell the truth that they want to hide? For those old men, distinguished family men or honorable fathers who want to marry us off without worrying about whether or not we are happy? For those young men who have the world at their fingertips, and who don't know of you because that's not their problem? No, I daresay that you are writing for me, for us, for young women thinking about their future.[59]

Another young woman took aim at boys (*garçons*) her age:

> I've noticed again that boys have idiotic ideas about women. Either they treat us like little birds, or they think we are floozies (*debauchées*). There's no middle way. You can't simply enjoy yourself in their company without having to deal with their ulterior motives. We went up to a room with a group of them, and they imagined that we would fall, like larks, into their arms.[60]

This rebellious "sex consciousness," as Virginia Woolf had called it, was emphatically young and exuberantly contemptuous of an older model of femininity with which it would brook no compromise. As we open the archival folders of readers' letters from the mid-1960s, generational differences begin to matter in a new, deeper, and more defining way. Older readers were far more likely to write with an awareness of compromises they had made. Marriage or, especially, pregnancy had made them old in a hurry. (As Annie Ernaux wryly pointed out, all it took was for one egg to meet one sperm; if they came together, you were suddenly in a different world.)[61] Even correspondents in their late twenties and thirties frequently struck what one might call a tone of gender pessimism. These older letter writers felt implicated in what younger ones considered "ridiculous" or "pathetic about the destiny of women"; they spoke of their "shameful inferiority," or a feminine "complex" that they needed to "conquer." "My aspirations to autonomy are buried in guilt (myth of *la femme au foyer*)," wrote one. "I still have many contradictions to destroy," wrote another.[62] "Sexed consciousness" could readily instill self-loathing or spark unease or contempt for women who seemed at home with their lot.

A Norwegian psychologist, age twenty-five, tried the hardest to express an even more visceral unease, which she sensed that Beauvoir shared. She wrote, awkwardly, in English. She emphasized that her "problem as a woman" was *not* the emptiness identified by Betty Friedan, and not so easily dealt with. She saw nothing she could do as an individual, and no collective outlet either. Her sense of herself as a woman was much more ambivalent than Friedan's analysis allowed for: "No matter how modern people think that they feel and think about equality of the two sexes—the problem is deeper still. I find a difference between men and women." She found it impossible to imagine "real liberation" within these parameters. "It [difference] still sneaks into identity and self-acceptance in a much subtler way than one thinks . . . I think that deep inside me I tend to despise women, and I am terribly afraid of feminine stupid women . . . These— very badly expressed thoughts—I have from you."[63]

Beauvoir's work was particularly apt to prompt disquiet. Despite the didactic, look-at-me aspects of her memoir volumes, she never hesitated to unfurl her hesitations or mixed feelings before her public, and in doing so virtually invited her public to share similar feelings with her. "Despite" may be inapt, however, for Beauvoir was performing different roles. She was a model or mentor in the project of self-emancipation, but also a confidant for mixed feelings and inner doubt about just what women's emancipation meant. What mix of inner change and social transformation was one striving for, and how did one set about it? Beauvoir captured as few others could the irreducible uncertainties of women's emancipation and a women's politics.

The unease was also there in a broader cultural "prompt" in the world these correspondents inhabited. Friedan's *Feminine Mystique*, like *The Second Sex*, Andrée Michel's *Condition de la Française*, and countless columns in the popular press, from *France Observateur* to *Elle* and other women's magazines, cast femininity as a thoroughly internalized combination of prescriptions and feeling—a "malaise" or, in more psychological terms, a "complex." "Complex" had different valences. For many, it sounded condescending and trivializing; it meant one was hopelessly neurotic, caught up in a drama that was entirely personal. The men who described their wives as resentful sounded these notes, and so did Beauvoir herself when she rolled her eyes at small-minded middle-class women.

"Complex," however, could also evoke sympathy and flag seriousness. A complex could not be banished by force of will or giving it a name; it required a more sustained reckoning that promised to be both troubling and productive. Beauvoir's analysis of women's problematic subjectivity as *interesting* pointed in this direction, as many correspondents told her. As one letter writer put it, the best measure of how deeply *The Second Sex* had been "integrated into my life" was that "for two years I have been in analysis." Like Beauvoir, she said, she had enjoyed her share of the thrills of travel and the "fascinating adventures of the exterior." But those did not compare with the adventures of psychoanalysis: "I so regret not being be able to convey in this letter that analysis is unlike anything that you can imagine, deduce, assume, or even have a premonition of from the outside."⁶⁴ Other correspondents asked her to elaborate on her slightly summary discussion of Freud in *The Second Sex*: "Don't you think that you could write a new work, and continue your study of women, taking the path of psychoanalysis?"⁶⁵ The efforts to forge new understandings of female subjectivity, like many of the currents of left and liberal thinking in the 1960s in which nascent feminisms were embedded, worked through Freud as well as against him. In the intimate world of these correspondents, that work took the form of a struggle to express and account for oneself but also to go further and to *theorize* it. To write was to bring it to consciousness.

What is more, in the idioms of the 1960s, a "complex" could refer to any number of psychological, economic, and political formations, from an "inferiority" complex to the "military-industrial" complex. So the project of theorizing the self and its relationship to the psyche or the world could draw on very different theoretical traditions or combinations of those traditions: Freudian, Marxist, and existentialist. The project was vast, daunting, and exciting. In the late 1960s, the process of changing minds or "raising consciousness"—what some call producing new political subjectivities—was a fascinating intellectual and cultural project.

"Is it too pessimistic to characterize the mutual recognition of womanness as merely the exchanged glances of those cornered in the same cells by the epithet 'woman'?" asks Denise Riley.⁶⁶ The answer is probably yes, but the tone of these letters to Beauvoir certainly underscores the aptness of Riley's question. It was one thing to identify with Beauvoir as a free spirit and a rebellious, accomplished woman, and another to enlist in a collectivity of "women"; indeed, the one militated against the other. It was one thing to find "the woman question" interesting and significant and another to embrace feminism as a political identity, especially at a historical moment when the post-suffrage women's movement still carried the image of being stolid, bourgeois, and narrow—unconnected to global struggles for liberation. The "invisible revolution" of the postwar decades created a palpable sense of change in the 1960s. The discourse of modernization and the felt acceleration of time meant that even a feminist like Andrée Michel, with her incisive writing and her radical political credentials, which she had earned in the resistance to both the Nazis *and* French colonialism in Algeria, could seem old-fashioned. That suffrage came so late in France and that it was decreed from above heightened the impression that feminism had only won yesterday's battles. It would prove difficult to redefine a political affiliation so associated with narrow class interests. As Jacqueline Feldman, one of the founders of the radical and brilliantly provocative women's liberation movement in the aftermath of 1968, wrote of her early years, "When I was a student, feminism was in its lowest point; a feminist was a ridiculous figure that you did not want to be."[67] Feldman's "ridiculous" echoes the 1963 letter from the sixteen-year-old. Andrée Michel's MDF never gained much of a foothold among young people. What Beauvoir considered the existential and ontological obstacles to women "saying 'we,' " or the political impasses of feminism, were not timeless but were rooted in the historical moment.

One too familiar storyline about Simone de Beauvoir casts her as "ahead of her time" in 1949 and "behind" it in the 1960s. In that later period, the story goes, she was slowed by the weight of her political commitment to socialism and class, her theoretical blind spots, or her absence of sisterliness but found herself paddling, hurriedly, to catch the cresting second wave of feminism in the aftermath of 1968. The history of feminism, like that of any social or intellectual movement, does not follow the predictable and regular rhythms of waves, however; it is much more interesting and volatile than the wave metaphor suggests. Beauvoir is more interesting as well, and thoroughly of her time, her hesitations and aversions widely shared. Her relationship with her readers, with the intellectual and emotional discomfort that relationship produced, is a striking micro-politics of feminism in the mid-1960s. That micro-politics is also fully on display in her dialogue with letter writers about how to navigate the shoals of romance, love, and marriage.

7

Couple Troubles

Come on, be a little more Simone-de-Beauvoirian.
April 6, 1967

In 1967 an Austrian woman who had been reading *Das andere Ge-schlecht*, or "The Other Sex," as the German translation was titled, sent Beauvoir her reflections on the sections concerning marriage. The reader was passionate, appreciative, not a philosopher, and cast Beauvoir's argument in terms very much her own.

> You see the role of woman today exactly as it is—an eternal battle against evil, a battle without hope . . . Oh yes, Madame, that's how it is, *that's how it is*!!
> . . . You wrote that a woman is unhappy *because she isn't married*, or *isn't married yet*, or *isn't married anymore*. But in fact, most women are very unhappy *because they are married*.[1]

A great many of the letters to Beauvoir concerned marriage, which loomed over the lives of the letter writers as much as the Algerian war loomed over the Republic. Many struck a similarly melodramatic tone. Marriage was an almost inescapable lifelong drama with many ramifications: even the unmarried were implicated in marriage's galling legal and economic dependencies, the encompassing power of conjugal love as a metaphor for harmony and altruism, and the knots of love and resentment, submission and resistance, duty and disenchantment that tangled family life.[2]

Broad social and cultural changes in the 1950s and 1960s helped to create a wave of unhappiness about marriage, and many things about Beauvoir virtually guaranteed that women's complaints would swamp her mailbox: her riveting personal life, the ways in which her memoirs laid out what many read as rules for relationships, and the vividness of *The Second Sex*'s passages on marriage. The cumulative effect of all these made her an iconoclastic expert on the subject. As on other matters, Beauvoir found her correspondence on this subject gratifying but also frustrating. In 1968 she published a short story, "The Woman Destroyed," aiming to show her disappointed-in-marriage readers that they had not grasped her radical critique. The problem was not that marriage made women unhappy; the problem was that women pursued "happiness" rather than liberty, and that they invested their hopes in an institution that was based on and perpetuated the asymmetry and inequality of the sexes. "The Woman Destroyed" and Beauvoir's effort to correct her readers' misinterpretations of it elicited even more misunderstanding—and more disappointment from the author. It has become a classic case study of reading, misreading, and writing; it has drawn attention from literary critics for decades. The readers' letters, however, add new voices and texts to those discussions.[3]

The subject of marriage provides an especially revealing example of Beauvoir's fraught relationship with her readers. More generally, the mutual disappointment and misunderstanding capture the tense encounter between feminism and the "intimate public" of women's culture. An intimate public, as Lauren Berlant lays it out in her sympathetic and brilliant analysis, is an imagined or affective community that surrounds the writing and media that address women, from literature and magazines to radio programs and so on. That community elicits and values a feeling of belonging. What its members share is less a social condition than a set of aspirations and feelings, an orientation toward emotional knowledge, or a collection of strategies to manage recurring disappointments. The intimate public provides "a complex of consolation, confirmation, discipline, and discussion." Feminism, Berlant says, is a "kind of nosy neighbor" of this intimate public.[4] The metaphor is well worth pursuing; it is a suggestive way to think about Simone de Beauvoir and the very conventional women who made up a large swath of her public. A nosy neighbor listens to conversations, intervenes in her neighbors' debates, and stirs up trouble; while she often tries to set herself apart from her neighbors, she lives, inescapably, in the same community. Beauvoir certainly did not consider women to be locked in what her Austrian reader called an "eternal battle against evil," and seeing *The Second Sex* transformed this way into melodramatic lament surely made her uncomfortable. But the very proximity of Beauvoir's work to the intimate public is essential to understanding Beauvoir's relationship with her readers and, more broadly, some of the enduringly difficult dynamics of feminism's history, especially the ways in which female complaint and feminist critique simultaneously overlap and undercut each other.

An Improbable Expert on the Modern Couple

The wave of conjugal unhappiness in these letters was the reverse side of the post–World War II romance of the couple. Economic expansion and the transformative social changes that came with it in the 1950s and 1960s scuttled older assumptions and practices surrounding the family. Popular culture in the late 1950s swooned over "the couple," a heterosexual twosome, freed from many constraints of the past, and now negotiating an intimate partnership that involved work, love, sex, and the union of two emphatically distinct if dreamily complementary individuals. This was an ideal, but a culturally resonant one, standing for the expansive possibilities of the postwar world.[5] The ideal accompanied the emergence of new patterns of marriage from the middle of the twentieth century on. Men and women socialized and found partners earlier than they had before the war. They set off on their own more often and married younger—men in their mid-twenties and women even earlier than that. Families were being created more quickly and they produced more children. In 1939, just before the war, for every thousand French women of childbearing age, there were sixty-four children. After the war, that number quickly rose to eighty-one.[6] This was the now famous and nearly worldwide "baby boom" of the postwar. By the 1950s, young men and women from the middle classes were less likely than before to ask for their parents' consent and wait for any property or inheritance. They banked instead on decent jobs in expanding economies as well as on government benefits to families. (In France, the baby boom did not lessen the government's commitment to continuing pro-natalist policies, which included tax breaks for families with children, family allowances, and salary supplements for single-earner households.) Young women and men hedged their bets, however; they remained very likely to marry someone from the class and region into which they were born. Marriage, then, was rarely a way to move up the social ladder. Neither was it a leap in the dark, although conservative commentators clucked about young people's reckless romanticism and disdain for tradition in pursuit of *le grand amour*—the love of one's life.[7] Expectations did change; emotional and sexual rapport became the benchmark of a satisfying marriage or coupledom.

By the late 1950s and 1960s those new aspirations surfaced often in the women's press, highlighted in quasi-statistical studies like *La Française et l'amour* and stoked by frequent splashy "polls," such as *Elle* magazine's survey "The Joys and Worries of Women," which showed that "love" topped women's list of joys. "Success in marriage is thoroughly confused with self-realization," sighed a commentator in 1958, who also rued that "women's literature does nothing to stem the tide that carries women in that direction."[8] Wrote the French sociologist Edgar Morin in 1962, "We believe in love." He called love "an institution, in the Durkheimian sense," a powerful sociological constraint that molded the unformed.[9] In the words of the prolific French feminist journalist and sociologist Evelyn Sullerot, marriage was now a "boat" into which you loaded all your needs: "sexual, affective, intellectual."[10] Love was understood to go hand in hand with sexual attraction and pleasure. The eroticization of marriage, or the belief that sexual desire accompanied love and commitment rather than endangering them, was one of "the great dramas" of the century.[11]

That drama had genuinely emancipatory potential, tied often to "an effort to make women's sexual agency and experience look like a positive good rather than a source of shame and dishonor."[12] But the result was even more drama: complicated new scenarios, heightened hopes, bitter disappointments, and lingering dissatisfactions. Experts of all sorts zeroed in on conjugal harmony and ways to promote it. During the 1950s and

1960s, psychologists, social workers, and advice givers concerned with children and child raising called cultural attention to marriage: unhappy couples and unhappy families were the root cause of juvenile delinquency and social disequilibrium.[13] For all of these reasons, stories of couples, whether they were married or not, captivated the French public. If Françoise Giroud and Jean-Jacques Servan-Schreiber, the attractive, spectacularly successful globe-trotting coeditors of *L'Express* magazine, were a famous and much-discussed duo, Beauvoir and Sartre were even more so. It is hard to exaggerate the fascination with the counter-conventional existentialist duo.[14]

In France and beyond, people who followed Beauvoir and Sartre knew that when the two were in their twenties, they made a nonmarital "pact," renewable every two years, which allowed both to take other lovers but required that they be honest with each other. Later, their letters to each other would lay bare some of the discomfiting features of this open non-marriage.[15] So would Beauvoir's letters to her lover, the Chicago writer Nelson Algren. Beauvoir's sexual relations with Sartre were unrewarding from the start, and in Beauvoir's words, "it seemed useless, even indecent, for us to keep sleeping together."[16] They remained each other's primary life companion, but for Beauvoir, their companionship seems to have entailed aiding and abetting Sartre's sexual projects. She pushed several women with whom she was involved toward Sartre, and once they had slept with him, she compared notes and denigrated them. Several of these women were her former students or the couple's protégées.

Beauvoir and Sartre were "continuously involved in tortuous and sometimes rather shabby relationships with others," writes Toril Moi.[17] Moi is putting it mildly. Bianca Bienenfeld was from a Polish Jewish family that had taken refuge in Paris in the 1930s, studied with Beauvoir, started an affair with her, then acceded to Sartre's advances (her first heterosexual experience), only to be precipitously dropped by both. Bienenfeld charged that the couple's callousness in love set the stage for a crueler betrayal: when the Germans arrived and Vichy took over, making France enormously dangerous for immigrant Jews, neither Beauvoir nor Sartre expressed the least concern for her or for members of her family. Several of her relatives were deported and died in the camps.[18]

Sartre went well beyond having and honestly acknowledging many affairs with women. He recounted them to Beauvoir in very great detail, with a combination of cynical pleasure in seduction, open contempt for the seduced, and narcissism. Beauvoir reported Sartre's pursuits in letters that are disturbing for what they reveal about her powerlessness, her complicity with him, or both. In 1960 she and Sartre made two political tours of Latin America, including a visit to Cuba to honor the revolution. During the second trip, they stayed for two months in Brazil, where Sartre became involved with a young Brazilian woman. Beauvoir described the unfolding melodrama to her lover Nelson Algren (English hers):

> He [Sartre] decided it was not enough to have one dark Algerian girl, one fair-haired Russian, and two fake blondes. What was he lacking? A red-headed one! He found her and began an affair with her: she is twenty-five and a virgin (as her thirty and twenty-three-year-old sisters are). In the north of Brazil, well-bred girls don't sleep with men. I like her very much, but I am scared of what is going to happen again to crazy Sartre if he succeeds.

A month later Beauvoir continued the report. She was in the hospital with typhoid, Sartre was exhausted, and the young woman was increasingly bewildered by the situation and anxious that she was about to be dropped. The whole entourage was swimming in alcohol and barbiturates.

> The girl was very much interested in Sartre, she has a will and personality, and she saw him a lot; but she resented being blamed by her family, her friends, and the whole town . . . They quarreled. Sartre had a hell of a life in this dreary hostile town [Recife], with me in the hospital and the half friendly, half scared red-headed girl . . . The girl drank too, when I had recovered we spent a crazy night, she broke glasses in her naked hands and bled abundantly saying she should kill herself, because she loved and hated Sartre and we were going away the next day. I slept in her bed, holding her wrist to prevent her to jump by the window, after giving her a heavy dose of gardenal, too. She is a nice, attractive girl, I must say, she will come to Paris and Sartre says maybe he will marry her! What of the Algerian one then? Well, that is the future.[19]

Did Beauvoir identify with Sartre or with the young women he seduced? Did she think she was protecting him or them? It is impossible to discern.[20] But her complicity suggests the kind of bad faith with which she sometimes charged others. A few years later, an admiring male reader shared with her a long account of the collapse of his marriage and his rocky, jealousy-riven affair with a younger woman, which was also ending unhappily. He asked for advice. This is one of the few occasions on which we know how Beauvoir responded: she told the reader his affair was in "bad faith," and she admonished him for believing that his tumultuous love life had "anything in common with my pact with Sartre."[21] Not only did she deny how much similar hurts and vulnerabilities troubled her relationship, but she also refused him the privilege of living and understanding his love life through hers.[22] For someone who valorized honesty and self-knowledge as essential to intimate relationships, Beauvoir sometimes displayed very little of it.

The Prime of Life (1960) and *The Force of Circumstance* (1963) barely hinted at the tawdry aspects of the Beauvoir-Sartre ménage. Still, what Beauvoir *was* willing to tell at the time provided more than ample fodder for admiration, disapproval, speculation, and debate. Issues of love, partnership, and sexual, existential, or emotional fulfillment figured as central points of readers' identification with Beauvoir and, increasingly, their disappointment and anger with her.

The Prime of Life, the second volume of Beauvoir's autobiography, narrated her feelings as a young woman passionately in love with both a man and her liberty. She called it "a biography of us."[23] Her rebellion against bourgeois values and her efforts to build a relationship in "radical freedom" formed the heart of her story.[24] She and Sartre swore to avoid the constraints and tediousness—or, in her more pungent words, the "decay"—that menaced any long relationship. Beauvoir acknowledged that the rules the two set for themselves were fraught with psychological dangers. She struggled with her desire for security. She fought against the dangers of becoming what Sartre called a *"femme d'intérieur"* (a stay-at-home woman). She confessed to feeling puritanical and stiff by comparison with Sartre's more carefree lovers.[25] The couple's pledge to tell each other all, she admitted, had caused immense pain. (She was revealing to her readers only a fraction of what the couple actually told each other.) *Elle* published excerpts of *The Prime of Life* several months before the book came out, a measure of its popular appeal and a boost to its sales.

In *The Prime of Life,* Beauvoir allowed that the "contingent loves" that both she and Sartre wanted the freedom to enjoy were not easily contained. She discussed the first case in point: the Sartre-Beauvoir trio with Olga Kosakievicz. Olga was Beauvoir's student in Rouen; she was seventeen and Beauvoir twenty-five. Olga's father was a White Russian noble who had fled the revolution; her mother was French and a devotee of the right-wing Action Française; her friends were a "band of Romanian and Polish Jews, driven from their country by anti-Semitism." She caught Beauvoir's attention in 1935 as a shy, high-strung, unconventional student in her philosophy class. Beauvoir introduced her to Sartre. By Beauvoir's account, the trio that ensued was a "stunning success"—that is, until Olga turned out to have demands and desires of her own, at which point the "kid [*gamine*] threatened to take over the couple." The trio later became a foursome, adding one of Sartre's students, Jacques-Laurent Bost, who became Olga's husband while remaining Beauvoir's friend and occasional lover for nearly a decade.[26]

The next volume, *The Force of Circumstance* (1963), revealed more "fleeting romances," and "friendships or camaraderie with lovers (*amitiés ou des camaraderies amoureuses*)."[27] The volume's spotlight, however, shone on the three contenders for lasting relationships: "M.," or Dolores Vanetti Ehrenreich, a young French woman Sartre met in the United States, and the source of the first seriously disconcerting trouble for Beauvoir's "pact" with Sartre; Nelson Algren, with whom Beauvoir fell in love in 1947 and addressed as her "husband" until she refused to leave Sartre and her life in Paris for him in 1951; and Claude Lanzmann, journalist, member of the editorial board at *Les Temps Modernes*, and future director of *Shoah* and other remarkable documentaries. Beauvoir was forty-four when she met Lanzmann. He was seventeen years younger. She believed that she was too old for love and that he was too young for her, but their affair lasted seven years.

Few women had access to such romantic adventures, but Beauvoir nonetheless generalized her experience. The balancing act in her love life was a challenge faced by many others, "how to reconcile fidelity and liberty." As she saw it, "Many couples have made more or less the same pact that Sartre and I did, trying, through all our challenges, to maintain a 'certain fidelity.' "[28] The British and American press had already cast her as the French specialist on "love." In 1959 *Esquire* published "Brigitte Bardot and the Lolita Syndrome" and the *Daily Express* commissioned "The Chemistry of Love," running it alongside pictures of both Clark Gable and his wife, and Arthur Miller and Marilyn Monroe.[29] Beauvoir had deliberately steered clear of anything like a romantic or erotic memoir, highlighting instead her emotional conflicts and philosophical conundrums.[30] Still, her story was riveting, and she certainly appeared to present herself as an expert on the couple. "Observe, she seems to say, the model couple; with the right relationship at work between man and woman, see how I escaped those inequities that are the lot of 'the second sex,'" Germaine Bree wrote in reviewing the English translation of *The Prime of Life*, irritated by what she found the memoir's didactic tone.[31] Others, however, felt that Beauvoir revealed enough of her vulnerabilities and unhappiness to make her credible. In any event, her story and intellectual prestige commanded attention. New Wave director André Cayatte asked her to work with him on a film about the "problems of the couple" and divorce. Beauvoir agreed, partly on the grounds that she had received so many letters on the subject.[32] The project fizzled, but her reputation as an expert endured. Marriage counselors in Heidelberg invited her to come speak on the "conditions of love."[33] It is a testament to Beauvoir's skill as a memoirist, her careful cultivation of the Sartre-Beauvoir myth, the public's interest in coupledom, and, above all other factors, the visibility of marriage as a node of gendered and sexual power, feeling, and privilege that so many wrote Beauvoir to applaud her choices or to argue about what they signified.[34]

Beauvoir's refusal to marry thrilled some and worried others. "How can the narration of your relationship with Sartre, Algren, Lanzmann, and above all, with yourself, and of all else that happened to you . . . fail to move and abide with thousands of your readers?" wrote one reader (in English). "You are a model for all of us . . . love without pettiness, without jealousy, a fraternal love of which you give us such a sterling example," wrote another, though she added that not all shared this view. Indeed, dissent appeared in the response of parents who puzzled over young people's enthusiasm for Beauvoir. "I'd like to understand the relationship that makes so many young people wish that their couple could resemble the Sartre-Beauvoir pairing [*jumelage*]. I appreciate your intelligence, spirit, style, and honesty, but I don't think yours is a better way to live [*mode de vie*]—or even that it is good," argued one parent.[35] "I have two young impressionable teen-agers and must protest," wrote a woman from Southern California. "I wouldn't think of intruding on your private affairs if you didn't make them so public. But you say, 'Look world, look youth!' "[36] A Catholic mother from France fretted about Beauvoir's hold on her son's fiancée: "Needless to say I'm concerned about whether or not my future daughter-in-law will succeed in life." Had Beauvoir read Paul Bourget's *The Disciple* (an 1889 novel about the powerful sway of a materialist/positivist philosopher on a vulnerable young student)? "When I was 18 his books were as much in vogue as yours are now." *The Disciple* was an object lesson on the baneful influence books could wield over twenty-year-olds, shaping "their entire lives." What, the woman demanded, "is going to happen if my future daughter-in-law becomes enthralled with your work? Consciously or not, she may model her life plan on what you propose—Will she find happiness? What do you think?"[37]

Objections from other quarters underscored a growing gulf in opinion (in France and elsewhere) on the issues of sexual mores and conjugal conventions. Beauvoir's repeated assertions that her pact with Sartre was one of her greatest accomplishments strained many readers' credulity. "This part on your relationship with Sartre?" queried a reader à propos *The Force of Circumstance*. "I am sorry to be aggressive, but I don't agree with the charade of liberty that you acted out for each other . . . M. [Dolores Vanetti], Algreen [*sic*]—these are failures—for them and for you." The reader waxed enthusiastic about Beauvoir's account of the Algerian war, which, she said, perfectly captured what she and many her age remembered as their first political experience. She was insulted, however, by the conventionality of the volume's epilogue, which opens with Beauvoir calling her relationship with Sartre the "one sure success" in her life: "You can't do that to us!" Another was "really surprised by your submissiveness to Sartre. My mother seems less submissive to her husband than you??" she said, with question marks to emphasize her incredulity. A nervy young man of seventeen, who had been "struck by her personality" and was interested in "very free relations between the sexes," apologized for having questions about Beauvoir and Sartre that "might seem indiscreet." What was their relationship about? "Friendship seems to me a little banal, but love is a little strong." He wanted an answer, and one that did not condescend to his youth. He did not want to be mistaken for "an emotional adolescent," susceptible to Beauvoir's intoxicating influence. "In all modesty," he added, "I think I have a certain equilibrium, and you are not going to do me harm."[38]

The many letters along these lines register readers' impatience with the constraints of the discourse of "modesty" in which discussions of sexuality had long unfolded, especially in France. Beauvoir had shown herself to be a writer willing to talk about the body, and they wondered about how cautious she proved in the memoir. "Why not tell your readers more about your own experiences, from the physical point of view?" wrote a thirty-four-year-old woman, a teacher, married and the mother of two. "Modesty? [*Pudeur*?] . . . I am surprised, Madame, and trying to understand." She was quite insistent. "Physical love is no mystery to me . . . My desire to understand better stems only from my interest in you."[39]

Beauvoir's account of the "trio" may have raised some eyebrows, but it elicited a brilliant letter from one especially irreverent reader. This reader was disappointed. She thought she had found in Beauvoir a bold fellow thinker, an intellectual who did not shy away from reflecting about herself as a woman, a brilliant and intimate companion: "Finally a woman whose books speak about problems that I often thought I was alone in asking myself. It is so difficult to find a woman among those around one who is both intellectual and interested in her way of being a woman, so difficult to have the time to take up intimate subjects and dare to take them all the way." But this reader found Beauvoir surprisingly timid in matters of love and sex. Henry Miller didn't describe "experience," the reader protested; Miller relished being "in his skin." Quite apart from her impatience with Beauvoir's timidity, she offers a nicely pointed critique of Beauvoir's category of experience as too cerebral, too already processed. To be sure, Beauvoir had never promised "juicy passages" (*passages croustillants*) on her love life. Still, she remonstrated, "the warmth [*chaleur*] of your love for Sartre disappears completely." This reader also suspected that Beauvoir was in fact enjoying more pleasures of the flesh than she let on in the autobiography: "And finally, the TRIO—Let's talk about that. There would be a lot to say. You say too much or too little . . . [T]he reader is turned into a detective, trying to match your story to an actual situation . . . The husband. The wife. The wife's friend who becomes the husband's mistress." All that was utterly conventional, she continued. She pressed forward, spinning out less traditional possibilities—and she illustrated those possibilities with two delightful pages of intricate sexual triangles, the points connected by one- or two-way arrows and question marks. Who, exactly, was pleasuring whom? JP→?S[imone] ← → O[lga] ← → M?[40] This reader had a keen queer eye for sexual arrangements. With that sensibility and her drawings, she sketched out how much the supposedly scandalous celebrity was concealing from her readers. Her disappointment reflected just how much Beauvoir had come to represent for many of her readers the possibilities of female desire.

The Second Sex

Beauvoir wrote vividly about not only *her*self, but also *the* self. Readers' letters about marriage responded not just to her memoir but to the rekindled interest in *The Second Sex*. Marriage, "the destiny traditionally offered to women by society," loomed large in Beauvoir's analysis of women's confounding struggle for personhood and self-sovereignty. She indicted the hollow promises of bourgeois equality and the annihilation of the female self in a critique that drew on ideas ranging from the then new structuralist anthropology of Claude Lévi-Strauss to existentialist ethics. "The past that it perpetuates," Beauvoir wrote of modern marriage, is anchored in the "exchange of women," in which "male groups help each other fulfill themselves as [*s'accomplir comme*] fathers and husbands . . . A woman is always given in marriage to certain males by other males." She insisted an institution so rooted in the asymmetry of the sexes was morally bankrupt. Sexuality in the absence of freely assumed desire and pleasure, reduced to "no more than an animal relation," was necessarily "obscene."[41]

Three of Beauvoir's themes seemed particularly to resonate with readers. The first was material: the repetitive grind of household work as a "torture of Sisyphus." As Beauvoir described it, "the clean becomes soiled, the soiled is made clean, over and over, day after day." Domestic labor, Beauvoir argued, "gives [a woman] no autonomy, it is not directly useful to society, it does not open out on the future, it produces nothing."[42] Historians have written at length about mass consumerism in postwar Europe, detailing the soaring sales of stoves, vacuum cleaners, washing machines, and cleaning products for the home. Indeed, by now we know more about labor-saving devices than about work. But as one historian pointedly reminds us, the "home absorbed more labor power than any other 'industry' in France."[43] Countless married women wrote to thank Beauvoir for her analysis of the numbingly lonely and exhausting world of housework.

The second was psychological: Beauvoir's withering indictment of "bourgeois optimism" and its accompanying chorus of romantic disappointments, which rang through women's magazines. "What bourgeois optimism has to offer the engaged girl is certainly not love," Beauvoir writes. "The bright ideal held up to her is that of happiness, which means the ideal of quiet equilibrium in the midst of repetition and immanence."[44] ("Transcendent" projects are creative and open onto the future; "immanent" ones simply maintain existence.)

Beauvoir's warnings of the gothic psychological dramas that erupted when women, almost inevitably, rebelled against these arrangements likewise struck a powerful chord among her readers. If marriage "incites man to capricious imperialism," she argues, it drives women to venom and self-destruction; women become "leeches," "praying mantises"; they use an "arsenal of tricks," such as refusing to have sex. These conflicts, she maintains, sometimes blow up a marriage; more often they slowly poison the relationship. In Beauvoir's words: "As a rule, a woman wants to 'hold onto' her husband while resisting his domination. She struggles with him in the effort to uphold her independence, and she battles with the rest of the world to preserve the 'situation' that dooms her to dependence. This double game is difficult to play and explains in part the disturbed and nervous state in which many women spend their lives."[45] Beauvoir makes these warnings hard to avoid. She reiterates them in the conclusion of *The Second Sex*, which evokes the war between the sexes and the battles that will go on "as long as femininity is perpetuated as such." Beauvoir laces her philosophy with nightmarish imagery and vivid prose: "The woman who is locked up in immanence endeavors to hold man in that prison also; thus the prison will be confused with the world, and the woman will no longer suffer from being confined there." Inequality produces resentfulness and contradictory flailing—demands for both "old-fashioned respect and modern esteem." The man, Beauvoir continues, becomes "irritated" and "defensive"; he accuses the woman of playing unfairly, although wittingly or not, he has stacked the deck against her.[46]

These passages come immediately before the famous articulations of woman's doubled consciousness and the impossible subjectivity of being self and Other. Beauvoir sets out the heart of *The Second Sex* in this single compelling passage: "Since woman is opaque in her very being, she stands before man not as a subject but as an object paradoxically endowed with subjectivity; she takes herself simultaneously as self and as other, a contradiction that entails baffling consequences."[47] The relationship between woman and man is a very particular kind of bond between two consciousnesses, one in which antagonisms and inequality are complicated by invitations to complicity and identification. Intimacy, love, and sexual desire therefore had vastly different stakes for women and men. For Beauvoir, marriage was only one instance of the annihilation of the female self. For many women readers in the 1960s, however, that institution towered over their life trajectories.

Beauvoir's critique of the institution was radical, her prose gripping, and her scenarios dreadful. Not surprisingly, she drew readers into confession, introspection, alliance, and rejection. Beauvoir's words became for men as well as women scripts to be used in their own lives. "Your book is a work of art . . . [S]ome of the phrases from your book have become things singing in my mind—like marriage oppresses a man but annihilates a woman," wrote a man from the United States.[48] Married readers even made a point of saying they had read Beauvoir together, and that they were using *The Second Sex* to manage their lives as a couple. A mother of two from Madrid penned a remarkable letter disclosing just this practice. Her husband, a typesetter, had encouraged her to read *The Second Sex* before their wedding. Both of them now saw Beauvoir as "a symbol of the dignity of the female human being." In this letter, which is short, but long on how cramped its author felt by her narrowed horizons, Beauvoir becomes a protagonist in the couple's conversations: "When I was drowning in the everyday worries of the household and children, and, at the same time, unhappy about the confines of my world, my husband would say to me, 'Come on, be a little more Simone-de-Beauvoirian.' "[49] The letter is inescapably ambiguous about her husband's affect during these discussions.

This same writer went on to evoke the difficulties she faced in a "milieu that is very different from yours," where "independence" and "liberty" could be nothing more than abstractions. Thwarted longings for a more egalitarian relationship ran through many letters to Beauvoir. Correspondents wrote of the obstacles to their aspirations and the succor they received from her personal example. As one woman expressed it:

> My husband and I try to have an egalitarian marriage, but it is difficult, and
> on many occasions it is your books that have clarified the issues and given

me support. I know I don't have your fearlessness, your disdain for public opinion . . . But there are also real barriers, the power of a social, professional, and economic milieu. How can you hold up against all that? That's when books like yours are invaluable . . . They confirm your feeling that you're not completely wrong.[50]

Similarly, "I don't know any other couple trying to do things the way we are," wrote an American woman chafing at the combination of financial straits and provincial boredom as she watched her second marriage deteriorate. "I'm not cynical or bitter, just wondering if I can be a whole, complete independent person and still be married. How I wish I had only a small part of your wisdom and drive at such a young age as you experienced."[51]

Letters to Beauvoir reveal that the soaring hopes of the 1950s and 1960s for conjugal fulfillment could be quickly dashed; the "boat" into which one loaded "sexual, affective, and intellectual needs," in Sullerot's terms, could quickly take on water. A twenty-seven-year-old woman from Bogotá had counted on her marriage to be a "physiological and psychological culmination," and her language captures the expectations of the period. But a husband with no intellectual interests and four pregnancies back-to-back had upended that scenario: "What can I do? Not daring to cause a scandal in society, to pain my parents, or to upset the children by distancing myself from him, I am resigning myself to a bourgeois existence."[52]

Many of those who wrote had chosen to marry young, often in rebellion against their families. Even if these choices reflected new freedoms, the absence of contraception brought children in quick succession, overwhelming a young couple's economic and emotional resources. The woman from Bogotá blamed her situation on the "hypocrisy and blindness of the Church on the 'scabrous' subject of birth control."[53] Several social surveys of new mothers drew disquietingly similar conclusions, though without indicting the church. Roughly one third of mothers interviewed while they were in maternity wards in Paris, Grenoble, and Lyon in 1960 reported that they would have used a contraceptive had it been available.[54] Some letter writers blamed themselves for a series of bad choices. "If I had followed your example, worked hard, and been serious, none of this would have happened," wrote a correspondent who had married to escape her parents. She now had three children and lived with her husband in a one-bedroom apartment: "As stupidities go, that's colossal, don't you think?"[55]

Another, born into a Jewish family in the Périgord in southwest France, had long wanted to leave the region, but her father had died when she was young, her brother had been deported to Dachau during the war, and she needed to stay near her mother. She "took refuge" by marrying a cousin, with whom she had three children. She wrestled with how to act ethically in the face of what she considered her mistakes. "Children notice everything," she wrote. "They are dreadfully open and lucid, but they are going through a period where they need their parents to be . . . [her ellipses] virtuous. Forgive me the word. I detest it. But I know that their demand is logical, legitimate. They are born of our cowardice; at least I try to take responsibility for that as best I can." Another Jewish woman, who had survived the camps and ended up in California, wrote a confusing letter but one that captured a similar and utterly plausible combination of rage and self-laceration. "My marriage is falling apart. I hate him," she wrote of her husband. "I think I hate him because I feel guilty for not having chosen a better spouse."[56] Later, she thanked Beauvoir for responding.

Several letters revealed struggles with domestic abuse and violence, issues that were virtually taboo in the mushrooming psychological counseling literature well into the 1970s. Of the many letters that hesitantly broached the subject, the following is the most striking, both for its description of the problem and for what it conveys about the role of letter writing in a reader's life:

> I married very young to be rid of my parents and I am not happy at all with my husband.
> . . . I've been thinking about divorce for a long time but I never had the courage. He is very sensitive and very violent . . . There are many scenes . . . This time was more serious, more violent, longer. The truces are shorter. So I have made up my mind. I am at my nerves' ends . . . A friend of my husband's comes to talk to me . . . He tells me I'm crazy. That I will fail. That I don't have the right to do this to my son. I thought I was right; now I am disoriented. My husband can no longer hope for anything from me. I don't love him. Suddenly it seems obvious that I have to sacrifice myself. I cried. I don't want to. I want to live.

Amid the din of her husband's rage, the meddling of friends, and memories of her mother's voice, which, she said, had come "back to haunt" her, she found a comfort in her "conversation" with Beauvoir. "Writing you," she put at the end, "has soothed me."[57]

Women spelled out the conditions that made marriages at once unhappy and seemingly impossible to escape: economic precarity, pressure from family elders as well as children, the prosaic but very real burdens of cramped and grossly inadequate housing, and exhaustion, depression, and ill health.[58] They had not anticipated the repercussions of marriage when they entered into it—how many duties, assignments, and expectations the institution imposed; how quickly marriage could go bad; and how many resources they would have to muster to escape. "I wanted to have children and all the rest came . . . I was ready to leave. I didn't do it . . . [S]ometimes I tell myself I'm a coward, other times that it is my duty to stay—and also that leaving is a ridiculous desire at my age." (She was fifty). "I was a heap of entrails," wrote one with a doctorate, borrowing a phrase from Rimbaud. "I fought for a long time, though. I fought against a husband who wanted to enslave me, invasive children, an exhausting family. I could fight then, for I was young." They shuddered at the banality of their situation. "Here I am, a doctor's wife, petty bourgeois, faithful and calm—me!" wrote the mother of four children, wondering if she could "reinvent" her life at such a late age. (She was thirty-six.) Some told operatic stories about partial escapes—having affairs, hiding their lovers' letters from their husbands, meeting lovers at train stations, or falling into complicated foursomes (several of those with both female and male lovers)—but putting on the brakes in the name of preserving the ideals of one *true* love and happiness (*bonheur*). Other stories were simple and tedious. "What am I going to do about my husband?" wrote a woman who badgered Beauvoir with several letters on her marriage, none of which seem to have been answered. "We started all over. Now he's sick and I am stuck."[59]

Letter writers borrowed Beauvoir's words to explain themselves. One characteristic letter described reading *The Second Sex* while the woman was in a state of "full conjugal disarray." She described her emotional chaos in terms straight from various scenes in *The Second Sex*: "Housewife for two years and unsatisfied (although I wanted this situation), I am destroying my husband and myself, without ever breaking free. I had a propensity to the passivity of a mistress of the house, this narcissist, this woman who is devouring and being devoured, this woman in love who is at the same time slowly becoming frigid, even this slumbering erotomaniac."[60] It was as if Beauvoir had named and even created the tensions that readers then felt compelled to write about.

"The Woman Destroyed"

"Conjugal disarray!" "Failed marriage." "My life is ruined." It is easy to imagine any author tiring under such a barrage of unhappiness, disappointment, and self-laceration. It is startling, however, to see that Beauvoir used what she herself described as readers' "confidences" as grist for her authorial mill. A (long) short story or novella she published in 1968 did just that. The story involves a woman reeling in confusion as she learns that her husband has been having an affair. The story is titled "La femme rompue"; *rompre* means to break off, as in a relationship, and *rompue* means broken, but also exhausted or worn out. The English title is "The Woman Destroyed." (It is one of three short stories in a collection titled *The Woman Destroyed*.) Beauvoir later explained the origins of the story and her purpose. The story itself was "commonplace" or "banal," she said. "I had recently received letters in which several women in their forties confided in me . . . They understood nothing of what was happening to them. Their universe was crumbling, and they no longer knew who they were." She created a heroine and constructed her diary with an eye to showing how her protagonist "tried to flee her truth." Beauvoir was referring, of course, to letters just like the ones I have quoted. Her tone heightens one's sense that she had exploited her readers' trust.[61]

   "The Woman Destroyed" is stiff and didactic. It hinges on a crisis in the marriage of Monique, who gave up a medical career to stay at home with her two children, now grown, and Maurice, an oncologist who, it turns out, has been having an affair for years. Beauvoir begins at the moment when Monique first learns of the affair, and writes it as Monique's diary, inviting the reader to join her in observing Monique's flailing efforts to sort through what her marriage has meant, taking note of her "fabrications," "omissions," "mistakes," and self-deceptions. Monique persuades herself that Maurice's lover, Noëllic, a lawyer, is a superficial, materialistic, fashion-obsessed *arriviste*; Maurice cannot have feelings for her.

Monique dizzies herself wondering whether she should battle to win Maurice back or demonstrate her patience and resolve by waiting out the storm. She vacillates between trying to stay calm and berating herself for "cowardice," between believing she understands and understanding that she doesn't. Monique seems to know that every line in her diary is tangled by denial. "In truth, I am disarmed because I never imagined that I had rights," she confesses in her diary. "I wait, and I even ask [*demander*]. But I don't know how to require [*exiger*]."[62] The distinction between *demander*, to ask—seen as wheedling—and *exiger*, to require or claim, is signature Beauvoir. Indeed, Monique is a barely fictionalized version of the unhappy married woman in *The Second Sex*, unable to "win possession of herself" and twisted by resentment and neediness. But as literary critics have pointed out, the story also reads like a *roman de la gare* (a railroad station novel, the pejorative French term for cheap commercial literature), a dime store romance, or the kind of romantic fiction found in women's magazines. The voice is confessional, the tone is intimate, and the plot makes "love" the solution to problems as well as the source of them. What is more, the drama is entirely personal: no social and material constraints shape the characters' feelings or actions. Beauvoir sets the story in the swank seventh arrondissement of Paris; her characters leave the neighborhood only for vacations in Italy. That the story was first published in *Elle* (in five issues from October through November 1967) accentuated its romantic-fiction features.[63] To put it simply, the line between dime store banality and the deliberate mocking or critique of that kind of story becomes all but imperceptible.

"The Woman Destroyed" flopped with the critics. Highbrow reviewers in *Le Monde des Livres*, *Les Nouvelles Littéraires*, and *Le Figaro Littéraire* deemed it unworthy of being called literature: sloppy, lifeless, and "suffocatingly conventional." As one reviewer put it; "Truly, 'The Woman Destroyed' is a whole women's magazine by itself. It is *Elle* in *Elle*. So far, only the horoscope is missing." The sixty-year-old author was now embarrassingly passé.[64] Many readers shared those critics' views, which stung. But by Beauvoir's own account, vastly more frustrating was the effusive praise from married forty-something women very much like those whose letters had prompted the story in the first place—in other words, the models for the clueless Monique. "I was immediately besieged by letters from women who had broken up, partly broken up, or were in the midst of a break-up," complained Beauvoir. Those letter writers thanked her profusely for writing about them with such insight and capturing their experiences with exceptionally sympathetic understanding. Exasperated, Beauvoir wrote that their reactions "rested on an enormous misunderstanding," and she called her readers as "blind" as her muddled fictional character.[65]

Beauvoir's unusually detailed account of her intentions, her readers' misreadings, and her reactions to those misreadings have made "The Woman Destroyed" a lively and absorbing case study in literary (mis)reception, authorial intent and how it can go awry, projection, identification, and the power in play between author and reader.[66] That discussion, though, has to rely on Beauvoir's version of the exchange. The archive provides our first view of the readers' letters and how reader and author engaged each other; it brings new texts into the picture. As far as the story goes, the lives and dilemmas of her readers make "The Woman Destroyed" look dull by comparison, and their letters make Beauvoir's account of them seem blinkered and unappreciative.

To begin with, many letter writers had no trouble grasping the basic tenets of existentialism. One reader who understood perfectly well that Beauvoir's characters referred to concepts in her other works still could not fathom the author's purpose: "What did the author want to show us? The woman-child, I suppose, the dependent and mystified woman whom she speaks of elsewhere, trapped in a situation she can't overcome; stuck in an attitude she has made absolute, and therefore unable to become a real adult, conscious, autonomous, free—the old enslaved and colonized woman." But by this reader's lights, Beauvoir's Monique was a woman "perfectly infantile and ridiculous," without any mooring in the contemporary world. By the mid-1960s, she wrote, women left their marriages without losing all composure. "I'll tell you something else," the reader added: *women* as well as men had affairs. Judgments from the "connoisseurs of institutionalized hypocrisy" notwithstanding, the traditional double standard "is being turned upside down, across social classes, and regardless of political inclinations." Monique, she charged, was an anachronism. A thoughtful intellectual would have written about marriage as it actually existed and advocated reforming the laws on divorce so that even formerly married people could "lead their own lives."[67] Many other readers found the central issues too narrowly cast to be interesting. In *The*

Prime of Life, Beauvoir had already discussed whether intimacy required transparency. "The Woman Destroyed" offered a stilted and unsatisfying version of the story, devoid of the lived tensions of sustaining both intimacy and total truth-telling that had strained her pact with Sartre. Beauvoir's story was neither personal enough to be gripping nor sufficiently political to be genuinely provocative.

Other readers were put off by the bourgeois *mise-en-scène* of the story, which stripped away any material dimensions of the marriage, sealing off its psychological and existential aspects in a separate, privileged zone. A few letter writers suggested that whether or not partners could contend with the truth about "contingent loves" was rather less pressing than other concerns, like battling with a husband over one's work or earnings, looking for employment after years out of the labor force, or searching for housing when single, especially with children in tow. A woman who had just left her husband after "a very violent discussion" about whether she could work on her own and "keep everything for herself" wrote that she needed to turn to "the immediate issue: first you have to find a place to live, which is difficult with children, and a job." Another woman, with serious health problems, had been living with her grandmother, husband, and small child for two years; her husband, deep in debt, was applying unsuccessfully for social housing. Her grandmother paid the gas and electricity bills and took the infant to sleep in her room, while the woman's husband was becoming increasingly violent and abusive toward all of them. These were the scenarios one reader may have had in mind when he asked Beauvoir if she could create some plausible characters, for example, with problems with money, at work, or with health.[68] Not much authorial imagination seems to have gone into Beauvoir's main characters' options. Maurice reproaches Monique for losing intellectual interest in his work and stopping her own, recapitulating Sartre's warning to Beauvoir that she should not become a "stay-at-home woman" (*femme d'intérieur*).[69] Monique's therapist can recommend nothing more than finding a job.[70]

Many readers, nonetheless, were enthralled: "You can't imagine how interesting I find 'The Woman Destroyed' . . . Every week I get more impatient for Saturday, the day that *Elle* comes out"; "What is going to become of your heroes? I will know it in the next issue of *Elle*." Another wrote, "I don't usually read *Elle*, but I can't wait for the next issue." Appreciative letters poured in from women who recognized themselves in Monique and her situation. "My life, my story, my suffering, my distress as a woman who was betrayed and abandoned by her husband; even the name, Maurice, even the profession, doctor, are the same," wrote a woman from Israel. "Just like your heroine I asked my friends thousands of questions," a Parisian woman confessed. "I read the Bible . . . I took tranquillizers . . . Finally I had had enough, and you helped me put my life back together." Another writer admitted, "I had the whole thing . . . children, money worries, sickness, and then a splendid story of adultery." Her effort to reconstruct her marriage resulted in "another illusion! A total fiasco!" Her nerves were shattered, and her husband had become sexually impotent. One reader indignantly dismissed a nasty review of "The Woman Destroyed" as "stupid." "You probably know this, Madame, but it has to be repeated," she continued, "that we are a very great many for whom your testimony is exemplary." One writer, for example, shared how her "husband left home last Thursday . . . taking all his things and leaving us hardly anything."[71] In an "irremediable situation," wrote another, the only consolation came from knowing you were not alone, not "damned."[72] These letters have the classic features of what Lauren Berlant calls the "female complaint," with their laments about bearing the burdens of an unjust world (or fighting an "eternal battle against evil," in the words of the Austrian woman quoted earlier) or of being abandoned by their protectors; these are stories of adapting to "scenarios of necessity," of expecting to share experiences, and of finding consolations in belonging.

Even distressingly conventional readers, though, could be extraordinarily articulate about how they reacted to Beauvoir's work. The woman from Israel, who found so many of the details of "The Woman Destroyed" familiar, reflected that the story had given her some detachment. Her relationship with Monique involved less identification than alienated self-recognition: "If we can read it as a story, it seems after all an ordinary story, and not something that destroyed my life." A recent divorcee wrote that she probably would have left her marriage even without Beauvoir's help, but that reading her nonetheless made a difference: "We're carried by so many currents, interior and exterior, but I wouldn't have understood the urgency of the situation. You gave me reasons for being."[73]

Moreover, Beauvoir's remarks about her muddled and lost forty-something correspondents sound like caricatures. Some did see their "universe crumbling," but others could feel a new world taking shape. "For two months my life has been in revolution," one exclaimed. "Now a first stage is over, and I need to tell you how that happened." A Japanese woman wrote that she loved her husband, but she was "tired of marriage." She wrote in English: "Just 3 days ago I began to live alone (not yet divorced). Then today I read your book, *Le Deuxième Sexe*. Your book made me awake. I understand that my difficulties are not personal ones. How your words encourage me!" These women were not looking for consolation, asking for advice about new love, or doubling down on their bad bets. They were finding and confirming a more substantive reckoning with their condition, casting it as collective. If many of the letter writers were stuck, they were not necessarily muddled. One called her marriage a failure "on the physical level, where it was total, but also on the moral and intellectual level." She had hoped children would save her relationship but found motherhood stifling. She had just moved in with a new lover. Her "very religious" husband was pulling out all the stops: refusing to give up the children, telling the family that she (the wife) was suffering a temporary nervous breakdown, and mobilizing her own parents and his priest to recall her to her "duty as wife and mother." Should she leave her children, she asked Beauvoir, or take them away from a father whose only fault was not having been able to love her? "I've been turning this problem over for months and I see no way out; this is why I'm asking for your advice."[74] Like many in the late 1960s, she emphasized that hers was not an issue to be addressed in an advice column (*un courrier du cœur*).

Indeed, many who wrote to Beauvoir very specifically repudiated the voice of the "intimate public." By the late 1960s, the *courrier du cœur* loomed as a specific negative example. The letters to Beauvoir were marked by a growing insistence that the problem at hand was not trivial or merely personal. Many a letter writer stressed that she was not "the advice column type" ("*genre courrier du cœur*"), that she knew better than to ask for consolation or formulaic advice, and that while she did want someone to *listen* while she thought out loud, she was actually thinking for herself. I'm writing *directly to you*, not airing my grievances to the world, many letter writers underscored; their imagined audience was not the other readers of a women's magazine but a brilliant and unconventional radical philosopher. They were painfully self-conscious that the very act of taking their intimacies to a public figure threatened to draw them into the force field of the intimate public, warping and trivializing their concerns. They winced at the contempt they knew others felt for that genre. As one reader commented regarding a condescending review of "The Woman Destroyed" in *Le Monde*, the story's language was indeed "borrowed from the pettiness of the everyday." But, she continued, while the woman's situation might be *misérable* (wretched), it was not *méprisable* (contemptible).[75]

Beauvoir's forays into the commercial women's press or the intimate public had polarized her readers for some time. When excerpts from *The Prime of Life*, most of them on marriage, ran in *Elle*, many correspondents were indignant: "If you want your work to be lucid and moral, it should not be vulgarized. I was shocked to see your name and Sartre's on the same pages as recipes and the Courrier du Cœur." Publishing "The Woman Destroyed" in the same magazine sparked similar reactions. "*Elle*??" asked a one-time admirer. Furious, she vowed never to read Beauvoir again. "You have allowed your novel to be divided up like a vulgar serial, and published surrounded by silliness," wrote another. "What is happening? It is hard to swallow." Wrote one of Beauvoir's longtime friends, "They'll never forgive you for publishing in *Elle*."[76]

Were the *Elle* readers too blinkered to see that Monique was unsympathetically hapless? They sensed—rightly—that there was more of Beauvoir in Monique than she acknowledged to herself, and also that Beauvoir shared the same troubles they reported to her. They stoutly refused to hear the condescension in Beauvoir's voice, wanting to believe that a powerful literary figure was speaking for—rather than at—them. If that was wishful thinking as well as pride, the author had encouraged it. There was no less wishful thinking in Beauvoir's belief that a writer could simply instruct her readers, or that by force of writerly power her work could model and constitute an escape from the intimate public.

Beauvoir believed a bright line separated "female complaint" from rebellion—or the needy resentment produced by accepting one's dependence from "taking responsibility" and assuming one's liberty. Beauvoir's negative models, like the married woman in *The Second Sex* or Monique in "The Woman Destroyed," rebel sporadically, but their revolt is self-destructive and illusory. Beauvoir's positive models, like herself in *The Prime of Life* or the independent woman in the final chapter of *The Second Sex*, have the courage to trade "happiness (which is not guaranteed in any case)" for liberty. They take the high road, authentically assuming the status of a subject. But what this meant, concretely, apart from eschewing marriage or getting a job, was hardly clear. In any event, as the letters show, women took the high road, the low one, and many in between.

In a popular culture and at a historical moment so infatuated with *le grand amour*, Simone de Beauvoir's indictment of "bourgeois optimism" and its romantic illusions was bracing and resonant. Yet Beauvoir's categories of analysis did little to capture her readers' emotions, their aspirations, or the political reverberations of their feelings. It is true that many of the complaints that filled Beauvoir's mailbox seem to have been driven by "fantasies of conventionality." It is also true that readers registered *disappointment* with the promises of marriage, not necessarily disenchantment with the institution itself. As Berlant puts it, "In the literature of the intimate public, the *restlessness that desire creates is not the same thing as an imminent politics.*"[77] Feelings such as these would not necessarily create transformative social movements. But Berlant's appreciation for "restlessness" captures better than Beauvoir did the emotions summoned up by reading Beauvoir and corresponding with her. What is more, this "restlessness" forms one terrain on which feminism is obliged to work.

It is impossible to ignore how powerfully heterosexual marriage unequally distributes legal privileges, social duties, labor market advantages, and emotional burdens along gendered lines. Social and political theorists, anthropologists, and historians have amply demonstrated the extent of cultural and political investment in that institution.[78] Many of these correspondents placed their hopes in marriage too, so it is not surprising that marriage became a node of existential unhappiness and sometimes inchoate complaint. What was striking in 1968–1970 was the rapid escalation of complaint into radical critique, and a critique that went well beyond marriage to the nuclear family and its embeddedness in patriarchal culture, to the illusions of "nature" and the female body and a reimagining of sexual pleasures and practices. It is equally striking that many of the radicals who developed that critique, like Shulamith Firestone, also wrote to Simone de Beauvoir, pulling out very different strands of her work.

Letters about marriage and "The Woman Destroyed" have taken us very far from what we might consider the center of action in 1968. Headlines that year were made by student protest, massive labor strikes, and civil rights militancy. But these letters show the currents that were troubling quieter waters. In fact, and even more important, it was not such a long step from these grievances about exhausting and mind-numbing domestic labor to the working-class dimensions of the history of 1968. Embedded in these complaints about marriage was a simmering protest against overwork—and overwork compounded by an egregiously unequal division of labor that assigned to women the burden of housework, childbearing, and the affective responsibility for the family. In the 1970s, the boisterously radical MLF—Mouvement de la Libération des Femmes, or women's liberation movement—would repudiate the "repetition and routine" of marriage. When a 1971 MLF demonstration happened to pass in front of a wedding taking place in a small church off the boulevard de la République in Paris, marchers peeled off from the demonstration and ran into the church chanting, "Liberate the bride!" Marriage "claims to assure security," wrote one activist, "but only organizes dependence." The MLF, she asserted, was voicing "women's long-standing grievances with the 'diabolical machine' by which society condemns them to be complicit in their own oppression." By the 1970s, the restlessness of the "intimate public" would become thoroughly entangled in the extraordinary upsurge of radical feminist politics.[79]

Even before that upsurge, however, the discontent reflected in these letters to Beauvoir had helped to produce a series of important marriage law reforms establishing married women's equality and independence, their right to open bank accounts, to sign contracts, and to appear in court. By modifying laws governing the separation of goods in case of divorce, changing "paternal" to "parental" authority in matters regarding children, and simplifying divorce, such reforms hastened the "decolonization of married women," in the entirely characteristic imagery of the moment.[80] None of this would have happened without the simmering of female complaint. The starkest evidence of discontent came with the abrupt end of rising marriage rates. In France (and elsewhere), marriage rates peaked in 1972 and have fallen steadily since.[81]

In 1960, Paul Ricœur wrote in the progressive Catholic journal *Esprit* that sex was no longer sacred, and rightly so. How would that desacralization change "the conjugal ethics of modernity?" he asked. Marriage, Ricœur observed, had been "our culture's cardinal bet regarding sex."[82] A decade later the answer was clear: the bet was off.

8

Sexual Politics and Feminism

We want to know the real explanation for the explosion of this time
bomb . . . for this violently emotional tone and interpretive delirium!
March 9, 1972

Throughout the 1960s, letters to Beauvoir simmered with grievances
about stifling marriages, constrained choices, the grind and boredom of
housework, the absence of contraception, serial pregnancies, criminalized
abortion, and the affective burdens of family—responsibility for everything considered the lower province of women. These issues, contraception in particular, mattered in the politics of the mid-1960s; in 1967 the
French legislature legalized contraception; women swelled the ranks of
labor unions; books on the female condition filled bookstores; feminism
was a recognizable topic. In May 1968, the explosion of student radicalism and the enormous general strike of labor that were the most distinctive features of that famous year in France pushed these matters to the
side. The salient categories of identity were class and youth; the slogans
that mobilized concerned wages and quality of life, opposition to hierarchy and authoritarianism, personal freedom, and sexual liberation. The
last was understood to be male and heterosexual; at least it was rarely in-
flected by reckoning with its gendered or queer dimensions.

Feminism, transformed and renamed women's liberation, emerged with immense force in the aftermath of this movement, as a second '68. By 1970, a movement the French press called the Mouvement de la Libération des Femmes, or MLF, had emerged, although the movement encompassed a series of different and often rival groups and tendencies, and the name would always be contentious. Within a year, women's liberation had alternative newspapers, general assemblies in the lecture halls of the Sorbonne and the École des Beaux-Arts, massive grass-roots support, and international networks. These were exhilarating days. They brought Beauvoir letters from Germany, Great Britain, Belgium, Spain, the United States, and Argentina. One correspondent had just returned from Paris to Buenos Aires, where her political world and her own center for research had been wrecked by military rule and repression. What continuity she felt in her life came from feminism and the "sisterhood" she felt with her comrades.[1] Gay liberation, too, was part of this "second '68" and part of rethinking sex—with all that sex meant, from gender roles to sexual difference and from desires to intercourse.

Beauvoir's correspondence captures many dimensions of this period and its turmoil. Gone, for the most part, were the days when her readers treated her as an oracle, an expert, a source of sexual knowledge. As the writer Annie Ernaux irreverently put it, the only thing one learned from Beauvoir was that "it was a misfortune to have a uterus."[2] Still, Beauvoir remained a magnet for the various currents of the new politics: its sudden radicalization, its different constituencies, its internationalism, its highly charged affect and changed emotional register, and the interplay of feeling, identifications, and politics.

The Scandal of Abortion, 1949–1970

From 1970 on, the legalization of abortion would become *the* defining issue of the new movement: its most striking and resonant demand. In ways that are hard to imagine today, the call to legalize abortion united metropolitan and provincial opinion; it bridged social class and, strikingly, sexual orientation. It was an international movement as well.[3] Beauvoir's reputation in 1970 had everything to do with her well-known and longtime stance on the matter. For decades her outspoken radicalism had elicited scores of letters and visits from unhappily pregnant women asking for help, money, or the address of a doctor who might perform an abortion. Correspondents had vented their rage at the double standard: men could both wax poetic about the joys of fatherhood and walk away from responsibility for pregnancy, while women seeking to end a pregnancy were charged with being "weak, despicable, disgraceful, criminal, and so on."[4]

"Abortion is considered a revolting crime, to which it is indecent even to refer," Beauvoir wrote in *The Second Sex*—and then proceeded to defy decency, speaking about it at length and in detail.[5] In *The Second Sex*, she opened the chapter on "the mother" not with the woman's happy embrace of a natural destiny but with abortion and birth control, which she presented as a constitutively *human* rebellion against species being and the dictates of nature. It is impossible to exaggerate the centrality of bodily unfreedom to Beauvoir's understanding of women's condition, or a woman's dread of being "caught" by pregnancy to the philosopher's vivid portrait of immanence. Self-sovereignty, responsible ethical action, equality, and real love (or, simply, decent relationships) between men and women were inconceivable if pregnancy and motherhood awaited women like a trap.

In 1960 Beauvoir was asked by Dr. Marie Andrée Lagroua Weill-Hallé, an obstetrician and the head of the French Family Planning, to preface the doctor's collection of fifty case studies of her patients, all of them unhappily pregnant (*The Great Fear of Loving*, 1960). Weill-Hallé opened her book by reciting the familiar grim facts. "Getting an abortion" when abortion was illegal commonly meant inducing a miscarriage, inserting or having someone insert a probe or knitting needle into your uterus and waiting for the blood to flow. The process often took several days. It often required reinserting the probe. It usually landed you at a clinic or hospital for an emergency D&C, a dilation and curettage, or scraping the uterine lining.[6] Many women who had given themselves abortions this way described being "punished" for their misdeeds by the clinic doctor, who understood all too well the cause of the miscarriage and performed the D&C without anesthesia. Weill-Hallé's stories of her patients aimed to put a face on the suffering and irreparable damage to women's health caused by the laws (in France and elsewhere) that criminalized abortion, contraception, and public discussion of either.

In France, that legal regime had been put in place in the early 1920s, in the aftermath of the tremendous losses of World War I. Helping a woman procure an abortion was punished with up to five years in prison and stiff fines, and those penalties had been raised in 1939 and again in 1942, when the Vichy regime made abortion a crime against "the French race."[7] Although the Vichy-era law was repealed, abortion, contraception, and discussion of contraception ("anti-natalist propaganda") remained illegal. (Teaching about the church-approved "natural" method of taking one's temperature to track ovulation was an exception.) Those laws were neither popular nor effective, to judge by the rates of illegal abortion. Weill-Hallé was hardly the first to speak out on the "scandal" of abortion. By 1960, the law's cruelties as well as its inefficacies were manifest.[8] That did not mean the laws would be changed. To the contrary, as Luc Boltanski has argued concerning the history of abortion in general, almost everywhere, abortion has been condemned but tolerated. The role of legal prohibition is not to halt the practice, Boltanski argues, but rather to hold the line between "official" knowledge, which is "public, solemn, and collective," and "unofficial" knowledge, secret, shameful, and individual. The law's purpose has been "to prevent the moral dilemmas associated with abortion from entering into the public sphere."[9]

Beauvoir's preface to *The Great Fear of Loving* was scathing on the way the issue was kept out of public discussion. Silence and denial concealed its everydayness even from women themselves, who faced unwanted pregnancies in criminalized isolation, as if their pregnancies were unhappy "accidents" rather than constitutive features of women's situation in a world where contraception was illegal and unacceptable. Doctors, who presented themselves as experts on women's bodies and interests, and who wielded enormous power over women looking for advice on contraception and pregnancy, professed themselves unable to change the law. Under these circumstances, Beauvoir concluded, more testimony was almost futile; it would barely dent the wall of silence and taboo.[10]

Nineteen sixty was also the year when the arrest and torture of Djamila Boupacha created such a scandal, and Beauvoir's preface to Weill-Hallé's book struck the same chords as her writing on Boupacha. In Beauvoir's presentation, the "scandal" of torture resembled the "scandal" of illegal abortion: the most scandalous aspect of both was that the public had grown used to them.[11] Both practices were open secrets, practices that offended professed moral codes or violated laws in a way that showed those codes and laws to be hollow. Their very everyday-ness was numbing: that the "revelations" promised to continue only deepened the gulf of denial. Torture was the scandal of a state-sanctioned colonial war, abortion the scandal of criminalized contraception and women's sexual unfreedom; both were known but unacknowledged, and thus permanently shocking.

In Beauvoir's preface to Dr. Weill-Hallé's book, the women patients seem to share much with the young Algerian woman in her prison cell. They are "exhausted, harassed, terrified, hunted down." Isolation compounds their powerlessness and terror. "How do other women manage?" one asks. A feeling of criminal wrongdoing that women at once internalized and also understood to be unfair; a sense that their case or their "condition" was not, in fact, singular; the belief that justice or knowledge *should* be available somewhere—these feelings and this situation were present in both cases. In Beauvoir's analysis, both situations exemplified the ways in which law, culture, and bad faith foisted suffering or, in the case of abortion, impossible ethical choices on women.

Putting these two cases together in this analysis of law, crime, punishment, and consciousness also reprised themes and language from *The Second Sex*. Beauvoir wrote there of the woman who finds herself in a clinic for a D&C after provoking a miscarriage: "She is punished *sadistically*." The medical procedure (D&C), Beauvoir wrote, was not "suffering" but rather "torture." Between the two lay a world of difference: the honorable *suffered* what happened to them by accident or fate; the presumptively criminal were *tortured* intentionally. An unhappily pregnant woman was forced to beg for addresses, to find accomplices to her crime, and to risk herself and her body; she had allowed herself to be trapped; she was made to feel it was her fault: "It is difficult to imagine abandonment more frightful than that in which the menace of death is combined with that of crime and shame . . . Pain, illness, and death take on the appearance of a chastisement."[12] The impossibility of escaping one's body, or the experience of that body as a trap, was one of the most vivid examples of what Beauvoir termed "immanence."

One of those to recoil from Beauvoir's stance in 1960 was Weill-Hallé herself, who wanted to steer clear of Boupacha's case.[13] She worried that Beauvoir, for her part, was drawing back from her support for Le Planning Familial. Why, Weill-Hallé asked, would Beauvoir not return her phone calls and letters? She was apprehensive that the famous intellectual, whose name brought Planning audiences to their feet, would skip the press conference called to publicize *The Great Fear of Loving* and the group's cause. Beauvoir did attend the press conference. But in her later account of the event (*The Force of Circumstance*, 1963), she was biting about Planning's timidity. Weill-Hallé appeared "virginal" with blonde hair and a white dress, and the experts assembled—doctors, psychoanalysts, and other "more or less credentialed specialists in matters of the heart"—dutifully accommodated France's code of "modesty" (*pudeur*) and avoided shameful topics. Not one person at the press conference used the terms "birth control" or "contraception," Beauvoir commented caustically. "At the word abortion, they covered their eyes; as for sex, it was nowhere."[14]

Planning did in fact "cover its eyes." The organization had only just given up its former name, "Happy Motherhood" (La Maternité heureuse); it remained very much in the thrall of the politics of improving conjugal life and protecting the "emotional equilibrium" of heterosexual duos.[15] Abortion was the problem and contraception the cure-all; legal birth control would sweep aside all unhealthy impediments to "love" or the happiness of "the couple." Rape and sexual violence had no place in this picture of happy heterosex. Neither did gender or racial inequality or male sexual privilege. Planning steered very clear of any of the connections Beauvoir's work suggested between colonial or racist violence and misogyny, or between sexualized domination and intimacy (or the sexual *tout court*).

In fact, one look at Weill-Hallé's book shows her racism to have been undisguised. The very first of her case studies was titled (with my italics) "She *Could Not* Get Married." The patient is young, bourgeois, of a "discreet elegance." Her face hardens when her obstetrician (Weill-Hallé) tells her she is pregnant. Out of the question to have "this one," she tells the doctor, for she can't marry the father. "He is a black African." In pointed contrast, the next case concerns a woman with what Weill-Hallé calls a "serious boyfriend"— "One Who *Could* Get Married," if only the couple could afford a child.[16] One might say that Weill-Hallé was describing the social pressures of this woman's world, but the language makes clear that she too saw a public revelation of interracial intimacy as unacceptable.

It is not news that family planning movements worldwide often appealed to white, middle-class privilege, racism, and eugenics, the science of improving population. One stark illustration: the 1920 French law that banned contraception and distributing information about contraception never applied to the territories and colonies. According to a legal agreement, "special circumstances" could warrant altering metropolitan laws in the colonies. French officials in Guadeloupe and Martinique worried about how to *reduce* fertility, and in the 1960s they gave Family Planning free rein to set up clinics. Thus contraception was not only legal there; it was free to women over fifteen.[17] Even against this eugenicist biopolitical background, however, Weill-Hallé's racism stands out in its conjuring with the vice of miscegenation and casual assertion of the impossibility of interracial marriage or child raising.

That Beauvoir agreed to write the authorizing preface to Weill-Hallé's book is shocking; the book's racist presuppositions were so widely shared that they were invisible. Planning as an organization did have some claim on Beauvoir's loyalties. What is more, the social workers, family assistants, and medical personnel who staffed its local branches did not necessarily subscribe to these eugenicist views. Planning had to confront the Catholic Church, obviously, but also the Communist Party, which until 1965 insisted the real issue was better wages, working conditions, and housing so that working-class women could have more children. (Whether or not women *wanted* to have more children was not judged an important question.) Beauvoir treated the invitation to preface the book as an occasion to restate her own position, and was either blind to or complicit with the book's racism. I found only one correspondent willing to confront these views, a fact that is telling about the circles of Beauvoir's readers and their racial privileges and assumptions. It is true that the rhetoric of sexual politics would change so quickly in the following decade that Weill-Hallé's book, with its paeans to happy motherhood, heterosexual equilibrium, and eugenics, quickly faded from view. But this passage stuck in the minds of those who later used the book and its preface to underscore the narrow vision and constitutive racism of white European women's feminism.

The Sexual Politics of Radical Feminism

Planning radicalized dramatically in the 1960s, driven to the left mostly by local activists. Those activists smuggled illegal contraceptives into France, sometimes through the same networks that had given clandestine support to the FLN. They defied both French law and Planning's national leadership by setting up clinics to provide information on contraception. The first clinic opened in 1961 in Grenoble, where Planning was directed by Henri Fabre, a veteran of the Resistance and a Trotskyist who had left the Communist Party.[18] In 1967, when what became known as the Neuwirth Law very cautiously began to liberalize access to contraception, Planning's ranks grew. When it became clear how strictly the French state was trying to limit the manufacturing of contraceptives, their market, and public access to them, Planning's membership expanded again. The obvious shortcomings of the new law and efforts to sabotage it encouraged polemics, more publicity, and defiance.[19] So did the papal encyclical of 1968, which condemned contraception and the loosening of sexual mores; the encyclical infuriated not only activists but also many people with no particular political affiliation who expected the pope to temper the church's position and to accommodate, in some small measure, the well-established everyday use of contraception by Catholic men and women in Europe.

After 1968, however, Planning was outflanked on the left by the upstart MLF, which was imbued with the urgent, take-charge-now spirit of the global unrest of that year. Its founding members were brilliant political provocateurs. The MLF made the central issue not just contraception—and emphatically not "happy motherhood" or "planning"—but instead sexuality, sexual freedom and pleasure, and the psychic structures of femininity. The MLF infused feminism with an entirely new dynamism.

What had happened? How do we account for a transformation so rapid that it seems almost a wrinkle in time? The legendary May 1968 in France combined an explosion of student protest with one of the biggest general labor strikes in history. The rebellion had many targets: the relentless pace of production during the postwar economic boom, the failure of economic expansion to provide a better quality of life, rigid hierarchies in the workplace, heavy-handed regulation of state-controlled radio and television, overcrowded and underfunded universities, paternalistic rules governing student life, and the authorities' ready recourse to police repression. Rebellion in 1968 was international; even a short inventory of hotspots would include Rome, Mexico City, Tokyo, São Paulo, Berkeley, and Chicago as well as Paris. The Prague revolt against Soviet rule and the Tet offensive in Vietnam were among the most portentous events of the year. The American war in Vietnam and the civil rights movement were the most glaring examples of the hollow promises of postwar democracy and they mobilized international opposition. In France, the Vietnam war revived memories of France's own colonial violence. The French government, like other states, was shaken by 1968 but regrouped, though its image and legitimacy were tarnished. The mobilization of young people remained. So did the new attention to personal liberties and the impatience with long-overdue reforms and reformism in general. The heady sense of internationalism also endured; it infused the women's movement with a new radicalism.

The new feminists drew from the same sources as other radicals of their generation: the critical theorists who were using Freud to reread Marx and rework conceptions of human subjectivity and revolutionary practice. Wilhelm Reich was only one of these Freudian Marxists, but his work became especially important for young radicals because he so passionately believed that youth stood at the vanguard of revolution and that youthful sexual desire had transformative potential.[20] Sexual life was a locus of emotional, psychological, and bodily oppression and unhappiness. Freeing youthful desires was not a trivial distraction from real political concerns; banishing shame, fears, fetishes, and taboos around sexuality had wider ramifications. "The struggle to solve the sexual question of young people is tied to the struggle to overturn the capitalist regime," declared Reich.[21] His major work had been written in the 1930s, but by 1968 he had so captured a generation's attention that his work was mimeographed, bootlegged, excerpted, commented on in conferences, discussed in reading groups, and translated all over Europe. When Reich's championing of sexual freedom was joined to the critical theory of everyday life and the "decolonization of the soul," it was electrifying. The sexual radicals of '68 often cited Reich when they called for making contraceptives available to everyone, including minors, without a prescription, and for decriminalizing homosexuality.

The role of sexual subjectivity in the student movement of 1968 was eye-catching. So were the glaring blind spots and sexism of that movement, and those did much to metabolize feminist anger. As one early radical feminist acerbically observed, the leaders of May '68 had made much of the "sexual poverty" of student life. *That* impoverishment was "laughable" (*dérisoire*) compared to what women lived through. What about "frigidity, conjugal duty, rape, accidental sterilization?"[22] The new left's blinkers on this score could hardly be more painfully obvious. Indeed, the famous pamphlet she was citing, "On the Poverty of Student Life: Considered in Its Economic, Political, Psychological, Sexual, and Particularly Intellectual Aspects, and a Modest Proposal for Its Remedy" (Situationist International, 1966), is a helpful reminder of the discourse from which both radical feminism and gay liberation recoiled in anger. (The Situationists were inspired by Henri Lefebvre's critique of everyday life and his call to reclaim the humanity of urban and capitalist space. Their slogans, such as "take your desires for reality," became the poetry of the streets in 1968.) In the pamphlet, "sex" figured as a stand-in for a thwarted and repressed but potentially revolutionary life force—for real as opposed to "manufactured" or "colonized" desire. The pamphlet scoffed at the timidity of "bohemians," who dared not venture beyond "most traditional practices of eros and love, reproducing at this level the general relations of class society . . . Even old ladies in the provinces could do better." The pamphlet judged bourgeois rebels dismayingly conformist, "impotent," and afflicted by a deadening "menopause of the spirit." Priests "sodomizing thousands of students" figured the pamphlet's attack on Catholicism.[23] The Reichian theories of sexual subjectivity and revolution made very little room for gender or sexual difference. When reduced to slogans and tied to an overwhelmingly male student movement, they became obnoxiously masculinist. If sexuality was the privileged expression of freedom, women's vulnerabilities (or the asymmetry of the sexes) could hardly be more portentous or the limits of the sexual revolution more obvious. This is the context in which legalized abortion became so important.

The new MLF, born out of a smattering of women's groups in 1968, was unimpressed by earlier legal reforms. The group did not tarry over the obvious shortcomings of the 1967 Neuwirth Law. Unlike Planning, the MLF was not interested in "widening permission" for women to use contraception or liberalizing medically authorized "therapeutic" abortion. It offered a different biopolitics, a repudiation of the state's "claim to control demography," making the issue a matter for women.[24] Unlike Planning, the MLF put women themselves, not medical and scientific experts, at the center of the debate and decision making. Unlike Planning, which courted respectability and connections, the MLF deliberately provoked. Unlike Planning, the new movement did not see contraception as the *solution* to the *problem* of abortion.[25] The *problem* was the freedom of the body. Abortion was the "habeas corpus" of the new generation, wrote a commentator at the time: the great writ, the fundamental freedom of the subject and body from the state.[26] For the new women's movement, fully legal abortion was not an "ultimate goal" but only "its most elementary demand."[27]

The demand had a bracing shock value. Here is how one of the movement's founders describes the bold discussion at one of the early meetings (1970) of what would become the MLF: "We talked about abortion at the first meeting I went to. We gave one another addresses. Abortion was a dangerous subject; you had to have plenty of confidence to talk about it like that in a big group. That was Monique Wittig [who had spoken], I remember. I was thrilled."[28] Abortion, she continued, was as dramatic and high stakes as any cause embraced by the left: "Here was a real tragedy for women, a tragedy that involved their bodies, a scandal that cost lives. This was a hard-hitting subject. I couldn't believe I was meeting women who dared take it on." The provocation was fearless and deliberate. At issue were the primal psychic structures of femininity: conceptions of what it meant to inhabit a woman's body, and the habits of feeling surrounding love, sexual desire, femininity, the self, and one's future.[29]

In 1970 Beauvoir was a prestigious intellectual, but more a figurehead than a firebrand. By her own account, she stood on the sidelines during 1968. She found the student occupation of the Sorbonne disconcertingly chaotic. But a daring and radical women's movement was now raising issues on which she had well-established positions. The politics of abortion figured prominently in the first manifestos of radical feminism. Why was abortion illegal, and what did that say about the position of women? asked the first article in "The Liberation of Women: Year 0," published as a special issue of *Partisans* in 1970. Quite a lot, Beauvoir had been saying for two decades. Thus, when a group from the MLF started to draft a splashy statement on abortion rights in 1971, she was an obvious recruit, and she threw herself into the cause.[30] In April 1971, on the front page of the *Nouvel Observateur*, 343 women declared: "Every year in France, 1 million women have abortions . . . I am one of them." The manifesto was signed by stars from the worlds of French letters, stage, and screen (Beauvoir, her sister Hélène, Marguerite Duras, Catherine Deneuve, Françoise Sagan); feminist militants like Monique Wittig, Christiane Rochefort,

Christine Delphy, Cathy Bernheim, and Anne Zelensky; and hundreds of less-well-known women. It proved spectacularly successful. The satirical journal *Charlie Hebdo* gleefully rechristened it "The Manifesto of 343 Sluts!" capturing the moment's exuberantly in-your-face character, or militant shamelessness. As in the Boupacha case, Beauvoir joined forces again with Gisèle Halimi to form a committee that would provide legal defense for those who signed the petition should they need it.

While Beauvoir did not organize the manifesto, its tone and argument were very Beauvoirian: determined to shake up categories of "decency" and declaring that women would no longer live their bodies or condition as shameful. It confronted head-on the contempt for women that lay behind relegating abortion to the shadows: "Abortion: This is something that concerns women [*bonnes femmes*, which is condescending]; it's like cooking, or laundry—something dirty. Fighting for legal and free abortion is seen as pathetic. Women are always trailing the smell of the hospital, food, or shit." This was a nicely pungent version of the argument that abortion has almost always been tolerated as long as it remains illegal, confined to the shadows, and does not become an occasion for collective deliberation and knowledge. The manifesto declared that women would no longer be "shamed" for being "caught" or "trapped" (*prise*). In French, *prise* was a common idiom for getting pregnant, one that captured the riskiness of sex for women (what Beauvoir had theorized as the inescapability of the body), and also the sense that as a woman, you had tried to get away with something, namely, using your body for sexual pleasure.

It bears emphasis that the language of the manifesto was broader and more radical than our current discourse of "reproductive rights." It took aim at a social division of labor that delegated to women responsibility for managing invisible and undervalued affective and physical labor—the backstage work of society. It focused on internalized misogyny and a dark landscape of the "abjection" of the feminine. Against that backdrop, the changes and reforms of the postwar period—economic developments that brought more women into the labor force and labor unions, consumerist prosperity that prompted coy discussion of desire in women's magazines and media, halting liberalization of laws on contraception, and changing norms that led universities, reluctantly, to allow women students in male students' dormitories—were so paltry as to be beside the point. If sexuality was to be a good, or, as it would be put in liberal discourse, healthy, it could not be a trap. This was the context in which abortion became such a powerful symbol and also such a resonant issue.

Journalists were astonished by the extent and the intensity of popular support for the new abortion campaign to legalize abortion. In the words of one reporter: "Who knows how, but this movement has become a mass organization . . . Even the demonstrations against the Algerian war never produced anything like this. For the first time, the protest is not simply intellectual and political. It is based on popular opinion. This is a problem that touches every woman in her flesh."[31]

As the manifesto, countless feminist tracts, and letters to Beauvoir showed, abortion was thoroughly bound up in other matters that "touched women in the flesh": discrimination, disdain, and open misogyny in the labor force and at home. "You don't call this work?" asked *Le Torchon Brûle* under a sketch of a woman bent over the floor with a mop, clutching her back, and surrounded by her crying children. "Enough!," reads the caption. Wrote feminist Christiane Rochefort in an accompanying article, "We've shed enough blood, we've obeyed your laws long enough, we're tired of serving you. We've done enough to fill your Métros, your supermarkets, your housing projects, your unemployment offices, your insane asylums—we want to be free."[32] *Le Torchon Brûle* (literally, the burning dishrag) was the most irreverent of the new feminist newspapers in the 1970s. Its title means roughly "it's war between them," and might best be translated as "the house is on fire." *Le Torchon Brûle* brilliantly mined for comic political effect the same anger that ran through letters to Beauvoir.

The Manifesto in the Intimate Public

After the manifesto, as during the Boupacha affair in 1960, Beauvoir's mailbox overflowed with testimony. Many letter writers were eager to endorse the taboo-defying courage of those who had signed. "Bravo to all, especially those who are well known, for your courage!" wrote one who described herself bitterly as one of those supposedly "happy mothers" who wanted nothing to do with abortion rights. She had had an abortion after bearing five children: "If more testimony would be helpful, you can use my name." The manifesto read as an invitation to testify. "When I discovered that other women were starting to say out loud what I think to

Figure 4. The first issue of *Le Torchon Brûle*, the radical feminist journal published monthly from 1971 to 1973. (*Menstruel* is a play on *mensuel*, or monthly.) The artists who drew for the journal were known only by their first names.

© Marine, with thanks to the Bibliothèque Marguerite Durand, Paris.

myself, I cried. I was not alone," wrote another. She spelled out the toll that the law and social contempt had taken on her body. Like others, she was furious at what she identified as systematic exploitation by "male society," writing: "I have had four children without once feeling pleasure in making love . . . Male society has robbed me; it has robbed me of my strength, my youth . . . [I]t has made me have abortions three times, squatting in the bathroom." Wrote another, "I've had two abortions on a dirty crowded [clinic] table, and I've done it to myself as well," adding, "When you've been through what I have, and you think that there are others out there sobbing in despair for the same reason, you want to strangle these men." The thing that "makes me mad," wrote one infuriated by the web of complicity and denial that surrounded abortion, is that women make the sacrifices, men are hypocrites, and "no one really denounces the system—even women who've had abortions."[33]

Many who wrote Beauvoir were particularly galled by the availability of abortion elsewhere, which highlighted French hypocrisy and encouraged exploitation and fraud. "I've had two abortions in Switzerland, with a medical referral . . . We should be able to have abortions in France under the same conditions," argued one woman. Another angrily recounted her recent experience in London, in a clinic to which she had been referred by her French doctor. Abortion had been decriminalized in England in 1967, the same year the French state only grudgingly lifted its ban on contraception. The legal differences had entirely predictable results: "You probably already know that London is swarming with abortion agencies that are directed towards patients from other countries . . . Let me tell you right out: these organizations flagrantly exploit the panic, shame, and ignorance of foreigners." She continued:

> The doctor (woman) in France said I was 16 weeks pregnant and gave me the address of an agency in London that makes arrangements to get an abortion in London. . .
>
> Now I realize that the doctor who gave me the address didn't know how the agency worked and how much they charged . . .
>
> I spent a whole week at the office of the London Advisory Agency, 25 York St., London SW, tel. 935–0361. First, they refused to take a money transfer; then the money transfer was taking too long; I had to go back to France, get the money, and come back to London. Finally, I had cash and got the operation the next day.

The majority of this letter writer's fellow patients were French and German: "Like me, they were completely panicked, and totally dependent on this organization to get them out of their jam." Two women secretaries—one French, one German—worked at the agency. Two men ran it. The agency asked at first for 3,500 francs, and then 3,250; in the end, she paid 3,000 francs, 1,000 of which went to the agency as a commission simply for making the appointment.[34] "I didn't expect angels of charity," she wrote, "but I was shocked . . . It is a racket." The nurses in London let her know that she could have called the doctor directly; in fact, the doctors preferred not to have to deal with agencies. So the correspondent passed on to Beauvoir the doctor's name, address, office, and home telephone numbers. "I wonder how many French doctors have handed French women over to these swindlers," she asked bitterly.[35] The answer was a great many. Between 1972 and 1973, 35,000 French women had traveled to England to have an abortion.[36]

A French woman who administered one of those London agencies wrote to Beauvoir offering a similar account, although she believed that at least England "had spared these women the humiliation and degradation of illegal and criminal abortion." She also prided herself on comforting women seeking abortions when they arrived, "embarrassed, worried, and anxious." As she said, rich French women did not need to travel across the channel; "they could easily pay a gynecological assistant to do this little operation" in France. Poor women, by contrast, were driven to "charlatans" and fell prey to "lucrative scams."[37]

The political sentiments expressed in these letters were not confined to metropolitan radicals. In 1949 Beauvoir's bluntness about abortion had made her unusual. By 1970–71, testimony, confession, and opinion about abortion poured out in the pages of women's magazines, across the airwaves on radio programs for women, and elsewhere in the intimate public. The daily write-in and phone-in afternoon women's radio program hosted by the psychoanalytically minded journalist Menie Grégoire, which launched in 1967, is a sterling example, and Grégoire's audience sometimes overlapped with Beauvoir's.[38] Grégoire devoted hours of airtime to questions and comments from her listeners on the hypocrisy of legislators, the medical profession as a body, and men in general; the censoriousness and willful ignorance of most ob-gyns; the taboos surrounding reproductive basics; and the public ignorance those taboos produced—the misinformation about hormone shots, and folk remedies for "getting your period back." Grégoire was no sexual radical; on the contrary, she was conservative about the family, marriage, and the need for heterosexual "equilibrium." She is an excellent example of authoritarian neo-Freudianism. But she did not hesitate to support the right to abortion and was not reluctant to discuss it. The fact that she gave so much time to the subject measures the overlap between the themes of radical feminism and those of the provinces.

The intimate public now spoke in a feminist vernacular. Grégoire's listeners were overwhelmingly working class, from the provinces and the industrial centers (*grands ensembles*) of northern France. Many were also Catholic. Their letters and phone calls mixed folksy-sounding expressions like "You know, you don't have children like you bake a cake" with recognizably new feminist claims that "a woman's body is her own." They were defiantly matter-of-fact: "Religion, the government, and the pope have no business in this."[39] A devoutly Catholic mother of three was unafraid to say that despite her religious beliefs, she was "still for abortion." A self-described "practicing Catholic with 5 children" who had just had an abortion wrote, "I don't regret anything," adding, "I don't feel like I've committed a crime."[40] Grégoire refused to dispense the addresses of abortion providers, but that did not stop hundreds of listeners from requesting them or passing on information about clinics in England and Switzerland. "I also have a niece with two children who went to have an abortion in Switzerland," one listener told Grégoire. "I can give anyone the address; in the last few years it cost about 150,000, and you have to bring your family book [*livret de famille*], because the doctors will give you an abortion only if you've already had two children. I'm writing this letter so you can give this information to the unfortunate women who are in the same situation."[41]

Women continued to plead for help or muddle through on their own. The accumulation of requests like the ones that follow is remarkable testimony about the mood of a historical moment. While the anger was audible, change still seemed a *very* long way away.

To Beauvoir, from a woman from the upscale suburbs of Paris: "Excuse my indiscretion, but I urgently need to have a *very short* conversation with you. Honestly, five minutes will do, but I cannot put it in writing . . . I live in the suburbs, with a large family, and I am in Paris today. If you could give a few minutes of your time you will help me more than you could imagine."[42]

To Grégoire, with more anger and resolve, from a young woman with a fifteen-month-old child, pregnant again: "I loved my husband. I didn't know how to keep him away from me. I swallowed every kind of pill; the doctor told me to come back [for a D&C] when I was bleeding." [In other words, the doctor would give her a D&C if she were already miscarrying.] "So I dealt with it all on my own [*je me suis débrouillée toute seule*]."[43]

To Beauvoir: "I am writing you with a request. I am one month pregnant, and for financial reasons, I cannot keep this fourth child."[44]

To Grégoire: "I know that a lot of women 'manage' [*se débrouillent*], as they say. Aren't they worried about their own lives? I only see one solution—a legal abortion with a doctor, but where do you go for that? Despite all the talk about this matter, it's hard to find an address. I'm thinking of Switzerland. Can you get me some information? I'm only two months pregnant and want to do something right away."[45]

The manifesto of 343, then, was only one spark in an explosion of testimony.[46] The testimony was unapologetic, coming as it did from defiant *débrouillards*, who had long been capable of "managing" on their own and were now no longer willing to remain in the shadows, quietly shouldering the burden of being discreet.

"Your Sexual Revolution Is Not Ours"

Equally striking, and strikingly counterintuitive, was the lesbian and gay mobilization behind the campaign to legalize abortion. The FHAR (Front Homosexuel d'Action Révolutionnaire, or Homosexual Front for Revolutionary Action) first came together at a protest against a right-to-life rally in February 1971. The rally was called by a prominent pediatrician and geneticist who opposed legalized *contraception*, let alone abortion. Feminist and gay militants, including Françoise d'Eaubonne and Pierre Hahn, showed up to protest, demanding abortion as a woman's right. Scuffles followed. Heads were knocked. In the aftermath, the group around Eaubonne and Hahn named itself FHAR.[47] Its manifesto, the "Letter to Those Who Think They Are Normal," published in the famous twelfth issue of the leftist newspaper *Tout!* later that year (April 1971), declared that contempt for women and for homosexuals were of a piece: both were the "doormats" of bourgeois culture. *Tout!* took on "the sacrosanct institutions of family and patriarchal monogamy" and what was "stupidly called the law of nature." It rejected normalizing psychology or "Oedipalism" and cast a very skeptical eye on the limited pleasures of heterosexuality and compulsory reproduction. It also published the manifesto of 343 "men who have been buggered by Arabs," confronting the sexualization of racial Others and, by the same token, the racialization of sexual Others.[48] The French writer Frédéric Martel calls FHAR the "bastard child" of women's liberation, but it might be more apt to think of the two movements as siblings, with the proviso that every child sometimes feels as if she or he was born into a different family.[49]

While the battle for legal abortion of 1971 championed women's agency, lives, and choices, then, it was not necessarily either female or heterosexual. It was thoroughly entangled in the feminist and gay critique of the ongoing "sexual revolution" and the male New Left's "aberrant cult of virility." Family Planning had emphasized foresight, responsibility, and happy heterosexuality; lesbian and gay groups sounded the bolder themes of bodily freedom and self-sovereignty. The alliance between the different constituencies was fragile, however. The very resonance and drama of abortion as an issue threatened to drown out other concerns. The feminist and lesbian Cathy Bernheim captured the radical appeal of women's liberation as well as anyone. For her, abortion distilled better than any other issue the larger demand to reclaim the body, to speak concretely about women's lives, and, perhaps most important, to dramatize the self-evidently *political* character of personal life. In fact, Bernheim mused later on, abortion rights did so much political work for feminism that she and other lesbians in the movement kept their sexual identities and preferences on the back shelf, concealing "a fact that for some of us was at least as important as the conditions of abortion in France."[50]

Debunking myths about conventional hetero-sex, female "frigidity," and vaginal orgasm, claiming alternative pleasures and sexualities—all this was central to the women's liberation project and could sweep together lesbian and heterosexual women. In the words of Anne Zelensky, "We were no longer condemned to mono-sexuality."[51] Christine Rochefort called the dominant culture's insistence that orgasms were vaginal a form of damaging "psychological warfare." Heterosexual coitus was as bound by social convention as any social act, Rochefort acerbically noted; the point was to "question the present system of fucking."[52]

We are a very long way from Weill-Hallé, Happy Motherhood, and Family Planning. Representatives of that earlier feminist tradition, indignant, wrote Beauvoir, telling her to rein in the MLF feminists whose positions she endorsed by signing petitions and joining marches. Mireille Godet, the daughter of neo-Malthusiam and birth control advocate Nelly Roussel (1878–1922), seethed in indignation at the "scatter-brained girls of the MLF" and their "so-called feminist publications."[53] Godet fumed that *Le Torchon Brûle* peddled only "obscenities." Talk such as that only "played into the hands of those who confuse advocating contraception with promoting pornography." That confusion had prompted the law of 1920 banning contraception in the first place, she argued. "Feminism can easily be degraded." Godet repeated her point for emphasis: "We have to be careful . . . serious, and careful."[54]

Beauvoir had never cared about being careful. But she had her own reservations about the new feminist stances on sexuality and pleasure. In her discussion of feminism in *All Said and Done*, the last volume of her memoir, published in the fall of 1972, she made a point of weighing in on the issue of orgasm, calling radical (and especially lesbian) feminists "dogmatic." Now, as so many times before, she felt compelled to correct her allies and to restate her position: "Some feminists claim that vaginal orgasm is a myth and the only real pleasure comes from clitoral orgasm, and that contrary to what Freud says, a woman has no need of a man for sexual pleasure." But some women found "penetration" more "rich and satisfying." In any event, she continued, sex was about persons, not bodies or genitals, and orgasm was a classic case of a "psychosomatic phenomenon."[55] More baffling, she added to this restatement a footnote to the work of the French sexologist Gérard Zwang, who buttressed his theory that women responded to vaginal stimulation with ethnographic evidence gathered in Polynesia and the Andes.[56]

Beauvoir's radical interlocutors and correspondents would have none of this. "I'm not really persuaded by what you write about vaginal orgasm," wrote a young feminist from Luxembourg. She had just spent what she described as a lovely languorous rainy afternoon enjoying *All Said and Done*. But why, she asked, was Beauvoir citing a long passage from Zwang on Polynesian and Andean vaginal masturbation? "As far as

I'm concerned, the fact that Polynesian, Andean, and other peoples have decorated penises (or whatever they shove into women's vaginas) doesn't prove much at all, especially since, as always, men want to exaggerate the importance of this kind of physical contact . . . Personally, I have to confess that this kind of stuff never did anything for me, but I have felt powerful clitoral orgasms."[57] Women faked orgasm all the time, this correspondent continued. As she pointed out, Beauvoir herself had explained how women could internalize cultural expectations about the pleasures of penetration and hetero-sex. The letter writer found Anne Koedt, author of the already famous "Myth of the Vaginal Orgasm," vastly more persuasive than either Zwang or Beauvoir. Nonetheless, she was appreciative and admiring: "What you have written will stay with me all my life." She closed by remarking impishly, "As always, reading what you write gives me *courage* and *pleasure*."[58]

The Seductions of Sisterhood

Beauvoir's letters show how much cross-cutting currents of homosexuality, homoeroticism, and homosociality buoyed the women's liberation movement and reoriented its understanding of sexuality. Correspondents who had been following newspaper coverage of feminism asked Beauvoir to "put them in touch with lesbians in the movement" or declared their "passionate love for women."[59] Feelings like these infused "sisterhood" with a new energy. Beauvoir has been charged, for good reason, with philosophical incoherence on lesbianism, with an inability to understand woman as anything besides the Other of man or lesbianism as anything but a rebellion against male domination. She has been indicted as well for her timid refusal to acknowledge her affairs with women.[60] Many readers in the 1960s and 1970s saw through Beauvoir's subterfuges and detected these relationships. Even without reading between the lines, however, the archive of letters shows that the story of Beauvoir's messages on lesbianism is complicated.

The Second Sex's discussion of the body as part of a "situation," and a fundamentally alienated situation at that, had long made Beauvoir seem an appropriate confidant for people reckoning with misfit experiences of body and sexuality. As one had written in 1956 about *The Second Sex*:

"For me, your book was a revelation, from the point of view of truths you bring out and the clear and precise way you lay them out." In the early years, those confidences, particularly from women, were oblique and metaphorical: one called herself "a rare bird" and virtually asked to be drawn out on the subject. "[I]t is so difficult to talk about oneself, one can only do it by answering questions." Other confidants were bravely straightforward, though fiercely secretive, such as this one from 1962, aware of the possibility of sex-change surgery:

> I am what is called a pervert, a lesbian. My friend and I have loved each other for years . . . We can only meet for about six weeks each year. The partings are agonizing. Could you give me the name of a doctor who could perform a surgical operation on me to change me into a man? . . . If you typed the name and address and put it into an envelope without signing it, that would relieve you of all responsibility.[61]

She was from England, and enclosed an addressed envelope and international postage.

By the mid- and late 1960s, the eroded tradition of "discretion" as well as a greater familiarity with the newer languages and concepts of sexuality made Beauvoir's interlocutors more inclined to actually engage her arguments. Their letters cast a revealing light on the deeply mixed messages of Beauvoir's work. On the one hand, as one letter writer pointed out, Beauvoir seemed to condescend to a young woman's love for another woman; while *The Second Sex* lingered over lesbian pleasures, it presented those pleasures as fleeting, youthful, or immature—very much a stage on the way to something else.[62] As the letter writer pointed out, Beauvoir said nothing about women who did not go to the next stage, or "evolve," but rather chose to "pursue the rites of Sappho . . . Tell me," she asked, do "you also consider my love the love of a 'beginner'? Do you really think it is impossible that I should love so much?" Several others fit themselves into the stage schema that Beauvoir had proposed, describing themselves as "unfinished" (*inachevée*).[63]

On the other hand, many correspondents zeroed in on precisely those passages in *The Second Sex* where Beauvoir debunked the reigning theories that psychosexual development should lead to heterosexuality, or the points where she took a stand against binary distinctions between hetero- and homosexuality or the interpretation of homosexuality as a struggle with a somehow alien self. She insisted that as far as nature was concerned, "every woman is homosexual."[64] That argument found many echoes. Finally, her passages on the natural and undeniable pleasures of touching a woman were quite intelligible to Beauvoir's inner circle, and they caught the attention of readers attuned to this kind of signal. As Michael Lucey has so well observed, Beauvoir's chapter "The Lesbian" could be read in any number of ways depending on the reader's situation; it was at once queer-friendly and impossible to pin down. As Lucey writes, its "intelligibility (to the extent that it is even clearly being sought after) is never confirmed, is always in doubt."[65]

Beauvoir's friendship and admiration for Violette Leduc, who was openly lesbian, was for many readers the frankest invitation to confidences.[66] After Beauvoir wrote the preface to Leduc's best-selling memoir *La bâtarde* in 1964, she received a series of letters from young women recounting their furtive lesbian relationships, their strategies for sneaking letters past their parents, or the subterfuge of going on vacations together as "friends." According to several letters, to mention Leduc was a quick way for young women to come out to each other.[67] For many reasons, then, Beauvoir seemed an appropriate person to whom one could express feelings that jumped the banks of conventional heterosexuality.

A striking number of correspondents borrowed Beauvoir's terms to articulate their multiple sexual desires. Wrote a thirty-eight-year-old woman, the mother of three children, "I have long been considered a homosexual, partly because of my appearance, but more because of my advanced thinking." Now she knew that homosexuality was "not an abnormality [*tare*], but a natural instinct, and often temporary." She knew, too, that "while one can be passionately in love with a man, that does not make sexual relations with him self-evident . . . [O]ne can have heterosexual relations and also accept passions for women." Wrote another, "I am both: hetero- and homosexual." A British woman who had started publishing a small magazine on women's psychological health (*Arena Three*) and also founded the Minorities Research Trust explained that she had never seen herself as an "exclusivist," and that her self-understanding was common. She reported on the letters she had received: "I have a great many letters from men and women of all kinds, many of them in difficulties—at home, at work, in marriage, school, university, in society generally—because of their not being able to conform to the 'exclusively heterosexual' image. In the main they seek reassurance that they are not alone in this backsliding from the official norm."[68]

Letter writers worked around the exclusiveness of hetero- and homosexuality by dwelling on how intimacy and friendship blurred with eroticism. Another mother of three (not surprisingly, many of the women who were coming out to Beauvoir had been married to men) wrote, strikingly, of a new and disconcertingly powerful friendship with another woman: "I have never experienced a feeling like this . . . [W]here are the borders between a passionate friendship, tenderness, and love? For two years neither of us has been able to see clearly." This is a *très belle histoire*, she wrote. "It makes me happy, but it also worries and troubles me."[69]

One of the most detailed letters along these lines came from a young woman in her twenties. She had passed through what she called the "normal stages" that Beauvoir laid out in *The Second Sex*. "But from the beginning, I knew, or maybe I should say I desired—that I wanted to be other. I never felt—I mean physically—more 'woman' than 'man' or 'man' than 'woman' . . . I have decided not to close myself off in either category." What is more, she had never thought that her "womanhood should automatically require this cortege of duties [*ce cortège de devoirs*], respect for men, bodily suffering, and so on." She had long resisted any experience of "the flesh" (*le charnel*), which she found alienating. From time to time, she caught herself looking at the face or body of a woman, but recoiled and "felt a profound disgust with [herself]." She had never experimented, she said, for she didn't fit what she understood to be the profile of a lesbian: "I have never felt the visceral hate for a man that lesbians feel. . . . No hate, just fear of certain acts, fear of rape, of penetration, horror of possession. . . . There is too much violence in heterosexual love, a battle that tends to affirm the inferiority of the woman." The letter writer was plainly tired of the thin orthodoxy of left thinking about her situation, namely, that lesbianism was a subset of the oppression of women, itself a product of the real problem, which was capitalism. She wrote, wearily, as if it were a litany she knew by heart: "It goes without saying that the present condition of women is tied to the evolution of capitalist society, and that the alienation of women (which is the principal reason for my revolt) is inseparable from a social and economic context." Yet she was not convinced that "socialist societies had completely resolved the problem."[70] If she was writing to Beauvoir, it was because she believed Beauvoir's work, unlike the left orthodoxy, acknowledged the body's ambivalences and the complexities of desire. We sense her impatience as well with a certain *feminist* orthodoxy, namely, that lesbianism had to be understood as a woman's revolt against male domination. Monique Wittig's later argument that lesbianism had to be conceptualized outside a binary conception of gender—that "a lesbian is not a woman"—would have helped her articulate her objections to the orthodoxies more clearly. She reported, poignantly, that she had fallen in love with a woman who was "panicked at the idea of being in any way classified as a lesbian." She had had to accept a "normal friendship" with the object of her affections. Like other readers wrestling with understanding their sexual misfitness and figuring out how to live it, she found in Beauvoir's work ample reason to confide in her.

A longing for intimacy had always run through the correspondence: since the 1950s, readers declared to Beauvoir that they knew her, or that they wanted to know her better, that they *had* to meet her, and, very often, that reading her writing had made them love her. The gulf between reader and author, especially when the author was a celebrated intellectual, often made those professions of attachment sound like schoolgirl crushes. In several cases, however, a bolder tone came through, and by the early 1970s it could be quite openly sexual.

A lovely example comes in a series of letters from early 1973, from a woman whose political and artistic circles overlapped with Beauvoir's. They had several friends in common, including Françoise d'Eaubonne. This correspondent wrote seven letters over two months. She introduced herself to Beauvoir and they conversed by phone; she wrote Beauvoir about a woman on whom she had a crush, and she copied out and sent to Beauvoir the letters she and the woman had exchanged. She was also eager to plunge into politics. Eaubonne had "really shaken up the little world of the MLF and the FHAR." She was going with Eaubonne to a meeting of Choisir, and then they were off to plaster the walls with feminist posters. "Finally, some action! We were suffocating—if only this will last." (This was during the legislative elections of 1973.) She met Beauvoir and was smitten: "Madame my darling I am thinking of you and my heart is jealous . . . I want to hold you very close . . . I want to leave everything outside the door—your Sartre, your Claude, your Nelson, your Sylvie, your leftists—open your door for me." Beauvoir had apparently given her reason to believe the feelings were mutual, for she continued: "And should you want to meet me as well, not for some reason or another, not from kindness, but from the heart, and because of the heart—[my] heart is beating, trembling, troubled; one short note will make my heart leap with happiness. Let's be simple. I am waiting. ["I am waiting" is in English.] So YES? Soon? Alone?"[71] As it turned out, she settled for an abiding friendship with Beauvoir. But her letter, like so many others, brilliantly captures the whirlwind of feminist politics, lesbian and gay camaraderie, and the passions of sisterhood that characterized this historical moment.

How one's sexual subjectivity should flow into politics was not always so wonderfully simple. In the middle of the upheaval of May 1968, a young man involved in the homophile organization Arcadie asked Beauvoir if she would participate in a colloquium on "homosexuality in contemporary society." He added apologetically: "I know well that much more important problems demand your attention, and *should* entirely mobilize mine. In the moment of the Vietnam War, spending our time on our little problems can seem inappropriate or frivolous, especially as those who talk about and debate these problems always have a faint air of ridiculousness—in the French cultural context." But discrimination was real, and he was taking up the project of gay rights even though he was slightly "embarrassed" to do so.[72]

Another gay man was less apologetic but no less conflicted. "There is such turmoil in my head," he wrote, "that I scarcely know how to raise the sensitive problem this letter is about . . . But I know you have an open mind, and for a long time I have wanted to confide in you. You were the first person to make me conscious of all this bourgeois shit," by which he meant class-ridden society. He had been radicalized by May '68 but quickly found other militants to be "sectarian." He continued: "I am homosexual. Is sexuality something entirely secondary? I don't think so. I think it has its place in the happiness (or unhappiness) of each." The emergence of the FHAR had helped him reach new conclusions. "I don't think anyone can doubt this movement's revolutionary credentials. What's more, we—homosexuals—are exploited by a society based on *famille travail patrie*" (Vichy France's infamous mantra: Family, Work, and Country).[73] But could this movement really be his only political engagement? he asked Beauvoir.

The letters register extraordinary transformations afoot in the intimate public and also within radical movements. Letter writers raised newly pressing questions about priorities, commitments, and ethics. They knew they were straying from the kinds of politics and political identities Beauvoir had long championed: socialist, antifascist, and anti-imperial. They were naming and inhabiting new structures of feeling and thought, providing the vocabulary for a pluralized politics. They were doing that *against* the grain of some of her ideas and in political argument with her. Her visibly wavering Marxism, her new embrace of feminism, and her obvious sympathy for the varieties of sexual desire made her, now, a valuable interlocutor for many trying to bring their sexual selves and the new politics into alignment.

Bobigny and a Tale of Two Trials

In the fall of 1972 Beauvoir published the last volume of her memoir, *All Said and Done*. As it happened, that volume came out at the same time as the now famous Bobigny trial. Bobigny was what is called a "judicial event." It involved two trials and five accused: first, Marie-Claire Chevalier, a seventeen-year-old woman on trial for having an abortion; and next and separately Marie-Claire's mother, Michèle Chevalier, and three of her colleagues for complicity in abortion. For the government to bring these charges in 1972, against the backdrop of the popular mobilization I have sketched, was bound to create a scandal, and it did. Marie-Claire had been raped, and she was informed on by the young man who had raped her when the police picked him up for something else. Marie-Claire's mother had taken her to a gynecologist, who did not refuse to perform an abortion but demanded an astronomical sum to do so— three times her mother's monthly salary. Her mother reached out to a neighbor and her fellow workers. Unsurprisingly, by word of mouth they found a woman who knew (more or less) how to perform abortions and agreed to do so for one quarter of the price. Marie-Claire's ordeal took sadly common bad turns. The woman came to Marie-Claire's apartment five times, each time inserting a probe; after two weeks Marie Claire, hemorrhaging and with a fever from an infection, ended up in a public clinic; the clinic demanded 1,000 francs for a D&C; her mother wrote a check; the check bounced; the clinic reported her; and the police started to investigate.

The class dimensions of the case could hardly have been starker: a wealthy woman would simply have paid the 4,500 francs the gynecologist wanted or gone to Switzerland or England to get an abortion. Michèle Chevalier was a single mother with three daughters. The family lived in a two-bedroom apartment in rent-controlled housing, which Michèle left every day at 11 am for work, returning at 8 pm. All of the women accused were working class, employees of the RATP, the Parisian transportation administration. In fact, their networks of underground knowledge ran along the number nine line of the Paris Métro, where they were all employed. None of them denied or apologized for what they had done. The mother did not regret helping Marie-Claire decide to abort. The woman who did the abortion had learned the procedure on herself when her husband had told her to "deal with it" (*débrouille-toi*).[74] The trial also exposed the divisions within the medical establishment, showing many doctors to be either corrupt (gouging desperate clients) or disgusted with the law, which they considered cruel and ineffective.[75] The schools offered no sex education.

The lead defense lawyer in the Bobigny cases was the same human rights attorney who had led Djamila Boupacha's defense in 1960, Gisèle Halimi. Like Boupacha's trial, Bobigny brought together Halimi and Beauvoir, here as leaders of Choisir, the organization formed in case the 343 signers of the manifesto on abortion needed legal defense.[76] Like Boupacha's trial, Bobigny became a political event aimed at public opinion, with political and media personalities, press coverage, and at the end, a book that defied the state by publishing the trial transcripts of what was supposed to be a confidential hearing. Halimi, for whom the courtroom provided an arena to orchestrate testimony and put the legitimacy of the law on trial, called it a "trial on behalf of a new feminism." It should be conducted, if possible, by women themselves.[77] In the good French tradition, Bobigny like Boupacha became an "affair" or "scandal"—a moment that showed just how hollow the legal system was.

The courtroom spectacle was remarkable. Male judges found themselves obliged to listen to testimony from a lineup of defiant women. The *procureur*'s questions to defendants accused of "complicity" in the case of Marie-Claire had the effect of exposing how familiar illegal abortion was, particularly among working-class women. All the women involved in Marie-Claire's case knew the risks of abortion. Once the woman in charge realized that infection had set in, she got the address of a sympathetic gynecologist at a clinic who could "save this girl's future"—keeping her from "ruining her life" as a woman. "We talk about this between women," she said—a comment that applies to the much broader underground of abortion knowledge.[78] Proving the defendants' complicity with one another required asking about disagreeable details: who had placed speculums and probes, and how; who had boiled the water or provided the alcohol in the unsuccessful efforts to sterilize the instruments.

Halimi brought in many well-known women to testify. She managed to ask whether they had had abortions themselves. They had. "We are not interested in this," declared the judge, defending courtroom protocol and the now battered cultural codes of discretion and decency. "This display is unpleasant. Now is not the time." If Halimi kept these witnesses coming, "we will be here until the end of the year."[79] Beauvoir testified that she had helped women find addresses and lent them money. That testimony brought kudos from several correspondents and yet more letters like the ones she had received for years pleading for a quick face-to-face meeting or an address.[80]

The trial also exposed the fault lines that lay under the new sisterhood, however. Solidarity with women who actually performed abortions was in short supply. The *Nouvel Observateur* championed the campaign to legalize abortion but refused to publish a story about a woman who had been sentenced to six months in prison for performing an abortion. She was seventy-nine, in poor health, and died after three weeks in prison. A friend of hers wrote Beauvoir, furious. Beauvoir, Halimi, and the manifesto represented "the height of hypocrisy." If they believed it was courageous to declare that one had had an abortion, why wouldn't they help those who were being prosecuted for providing one?[81]

Radical feminists from MLF contested Halimi's courtroom tactics. Halimi marshaled testimony not only from women celebrities but also from Nobel Prize–winning doctors, who criticized the law and acknowledged that they had either performed abortions—or would do so—or counseled women to have them. The prospect of prominent men offering their expert judgment on the law, baring their consciences and confessing their ethical dilemmas, infuriated most MLF militants, who noisily protested outside. Nor did MLF radicals appreciate Halimi's emphasis on what she called Marie-Claire's "social tragedy": a family with three daughters headed by a working single mother, and too poor to afford a new baby.[82] For the feminist radicals, women were women, wealth and class position notwithstanding; their bodies were their own; the choices were theirs to make; and the point should be made with "un-dramatic" stories.[83] Beauvoir's sympathies lay with this liberty-of-the-body argument: class differences mattered less than a common female condition under male domination. When Halimi (and her client) refused to let a well-to-do MLF militant testify about her illegal and frightening abortion, Beauvoir resigned her position in Choisir, attacking the organization's cautious "reformism." From the other side, activists who simply wanted Marie-Claire to be acquitted wrote Beauvoir to deplore the "politicization of the debate" and to demand that the radical feminists who attended the trial "behave like adults and stay calm."[84]

Beauvoir's stance on Bobigny and the politics of Choisir also earned her a long and surely painful missive from Jacqueline Manicom, a leader of Choisir, a writer from Guadeloupe, and a midwife with decades of experience in the Antilles and the public hospitals of Paris. Manicom had testified at the Bobigny trial. Now she had a testy political exchange with Beauvoir. So Beauvoir and her allies in the MLF considered Choisir "reformist"? Did Beauvoir imagine herself to be a "revolutionary"? "You rarely find a copy of *The Prime of Life* or *The Second Sex* in public housing." Beauvoir's books served only to "decorate the bookshelves of bourgeois men and women." Beauvoir thought that Choisir's emphasis on class was shouldering "bourgeois" women aside? Precisely, wrote Manicom: "The real problem is to know which women we want to liberate."[85]

Manicom pointedly asked Beauvoir to recall Weill-Hallé's *Great Fear of Loving* and the case of the bourgeoise pregnant by a "black man." Did this woman think "her body was her own," or was she instead "traumatized by giving birth to a child of color"? "I will not be in solidarity with a woman like that." Weill-Hallé had never been anything but a "technocrat of contraception," but Manicom expected Beauvoir to be something more than a "technocrat of the liberation of women"—able to understand the salience of race and class to questions of women's rights. This is one occasion when one wishes we had Beauvoir's response. Shortly thereafter, at a public meeting at the Maison de la Mutualité in Paris, Manicom angrily denounced the absurd cruelties and shameful racism of French laws. She pointed out that the French state prosecuted Marie-Claire for abortion while encouraging contraception and abortion in the French Caribbean. France "might want a France with one hundred million inhabitants, but not too many little negroes." Manicom's own collection of case studies of her patients and fellow workers, who were from Caribbean France as well as immigrants, published in 1974, was an implicit rebuke to Weill-Hallé.[86]

The Manicom exchange leaves us with a poignant image of Beauvoir standing at the edge of the new feminism, reveling in the political explosion but inevitably singed by it. It is a glimpse as well of the ways in which racial inequality and anticolonialism would soon figure differently in metropolitan politics—no longer simply as useful analogies to radicalize middle-class women's (and men's) understanding of their subordination, but as critiques of that abstract, universalizing radicalism, forcing militants of the first and second "'68s" to reckon with their class and racial privilege, and challenging movements to reimagine bonds and alliances that could reach across difference. The archive of letters is a microcosm of both the exhalations and also the awkward tensions of second-wave feminism.

In 1972 Beauvoir shared her views on the new women's movement in an interview with the German feminist and media personality Alice Schwarzer, which was published in *Le Nouvel Observateur*. She applauded the MLF for defying taboos, declaring its autonomy, breaking with stodgy incrementalism of feminisms past, and making feminism a fulcrum of broader social transformation. Beauvoir had long refused to "close herself off in feminism." She embraced it now. She had been wrong, she said, to have argued that "women had to challenge only the system." That was "too abstract . . . They also had to challenge men." When Schwarzer asked her about the lesbian (*homosexuelle*) current in the MLF, Beauvoir replied: "Yes, some women are fully radical, and refuse men completely. They will bring along women who would otherwise be inclined to make certain compromises." These were not necessarily the terms in which lesbian activists would conceive of themselves or their politics.[87] But the magazine underscored Beauvoir's support for gay and lesbian militancy with a bold inset quote: "THE ROLE OF HOMOSEXUALS."[88]

The interview brought a barrage of letters. "I was so happy to hear your voice again . . . assured, calm, and confident," wrote one woman after reading Beauvoir's interview. "Your words count more than all the others together . . . You are not afraid of being mocked." Beauvoir showed that feminism was not a "false problem for bourgeoises and neurotics." She herself wanted to join the "collective action." But, she wondered: "How? Can you give me a date, a telephone number, an address? Please tell me that this letter has been read." A midwife wanted to put her skills to work for the cause and also to write something "revolutionary" about women's first sexual experiences. A young woman from Lyon wrote to endorse what Beauvoir had said about refusing the "servitude of marriage." She was "only a modest worker from a farming family." Growing up, she had watched "too many women submit to their husbands." Things had changed, though—in the countryside as well as the city. Widowed women she knew might have "liaisons," but they declined to marry again. Peasants and workers alike had "learned to fight for themselves," she observed. "It is surely easier to find feminists in your intellectual circles." But she was writing this letter "to tell you that although Paris is very far, we are following everything you do."[89]

Skeptics scoffed that she was jumping on the revolutionary bandwagon. "Enough is enough!" fumed one. "You can't open any newspaper these days without finding an article treating the revolt of women." Angry readers, many of them from an older left, demanded that Beauvoir explain her sudden dogmatism, her attacks on male former allies, and what one called her "violently emotional tone" and "interpretive delirium."[90]

Schwarzer described her interview with Beauvoir as "historic" and said that it marked Beauvoir's "conversion." It represented both less and more than that. Beauvoir signaled no intention to revise her philosophical premises. She felt no need to resolve the tensions between her Marxism and her existentialism, between her analysis of deep structures on the one hand and her calls for individual responsibility on the other. Yet her new stance was not as simply strategic as she contended.[91] It represented a remarkable banishing of Beauvoir's open and long-standing ambivalence about feminism, which has been one through-thread in the chapters of this book. In this sense her about-face *was* historic. It is revealing about the dynamics of historical change and, as the very mixed reactions of her readers show, the interplay of feeling, identification, and politics in historical change. The testimony from letters and contemporary accounts is about feelings that vacillated between visceral loathing for "women" to love, from alienation to belonging. They are about a powerfully idealized political subjectivity in which one has to fully inhabit one's politics, about politics as passion and desire and the wholeness of the political actor.[92]

The explosion of feminist militancy in the early 1970s surprised its advocates as much as its adversaries. To be sure, protest arose from the kinds of grievances we have seen simmering in Beauvoir's correspondence. But the *militancy* was abrupt, and broke through the impasses of the earlier 1960s. The heady sense of power and near success in 1968 emboldened radicals. Paris was virtually shut down for a month, and while Paris was not the center of 1968, it gave the global events of that year a revolutionary genealogy. The events of 1968 changed the metabolism of the left, hastening the speed with which new groups and radical ideas were generated. The startlingly violent confrontations between workers or students and the forces of order valorized anger, defiance, transgression—and joy. A bold, radically different sexual politics in particular repudiated the venerable tradition of decency, modesty, and shame. It changed the repertoire of acceptable political emotion. Beauvoir's correspondents underscore the political, social, discursive, and affective dimensions of the historical moment. They capture the elation, rage, and seductiveness of women's and gay liberation—as well as the tensions between and within those movements.

Even in these exciting days, the term "feminism" continued to arouse mixed feelings. The new term "women's liberation" did more than "feminism" to join the new movement to socialism, the working class, or student, civil rights, or anticolonial movements.[93] It expressed well a claustrophobic discomfort with "women" and already-existing feminism; that discomfort was virtually constitutive of the early MLF. "Feminine, to use the word was to renounce all dignity," wrote Anne Zelensky, a breakaway member of the older Mouvement Démocratique Féminin (Women's Democratic Movement). "Woman" was "used by reactionaries to lock people into a given historical situation and not let them out," a reader told Beauvoir.[94] Christiane Rochefort described how *"femme"* and its derivatives set her teeth on edge: "The rubric of 'feminine issues' gets on our nerves: political problems can only be [are always] common problems . . . We don't like segregation . . . What's more, many of us don't like the word 'feminist.' "[95] The unease with "woman," the gritting of teeth at "feminism," or the powerful attractions to and identifications with other women—these were not halfway points on the road to a resting place and the happy resolution of conflicts. The presumption of affective sisterliness and the obliteration of difference was already problematic. It would become more so.[96] Ambivalence was not going away. And as far as the politics of sexuality were concerned, in the 1970s as in the early 1950s, the many issues bound up in sex—not to mention the mixed feelings that individuals brought to it—meant that it would continue to spark polarizing debate.[97]

CONCLUSION

In the spring of 1968, Shulamith Firestone and Anne Koedt, American feminists representing the New York Radical Women (1967) came to Paris bearing just published copies of their new newspaper *Notes from the First Year*. Firestone and Koedt wanted to deliver a copy to Beauvoir in person. They went away disappointed. As Firestone wrote her sister from Paris: "Anne and I went to see S de B. on Sat . . . She wasn't home & a horrible woman concierge barked at us that we need an appointment date."[1]

Did this missed connection prefigure relations between Beauvoir and her followers in the future? That Beauvoir was not at home was an understatement. By her own account, she felt out of place during the protests of that famous month of May 1968. She was dismayed by younger leftists' opinion of *Les Temps Modernes* as an all-too-well established journal.[2] Her interventions in international politics had misfired badly. Beginning in 1965, she, Sartre, and Lanzmann had tried to mediate dialogue among intellectuals in the Middle East. In 1967 they met with political and intellectual interlocutors in Cairo and Tel Aviv and put together a fraught one-thousand-page-long special issue of *Les Temps Modernes* on the Arab-Israeli conflict. The special issue hit the newsstands exactly twenty-four hours before the Six-Day War broke out.[3] At that point, Sartre's and Beauvoir's (conditional) support for Israel and (cautious) condemnation of Arab aggression branded both of them traitors to the Arab cause and mooted their entire undertaking. The missteps continued. In the fall of 1968, Beauvoir and Sartre visited Prague, where Warsaw Pact troops had crushed the liberalizing efforts of the Dubček government. They returned having managed to reassure themselves that socialism in the Soviet bloc was successfully reforming from within. Finally, at the very moment when *youth* rebellion was grabbing the headlines, and young radicals like Firestone and Koedt were trying to visit her, Beauvoir was away from Paris working on a sociological study of aging, *Old Age* (*La vieillesse*), which came out in 1970. In short, she seemed to be doing all the wrong things. The global arc of left politics was bending away from metropolitan French intellectuals. "It happened so fast," she said later. "One day we were the main attraction, and the next . . ."[4] A twenty-six-year-old correspondent who considered Beauvoir and Sartre his generation's "philosophical tutors" bluntly asked if their thought was relevant any longer.[5]

Beauvoir did remain relevant to the feminist avant-garde, if largely as a symbolic figure. Shulamith Firestone, undeterred by her unpleasant encounter with the concierge, dedicated her best-selling radical manifesto *The Dialectic of Sex: The Case for Feminist Revolution* (1970) to Beauvoir.[6] That dedication gave radical American feminism a European philosophical genealogy and connected Beauvoir to another cohort of readers. *The Second Sex* nonetheless seemed like a stodgy classic compared to Firestone's *Dialectic of Sex* or Kate Millett's *Sexual Politics*, which was also published in 1970. By the late 1970s, developments on Beauvoir's side of the Atlantic—Lacanian psychoanalysis, structuralism, poststructuralism, and deconstruction—would seem to have scuttled the premises of Beauvoir's version of feminism, seen as tethered to an insistence on individual freedom and in quest of an illusory authentic self. These theoretical developments laid the ground for the late twentieth-century renaissance of feminist thought or, rather, for a new strand of critical theory in which feminist rethinking of language, subjectivity, and sexual difference led the way. The figures Americans called the *new* French feminists—Luce Irigaray, Hélène Cixous, and Julia Kristeva—whether they were rewriting the history of philosophy or revising the language of psychoanalysis, all sought to decenter female subjectivity rather than embracing a philosophy of consciousness or presence. Their work was many steps away from Beauvoir even as they were thinking through issues that Beauvoir herself had raised. It is a testament to both the wide range of feminist critical theory from the 1970s through the 2000s and also the richness of Beauvoir's philosophical concepts that her writing could be reappropriated for so many different positions.[7]

The story of Beauvoir's relations with her readers, however, is not only about her legacy to feminism. *Old Age* has received relatively little attention, but it was not a detour from either Beauvoir's central interests or her readers' concerns. Mortality was the most existential of matters. It had been central to the epilogue of *The Force of Circumstance* and to *A Very Easy Death*, the bitterly titled account of Beauvoir's mother's passing.[8] Like those earlier works, *Old Age* elicited hundreds of appreciative letters. Beauvoir's scandalous and bracing "indiscretion" was again on full display as she struck out onto intimate territory others avoided. Beauvoir may have rued her choice to turn to *Old Age* at a time when everyone else was talking about youth or feminist radicalism, but the topic was surprisingly timely. The upshot was a book and an outpouring of letters that reprised earlier episodes in her career, summing up much of her legacy and pointing to the dynamics that repeatedly renewed her bond with her readers.

In *Old Age* as in *The Second Sex*, Beauvoir combined sociology with testimony, case studies, and cultural criticism. Culture cast the elderly as the Other, "not as fellow humans." The aged were isolated and shunted off to the shadows; poor, disparaged as unproductive, and embarrassing, even repellent, in their neediness and infirmity, with their slack flesh, failing eyes and ears, missing teeth, confusions, or dementia. Beauvoir did not spare the gory details about aging as a bodily experience. Yet the obstacles the elderly faced were not simply or even primarily biological-medical but rather sociocultural, produced by public policy, political economy, institutions and medical practices, family structures, and cultural reflexes—especially the denial of mortality. Economic and physical precarity made aging and the aging body sites of intense vulnerability, shame, and fear. As in *The Second Sex*, Beauvoir defied taboos and stirred up a hornet's nest of feeling.

Many readers charged *Old Age* with "obscenity," "indecency," and "irreverence." "I'm glad I didn't waste my money on it, since I usually don't collect horrors and filth," wrote one correspondent, who went on to berate Beauvoir for "the sadistic pleasure" she seemed to take in describing the "decrepitude" of old people and lingering on clinical descriptions of failing bodies. In 1970 as in 1949, that project elicited charges of prurient sensationalism, a desire to humiliate, or irreverence. Religious readers (Catholic and Jewish) scolded Beauvoir that her atheism had prevented her from "nearing the turn of the bend" with equanimity. If she were religious, they advised, she would be able to contemplate aging without fear. Appreciative readers, by contrast, fully agreed with Beauvoir that "aging itself constitutes one of the most terrifying aspects of the human condition." They found reading the book excruciating but important. While the subject was decidedly not "polite conversation," as one put it, even six hundred densely detailed pages were not too much, for "each page pushes the reader to reflect" and to rethink their opinions.[9]

These elderly letter writers, encouraged not only by the author but also by some of the defiant (or shameless) spirit of post-'68, refused to be "discreet" about their no longer robust bodies, their sickness, loneliness, and humiliations. They tallied up their social security payments to show just how short those fell of their former wages or salaries. They wrote about housing problems, which were compounded by poverty, the indignity of being refused leases on apartments, and what one letter writer called a "deliberate policy of social segregation." They reported on overcrowding in understaffed nursing facilities and psychiatric institutions. Anger at the "ingratitude" of children was an inevitable theme in a world that was so militantly youthful, and it borrowed the 1960s radicals' critique of capitalism's infernal cadences: "Thank you and bravo, Madame, for paying attention to old people. I hope your book will be widely read . . . and that those who are now young will see what awaits them—unless they stop scorning those who are no longer 'productive.'" This letter writer winced at being obliged to get a library card under his daughter's name—at having to identify her as head of the household. He had gone to buy his daughter a television set on credit, only to be told that he had to go through her account, and with her authorization, for his pension was presumptively inadequate. "Humiliating, all of that." Or "I feel like a stranger in my own country," wrote another. "You are refused everything." Or again "Old age is a calamity . . . [Y]ou [Beauvoir] understand it so well, even though you are very far away from it."[10]

Old Age was widely reviewed in France and almost immediately translated into English. That interest stemmed partly from Beauvoir's high profile but partly too from the heightened significance of aging as a social and political issue. Beauvoir received letters from gerontologists and hospital directors in France and across Europe, from France's Administration of Social Services and the United States national and White House councils on the aging. "The theme of 'aging' interests, concerns, perhaps even obsesses *the world*," as one reader wrote to Beauvoir.[11] Increasing life expectancy had placed aging on the agenda. So too had heightened political attention to poverty, hunger, employment, quality of life, security, and dignity. The elderly were no less intent than other social groups on demanding their share of social provisioning and state resources, and they had their own critique of the productionist rhythms of postwar economic expansion and consumer culture. Their letters to Beauvoir place these aging writers, indeed their generation, squarely in the history of the 1960s.

Old Age prompted letter writers to reflect on the meaning of the searing experiences of the twentieth century. An eighty-year-old woman from the Dordogne, in southwest France, wrote that after enduring two world wars, she found "facing the possibility of nuclear annihilation" to be "more horrible than the human heart can imagine." Still, she pluckily described herself as a "perpetual rebel, despite my advanced age." She thanked Beauvoir for her life's work, which she called "a veritable fireworks of sincerity and truth." A somewhat younger woman, sixty-nine years old, a former doctor, originally from Hungary, had lived through the war in the center of Europe and was much more scarred by her past. She had been widowed twice. Her husband of twenty-three years had been killed by militias of the fascist Hungarian Arrow Cross; she and her three children survived. She met her second husband, a fellow doctor, "charming and admirable," at a center for repatriated political prisoners. He had survived Auschwitz, but he never recovered his health and passed away after a long and painful illness. She felt lonely and without purpose, and she knew her loneliness made her a burden on her children and grandchildren. The depth of feeling in her letter had many sources: painful memories, longing for companionship, identification with a well-educated writer who shared some of her points of reference, and the knowledge that Beauvoir was interested in the existential complexities of women's lives.[12]

The Hungarian woman's letter was eloquent about letters in general and the way absence intensified intimacy. She cast Beauvoir in the patient, unhurried posture of a therapist. She opened her letter with the same ritual phrases as countless correspondents, imagining a dialogue. But her explanation of the advantages of writing a letter—being literally invisible—was especially poignant:

> I wish I could send one sentence and you would understand. But no. I have to try to describe everything, and to be concrete. I console myself by saying that I may find comfort in getting at least some of my torment off my chest in writing . . . It is good to communicate ideas in writing; you aren't disturbed by a possible gesture of impatience from your partner, or by the boredom that you see appear on their face.

While she wrote in educated French, like many of the other letter writers she apologized for being unable to meet the epistolary challenge of putting everything in words:

> That's my life, and you can feel it with me, even if I cannot express it very well . . .
>
> Why did I write all of this to you? Because I have never felt such a human closeness as I do with you, Madame, whose writing can express the whole gamut of emotions.[13]

Her missive captures especially well the feelings and needs that ran through so many of the letters in this archive, feelings and needs that shaped this reader-author relationship. Those feelings were existential and historical: an urge to add one's voice to testimony about the century, which often entailed reliving traumatic events, and the desire to give both one's life and one's historical moment meaning by framing them together. Her letter also distills the longing to account for and understand one's experience as well as the difficulties of doing so, and it is a lovely portrait of the trust that Beauvoir elicited—the conviction that she had the resources, concepts, and perspective to understand what her readers found too hard to say.

Beauvoir received letters until she died in 1986 and, in fact, beyond; anyone who visits her grave at the Montparnasse cemetery will find it scattered with admiring notes, often scribbled on Métro tickets. But the volume of letters in this archive diminishes after *Old Age* and Beauvoir's last autobiographical volume, *All Said and Done*, in 1972. Beauvoir remained fully engaged in feminism and international politics. She gave interviews in the media, joined in campaigns to make rape a crime rather than a misdemeanor, and made a section on "ordinary sexism" a regular feature in *Les Temps Modernes*. She lent her name and energy to radical feminist journals that addressed sexual violence and the racism that often infused debates about it, the respective places of materialism and new critical psychoanalysis in feminist theory, and whether what Monique Wittig called "straight thought" (*la pensée straight*) had any relevance for lesbian feminists.[14] Those contentious questions stimulated new work in philosophy, history, and literature, but authors of that work took to print themselves rather than routing their thoughts through a letter to Beauvoir.

The central drama in the letters in this archive is the readers' appropriation of Beauvoir's ongoing interpretation and reinterpretation of her life and times. Thus the end of Beauvoir's autobiography marks a fitting moment to stop and conclude by reflecting on the reader-author relationship, Beauvoir's legacy, and the archive as an artifact of the packed moments of the postwar and the cultural history of the twentieth century.

This archive tells the story of a remarkable author-reader collaboration. That collaboration was complex, with several dimensions: deliberately nurtured and mutually affirming, conflicted and power-laden, philosophical, literary, historical. It instantiated Beauvoir's understanding of what it meant to be a writer. As she repeatedly argued, readers anchored a writer and her work in a collective social reality; they were vital to her engagement with the world. For Beauvoir, both philosophy and literature investigated the meaning of experience(s) and consciousness in the world. Indeed literature, with its ability to convey the texture and meanings of experience, could do this as well as philosophy.[15] That conviction lay behind Beauvoir's autobiography: writing *particularized* existence and made consciousness present to itself, and writing one's life was a form of philosophical practice. That belief animated her interest in her readers and the singularity of their lives. Readers, for their part, were moved to write about themselves, for they found in Beauvoir's grammar of "experience" a way to express the process of knowing the world and themselves.

For countless readers, the realm of experience-to-be-interpreted was in the hidden, isolated spaces of the supposedly "personal" and "private," where feelings and memories could be reexamined and found to fit into structures and constraints—social, political, psychological—that could be named and reflected on. For countless others, the realm of experience was History with a capital *H*. What they warmed to in Beauvoir was first, her long and detailed reflection on the connections between world-shaping events and one's own life, or the bridge between the historical and intimate, and second, her abiding interest in the exhausting, exhilarating, crushing, or generative dimensions of feeling, in other words, her phenomenology of emotion. The memoirs provided historical scaffolding for reconstructing and working through one's own memories, and for excavating and revisiting the feelings involved. No wonder, then, that Beauvoir's readers wrote to her about such an extraordinary range of subjects, from the mundane to the world historical, their childhoods, their marriages, their illnesses, their dilemmas about contraception, how to categorize their sexual desires, their desire to write, how to organize against colonialism or for feminism, about labor in the workplace, families, sexual desires and political ambition, romantic disappointments, and political failures.

Looking at Beauvoir's work through these letters says much about what literature can stir in readers. *What Can Literature Do?* (1965) laid out Beauvoir's views on how literature could reshape a reader's world, the powerful identifications that literature could produce, and the "intermingling" of reader and author: "That is the miracle of literature, which distinguishes it from information: that another truth becomes mine without ceasing to be other. I renounce my own 'I' in favor of the speaker; and yet I remain myself. It is an intermingling ceaselessly begun and ceaselessly undone, and it is the only kind of communication capable of giving me that which cannot be communicated, capable of giving me the taste of another life."[16]

The deluge of letters Beauvoir was receiving in 1965, when she wrote this, might well have fortified her views. Men as well as women were voluble about just this intermingling, recognizing themselves in her and merging her memories with theirs. They reported their own versions of being overwhelmed by reading, and transformed in a manner that reshaped their sense of self or enabled them to see the world with new eyes—the importance of the "taste of another life." This testimony could provide gratifying evidence for Beauvoir's understanding of literature and proof of her own success as a writer. While Beauvoir's conceptions of an author's power to "transport" and "take over" a reader are sometimes startlingly heavy-handed, they were certainly encouraged by enthusiasts in her public.

The author-reader relationship was far from simple or transparent. At the beginning of *The Force of Circumstance*, Beauvoir was almost breezy about the challenges of unfurling herself before the public. In writing, she was in control: "Perhaps my image projected in another world [*un monde autre*]—that of psychoanalysts, for example—would disconcert or embarrass me. But if I am the one who is depicting myself, nothing frightens me." Even though she was depicting herself, however, she was also projecting herself into other worlds in which she had little control. Beauvoir's relationship with readers had more of the dynamics of psychoanalytic exchange than she wanted to recognize. It was deepened and also distorted by feelings that remained opaque and that neither party to the exchange mastered: identification and misidentification, desire, seduction, fantasy, and projection. The relationship that she entered so fearlessly had many dimensions from which she recoiled: the expectations of intimacy that came with both celebrity and having her work circulate in the women's press; the members of the public who read her fiction as dime store romance; and not least, the emotional and political misrecognitions that were a recurring feature of her rapport with the public.

As many scholars have pointed out, the memoirs readers so loved hid as much as they disclosed. Beauvoir's rhetoric of existential authenticity fits awkwardly with her cagey refusal to acknowledge any number of important political missteps, as well as personal compromises, vulnerabilities, and failures.[17] For Marie-Jo Bonnet, those shortcomings and betrayals go beyond Beauvoir's analysis of lesbianism as a fleeting and "immature" stage or her denial of her own sexual relations with women; Beauvoir's self-deceptions produce an above-it-all tone, a stance of haughty exteriority to her subject. She condescends to the women about whom she is writing. Bonnet notes: "I have often been surprised by the effect of *The Second Sex* among women. And not only in the West. In China, in Japan, the book is known, read, and commented on. How can so many women recognize themselves in the scornful portraits of submissive women that Simone de

Beauvoir painted of them?"[18] Was Beauvoir scornful, and if so, why did readers not see that? Questions like these have been raised by critics since *The Second Sex* first came out in 1949.[19]

The archive upends those questions, for what the letters lay out is not reducible to encountering scorn or finding sympathy, submitting to Beauvoir's judgments or resisting them. Here, for example, is a reader who encapsulates the complicated politics of reading and writing Beauvoir. As she works through a crisis in her life, she rereads parts of *The Second Sex*, including the chapter on lesbianism that Bonnet and others so rightly find wrong-headed. The letter is from 1972 and in English:

> The last five years have been painful and my marriage is not a successful one, although my husband is a fine man. In an occasion of all too frequent despair I have just turned to glance once again through your book . . .
> I read the chapters on the Formative Years and on Marriage over. You are right, you are still right. You have understood. It is a work of genius and I can only give you my thanks for the comfort it gives me to know I was not born evil, that I am possibly a product of what I cannot yet wholly grasp . . . I am one of your "failures" . . . I find the knowledge of what I am as woman devastating. But you, at least, understand all of it. It is a magnificent book. Thank you.[20]

It is an unexpected and tightly packed bundle of conflicting feelings and readerly reactions: grief, anxiety, gratitude, certainty, and resolve. Like the woman cited in chapter 8 who knew Beauvoir would describe her as "unfinished," or "incomplete," she has borrowed Beauvoir's terms ("one of your failures"). Like that other reader, this letter writer is not simply adopting those terms and Beauvoir's judgments but reworking and recasting them, using them as she recalibrates her inner compass. She is devastated as she faces the end of her marriage and the heterosexual identity she has tried unhappily to inhabit; in 1972, a world of conventional expectations has been built around both. But she is grateful for finding her not yet specified sexuality intelligible. Above all, she is taking on some of the "magnificent" authority of the book for herself.

One could be effusively grateful without being in the thrall of Beauvoir's concepts. Letter writers like this one continued to negotiate their worlds in ways that cannot not be categorized simply as submission or resistance. Some were angry that Beauvoir asked too much (no collaboration or compromises!) or that her program (freedom, responsibility, and self-creation) provided too little. They were perfectly capable of ignoring Beauvoir's sometimes patronizing tone and identifying with her, the authoritative author. That identification could take them out of themselves, fuel their own ambitions, or provide respite from the requirements of femininity. Letter writers repeatedly said that *The Second Sex* made the condition of women *interesting* to them. It defamiliarized that condition. They used her work to convert an unhappy feeling into a puzzle—to become intellectuals.

Reading the admiring letters in this archive does not cast Beauvoir in a flattering light. She *did* condescend to many of those who followed her so avidly. She exploited her readers' confidences. *The Woman Destroyed* caricatured the unhappily married women who had poured out their grievances to her, expecting understanding. Beauvoir sniffed in disdain at the literary ambitions of middle-class women who tried to "overcome their condition" by writing, with only narrow and uninteresting work to show for it. Many of her correspondents were just such aspiring writers, often women at home for whom writing was a precious and protected space for intellectual engagement, expression, or self-reflection. This relationship was certainly unequal and sometimes cruel in its illusions. To see that it was also compelling and generative, however, is to open a window onto the long and often hidden history of followership.[21]

The postwar French cultural world was hierarchical. So were the international literary worlds in which French thinkers loomed so large and the local educational and political cultures attached to them. Even in socialist and radical circles, younger readers devoted to their teachers and their causes would find constant tutoring a sign of engagement; it conveyed an expanded sense of their possibilities *and* a confirmation of the significance of their lives. If Beauvoir came across as didactic, it was often in response to calls from followers to issue authoritative statements on subjects that ranged from the quality of their writing to marriage and socialism. The dialogue in these letters nonetheless marks a certain democratization of thought, expression, and affect. That dialogue was a newly direct conversation with a secular authority, a literary mandarin who was interested in ordinary life, a *philosopher* who wrote about women and the body. Those conversations were more frank than before, though in the 1950s very few letter writers could be as plainspoken as Beauvoir on matters of sexuality. Their queries offer a sobering glimpse of just how unevenly sexual knowledge was distributed and why: the medical profession guarded its monopolies of medical knowledge and power; codes of decency differed by class, religion, and milieu; and circuits of clandestine, or "unofficial," knowledge were necessarily patchwork, walled off from public deliberation by denial and opprobrium. Increasingly, however, the letter writers voiced not just a need but a *demand* for sexual knowledge. They also spoke of a "right to respond" to Beauvoir's work. An eighteen-year-old Mexican woman was disappointed to have missed meeting Beauvoir when she visited Mexico City: "I have to tell you how much you have given me and how grateful I am." But she wanted more. She wanted direct engagement: "I claim the right not to listen to you, but to ask you questions." The push to travel to a bookstore or library, probably at the suggestion of a local teacher, political ally, or friend, to read a difficult text or a challenging memoir, and to write the author, asking questions, came from below. Focusing too much on the pull of French intellectuals—or intellectuals in general—can obscure the steps, institutions, and intermediaries that led readers to engage with their work in the first place.

"The letters that one keeps and transmits from one generation to another become part of the '*lieux de mémoire*' of a family," writes French anthropologist Daniel Fabre.[22] This correspondence is a remarkable *lieu de mémoire* of the existentialist family: its global celebrity, the ease with which it was assimilated into popular culture and pop psychologizing, its polymorphous political implications, from blandly liberal to revolutionary, and the linkages that helped it circulate with such ease between metropolitan France and the era's revolutionary anticolonial movements and thought. The 1950s and 1960s were a moment of keen interest across the globe in existentialism's call for self-liberation and its emphasis on psychological and political possibility—possibilities to be realized by working one's way out from under the encrusted hierarchies of colonial rule, racism and Jim Crow, the resurgence of authoritarianism, capitalism and consumer culture, and male domination. That project could bring together North and West African, Afro-Caribbean, African American, and French thinkers. If the "decolonization of the soul" proved the most resonant metaphor of the period, that was because it spoke to such a variety of human conditions. Existentialism seemed to reinvigorate Marxism's dream of universal emancipation. Beauvoir's followers no less than Sartre's were woven into the international discussion on these issues.

That existentialist moment waned. The revolutionary center of gravity shifted away from Europe; colonialism's networks of exchange weakened; literary hierarchies and French universalism wore thin. Systems of racial, colonial, and gender subjugation *might* be analogous in the ways that the existentialists like Beauvoir suggested. Historically, as letters to her demonstrate, recognizing those analogies might be radicalizing. Yet it quickly became apparent that those systems did not run parallel but rather intersected; they overlaid and cut across each other in ways that divided and confounded the movements against them and undermined the power of existentialism's once resonant and capacious abstractions.[23] Structuralism and its heirs offered more compelling ways of thinking about the puzzles of power and difference.

The archive is also a *lieu de mémoire* of feminism. It vividly records some of the conditions that fueled so much gender anger during what is traditionally seen as the long postwar period of prosperity, economic expansion, and stability: the egregiously unequal burdens of household labor; care for children, the ill, and the elderly; and affective responsibilities for family and marriage. These contradict our rosy image of these decades of economic expansion. The physical and emotional tolls of pregnancy were the dark side of the "baby boom" after World War II. So were illegal contraception and abortion, which made avoiding pregnancy a problem for women to deal with on their own, "discreetly," in the shadows. Despite the 1950s romance of the couple, marriage became an especially visible and resented node of gender and sexual inequality. Disenchantment with marriage was remarkably abrupt. Disenchantment with conventional heterosexuality was less so but is ongoing. As Simone de Beauvoir pointed out long ago, inequality profoundly distorts intimacy.

The letters' most riveting testimony is about the halting transformation of political subjectivity: the dialectic of aspiration and disappointment, the process of trying out new ideas or analogies (between feminism and decolonization or civil rights), and, more broadly, the hesitations, evasions, political and ethical dilemmas and impasses, discoveries, productive misreadings, mischievous reinterpretations, and unexpected connections between abstract ideas and everyday dilemmas. Beauvoir may have been especially likely to elicit uncertainties and frustrations, lingering as she did on the traps that mined the condition of women, the contradictory knots of female subjectivity, and her undisguised ambivalence about feminism. The thoughts and feelings in the readers' letters, however, owe as much to the broader cultural "incitements" to self-scrutiny and new norms of the postwar moment, to a sense of responsibility for democratic renewal after the catastrophes of two world wars, Nazism, and fascism. This historical moment summoned Beauvoir's readers to become new kinds of people. That their letters make that striving so visible may owe most of all to the rituals of the epistolary "conversation," which virtually compels presenting and reworking the self, however provisionally, experimenting with ideas, and constructing a life story. In a letter, where textuality is all, the writer needs to lay out everything she can about what she wants to be known, borrowing and reworking others' formulations in the process. Finally, as a friend of mine observed, in a letter, unlike a conversation, the writer is allowed to finish her sentences and complete her thoughts—indeed, she or he is obliged to do so.

The archive is a remarkable record of the intimate and affectively charged relationships between feminists from different generations and with different political stances or sexual orientations. It deepens our appreciation for the exhilarations of solidarity, the desires for belonging, and the anger or disappointment at betrayals. The affective dimensions of 1960s radicalism are not unique, but they are particularly pronounced. The anger and joy of 1960s movements had the unabashedly transgressive charge of sexuality. Those same feelings helped to produce 1970s feminism's distinctively corrosive humor and seductive homoeroticism. They helped to spark its militant and world-changing shamelessness: its repudiation of "modesty" (*pudeur*) as a discourse, a set of limits on speech, a complex of fears, and an emotional discipline. Those feelings infused the idealization of sisterhood, and its expectations that relationships among women would be emotionally fulfilling as well as politically effective.[24] Seen from our point of view, Beauvoir's decades-long exchanges with her readers offer an extended, often tempering perspective on those hopes. They decidedly blur the image of Beauvoir as feminist heroine or leader. More important, however, the complex relationship that these remarkable letters express demonstrates both the difficulties and the strengths of feminism: the power of identification and discovery, the stubbornness of hierarchies, and the impossibility of leaving "the personal" for "the political," as if the two were separate realms.[25]

The letters to Beauvoir testify to some of the most elusive but profound kinds of historical phenomena. They offer a vantage point on the slow and hardly inevitable transformations of political subjectivity and underscore the affective dimensions of political mobilization or paralysis. They illustrate the power of books and also the power of the public, whether individually or collectively, to transform books and their meaning. They prefigure the soaring popularity of memoir and interactive reading experiences in our own time. They show that intellectual life is a collaboration. They are traces of a tangled and transferential relationship between readers and author, one whose historical significance overflows this single archive.

NOTES

Introduction

1. Mauricette Berne, "Elles écrivent," in *Cinquantenaire du "Deuxième sexe,"* ed. Christine Delphy and Sylvie Chaperon (Paris: Syllepse, 2002), 392–94; Simone de Beauvoir, Lettres reçues, subheading Lettres reçues de lecteurs, Manuscrits, Occident, Bibliothèque Nationale de France, N.A.F. 28501. At the time of writing the collection was still being organized, but at that point there were forty-six boxes and roughly eleven thousand letters.

2. I refer to her as "Beauvoir" rather than "de Beauvoir," following French usage.

3. The other scholar taking on the whole archive is Marine Rouch, who is doing the extraordinary work of tracking down Beauvoir's correspondents, interviewing them, and reconstructing Beauvoir's role as a literary mentor. See reports on her ongoing work at https://lirecrire.hypotheses.org/ and a series of articles, "Vous êtes descendue d'un piédestal": Une appropriation collective des Mémoires de Simone de Beauvoir par les femmes (1958–1964), *Littérature* 191 (September 2018): 68–82; "Vous ne me connaissez pas mais ne jetez pas tout de suite ma lettre," "Le courrier des lecteurs et lectrices de Simone de Beauvoir," and "Les féministes et leurs archives," in *Genre de l'archive: Constitution et transmission des mémoires militantes*, ed. Françoise Blum (Paris: Codhos, 2017), 73–83, 93–108; " 'Merci pour le message d'espoir': Ces femmes qui écrivaient à Simone de Beauvoir," *Le Magazine Littéraire* (April 2016): 79.

4. Joan W. Scott, *The Fantasy of Feminist History* (Durham: Duke University Press, 2010), 147.

5. Sylvie Le Bon, "Lettre au président de la BNF, January 23, 1995," in *Simone de Beauvoir*, ed. Eliane Lecarme-Tabone and Jean-Louis Jeannelle (Paris: L'Herne, 2012), 373–74.

6. In Beauvoir's lexicon, "describe" takes on extra weight: "The gesture of writing carries with it a theoretical aim." Geneviève Fraisse, *Le privilège de Simone de Beauvoir* (Arles: Actes Sud, 2008), 35. To describe oneself is to become a philosopher of one's own life. On Beauvoir's writing, see Toril Moi, "What Can Literature Do? Simone de Beauvoir as a Literary Theorist," *PMLA* 124, no. 1 (2009): 189–98, and "The Adventure of Reading: Literature and Philosophy, Cavell and Beauvoir," *Literature & Theology* 25, no. 2 (June 2011): 125–40. Beauvoir's thoughts on writing and reading are everywhere, but see especially *Que peut la littérature?* (Paris: L'Herne, 1965), 73–105, and *Tout compte fait* (Paris: Gallimard, 1972), chap. 3, esp. 193–205.

7. Tony Judt, *Postwar: A History of Europe since 1945* (New York: Penguin, 2005); Herrick Chapman, *France's Long Reconstruction* (Cambridge: Harvard University Press, 2018).

8. Mark Greif, *The Age of the Crisis of Man: Thought and Fiction in America, 1933–1973* (Princeton: Princeton University Press, 2007), 264–65.

9. I have used both "autobiography" and "memoir," but for a discussion of the difference, see Philippe Lejeune, *Le pacte autobiographique* (Paris: Seuil, 1975), 236; and Jean-Louis Jeannelle, "Les mémoires comme 'institution des soi,'" in *(Re)découvrir l'œuvre de Simone de Beauvoir: Du "Deuxième sexe" à "La cérémonie des adieux,"* ed. Julia Kristeva et al. (Lormont: Éditions Le Bord de l'Eau, 2008), 73–83.

10. Diary entry for Saturday, June 21, 1958, in Simone de Beauvoir, *Force des choses*, vols. 1 and 2 (Paris: Gallimard, 1963), 2:188, hereafter *FC1* for volume 1 and *FC2* for volume 2.

11. Sarah Bakewell, *At the Existentialist Café* (New York: Other Press, 2016), 216.

12. Beauvoir's analysis of the female situation did not draw a bright line between nature and culture. In the 1980s Judith Butler used Beauvoir to rethink the distinction between sex and gender that had been so central to second-wave feminism, opening the way for the enormously influential arguments in *Gender Trouble* (1990) and *Bodies That Matter: On the Discursive Limits of "Sex"* (1993). See Judith Butler, "Sex and Gender in Simone de Beauvoir's *Second Sex*," *Yale French Studies* 72, "Simone de Beauvoir: Witness to a Century" (1986): 35–49. A few years later, Toril Moi used Beauvoir's concept of *situation* as an "embodied intentional relationship to the world" in her critique of Butler and poststructuralist arguments about the body. Toril Moi, "What Is a Woman? Sex, Gender, and the Body in Feminist Theory," in *What Is a Woman? and Other Essays* (Oxford: Oxford University Press, 1999), 3–120. In her podcast, "La poudre," Lauren Bastide asks her guests, "Were you born a woman or did you become one?" https://www.nouvellesecoutes.fr/la-poudre/.

13. More recent discussions of Beauvoir have taken place in the fields that overlap in feminist critical theory. Literary critics took feminism seriously earlier than most philosophers did, so they led the renaissance of interest in Beauvoir. That renaissance owes an enormous debt to Toril Moi. See *Simone de Beauvoir: The Making of an Intellectual Woman* (Oxford: Oxford University Press, 2008); *Feminist Theory and Simone de Beauvoir* (Oxford: Blackwell, 1990); and *What Is a Woman? and Other Essays* (1999), one of the single best starting points for those interested in Beauvoir. On Beauvoir's theories of writing and reading, see "What Can Literature Do?" and "The Adventure of Reading: Literature and Philosophy, Cavell and Beauvoir." Literary critics have been particularly attentive to not only the philosophical dimensions of Beauvoir's fiction and autobiography but also the textual dimensions of her life. A lively short example is Anne McClintock, "Simone de Beauvoir," in *European Writers: The Twentieth Century*, ed. George Stade, vol. 2 (New York: Scribner, 1990), https://

dept.english.wisc.edu/amcclintock/beauvoir.htm. Elizabeth Fallaize pioneered the study of Beauvoir's fiction; see *The Novels of Simone de Beauvoir* (London: Routledge, 1988); her edited volume *Simone de Beauvoir: A Critical Reader* (New York: Routledge, 1998); and the essays in Fallaize's honor in *Women, Genre and Circumstance: Essays in Memory of Elizabeth Fallaize*, ed. Margaret Atack et al. (Oxford: Legenda, 2012). Fallaize also contributed to the English translation of previously unknown texts by Beauvoir that were published in Margaret A. Simons and Marybeth Timmermann, eds., *Simone de Beauvoir: "The Useless Mouths" and Other Literary Writings* (Champaign: University of Illinois Press, 2011).

On the evolving literary history of Beauvoir's writing, see Susan Rubin Suleiman, *Crises of Memory and the Second World War* (Cambridge: Harvard University Press, 2006), and the volume she edited with Christie McDonald, *French Global: A New Approach to Literary History* (New York: Columbia University Press, 2010); Elaine Marks, ed., *Critical Essays on Simone de Beauvoir* (Boston: G. K. Hall & Co, 1987); Emily R. Grosholz, ed., *The Legacy of Simone de Beauvoir* (Oxford: Clarendon Press, 2004); and Julia Kristeva, "Reading *The Second Sex* Sixty Years Later," *philoSOPHIA*, 1, no. 2 (2011): 137–49.

Beauvoir's works, particularly *The Second Sex*, are read through existential, phenomenological, and feminist lenses. For an overview of the philosophical approaches, see Nancy Bauer, *Simone de Beauvoir, Philosophy, and Feminism* (New York: Columbia University Press, 2001); Laura Hengehold and Nancy Bauer, eds., *A Companion to Simone de Beauvoir* (Hoboken, N.J.: Wiley, 2017), especially the essay by Stella Sandford. See also Claudia Card, *The Cambridge Companion to Simone de Beauvoir* (Cambridge: Cambridge University Press, 2003); Stella Sandford, *How to Read Beauvoir* (New York: W. W. Norton & Co., 2007); Penelope Deutscher, *The Philosophy of Simone de Beauvoir: Ambiguity, Conversion, Resistance* (Cambridge: Cambridge University Press, 2008); and, more recently, Lori Jo Marso, *Politics with Beauvoir: Freedom in the Encounter* (Durham: Duke University Press, 2017).

On Beauvoir and existentialism, see Michèle Le Dœuff, "Simone de Beauvoir and Existentialism," *Ideology and Consciousness* 6 (1979): 47–57, and *Hipparchia's Choice: An Essay Concerning Women, Philosophy, Etc.*, trans. T. Selous (Oxford: Blackwell, 1989); and Margaret Simons, *Beauvoir and "The Second Sex": Feminism, Race, and the Origins of Existentialism* (Lanham, Md.: Rowman and Littlefield, 1999). Simons has also edited countless translations of Beauvoir's work; English-language readers are deeply indebted to her.

On Beauvoir's place in the tradition of Husserl and Merleau-Ponty, see Debra B. Bergoffen, *The Philosophy of Simone de Beauvoir: Gendered Phenomenologies, Erotic Generosities* (Albany: State University of New York Press, 1997); Sara Heinämaa, *Toward a Phenomenology of Sexual Difference* (Lanham, Md.: Rowman & Littlefield, 2003); Sonia Kruks, *Simone de Beauvoir and the Politics of Ambiguity* (Oxford: Oxford University Press, 2012); and Wendy O'Brien and Lester Embree, eds., *The Existential Phenomenology of Simone de Beauvoir* (Dordrecht: Kluwer Academic Publishers, 2001).

For Beauvoir and feminist theory, see Ursula Tidd, *Simone de Beauvoir, Gender and Testimony* (Cambridge: Cambridge University Press, 1999); Eva Lundgren-Gothlin, *Sex and Existence: Simone de Beauvoir's "The Second Sex"* (Hanover, N.H.: Wesleyan University Press, 1996); and Mary Evans, *Simone de Beauvoir: Feminist Mandarin* (New York: Tavistock, 1985). *The Second Sex* has provoked much debate among feminist scholars. See Laura Hengehold, *Simone de Beauvoir's Philosophy of Individuation: The Problem of "The Second Sex"* (Edinburgh: Edinburgh University Press, 2017); Margaret Simon, "Guess What's Missing in *The Second Sex*?" *Women's Studies International Forum* 6, no. 5 (1983): 559–64; Elizabeth Spelman, "Simone de Beauvoir: Just Who Does She Think 'We' Is?," in *Inessential Woman: Problems of Exclusion in Feminist Thought* (Boston: Beacon Press, 1988); and Linda Zerilli, "Feminist Theory without Solace," *Theory & Event* 15, no. 2 (2012).

On the historical side, see Sylvie Chaperon, *Les années Beauvoir: 1945–1970* (Paris: Fayard, 2000); Delphy and Chaperon, *Cinquantenaire du "Deuxième sexe"*; Sandrine Sanos, *Simone de Beauvoir: Creating a Feminist Existence in the World* (Oxford: Oxford University Press, 2016); Ingrid Galster, ed., *Simone de Beauvoir: "Le deuxième sexe," le livre fondateur du féminisme moderne en situation* (Paris: Honoré Champion, 2004), with essays that assess each chapter of *The Second Sex*; and Ingrid Galster, ed., *"Le deuxième sexe" de Simone de Beauvoir: Textes réunis et présentés par Ingrid Galster* (Paris: Presses de l'Université Paris–Sorbonne, 2004), a comprehensive collection of early reviews of *The Second Sex*, hereafter *Textes*. See the extensive notes that accompany Simone de Beauvoir, *Mémoires*, ed. Jean-Louis Jeannelle and Éliane Lecarme-Tabone (Paris: Gallimard, 2018), the new edition in the Bibliothèque de la Pléiade; and Annabelle Martin Golay, *Beauvoir intime et politique: La fabrique des mémoires* (Lille: Presses Universitaires de Septentrion, 2013).

14. Galster, *Textes*, 22. 294–96.

15. Martin Weil, "Nelson Algren, Author Hailed as Poet of Chicago Slums, Dies at 72," *Washington Post*, May 10, 1981.

16. Moi, *Simone de Beauvoir*.

17. The roles of Beauvoir and Sartre as intellectuals on the world stage have been given a bracing and welcome reassessment by Sandrine Sanos, *Simone de Beauvoir*; and Yoav DiCapua, *No Exit: Arab Existentialism, Jean Paul Sartre, and Decolonization* (New York: Columbia University Press, 2017). The matter of Beauvoir's sexual identity has been thoroughly recast in Michael Lucey, *Someone: The Pragmatics of Misfit Sexualities, from Colette to Hervé Guibert* (Chicago: University of Chicago Press, 2019).

See also Bianca Lamblin, *A Disgraceful Affair: Simone de Beauvoir, Jean-Paul Sartre, and Bianca Lamblin,* trans. Julie Plovnick (Boston: Northeastern University Press, 1996); Suleiman, *Crises of Memory and the Second World War*; Margaret Simons's introduction to Simone de Beauvoir, *Wartime Diary* (Urbana-Champaign: University of Illinois Press, 2009), 1–35; and Louis Menand, "Stand by Your Man," *The New Yorker*, September 26, 2005, reviewing Hazel Rowley, *Tête-à-tête: Simone de Beauvoir and Jean-Paul Sartre* (New York: HarperCollins, 2005).

18. Simone de Beauvoir, *Le deuxième sexe*, vol. 1 (Paris: Gallimard, 1949), 13, hereafter *DS1*. For this phrase I use the Parshley translation. Simone de Beauvoir, *The Second Sex*, trans. H. M. Parshley (New York: Knopf, 1953), xxv, hereafter *TSS 1953*. Constance Borde and Sheila Malovany-Chevallier translate it as "Women . . . do not use 'we.'" *The Second Sex* (New York: First Vintage Books, 2009), 8, hereafter *TSS 2009*. On Beauvoir's conceptions of history, see Fraisse, *Le privilège de Simone de Beauvoir*, 93–108; Jo-Ann Pilardi, "Feminists Read *The Second Sex*," in *Feminist Interpretations of Simone de Beauvoir,* ed. Margaret A. Simons (University Park: Pennsylvania State University Press), 29–43.

19. Audre Lorde, "The Master's Tools Will Never Dismantle the Master's House," in *Sister Outsider: Essays and Speeches* (Berkeley: Crossing Press, 2007), 110–14.

20. Marie-Josèphe Bonnet, *Simone de Beauvoir et les femmes* (Paris: Albin Michel, 2015), 205.

21. Tamara Chaplin, *Turning on the Mind: French Philosophers on Television* (Chicago: University of Chicago Press, 2007), 23. As Chaplin notes, the French *philosophes* had long been known for writing in a variety of genres, and Beauvoir's turn to autobiography followed well-lit paths. On Paris as a "clearing house for modern European thought and politics," see Judt, *Postwar*, 210. On celebrity, see Sharon Marcus, *The Drama of Celebrity* (Princeton: Princeton University Press, 2019).

22. Simone de Beauvoir, Lettres reçues, subheading Lettres reçues de lecteurs, Manuscrits, Occident, Bibliothèque Nationale de France, N.A.F. 28501, February 6, 1970, Bogotá.

23. Ibid., August 25, 1968.

24. Ibid., November 24, 1970, Quebec.

25. Ibid., May 8, 1969.

26. Ibid., November 26, 1969, United States (in English).

27. Ibid., October 27, 1971. See also December 5, 1960, and November 17, 1960. In several cases Beauvoir and a letter writer corresponded for many years. One young man starting his military service in 1957 asked her to be his "war godmother"; July 7, 1957. War godmothers supported soldiers by writing letters, starting in World War I. On this practice and the history of correspondence, see Martyn Lyons, *The Writing Culture of Ordinary People in Europe, c. 1860–1920* (New York: Cambridge University Press, 2013), esp. 82–84.

28. Beauvoir, Lettres reçues de lecteurs, July 31, 1964.

29. Private collection, with many thanks to Kattalin Gabriel.

30. "After all, you attract correspondence by noting the many letters you received at the time of your earlier books—and how interesting they are." Beauvoir, Lettres reçues de lecteurs, undated, 1965, Paris.

31. Ibid., December 7, 1969, Belgrade.

32. Ibid., October 26, 1969.

33. Ibid., February 27, 1968, Saint-Quentin, Aisne, France.

34. Robert Escarpit, *La révolution du livre* (Paris: UNESCO, 1965), 28.

35. Chaplin, *Turning on the Mind*, 232.

36. "The Femininity Trap," *Vogue*, March 15, 1947; reprinted in *Simone de Beauvoir: Feminist Writings*, ed. Margaret Simons and Marybeth Timmermann (Bloomington: University of Illinois Press, 2015), 42–48. Many serious journalists, including Claude Lanzmann, wrote for *Elle*.

37. Judt, *Postwar*, 5.

38. Hans Ulrich Gumbrecht, *After 1945: Latency as Origin of the Present* (Redwood City, Calif.: Stanford University Press, 2013), 28.

39. On the problems with that terminology, see Kathleen A. Laughlin et al., "Is It Time to Jump Ship? Historians Rethink the Waves Metaphor," *Feminist Formations* 22, no. 1 (Spring 2010): 76–135.

40. Beauvoir, Lettres reçues de lecteurs, May 31, 1968, Ontario, Canada.

41. Beauvoir, *TSS* 2009, 3, 8; *DS1*, 13, 21.

42. Historians' turn to intimacy is part of a larger interest in subjectivity and emotion. Intimacy is also attractive precisely because it is unspecified; it directs attention to relationships or exchanges that do not fit easily into our already theorized categories. It has also become a way of asking open-ended questions about any set of intersubjective relationships and the play of expectations, obligations, vulnerabilities, and possibilities those relationship entail. See, for instance, Nancy Rosenblum's *Good Neighbors: The Democracy of Everyday Life in America* (Princeton: Princeton University Press, 2016).

43. Bruno Cabanes, "Negotiating Intimacy in the Shadow of War," *French Politics, Culture & Society* 31, no. 1 (Spring 2013): 2.

44. Niklas Luhmann, *Love as Passion: The Codification of Intimacy* (Cambridge: Harvard University Press, 1986), 158.

45. Lauren Berlant, *The Female Complaint* (Durham: Duke University Press, 2008), viii. The intimate public is neither an implacably ideological aspect of mass consumer culture nor a "counter-public" that nurtures opposition. Berlant usefully conceptualizes it as "juxtapolitical," writing, "Intimate publics usually flourish to one side of politics, referring to historical subordinations without mobilizing a fundamental activism with respect to them." Lauren

Berlant and Jay Prosser, "Life Writing and Intimate Publics: A Conversation with Lauren Berlant," *Biography* 34, no. 1 (Winter 2011): 180–87.

46. Berlant, *Female Complaint*, ix; Jürgen Habermas, *The Structural Transformation of the Public Sphere: An Inquiry into a Category of Bourgeois Society*, trans. Thomas Burger and Frederick Lawrence (Cambridge: MIT Press, 1989).

47. Beauvoir, *FC1*, 63.

48. Beauvoir, Lettres reçues de lecteurs, August 31, 1970.

49. Ibid., January 5, 1973.

50. For warnings on "the global," see Fred Cooper, "How Global Do We Want Our Intellectual History to Be?," in *Global Intellectual History*, ed. Samuel Moyn and Andrew Sartori (New York: Columbia University Press, 2013), 283–94.

51. Le Bon de Beauvoir, "Lettre au président de la BNF."

52. The archive of Menie Grégoire, who hosted a write- and phone-in radio program starting in 1967, is a telling contrast. She saved and indexed every letter and phone call she received. Grégoire saw herself as a radio psychoanalyst, so preserving the traces of her dialogue with the public was important. But she also saw herself as a sociologist of private life. She parlayed her research into authority as an expert who spoke for the broad public. I have written about Grégoire's archive in "From Interiority to Intimacy: Radio and Psychoanalysis in Twentieth-Century France," *Cultural Critique* (Fall 2015): 114–19, and in chapter 8 here.

53. Gérard Mauger, "Écrits, lecteurs, lectures," *Genèses* 34 (March 1999): 144–61.

54. Judith Lyon-Caen, *La lecture et la vie: Les usages du roman au temps de Balzac* (Paris: Tallandier, 2006); Carolyn Steedman, "State Sponsored Autobiography," in *Moments of Modernity: Reconstructing Britain, 1945–1964*, ed. Becky Conekin, Frank Mort, and Chris Waters (London: Rivers Oram Press, 1999), 41.

55. Hans Robert Jauss, cited in Mauger, "Écrits, lecteurs, lectures," 144; Hans Robert Jauss, *Toward an Aesthetic of Reception*, trans. Timothy Bahti (Minneapolis: University of Minnesota Press, 1982); Michel de Certeau, *The Practice of Everyday Life*, trans. Steven Rendall (Berkeley: University of California Press, 1984), esp. 165–76. See also Nicholas Adell, "Writing One's Life: The French School of the Anthropology of Writing," in *Approaches to the History of Written Culture: A World Inscribed*, ed. Martyn Lyons and Rita Marquilhas (Cham, Switzerland: Palgrave, 2017), 97–116.

56. Beauvoir, Lettres reçues de lecteurs, August 31, 1970.

57. Beauvoir, *FC1,* 60. See *Rethinking Modern European Intellectual History*, ed. Darrin McMahon and Samuel Moyn (New York: Oxford University Press, 2014).

58. For intellectual historians' debates about context, see Judith Surkis, "Of Scandals and Supplements: Relating Intellectual and Cultural History," Peter Gordon, "Contextualism and Criticism in the History of Ideas," and Samuel Moyn, "Imaginary Intellectual History," in *Rethinking Modern European Intellectual History*, ed. Darrin McMahon and Samuel Moyn (New York: Oxford University Press, 2014), 34–50, 95–107, 113–26.

59. See especially Lyon-Caen, *La lecture et la vie*; and Janice A. Radway, *Reading the Romance: Women, Patriarchy, and Popular Culture* (Chapel Hill: University of North Carolina Press, 1984). See the productive disagreement in Lauren Berlant, "Reading the Romance: Women, Patriarchy, and Popular Literature by Janice Radway," *Modern Philology* 84, no. 3 (February 1987): 346–50; and Janice Radway, "Cultivating a Desire to Become 'Not- Something': Lauren Berlant, the Idioms of the Ordinary, and the Kinetic Temporality of the 'Nearly Utopian,'" *Communication and Critical/Cultural Studies* 9, no. 4 (December 2012): 337–45. See also Robert Darnton, "Readers Respond to Rousseau: The Fabrication of a Romantic Sensitivity," in *The Great Cat Massacre and Other Episodes in French Cultural History* (New York: Basic Books, 1985); Carla Hesse, "Reading in Extremis: Revolutionaries Respond to

Rousseau," in *Into Print: Essays in Honor of Robert Darnton*, ed. Charles Walton (State College: Pennsylvania State University Press, 2010); James Smith Allen, *In the Public Eye: A History of Reading in Modern France* (Princeton: Princeton University Press, 2014); and the many works of Roger Chartier, including "Reading Practices and the Materiality of Texts," *French Historical Studies* 41, no. 3 (August 2018): 397–401.

60. Amélie Nothomb, *Life Form*, trans. Alison Anderson (New York: Europa Editions, 2012), 55–56. Nothomb is interviewed about the novel and her readers at https://www.youtube.com/watch?v=tNYyvqtcaE4.

61. Margaretta Jolly, *In Love and Struggle: Letters in Contemporary Feminism* (New York: Columbia University Press, 2008), 6.

62. Beauvoir, Lettres reçues de lecteurs, November 3, 1970, Canada.

63. Martha Hanna, *Your Death Would Be Mine: Paul and Marie Pireaud in the Great War* (Cambridge: Harvard University Press, 2006); Martyn Lyons, *Reading Culture and Writing Practices in Nineteenth-Century France* (Toronto: University of Toronto Press, 2008), and *The Writing Culture of Ordinary People in Europe, c. 1860–1920* (Cambridge: Cambridge University Press, 2013); Liz Stanley, "The Epistolarium: On Theorizing Letters and Correspondences," *Auto/biography* 12, no. 3 (2004): 201–35; Deena Goodman, "Letter Writing and the Emergence of Gendered Subjectivity in Eighteenth-Century France," *Journal of Women's History* 17, no. 2 (Summer 2005): 9–37; Thomas Dodman, *What Nostalgia Was: War, Empire, and the Time of a Deadly Emotion* (Chicago: University of Chicago Press, 2018).

1. The Intimate Life of the Nation

1. Sections of this chapter were published as Judith G. Coffin, "Historicizing *The Second Sex*," *French Politics, Culture & Society* 25, no. 3 (Winter 2007): 123–48.

2. Two anthologies edited by Ingrid Galster have been of immeasurable value to me: *"Le deuxième sexe" de Simone de Beauvoir: Textes réunis et présentés*, ed. Ingrid Galster (Paris: Presses de l'Université Paris-Sorbonne, 2004), hereafter *Textes*; and *Simone de Beauvoir: "Le deuxième sexe," le livre fondateur du féminisme moderne en situation*, ed. Ingrid Galster (Paris: Honoré Champion, 2004). Galster distills some of that material in "The Limits of the Abject: The Reception of *Le Deuxième Sexe* in 1949," in *A Companion to Simone de Beauvoir*, ed. Laura Hengehold and Nancy Bauer (Hoboken, N.J.: John Wiley & Sons, 2017), 37–47. Hengehold and Bauer deal with the difficulty of contextualizing *The Second Sex* by including five articles on the subject.

3. Jean-Paul Sartre, cited in Gisèle Sapiro, *La responsabilité de l'écrivain: Littérature, droit et morale en France, XIXe–XXI siècle* (Paris: Seuil, 2011), 674.

4. Simone de Beauvoir, *The Second Sex*, trans. H. M. Parshley (New York: Knopf, 1953), xiii, hereafter *TSS 1953*; *Le deuxième sexe*, vols. 1 and 2 (Paris: Gallimard, 1949), 1:13, hereafter *DS1* for volume 1 and *DS2* for volume 2.

5. Beauvoir, *TSS 1953*, 267.

6. Beauvoir, *TSS 1953* xxv; see *DS1*, 2.

7. Sylvie Chaperon, *Les années Beauvoir, 1945–1970* (Paris: Fayard, 2000), 169–201. See also Michele LeDoueff's comments in Catherine Rodgers, *"Deuxième sexe" de Simone de Beauvoir: Un héritage admiré et contesté* (Paris: L'Harmattan, 1998), 247–49.

8. For the same point regarding pornography, which "also describes things not apparently sexual in content," see Carolyn J. Dean, *The Frail Social Body: Pornography, Homosexuality, and Other Fantasies in Interwar France* (Berkeley: University of California Press, 2000), 7.

9. On culture and intellectuals in France, see Tamara Chaplin, *Turning on the Mind: French Philosophers on Television* (Chicago: University of Chicago Press, 2007); Alice

Kaplan, *The Collaborator: The Trial and Execution of Robert Brasillach* (Chicago: University of Chicago Press, 2001); and Sapiro, *La responsabilité de l'écrivain*.

10. Beauvoir published early versions of the chapters on mythology in *Les Temps Modernes* at the beginning of 1948. The more shocking chapters, including "The Sexual Initiation of the Woman," followed in the spring of 1949. Volumes 1 and 2 came out separately, in June and October 1949, respectively.

11. *Paris Match*, August 6, 1949, reproduced in Galster, *Textes*, 137.

12. Prouvost purchased *Paris-Soir* from the Havas news and advertising agency between the wars and hired writers like Colette, Jean Cocteau, and Antoine de Saint-Exupéry. By 1940, *Paris-Soir* had a circulation of 2 million. Prouvost very briefly served as Marshal Philippe Pétain's minister of information in the Vichy regime, stepping down by the fall of 1940 and trying to disassociate himself from the version of *Paris-Soir* that was written and distributed in occupied Paris. The charges of collaboration were dismissed in 1947. He opened *Paris Match* in March 1949. See Claude Bellanger, Jacques Godechot, Pierre Guiral, and Fernand Terrou, eds., *Histoire générale de la presse française*, vol. 4 (Paris: Presses Universitaires de France, 1975), 423; Jean Durieux and Patrick Mahé, *Les dossiers secrets de "Paris Match"* (Paris: Robert Laffont, 2009), 25–27; Galster, *Textes*, 339. *Marie Claire*, also part of Prouvost's empire, was shut down and did not reopen until 1953.

13. Galster, *Textes*, 339.

14. The editorial comments are from *Paris Match*, August 6, 1949, cited in Galster, *Textes*, 136.

15. *Paris Match*, August 6, 1949, cited in Galster, *Textes*, 136.

16. Galster, *Textes*, 138. An abridged opening to "The Data of Biology," appears in chapter 1 of Simone de Beauvoir, *The Second Sex*, trans. Constance Borde and Sheila Malovany-Chevallier (New York: Knopf, 2009), 21, hereafter *TSS 2009*.

17. Galster, *Textes*, 139.

18. Beauvoir, *TSS 2009*, 80. In her review of *Elementary Structures of Kinship*, Beauvoir praised Lévi-Strauss's totalizing ambition: "What he is trying to comprehend is the mystery of all of society, the mystery of mankind itself." Simone de Beauvoir, "L'être et la parenté," *Les Temps Modernes*, no. 491 (1949): 943–49. On Lévi-Strauss, see Camille Robcis, *The Law of Kinship* (Ithaca: Cornell University Press, 2014).

19. Galster, *Textes*, 146.

20. Montherlant's sexual politics had been vigorously debated by women writers in 1936. Beauvoir, characteristically, ignored that debate, refusing to situate herself as a woman writer continuing a discussion of the woman question. "She erased those traces," writes Margarete Zimmerman in "Montherlant ou le pain du dégout," in Galster, *Simone de Beauvoir*, 185–98, 95.

21. Galster, *Textes*, 156, 158.

22. Beauvoir, *DS1*, 377, 382–83. See the discussion in Christof Weiand, "Stendhal ou le romanesque du vrai," reprinted in Galster, *Livre fondateur*, 241–56.

23. *Elle*, November 21, 1949, 8–9. *Elle* would eventually become one center of revived feminist debate. See Chaperon, *Les années Beauvoir*, 201 and chap. 10.

24. Emile Littré, *Dictionnaire de la langue française*, vol. 3 (Paris: Hachette, 1873–74), s.v. *pudeur*, https://gallica.bnf.fr/ark:/12148/bpt6k5460034d/f1387, emphasis added.

25. Havelock Ellis, *Studies in the Psychology of Sex*, vol. 1, general preface (originally published London: Wilson & Macmillan, 1897, but then banned; this citation from the third edition, 1927), Project Gutenberg Online, http://www.gutenberg.org/files/13610/13610-h/13610-h.htm. For particularly clear discussions of thinking about sexual difference (and/or gender complementarity), their psychic dimensions, and the political

repercussions, see Joan W. Scott, "The Persistence of Gender Inequality: How Politics Constructs Gender, and Gender Constructs Politics," *The Institute Letter* (Fall 2018): 8–10, Institute for Advanced Study, https://www.ias.edu/ideas/scott-gender-inequality; and Judith Surkis, *Sexing the Citizen: Morality and Masculinity in France, 1870–1920* (Ithaca: Cornell University Press, 2006).

26. Centre National de Ressources Textuelles et Lexicales, http://www.cnrtl.fr/definition/pudeur.

27. Simone de Beauvoir, "La Lesbienne," *Les Temps Modernes*, no. 44 (June 1949): 1007.

28. Beauvoir, *TSS* 2009, 419.

29. Ibid., 996.

30. *Les Temps Modernes*, no. 43 (May 1949): 770; *TSS* 2009, 384. As Nancy Bauer notes, Beauvoir does not provide her readers with very much philosophical guidance. Nancy Bauer, "Must We Read Simone de Beauvoir?," in Rodgers, *"Le deuxième sexe" de Simone de Beauvoir*, 120.

31. *DS2*, 147; *TSS* 2009, 442.

32. Helene Deutsch, *The Psychology of Women*, 2 vols. (New York: Allyn & Bacon, 1943 and 1945). Sonya Rudikoff's "Feminism Reconsidered," *Hudson Review* 9, no. 2 (Summer 1956): 178–98, also illustrates Deutsch's powerful influence at the time. Beauvoir stuck to this position on vaginal orgasm through the 1970s. See chapter 8.

33. As a phenomenologist, Beauvoir examines a woman's distinctive experience of her body, how that body is given meaning *and* how that body shapes her experience of the world. Sexual difference does not in itself have meaning, but it cannot be ignored. Sara Heinämaa, *Toward a Phenomenology of Sexual Difference: Husserl, Merleau-Ponty, Beauvoir* (Lanham, Md.: Rowman & Littlefield, 2003).

34. Simone de Beauvoir, *Force des choses*, vol. 1 (Paris: Gallimard, 1963), 245, hereafter *FC1*.

35. The first editorial committee consisted of Raymond Aron, Simone de Beauvoir, Michel Leiris, Maurice Merleau-Ponty, Albert Olivier, and Jean Paulhan.

36. Almost nine hundred publications were closed, at least temporarily. Sandrine Sanos, *Simone de Beauvoir: Creating a Feminist Existence in the World* (New York: Oxford University Press, 2016), 59.

37. Jean Paul Sartre, "Présentation des *Temps modernes*," *Les Temps Modernes*, no. 1 (October 1945). Reprinted in Jean-Paul Sartre, *Situations, II: Qu'est-ce que la littérature* (Paris: Gallimard, 1948), 11–30.

38. Gisèle Sapiro, *The French Writers' War, 1940–1953*, trans. Vanessa Doriott Anderson and Dorrit Cohn (Durham: Duke University Press, 2014), 489. *Les Temps Modernes* folded in May 2019. Its storied past is well summarized in Mitchell Abidor, "'Les Temps Modernes': End of an Epoch," *New York Review of Books*, May 17, 2019. See also Mark Poster, *Existential Marxism in Postwar France: From Sartre to Althusser* (Princeton: Princeton University Press, 1975).

39. Beauvoir, *FC1*, 72.

40. Senghor, Césaire, and Damas had founded the review *L'Étudiant Noir* in Paris in 1935. Sartre's collection of "negritude" writings in *Black Orpheus*, a special issue of *Les Temps Modernes* (October 1948), spoke to collections of poetry published by Damas and Senghor in 1947 and 1948, as well as with the new journal *Présence Africaine*, founded in Paris in 1947.

41. For a discussion of the operation of race and gender analogies in *The Second Sex*, the connections among Alva and Gunnar Myrdal, W. E. B. Du Bois, Richard Wright, and

Beauvoir, and black feminist readings of Beauvoir, see Kathryn T. Gines, "Simone de Beauvoir and the Race/Gender Analogy in *The Second Sex Revisited*," in Hengehold and Bauer, *Companion to Simone de Beauvoir*, 47–58. Margaret Simons was one of the first to take on the subject in *Beauvoir and "The Second Sex": Feminism, Race, and the Origins of Existentialism* (Lanham, Md.: Rowman and Littlefield, 1999).

42. See Stella Sandford, "Beauvoir's Transdisciplinarity: From Philosophy to Gender Theory," in Bauer and Hengehold, *Companion to Simone de Beauvoir*, 15–27.

43. *FC1*, 73.

44. Simone de Beauvoir, "L'initiation sexuelle de la femme," *Les Temps Modernes* 4, no. 43 (May 1949), 773 *DS2*, 150; *TSS* 2009, 386. Julien Benda (1867–1956) was best known as the author of *The Treason of the Intellectuals* (1927).

45. Beauvoir, "L'initiation sexuelle de la femme," 785; *TSS* 1953, 386; *TSS* 2009, 398.

46. François Mauriac, "Demande d'enquête," *Le Figaro Littéraire* (May 30, 1949). Cited in Galster, *Textes*, 23.

47. "These educated idiots who dig their Louis XV heels [a fashionable form of high heel] into every sacred way [a reference to the road defended at enormous cost during the battle of Verdun in World War I] of our life, these pedantic screeching cunts, they need to be put in a nursery to wipe their bottoms and have their potties emptied until they die." From Jean-Louis Curtis, *Nouvelles lettres d'une vie* (1989), cited in Galster, *Textes*, 296. Mauriac was writing about Claude-Edmonde Magny, who had criticized him in an article in *Esprit*.

48. On Mauriac, see Jean-Luc Barré, *François Mauriac: Biographie intime* (Paris: Fayard, 2009); Nathan Bracher, ed., *François Mauriac on Race, War, Politics, and Religion: The Great War through the 1960s* (Washington, D.C.: Catholic University of America Press, 2015), and "The Cold-War Christian Humanism of François Mauriac," *Christianity and Literature* 52, no. 3 (Spring 2003): 387–408; Tony Judt, *Past Imperfect: French Intellectuals, 1944–1956* (New York: NYU Press, 1992), 68–71; Sapiro, *French Writers' War*, 230–39; and Claire Blandin, *Le Figaro Littéraire: Vie d'un hebdomadaire politique et culturel, 1946–1971* (Paris: Nouveau Monde, 2010), 102–3, 135–39. Mauriac had crossed swords with Sartre in 1939 on the politics of literature; that battle resumed after the war and was in full swing when *The Second Sex* came out. Beauvoir wrote that his son Claude Mauriac (also a novelist) exemplified pompous masculinity (*DS1*, 28; *TSS 1*, xxiv). See Galster's notes on Mauriac, in *Textes*, 335; and Claude Imbert, "A Woman Philosopher in the Context of Her Generation," in *The Legacy of Simone de Beauvoir*, ed. Emily R. Grosholz (Oxford: Clarendon Press, 2004), 12.

49. Mauriac, "Demande d'enquête," *Le Figaro*, May 30, 1949, cited in Galster, *Textes*, 21.

50. Ibid., 22.

51. See Galster, *Textes*, 29–31, on homophobic aspects of this attack.

52. "La question posée," *Le Figaro Littéraire*, June 6, 1949, cited in Galster, *Textes*, 29. The responses were published in *Le Figaro Littéraire* from June 25 to August 6, 1949. The whole inquiry is in Galster, *Textes*, 28–92.

53. In 1940 Mauriac asked if literature "had taken a wrong turn" and was "sowing the seeds of defeat." He hinted at resistance by wondering what direction literature might take in the future. Sapiro, *French Writers' War*, 50, 125.

54. See Henri Hersco's response in *Le Figaro Littéraire*, July 30, 1949, cited in Galster, *Textes*, 82; Bernard Prosen's response, June 25, 1949, 84; J.-P. Missofe's response, June 25, 1949, 41–42; and Michel Sinniger's response, July 2, 1949, 43–44.

55. L.-H. Nicolas's response in *Le Figaro Littéraire*, July 9, 1949, cited in Galster, *Textes*, 57.

56. Pierre de Boisdeffre and François Sant-Anne, "Témoignages en marge d'une enquête," *Liberté de l'esprit* (Summer 1949), cited in Galster, *Textes*, 105–6.

57. See R. Marchoix's response in *Le Figaro Littéraire*, July 16, 1949, cited in Galster, *Textes*, 68; and Jean Kanapa, "Extrait," *La Nouvelle Critique* (July–August 1949), cited in Galster, *Textes*, 101.

58. Maurice Dubois's response in *Le Figaro Littéraire*, July 2, 1949, cited in Galster, *Textes*, 50–51.

59. Fernand Houssin's response in *Le Figaro Littéraire*, July 9, 1949, cited in Galster, *Textes*, 66. See also 48 and 68.

60. L.-H. Nicholas, cited in Galster, *Textes*, 57.

61. François Nourissier's response in *Le Figaro Littéraire*, July 16, 1949, cited in Galster, *Textes*, 65.

62. Maurice Dubois's response, cited in Galster, *Textes*, 50.

63. "Conclusions de François Mauriac et lettre de Cécile Gariel," *Le Figaro Littéraire*, August 6, 1949, cited in Galster, *Textes*, 87.

64. Jean-Marie Domenach, cited in Galster, *Textes*, 34. See also Domenach's interesting memoir *Beaucoup de gueule et peu d'or: Journal d'un réfractaire (1944–1977)* (Paris: Seuil, 2001), 54.

65. Galster, *Textes*, 65.

66. Pierre Néraud de Boisdeffre in *Le Figaro Littéraire*, June 25, 1949, cited in Galster, *Textes*, 22; Pierre Duchateau, 34; Bernard Prosen, 37 (he was overstating the case; see interventions in the Mauriac forum, 63–64 and 66); Emmanuel Mounier, 225–31; unsigned letter, 117–18; Armand Hoog, 160; Jean Palaiseul, 119–22; Pierre Carrigue, 45.

67. Mauriac, "Notre enquête près de la jeunesse intellectuelle: Conclusions," *Le Figaro Littéraire*, August 6, 1949, cited in Galster, *Textes*, 88. See also Mauriac's review of Micheline Maurel, *Un camp très ordinaire*" (1957). The mystery of evil was not new. "But never has evil presented us with this carefully studied apparatus, this tested method for torturing and debasing a creature of God." François Mauriac, *D'autres et moi* (Paris: Grasset, 1966), 90.

68. On this testimony, see Emma Kuby, *Political Survivors: The Resistance, the Cold War, and the Fight against Concentration Camps after 1945* (Ithaca: Cornell University Press, 2019), 27–31; and Amy E. Vidor, "Testifying to Auschwitz and Algeria," (Ph.D. diss., University of Texas at Austin, 2019).

69. Francis Jeanson, *Revue du Caire*, no. 128 (March 1950), cited in Galster, *Textes*, 250.

70. Aimé Parti, "Y a-t-il un éternel féminin?," *Paru* (August–September 1949), cited in Galster, *Textes*, 184–85.

71. Beauvoir herself helped to incite these associations. She was oddly taken with the American Philip Wylie's best-selling *Generation of Vipers* (1942), which had assailed American culture as puritanical, repressive, and twisted by "Momism," or domineering women. Beauvoir quoted extensively from Wylie in *The Second Sex*, and she published translated excerpts from *Generation of Vipers* in a special issue of *Les Temps Modernes* on the United States. "American matriarchy" became a popular theme in the United States, and Beauvoir did her part to bring it to Europe.

72. Galster, *Textes*, 184–85, 167, 185, 230, 262–63. Beauvoir seems to have known several doctors who performed abortions, and referred women and men to them. Simone de Beauvoir, *A Transatlantic Love Affair: Letters to Nelson Algren* (New York: The New Press, 1997), 263, 289–90.

73. Gunnar Myrdal with Richard Sterner and Arnold Rose, *An American Dilemma: The Negro Problem and Modern Democracy*, 2 vols. (New York: Harper, 1944). See also

Appendix 5, "A Parallel to the Negro Problem" by Alva Myrdal, "drawing a parallel between the position of, and feeling towards, women and Negroes" as a "fundamental basis of our culture," ibid., 2:1073–74, 1078; Simons, *Beauvoir and "The Second Sex"*; and Toril Moi, *Simone de Beauvoir: The Making of an Intellectual Woman* (Oxford: Blackwell, 1994), 204–13.

74. The passages on race, on Myrdal's *An American Dilemma*, and on Richard Wright's influence on Beauvoir's understanding of American race relations were struck from the 1953 English translation of *The Second Sex*. Margaret Simons, *Beauvoir and "The Second Sex,"* 182. At the height of the Cold War, when other radical black intellectuals were being hounded by McCarthy, Wright's communism may have made such references to him too hot for the publisher, Knopf, to handle.

75. Odette Grosjean-Darier, "*Le deuxième sexe* de Mme Simone de Beauvoir," *Les Cahiers Protestants* (Lausanne) 34, no. 6 (November–December 1950), cited in Galster, *Textes*, 260. Darier was from a wealthy Huguenot family and was active in Protestant circles in Geneva.

76. Françoise d'Eaubonne, "Réponse," *Le Figaro Littéraire*, July 23, 1949, cited in Galster, *Textes*, 73; Maryse Choisy, "Phallocratie," *Psyche*, no. 32 (June 1949): 124–25.

77. Angie David, *Dominique Aury* (Paris: Leo Scheer, 2006), 169.

78. On her political conversion and her position at the Liberation, see David, *Dominique Aury*, 300. On her right wing past and editorial projects, see David, *Dominique Aury*, 230–31. Edith Thomas was a Communist (until 1949, when she left the party), an early member of the Resistance, a feminist, and the editor of a journal, *Femmes Françaises*, which launched at the Liberation. She would go on to write *The Women Incendiaries* (*Les Pétroleuses*, 1960), which was about the women radicals of the Paris Commune in 1871. On Thomas and her relationship with Aury, see Dorothy Kaufmann, *A Passion for Resistance* (Ithaca: Cornell University Press, 2004).

79. Dominique Aury, "Le visage de Méduse," *Contemporains*, no. 2 (December 1950), cited in Galster, *Textes*, 266–71. *Contemporains* was a small postwar monthly journal of culture.

80. Ibid., 267–68.

81. Régine Deforges and Pauline Réage, *O m'a dit: Entretiens avec Pauline Réage* (Paris: J.-J. Pauvert, 1975), 16, 72–73, 166. Aury was also writing an essay on Laclos's *Les Liaisons dangereuses*. Ibid., 63–64.

82. Manon Garcia's appreciation of Beauvoir underscores this point; see *On ne naît pas soumise, on le devient* (Paris: Climats, 2018).

83. This complicated story and intertext deserves more attention, but that will have to come in a separate work. The Marquis de Sade's *Juliette* (*Juliette, or Vice Amply Rewarded*), published anonymously in 1797–1800, circulated in the nineteenth century, but in clandestine editions. It was republished in 1947 as part of what the editor Jean-Jacques Pauvert promised would be a full collection of de Sade's work. Pauvert asked Beauvoir to write a preface to the new edition. She declined, but reflected on de Sade, his ethic, and morality in "Must We Burn de Sade?" ("Faut-il brûler Sade?", *Les Temps Modernes*, [December 1951 and January 1952]). Publishing de Sade got Pauvert into legal trouble several times over the next decade. It was part of a wave of interest in erotic literature in postwar France. On the twentieth-century revival of Sade, see Carolyn Dean, *The Self and Its Pleasures: Bataille, Lacan, and the History of the Decentered Subject* (Ithaca: Cornell University Press, 2016); Matthew Bridge, "A Monster for Our Times: Reading Sade across the Centuries" (Ph.D. diss., Columbia University, 2011), chap. 5, 214. Aury reviewed Beauvoir's book *The Mandarins* in *La Nouvelle Revue Française* (1954): 1080.

84. *FC1*, 245.

85. Aury, cited in Galster, *Textes*, 266.

86. Jane Albert-Hesse, "Esclave? Victime? Complice?," *Franc-Tireur* (November 3, 1949), cited in Galster, *Textes*, 204–6; Vergnas, "Le troisième sexe," *Les Nouvelles Littéraires*, September 8, 1949, 191–94.

87. *FC1*, 135–36.

88. Maurice Merleau-Ponty, *Sens et non-sens* (1948), trans. Hubert L. Drefyus and Patricia Drefyus (1964), cited in Edward Fullbrook and Kate Fullbrook, *Sex and Philosophy: Rethinking de Beauvoir and Sartre* (London: Bloomsbury, 2008), 145.

89. *FC1*, 72.

2. Beauvoir, Kinsey, and Midcentury Sex

1. François Mauriac, in *Le deuxième sexe de Simone de Beauvoir: Textes réunis et présentés par Ingrid Galster* (Paris: Presses de l'Université Paris-Sorbonne, 2004), 87–88, hereafter *Textes*.

2. Marie-Louise Barron, cited in Galster, *Textes*, 126.

3. The important exceptions are Sylvie Chaperon, "Kinsey en France: Les sexualités féminine et masculine en débat," *Le Mouvement Social* 198, no. 1 (March 2002): 91–110; and Dagmar Herzog, "The Reception of the Kinsey Reports in Europe," *Sexuality and Culture* 10, no. 1 (Winter 2006): 39–48. See also Jo-Ann Pilardi, "The Changing Critical Fortunes of The Second Sex," *History and Theory* 32, no. 1 (February 1993): 51–73.

4. "Talk of the Town," *The New Yorker*, February 22, 1947, 19–20. On the formative effects of reading Wright and others, see Margaret A. Simons, *Beauvoir and "The Second Sex": Feminism, Race, and the Origins of Existentialism* (Lanham, Md.: Rowman & Littlefield, 1999); Sarah Relyea, *Outsider Citizens: The Remaking of Postwar Identity in Wright, Beauvoir, and Baldwin* (New York: Routledge, 2006); Alice Yaeger Kaplan, *Dreaming in French: The Paris Years of Jacqueline Bouvier Kennedy, Susan Sontag, and Angela Davis* (Chicago: University of Chicago Press, 2012); Whitney Walton, *Internationalism, National Identities, and Study Abroad: France and the United States, 1890–1970* (Stanford: Stanford University Press, 2010); and Ursula Tidd, *Simone de Beauvoir, Gender and Testimony* (Cambridge: Cambridge University Press, 1999).

5. Knopf's list of potential readers illustrates the difficulty of placing *The Second Sex* in a single discipline. The "ladies' list" named Margaret Mead, Margaret Sanger, Helene Deutsch, Pearl Buck, Eleanor Roosevelt, and Lillian Hellman. The "men's list" included Max Lerner, Ashley Montagu, Philip Wylie, David Reisman, Benjamin Spock, and Kinsey himself, who declined. Alfred A. Knopf, Inc., Records, Harry Ransom Center, University of Texas at Austin, box 1177.21, Hannah Arendt, December 16, 1952.

6. Deirdre Bair, *Simone de Beauvoir: A Biography* (New York: Summit Books, 1990), 432.

7. Michel Bozon, "Les cadres sociaux de la sexualité," *Sociétés Contemporaines*, no. 41–42 (2001): 5–9.

8. Dagmar Herzog, *Sexuality in Europe: A Twentieth-Century History* (Cambridge: Cambridge University Press, 2011), 3.

9. Simone de Beauvoir, Lettres reçues, subheading Lettres reçues de lecteurs, Manuscrits, Occident, Bibliothèque Nationale de France, N.A.F. 28501, February 24, 1953, May 15, 1952, and May 11, 1953.

10. Françoise Dolto, " 'Paris en parle . . . Le comportement sexuel de la femme américaine,' par le Docteur Alfred Kinsey," *L'Express*, September 19, 1953.

On Kinsey in the United States, see Sarah Igo, *The Averaged American: Surveys, Citizens, and the Making of a Mass Public* (Cambridge: Harvard University Press, 2007); Miriam

G. Reumann, *American Sexual Character: Sex, Gender, and National Identity in the Kinsey Reports* (Berkeley: University of California Press, 2005); Donna J. Drucker, *The Classification of Sex: Alfred Kinsey and the Organization of Knowledge* (Pittsburgh: University of Pittsburgh Press, 2014); Lynn Gorchov, *Sexual Science and Sexual Politics: American Sex Research, 1920–1956* (Baltimore, Johns Hopkins University Press, 2003); Regina Markell Morantz, "The Scientist as Sex Crusader: Alfred C. Kinsey and American Culture," *American Quarterly* 29, no. 5 (Winter 1978): 563–89; and Lionel Trilling, "The Kinsey Report," in *The Liberal Imagination: Essays on Literature and Society* (Garden City, N.Y.: Doubleday, 1953). On sex surveys, see Jacqueline Feldman, "Les rapports nationaux sur les comportement sexuels: Un exemple de deux types d'interaction science-société," *Archives Européennes de Sociologie*, no. 16 (1975): 95–110.

11. Galster, *Textes*, 33, 39.

12. M. Ernst and David Loth, preface to *La vie sexuelle en Amérique* (Paris: SFELT, 1948). On different aspects of the troubling American presence, see Victoria de Grazia, *Irresistible Empire: America's Advance through Twentieth-Century Europe* (Cambridge: Harvard University Press, 2005); and Richard F. Kuisel, *Seducing the French: The Dilemma of Americanization* (Berkeley: University of California Press, 1993). On the difficulties of resisting American advances, see Mary Louise Roberts, *What Soldiers Do: Sex and the American GI in World War II* (Chicago: University of Chicago Press, 2011).

13. Marie-Louise Barron, cited in Galster, *Textes*, 128.

14. Jeannette Prenant, cited in Galster, *Textes*, 272–84; anonymous review, 117.

15. Jean-Marie Domenach, cited in Galster, *Textes*, 33–34.

16. "In This Corner, Woman," *Hartford Courant Magazine*, March 8, 1953.

17. *Boston Traveler*, March 5, 1953. The Alfred A. Knopf records at the Harry Ransom Center hold scores of reviews and clippings; box 1300.7.

18. Ashley Montagu, "A French Gauntlet Tossed to Dr. Kinsey," *Herald Tribune*, February 22, 1953.

19. Clyde Kluckhohn, "The Female of Our Species," *New York Times*, February 22, 1953.

20. Beauvoir, Lettres reçues de lecteurs, February 24, 1953, Vermont.

21. A. R. Mangus, undated clipping (1953), in Knopf records, 1300.7.

22. See Margaret Mead, "The Second Sex, by an Angry Woman," *New York Post*, February 22, 1953, and her contribution to "A SR Panel Takes Aim at *The Second Sex*," *Saturday Review*, February 21, 1953.

23. Undated 1953 clipping (1953), in Knopf records, 1300.7.

24. Margaret Park Redfield, "Book Review: The Second Sex," *American Journal of Sociology* 59, no. 3 (November 1953): 269. Redfield, like Mead, was an anthropologist. See also the letters from Clara Thompson, Abraham Scheinfeld, and others in Knopf records, 1177.21.

25. Elsa Maxwell, "Party Line," *New York Post Home News*, October 14, 1948.

26. Carle C. Zimmerman, "Review: Sexual Behavior in the Human Female," *Harvard Law Review* 67, no. 3 (January 1954): 539.

27. Judith Surkis, "Sex, Sovereignty, and Transnational Intimacies," *American Historical Review* 115, no. 4 (2010): 1093.

28. Lionel Trilling, cited in Mari Jo Buhle, *Feminism and Its Discontents: A Century of Struggle with Psychoanalysis* (Cambridge: Harvard University Press, 1998), 128. See also Joanne Meyerowitz, "'How Common Culture Shapes the Separate Lives': Sexuality, Race, and Mid-Twentieth-Century Social Constructionist Thought," *Journal of American History* 96, no. 4 (March 2010): 1057–84; and Rebecca Jo Plant, *Mom: The Transformation of Motherhood in Modern America* (Chicago: University of Chicago Press, 2010).

29. Bruce Bliven, cited in Chaperon, "Kinsey en France," 92.

30. Françoise d'Eaubonne, *Une femme nommée Castor: Mon amie Simone de Beauvoir* (Paris: Encre, 1986), 162.

31. Joanne J. Meyerowitz, *How Sex Changed: A History of Transsexuality in the United States* (Cambridge: Harvard University Press, 2002). See also John H. Gagnon, *An Interpretation of Desire: Essays in the Study of Sexuality* (Chicago: University of Chicago Press, 2004); Thomas Laqueur, *Making Sex: Body and Gender from the Greeks to Freud* (Cambridge: Harvard University Press, 1990); Arnold Ira Davidson, *The Emergence of Sexuality: Historical Epistemology and the Formation of Concepts* (Cambridge: Harvard University Press, 2001); Paul A. Robinson, *The Modernization of Sex: Havelock Ellis, Alfred Kinsey, William Masters, and Virginia Johnson* (New York: Harper & Row, 1977); and Jane F. Gerhard, *Desiring Revolution: Second-Wave Feminism and the Rewriting of American Sexual Thought, 1920 to 1982* (New York: Columbia University Press, 2001).

32. See Harry Oosterhuis, *Stepchildren of Nature* (Chicago: University of Chicago Press, 2000), and "Sexual Modernity in the Works of Richard von Krafft-Ebing and Albert Moll," *Medical History* 56, no. 2 (2012): 133–55.

33. Laure Murat, La loi du genre: Une histoire culturelle du "troisième sexe" (Paris: Fayard, 2006), 150–57.

34. Havelock Ellis, general preface to *Studies in the Psychology of Sex*, vol. 1 (1927 ed., Project Gutenberg Online), http://www.gutenberg.org/files/13610/13610-h/13610-h.htm.

35. While corresponding about *The Second Sex*, H. M. Parshley reminded Alfred A. Knopf that Ellis's *Studies in the Psychology of Sex* had been off limits to the general public: "How difficult it was to obtain those brown volumes! And now exact reprints in two volumes can be bought anywhere, case histories and all. May you be right in foreseeing a wide demand for the de Beauvoir, which we are in the process of supplying!" Parshley to Knopf, December 10, 1951, Knopf records, 689.13.

36. See George Chauncey Jr. "From Sexual Inversion to Homosexuality: Medicine and the Changing Conceptualization of Female Deviance," *Salmagundi*, no. 58/59 (Fall 1982–Winter 1983): 114–46; and, more recently, Heike Bauer, "Theorizing Female Inversion: Sexology, Discipline, and Gender at the Fin de Siècle," *Journal of the History of Sexuality* 18, no. 1 (January 2009): 84–102.

37. Tracie Matysik, *Reforming the Moral Subject: Ethics and Sexuality in Central Europe, 1890–1930* (Ithaca: Cornell University Press, 2008); Herzog, *Sexuality in Europe*, 18, 28–29. On Hirschfeld, see also Meyerowitz, *How Sex Changed*.

38. Heike Bauer, "Introduction: Translation and the Global Histories of Sexuality," in *A Global History of Sexual Science, 1880–1960*, ed. Veronika Fuechtner, Douglas E. Haynes, and Ryan M. Jones (Los Angeles: University of California Press, 2018), 5.

In France such research was dispersed in separate disciplines: medicine, psychology, and law. Some historians attribute the indifference to sexology in France to the relative permissiveness of laws on homosexuality, which, in the form of sodomy in private between adults, had been decriminalized in 1791 and again in the Napoleonic Code of 1810. But other repressive laws took their toll. The French law of July 1920 criminalized any action or literature that "describes, divulges, or offers to reveal procedures that prevent pregnancy or to facilitate the use of those procedures." The law had a genuinely chilling effect on research and discussion. Sylvie Chaperon, "La sexologie française contemporaine: Un premier bilan historiographique," *Revue d'Histoire des Sciences Humaines* 17, no. 2 (2007): 15; Sylvie Chaperon, *Les origines de la sexologie* (Paris: Louis Audibert Éditions, 2007); Alain Corbin, *L'harmonie des plaisirs: Les manières de jouir du siècle des lumières à l'avènement de la sexologie* (Paris: Perrin, 2008); Janine Mossuz-Lavau, *Les lois de l'amour: Les politiques de la sexualité en France de 1950 à nos jours* (Paris: Éditions Payot, 1991); Murat, *La loi du genre*.

39. Kate Fisher and Jana Funke, " 'Let Us Leave the Hospital; Let Us Go on a Journey around the World': British and German Sexual Science and the Global Search for Sexual Variation," in Fuechtner, Haynes, and Jones, *Global History of Sexual Science*, 51–69. Judith Surkis's work is particularly attentive to the colonial dimensions of sexual thought; see *Sexing the Citizen: Morality and Masculinity in France, 1870–1920* (Ithaca: Cornell University Press, 2006, and *Sex, Law, and Sovereignty in French Algeria, 1830–1930* (Ithaca: Cornell University Press, 2019).

40. Arnold I. Davidson, "Sex and the Emergence of Sexuality," *Critical Inquiry* 14, no. 1 (Autumn 1987): 21.

41. Buhle, Feminism and Its Discontents, 23.

42. "We know less about the sexual life of little girls than of boys. But we need not feel ashamed of this distinction; after all, the sexual life of adult women is a 'dark continent' for psychology." Sigmund Freud, *The Question of Lay Analysis* (1926), in *The Standard Edition of the Complete Psychological Works of Sigmund Freud*, James Strachey, ed. (London: Hogarth Press and the Institute of Psycho-Analysis, 1986), 20: 212.

43. For a short and lucid discussion, see Luce Irigaray, "Psychoanalytic Theory: Another Look" in *This Sex Which Is Not One*, trans. Catherine Porter (Ithaca: Cornell University Press, 1985) 49–55; and for much more, Buhle, Feminism and Its Discontents, 22–124.

44. "He concentrated in the attributes of sexuality every variety of emotion. Sympathy and attachment, respect and contempt, parental love and filial piety, friendship and enmity, bodily victories and symbolic defeats, aesthetic pleasures and an interest in the ugly—all are assimilated to this unifying source." Philip Rieff, *Freud: The Mind of the Moralist* (Chicago: University of Chicago Press, 1979), 152.

45. Meyerowitz, "Common Culture," 1057–58.

46. Serge Moscovici, *La psychanalyse: Son image et son public* (Paris: Presses Universitaires de France, 1961), 19, on *homo psychanalyticus*.

47. *Modern Woman: The Lost Sex* by Ferdinand Lundberg and Marynia Foot Farnham (New York: Harper & Brothers, 1947) made the conservative case in the terms of ego psychology, linking women's "lost function and value" to "effeminate" men and the disordered emotions that had produced fascism and Nazism. Beauvoir took on Lundberg and Farnham in the introduction to *The Second Sex*. For the American side of this story see Plant, *Mom*, 19–54; and Buhle, *Feminism and Its Discontents*, 175–79.

48. Dagmar Herzog, *Cold War Freud: Psychoanalysis in an Age of Catastrophes* (Cambridge: Cambridge University Press, 2017), 15.

49. Alfred C. Kinsey, Wardell B. Pomeroy, and Clyde Martin, *Sexual Behavior in the Human Male* (Philadelphia: W. B. Saunders, 1948), 23.

50. Robinson, *The Modernization of Sex*, 57; Kinsey, *Human Male*, 110.

51. Kinsey, *Human Male*, 22–23, 21, 34, 206–7, 19, 9. In *Sexual Behavior in the Human Female* (Philadelphia: W. B. Saunders, 1953), Kinsey put more emphasis on ordinary people's ignorance about their own sexuality (5–6).

52. Kinsey, *Human Male*, 18, 197, 59.

53. Simone de Beauvoir, *A Transatlantic Love Affair: Letters to Nelson Algren* (New York: New Press, 1998), 254, December 31, 1948.

54. Simone de Beauvoir, *The Second Sex*, trans. H. M. Parshley (New York: Knopf, 1953), xiii, hereafter *TSS 1953*; Beauvoir, *Le deuxième sexe*, vol. 1 (Paris: Gallimard, 1949), 13, hereafter *DS1*.

55. Beauvoir, *DS1*, 73; *TSS 1953*, 55; Simone de Beauvoir, *The Second Sex*, trans. Constance Borde and Sheila Malovany-Chevallier (New York: Knopf, 2009), 45, hereafter *TSS 2009*.

56. Beauvoir, *DS1*, 77; *TSS* 1953, 38; *TSS* 2009, 49. See also Toril Moi, *Simone de Beauvoir: The Making of an Intellectual Woman* (Oxford: Blackwell, 1994), 169.

57. Beauvoir, *DS1*, 92; *TSS* 1953, 95; *TSS* 2009, 102. Juliet Mitchell expresses her dismay at Beauvoir's misinterpretation of Freud and its legacy to feminism in *Psychoanalysis and Feminism: Freud, Reich, Laing, and Women* (New York: Pantheon, 1974), 310–11.

58. Marie-Christine Hamon, "Le point de vue psychanalytique," in *Simone de Beauvoir: "Le deuxième sexe," le livre fondateur du féminisme moderne en situation*, ed. Ingrid Galster (Paris: Honoré Champion, 2004), 53–68. As H. M. Parshley was translating *The Second Sex*, he worried that Beauvoir was borrowing too much from Deutsch—both *Psychoanalysis and the Sexual Functions of Woman* (1924) and *The Psychology of Women* (1944). Karl Menninger sharply noted Beauvoir's unfamiliarity with the psychoanalytic literature on femininity. See Forum, "A SR Panel Takes Aim at The Second Sex," *Saturday Review*, February 21, 1953, Knopf records, 1300.7

59. In 1949 Roland Dalbiez, *La méthode psychanalytique et la doctrine freudienne* introduced Freudianism and its associated debates to many French readers. Elisabeth Roudinesco, *Histoire de la psychanalyse en France*, 2 vols. (Paris: Fayard, 1994); Serge Moscovici, *La psychanalyse, son image et son public* (Paris: Presses Universitaires de France, 1961).

60. Simone de Beauvoir, "Brigitte Bardot and the Lolita Syndrome," *Esquire*, August 1959, reprinted in *Simone de Beauvoir: Feminist Writings*, ed. Margaret A. Simons and Marybeth Timmermann (Urbana: University of Illinois Press, 2015), 119.

61. Beauvoir, *DS1*, 105; *TSS* 1953, 49; *TSS* 2009, 53.

62. Herman R. Lantz, "Review: The Second Sex," *Marriage and Family Living* 15, no. 3 (August 1953), 276. Clipping in Knopf records, 1300.7. Alfred A. Knopf and H. M. Parshley exchanged thoughts on how readers might respond; see November 27 and December 10, 1951, Knopf records, 689.13.

63. Carl Victor Little, "New Books: The Second Sex," *Houston Texas Press*, February 27, 1953, Knopf records, 1300.7.

64. Clyde Kluckhohn, "*Sexual Behavior in the Human Female* and *The Second Sex*," *Perspectives USA* (Spring 1954): 144–47, compares *The Second Sex* with Kinsey's second report. Margaret Mead, for her part, lamented that the "sudden removal of a previously guaranteed reticence has left many young people singularly defenseless in just those areas where their desire to conform was protected by a lack of knowledge of the extent of nonconformity." Cited in Gerhard, *Desiring Revolution*, 63. His review in the *New York Times* similarly judged the book to be "primarily about sexuality." "Fowler V. Harper Book Review: *Sexual Behavior in the Human Female*," *Yale Law Journal* 895, no. 63 (1954): 895–99.

65. Brendan Gill, "Books: No More Eve," *The New Yorker*, February 28, 1953, 99. Gill welcomed Beauvoir's debunking of ideas about womanhood: "Nothing looks stronger or less in need of scrutiny than a commonplace—up to moment when, having outlived its usefulness, it begins to be called poppy-cock."

66. Kinsey, *Human Female*, on premarital coitus, 325–26, 578, on rape, 213, 287, and 321; *Human Male*, 237–38, 263–64, 391, 578, 608, 300. Unwanted pregnancy is a source of "post-coital regret," *Human Female*, 318, 345, 5.

Among the report's sample of "2094 single, white females" there had been 476 pregnancies. But, Kinsey argued, the "2094 women who had had coitus had had it approximately 460,000 times." Kinsey, *Human Female*, 327. Note his use of "white"; he commented that "European and Asiatic populations" might be different and did not mention African Americans.

67. Kinsey, *Human Female*, 582. Further discussion in Regina Morantz, "The Scientist as Sex Crusader," *American Quarterly* 29, no. 5 (1977): 571–73; Gerhard, *Desiring Revolution*, 29–43; Helene Deutsch, *The Psychology of Women*, 2 vols. (New York: Allyn & Bacon,

1943, 1945). Sonya Rudikoff, "Feminism Reconsidered," *Hudson Review* 9, no. 2 (Summer 1956): 178–98, also illustrates Deutsch's powerful influence at the time.

68. Barbara S. Andrew, "Beauvoir's Place in Philosophical Thought," in *The Cambridge Companion to Simone de Beauvoir*, ed. Claudia Card (Cambridge: Cambridge University Press, 2003), 38.

69. "Bardot and the Lolita Syndrome," 124.

70. Sally Wood, "The Truth about Women," *Kenyon Review* 15, no. 3 (Summer 1953): 484, 486–89, 485.

71. These included the new "homophile" journal *Arcadie*, founded in 1954, and the prolific left intellectual Daniel Guérin. See Daniel Guérin, *Kinsey et la sexualité* (Paris: Juillard, 1954), and *Essai sur la révolution sexuelle: Après Reich et Kinsey* (Paris: Éditions Belfond, 1969); Chaperon, "Kinsey en France," 100–103; and Julian Jackson, *Living in Arcadia: Homosexuality, Politics, and Morality in France from the Liberation to AIDS* (Chicago: University of Chicago Press, 2009).

72. On the popularity, persuasiveness, and authority of surveys, see Igo, *The Averaged American;* for this moment in France, Judith Coffin, "Between Opinion and Desire: *Elle* Magazine's Survey Research in 1950s France," in *The Voice of the Citizen Consumer: A History of Market Research, Consumer Movements, and the Political Public Sphere*, ed. Kerstin Brückweh (London: Oxford University Press, 2011), 51–73.

73. *Elle*, March 15, 1954, and June 27, 1955.

74. "La Française et l'amour," *Sondages: Revue Française de l'Opinion Publique* 23 (1961): 1, 37–85; *La Française et l'amour: Une enquête de l'Institut Français d'Opinion Publique*, ed. Jacques Rémy and Robert Woog (Paris: Éditions Robert Laffont, 1960). The film is in the Archives du Film at the Centre National du Cinéma.

75. La Française et l'amour, 15.

76. "La Française et l'amour," 40.

77. The young did not trust conventional authorities, but they "trusted and respected themselves," Giroud continued, arguing for the democratic aspects of the new research. La Française et l'amour, 170. Giroud had commissioned the study of "The New Wave," *La Nouvelle Vague*, a year earlier. She was not one to note all the significant differences of class, race and ethnicity, education, or cultural capital that simply disappeared in the aggregated version of a generation.

78. *Elle*, March 15, 1954.

79. The phrase is from Samuel Moyn's discussion of debates over context in intellectual history; it is not his position. Samuel Moyn, "Imaginary Intellectual History," in *Rethinking Modern European Intellectual History*, ed. Darrin McMahon and Samuel Moyn (New York: Oxford University Press, 2014), 116. See also the contributions of Peter Gordon and Judith Surkis to this same volume. Judith Surkis, "Of Scandals and Supplements: Relating Intellectual and Cultural History," in ibid., 95–107 and Peter Gordon, "Contextualism and Criticism in the History of Ideas," in ibid., 34–50.

80. Simone de Beauvoir, "The Chemistry of Love," *Daily Express*, August 11, 1959, 8, in Beauvoir, Coupures de presse, NAF 28501.

3. Readers and Writers

1. See Tamara Chaplin, *Turning on the Mind: French Philosophers on Television* (Chicago: University of Chicago Press, 2007), chap. 1; Julie Augras, "Écritures de lecteurs: Beauvoir lue. La réception des *Mandarins* (1954–1959)," *Revue d'Histoire Littéraire de la France* 116, no. 2 (April–June 2016): 387–408; Björn Larsson, *La réception des "Mandarins": Le roman de Simone de Beauvoir face à la critique littéraire en France* (Lund: Lund University

Press, 1988); and Sally Scholz and Shannon Mussett, eds., *The Contradictions of Freedom: Philosophical Essays on Simone de Beauvoir's "The Mandarins"* (New York: SUNY Press, 2005).

2. Sandrine Sanos, *Simone de Beauvoir: Creating a Feminist Existence in the World* (New York: Oxford University Press, 2017), 78–80.

3. Simone de Beauvoir, Lettres reçues, subheading Lettres reçues de lecteurs, Manuscrits, Occident, Bibliothèque Nationale de France, N.A.F. 28501, undated (late 1954), Queyrac-Medoc, Gironde.

4. Ibid., December 14, 1960. See also September 24, 1969.

5. Ibid., December 8, 1954, Brussels; September 21, 1956; August 6, 1956, Montreal; January 13, 1960, Lausanne, Switzerland.

6. See Beauvoir's archive at the Bibliothèque nationale de France for more on her appearances in *Match* and *Jours de France* (NAF 28509, Dossier 1954). See Chaplin, *Turning on the Mind*, chap. 2, and Sophie de Closets's *Quand la television aimait les écrivains* (Brussels: De Boeck, 2004), 86, on *Lecture pour tous* and Beauvoir.

7. Beauvoir, Lettres reçues de lecteurs, undated, January–June 1957.

8. Judith Lyon-Caen and Dinah Ribard, *L'historien et la littérature* (Paris: Éditions de la Découverte, 2010), 85.

9. Chaplin, *Turning on the Mind*, chap. 1.

10. Beauvoir, Lettres reçues de lecteurs, February 1960. By 1959 Beauvoir was theorizing stardom as well as enacting it. Simone de Beauvoir, "Brigitte Bardot and the Lolita Syndrome," *Esquire*, August 1959.

11. Beauvoir, Lettres reçues de lecteurs, July 7, 1957.

12. Ibid., March 16, undated (the letter is catalogued as 1957, but it was written after *The Prime of Life*, so it must be 1960).

13. Ibid., December 26, 1958.

14. Ibid., in English, undated, last letter in 1957 file.

15. Ibid., September 24, 1969, Durban, South Africa; February 12, 1969, London.

16. Sharon Marcus, *The Drama of Celebrity* (Princeton: Princeton University Press, 219), 6.

17. Beauvoir, Lettres reçues de lecteurs, October 27, 1954; January 27, 1961; May 11, 1957, Liège, France; February 13, 1959; February 11, 1961, Paris.

18. Lettres reçues de lecteurs, January 29, 1957; see also June 12, 1960; January 27, 1961.

19. "Il l'avait d'abord trouvée si gourmée qu'il lui avait dit en riant: 'Vous prenez la vie avec des gants de chevreau glacé.'" Simone de Beauvoir, *Mémoires d'une jeune fille rangée* (Paris: Gallimard, 1958), 302.

20. Bruno Cabanes, "Negotiating Intimacy in the Shadow of War (France, 1914–1920s)," *French Politics, Culture & Society* 31 (Spring 2013): 9; Martyn Lyons, *Reading Cultures and Writing Practices in Nineteenth-Century France* (Toronto: University of Toronto Press, 2008), 167–84.

21. Martha Hanna, *Your Death Would Be Mine: Paul and Marie Pireaud in the Great War* (Cambridge: Harvard University Press, 2006); Ferdinand Buisson, *Le dictionnaire de pédagogie et d'instruction primaire* (Paris: Hachette, 1886–1888), s.v. *correspondance scolaire* http://sites.utoronto.ca/sable/recherche/catalogues/manuels/index.htm.

22. For example, Lucien Heudebert, *La correspondance de tout le monde, lettres intimes, lettres commerciales, lettres diverses (Paris: Albin Michel, 1917; revised in 1926, 1930, and 1951).*

23. Beauvoir, Lettres reçues de lecteurs, December 23, 1970, Rome; March 31, 1970, Venice.

24. Cited by Cécile Dauphin, "Les manuels épistolaires au XIXe siècle," in *La correspondance: Les usages de la lettre au XIXe siècle*, ed. Roger Chartier et al. (Paris: Fayard,

1991), 229. See also Daniel Fabre, ed., introduction to *Écritures ordinaires* (Paris: Gallimard, 1999), 18.

25. Liz Stanley, "The Epistolarium: On Theorizing Letters and Correspondences," *Auto/biography* 12, no. 3 (2004): 208. See also Deena Goodman, "Letter Writing and the Emergence of Gendered Subjectivity in Eighteenth-Century France," *Journal of Women's History* 17, no. 2 (Summer 2005): 9–37.

26. Louis Lavelle, chap. 1, "The Adventure of Narcissus," in *The Dilemma of Narcissus,* trans. William Gairdner (Burdett, N.Y.: Larson Publications, 1993). Lavelle (1883–1951) was a French philosopher of consciousness and perception.

27. Beauvoir, Lettres reçues de lecteurs, October 25, 1960, Mons-en-Barœul, France.

28. Ibid., January 1965.

29. Ibid., January 14, 1959; May 11, 1957, Liège, France; undated, 1957; São Paolo; undated, 1957; December 28, 1957; January 1, 1955; February 11, 1961, Paris. On *The Mandarins* as a roman à clef, see Beauvoir's *Force des choses,* vol. 1 (Paris: Gallimard, 1963), 364–70, hereafter *FC.*

30. Beauvoir, Lettres reçues de lecteurs, February 25, 1959; see also December 13, 1958; December 13, 1958, Paris; November 17, 1958; February 13, 1959; November 26, 1960; and November 22, 1960.

31. Ibid., May 3, 1959; January 27, 1961, Montreal.

32. Nancy K. Miller, "But enough about me, what do you think of my memoir?," *Yale Journal of Criticism* 13, no. 2 (Fall 2000): 426–27.

33. Referring to Beauvoir's *Force de l'âge* (Paris: Gallimard, 1960), hereafter *FA;* Beauvoir, Lettres reçues de lecteurs, October 25, 1960, Mons-en-Barœul, France; December 1960, Romans-sur-Isère, France; November 11, 1967.

34. Beauvoir, Lettres reçues de lecteurs, May 3, 1959; October 27, 1958. For others, see January 16, 1961; May 21, 1959 (from a woman who was about twelve years older than Beauvoir); May 3, 1959. See also May 9, 1960; October 27, 1958, Hauteville, France; November 28, 1958.

See Carolyn Steedman, *Dust: The Archive and Cultural History* (New Brunswick: Rutgers University Press, 2002), 76–78, on readers' search for a sense of self, and the reading that "confirms them as they want to be, and *feel in some measure that they already are*" (emphasis added).

35. Beauvoir, Lettres reçues de lecteurs, December 27, 1960, Paris.

36. Miller, "But enough about me," 432.

37. Beauvoir, Lettres reçues de lecteurs, undated, 1958.

38. Ibid., June 24, 1964; undated, 1963; March 30, 1965, Montreal; June 13, 1964; January 30, 1964; undated, 1963, Montmartre (Paris); and scores of others.

39. Ibid., March 25, 1955; March 5, 1955, Algiers; June 19, 1960, Sarthe, France (one reader did send her diary); January 30, 1959; March 13, 1964; March 13, 1964.

40. Ibid., June 19, 1964, Garches, France; April 15, 1955, Paris.

41. Ibid., November 8, 1958; November 26, 1960; November 1, 1958; November 20, 1958.

42. Martine Sonnet, "L'émoi des demoiselles en voyage: Du voyage dans quelques journaux intimes de jeunes filles du XIXe siècle," *Genre & Histoire* 9 (Autumn 2011): http://genrehistoire.revues.org/1382. Philippe Lejeune and Catherine Bogaert, *Le journal intime: Histoire et anthologie* (Paris: Les Éditions Textuel, 2006); Françoise Simonet-Tenant, *Le journal intime: Genre littéraire et écriture ordinaire* (Paris: Nathan Université, 2001); Lyons, *Reading Cultures and Writing Practices,* 167–84.

43. Beauvoir, Lettres reçues de lecteurs, August 31, 1970.

44. See Lejeune and Bogaert, *Le journal intime*, 91–92.

45. Fabre, *Écritures ordinaires*, 20.

46. Jennifer Ebbeler, *Disciplining Christians: Correction and Community in Augustine's Letters* (New York: Oxford University Press, 2012).

47. Cited in Ann Fabian, *The Unvarnished Truth: Personal Narratives in Nineteenth-Century America* (Berkeley: University of California Press, 2000).

48. Kate Millett, "Simone de Beauvoir . . . Autobiographer," in *Critical Essays on Simone de Beauvoir*, ed. Elaine Marks (Boston: G. K. Hall, 1987), 202–3. On feminist dimensions of autobiography, see also Nancy K. Miller, *Subject to Change* (New York: Columbia University Press, 1990), 55. Sharon Marcus's *Between Women: Friendship, Desire, and Marriage in Victorian England* (Princeton: Princeton University Press, 2007) also suggests distinctive features of nineteenth-century "life-writing" and autobiography.

49. Beauvoir, Lettres reçues de lecteurs, September 8, 1960, Saint-Cloud, France.

50. Several sent their own *notes de lecteurs*. See, for instance, ibid., January 2, 1957.

51. See Anne Fabian's persuasive critique of Williams's argument in *The Unvarnished Truth*, 7.

52. Simone de Beauvoir, *Memoirs of a Dutiful Daughter*, trans. James Kirkup (New York: Harper Perennial, 2005), 191.

53. Beauvoir, Lettres reçues de lecteurs, August 29, 1957; December 1960.

54. Beauvoir, Lettres reçues de lecteurs, December 3, 1952.

55. Simone de Beauvoir, *Le deuxième sexe*, vol. 2 (Paris: Gallimard, 1949), 146–47. See also Lettres reçues de lecteurs, May 16, 1961 (in English), and undated, 1961, cited earlier.

56. Tamara Chaplin, "Émile perverti? ou 'Comment se font les enfants.' Deux siècles d'éducation sexuelle en France," in *Les jeunes & la sexualité: Initiations, interdits, identités (19e–21e siècle)*, ed. Régis Revenin (Paris: Éditions Autrement, 2010), 380.

57. Chaplin, "Émile perverti?"; Mary Louise Roberts, *What Soldiers Do: Sex and the American GI in World War II* (Chicago: University of Chicago Press, 2011); Alain Corbin, *Les filles de noce: Misère sexuelle et prostitution, 19e et 20e siècles* (Paris: Aubier Montaigne, 1978). In the French Caribbean, policies differed dramatically; there, the state promoted population control. See chap. 8, below, and Kristen Stromberg Childers, *Seeking Imperialism's Embrace: National Identity, Decolonization, and Assimilation in the French Caribbean* (New York: Oxford University Press, 2019).

58. Sarah Fishman, *From Vichy to the Sexual Revolution: Gender and Family Life in Postwar France* (Oxford: Oxford University Press, 2017), 98–99.

59. Sally Alexander, "The Mysteries and Secrets of Women's Bodies," in *The Routledge History of Sex and the Body: 1500 to Present*, ed. Sarah Toulalan and Kate Fisher (New York: Routledge, 2013), 165.

60. Beauvoir, Lettres reçues de lecteurs, November 30, 1957, Thiers, France. On Ogino-Knaus calendars, see Melanie Latham, *Regulating Reproduction: A Century of Conflict in Britain and France* (Manchester: Manchester University Press, 2002); Anne-Claire Rebreyend, *Intimités amoureuses: France 1920–1975* (Toulouse: Presses Universitaires du Mirail, 2009), 212–13.

61. Jacques Derogy, *Des enfants malgré nous* (Paris: Les Éditions de Minuit, 1956), 17.

62. Beauvoir, Lettres reçues de lecteurs, March 16, 1956; November 21, 1956; November 21, 1956. See also April 3, 1956; and November 21, 1956.

63. Michel Foucault, *The History of Sexuality*, trans. Robert Hurley, vol. 1 (New York: Vintage Books, 1990), 17, 27.

64. Beauvoir, Lettres reçues de lecteurs, undated, in 1961 folder.

65. Ibid., April 19, 1957.

66. Ibid., undated, 1961.

67. Ibid., October 13, 1958.

68. Ibid., January 19, 1958; and undated, 1961.

69. Mona Ozouf, *Les mots des femmes: Essai sur la singularité française* (Paris: Fayard, 1995), 295.

70. Menie Grégoire, "La presse féminine, la femme et l'amour," *Esprit* (July–August 1959): 17–34; Marcelle Ségal, *Mon métier le Courrier du cœur* (Paris: P. Horay, 1952) (Segal wrote the *courrier du cœur* column at *Elle* for forty years); Evelyne Sullerot, *La presse féminine* (Paris: A. Colin, 1963); Edgar Morin, *L'esprit du temps: Essai sur la culture de masse* (Paris: Grasset, 1962).

71. Morin, *L'esprit du temps*; Sullerot, *La presse féminine*; Christian Delporte, "Au miroir des Médias," in *La culture de masse en France de la Belle Époque à aujourd'hui*, ed. Jean-Pierre Rioux and Jean-Francois Sirinelli (Paris: Fayard, 2002), 305–7.

72. Beauvoir, Lettres reçues de lecteurs, December 28, 1957; June 18, 1964, Aixe-sur-Vienne, France.

73. As Nancy K. Miller puts it, the author of a memoir wishes "to be—somehow—encountered in this way, found on that particular shelf." Memoir is "the record of an experience in search of a community." Miller, "But Enough about Me," 423.

74. Beauvoir, *FA*, 644.

75. Beauvoir, Lettres reçues de lecteurs, November 30, 1960.

76. Tracie Matysik, "Belated Lessons from Freud: Why Historians Never Tell the (Whole) Truth," unpublished paper, Institute for Historical Studies, UT Austin, May 8, 2014. Thanks to the author.

77. Beauvoir, Lettres reçues de lecteurs, November 30, 1954, Lausanne, Switzerland.

78. Ibid., November 16, 1954; November 21, 1956. See also July 16, 1960, Paris.

79. Ibid., October 25, 1960.

80. Ibid., November 18, 1961, Paris.

81. Ibid., December 31, 1961.

82. Geneviève Fraisse, *Le privilège de Simone de Beauvoir (suivi de "Une mort douce")* (Arles: Actes Sud, 2008).

83. Ibid., December 31, 1961.

84. Ibid., February 12, 1960, London.

85. See Lyon-Caen and Ribard, *L'historien*, 90–100, for an excellent discussion of the "Rousseau phenomenon" and Romantic letter writing in general. Also Robert Darnton, "Readers Respond to Rousseau: The Fabrication of Romantic Sensitivity," in *The Great Cat Massacre: And Other Episodes in French Cultural History* (New York: Basic Books, 1984), 215–56; Philippe Lejeune, *Le pacte autobiographique* (Paris: Seuil, 1975); and Jim Miller, *Rousseau: Dreamer of Democracy* (New Haven: Yale University Press, 1984).

86. Lejeune is writing about social media: "C'est le frisson du direct, régime que le journal, au cours de sa long histoire, n'avait jamais connu, et qui le rapproche de la correspondance." Lejeune and Bogaert, *Le journal intime,* 226.

Beauvoir, Lettres reçues de lecteurs, November 11, 1964.

87. Her remarks sent some readers back to Rousseau: "I can't believe that man wrote that before Freud! He alternates between the purest bad faith and the most penetrating analysis of that bad faith." Beauvoir, Lettres reçues de lecteurs, August 24, 1960.

88. Carolyn Steedman, "State-Sponsored Autobiography," in *Moments of Modernity: Reconstructing Britain, 1945–1964*, ed. Becky Conekin, Frank Mort, and Chris Waters (New York: Rivers Oram, 1995), 55.

89. Beauvoir, Lettres reçues de lecteurs, September 24, 1959, Durban, South Africa.

90. Ibid., November 23, 1960.

91. Ibid., October 15, 1961, Sofia, Bulgaria.

92. Ibid., May 20, 1960.

93. *FA*, 11–12; *FC*, 1, 8.

94. *FA*, 29–33; Beauvoir, Lettres reçues de lecteurs, November 26, 1960.

4. The Algerian War and the Scandal of Torture

1. Ursula Tidd, "Simone de Beauvoir et les usages de la mémoire," in *Simone de Beauvoir*, ed. Jean-Louis Jeannelle and Eliane Lecarme-Tabone (Paris: Éditions de L'Herne, 2012), 241–46, especially engages with Michael Rothberg's *Multidirectional Memory: Remembering the Holocaust in the Age of Decolonization* (Stanford: Stanford University Press, 2009). See Sandrine Sanos, *Simone de Beauvoir: Creating a Feminist Existence* (Oxford: Oxford University Press, 2016); Annabelle Golay, "Féminisme et postcolonialisme: Beauvoir, Fanon et la guerre d'Algérie," *International Journal of Francophone Studies* 10, no. 3 (November 2007): 407–24; Judith Surkis, "Ethics and Violence: Simone de Beauvoir, Djamila Boupacha, and the Algerian War," *French Politics, Culture & Society* 28, no. 2 (Summer 2010): 38–55. See also Heidi Brown, "From Sensation to Representation: The Torture of Djamila Boupacha during the Algerian War," *Women in French Studies* 26 (2018): 83–95; Mary Caputi, "Beauvoir and the Case of Djamila Boupacha," in *Simone de Beauvoir's Political Thinking*, ed. Lori Marso and Patricia Moynagh (Champaign: University of Illinois Press, 2006), 109–26; Mairéad Ní Bhriain, "Public Opinion and Passive Complicity during the Algerian War: Simone de Beauvoir and the Djamila Boupacha Affair," *Irish Journal of French Studies* 10 (2010): 97; Julien Murphy, "Beauvoir and the Algerian War: Toward a Postcolonial Ethic," in *Feminist Interpretations of Simone de Beauvoir*, ed. Margaret Simons (University Park: Pennsylvania State University Press, 1995), chap. 14. General issues about French intellectuals or the attractiveness of their politics have been discussed by Tony Judt, *Past Imperfect: French Intellectuals, 1944–1956* (Berkeley: University of California Press, 1992); Benjamin Stora, *La gangrène et l'oubli: La mémoire de la guerre d'Algérie* (Paris: La Découverte & Syros, 1998); James D. Le Sueur, *Uncivil War: Intellectuals and Identity Politics during the Decolonization of Algeria* (Philadelphia: University of Pennsylvania Press, 2001); Yoav Di-Capua, *No Exit: Arab Existentialism, Jean-Paul Sartre, and Decolonization* (Chicago: University of Chicago Press, 2018); and Emma Kuby, *Political Survivors: The Resistance, the Cold War, and the Fight against Concentration Camps after 1945* (Ithaca: Cornell University Press, 2019).

2. Herrick Chapman, *France's Long Reconstruction* (Cambridge: Harvard University Press, 2018), 26–298.

The May 1945 massacre in Sétif is often considered the war's beginning. Celebrations of the European victory were accompanied by demonstrations for political rights. The police clashed with demonstrators. One hundred Europeans bystanders were killed. The French military, police, and settler militias responded with a week-long campaign of "pacification," killing thousands of Algerians. Sétif drove Algerian nationalism underground and mobilized it. In the fall of 1954, the FLN launched a series of attacks that marked the beginning of open war. Benjamin Stora, *Algeria, 1830–2000: A Short History* (Ithaca: Cornell University Press, 2001); James McDougall, *A History of Algeria* (New York: Oxford University Press, 2017), 179–80.

3. *Mémoires d'une jeune fille rangée* was written between 1956 and 1958. It was published the same year as Henri Alleg's *La question*, a scandal-making revelation of torture that François Mauriac likened to the Dreyfus Affair.

4. He was elected not by universal suffrage but rather by an electoral college, which would provide the transition to direct election in 1965. The referendum also gave the overseas

territories of France the choice between accepting the constitution or independence, with the immediate withdrawal of French aid. Guinea alone became independent.

5. De Gaulle pursued an ambiguous politics; while he talked about different routes to *"autodétermination,"* the FLN did not respond to his overtures.

6. In Algeria, 1960 opened with the "week of the barricades," when activists on the extreme right tried to mobilize European settlers against de Gaulle. Boupacha's first trial was in June 1960; Francis Jeanson's was in September 1960. For a detailed account, see Le Sueur, *Uncivil War,* 230–38.

7. On Halimi, see careful readings of her autobiographies in Mireille Rosello, "Gisèle Halimi entre plainte et plaidoyer: 'On naît avocate, on ne le devient pas,'" *Modern and Contemporary France* 12, no. 3 (2004): 287–98; and Vanessa Codaccioni, "(Dé)politisation du genre et des questions sexuelles dans un procès politique en contexte colonial: Le viol, le procès et l'affaire Djamila Boupacha (1960–1962)," *Nouvelles Questions Féministes* 29, no. 1 (2010): 32–45.

8. Simone de Beauvoir, Lettres reçues, subheading Lettres reçues de lecteurs, Manuscrits, Occident, Bibliothèque Nationale de France, N.A.F. 28501, October 10, 1960, Paris.

9. For details, see Jean-Louis Jeannelle's essay in the Pléiade edition of Simone de Beauvoir, *Mémoirs,* vol. 1 (Paris: Gallimard, 2008), 1395. Algerian independence came in July 1963.

10. Simone de Beauvoir, *La force des choses,* 2 vols. (Paris: Gallimard, 1963), 1:501, hereafter *FC1* and *FC2* for volumes 1 and 2, respectively.

11. On her inability to celebrate, see Beauvoir, *FC2,* 487–88.

12. As Beauvoir observed, she was echoing Jean Genet and Michel Leiris. Ibid., 57.

13. Beauvoir, *FC1,* 10.

14. Beauvoir commented on her readers in Francis Jeanson, *Simone de Beauvoir ou l'entreprise de vivre (suivi de deux entretiens avec Simone de Beauvoir)* (Paris: Seuil, 1966), 269–72; and in an interview with Madeleine Gobeil, "Simone de Beauvoir: The Art of Fiction, No. 35," *Paris Review* 34 (Spring–Summer 1965). See also Jean-Louis Jeannelle, "Notice," in Beauvoir, *Mémoirs,* 1:1415.

15. Simone de Beauvoir, *Tout compte fait* (Paris: Gallimard, 1972), 32, hereafter *TCF.*

16. Simone de Beauvoir, *La force de l'âge* (Paris: Gallimard, 1960), 411, hereafter *FA.*

17. Beauvoir, *TCF,* 38.

18. Simone de Beauvoir, "An Eye for an Eye," *Les Temps Modernes* 1, no. 5 (1946); Margaret A. Simons, ed., *Simone de Beauvoir: Philosophical Writings* (Urbana: University of Illinois Press, 2004); Alice Kaplan, *The Collaborator: The Trial and Execution of Robert Brasillach* (Chicago: University of Chicago Press, 2000).

19. Beauvoir, *TCF,* 43.

20. Ibid. On their postwar celebrity and how she experienced it, see *FC1,* 62–71. On the couple's division of political labor, see *FC1,* 359; *TCF,* 43. On fretting about how she might "engage" in the war, Jeanson and his politics, and her decision to turn to memoir, all circa 1956, see *FC2,* 126–29.

21. Pierre Mendès-France, November 12, 1954, in the National Assembly. Mitterand's speech was also delivered before the National Assembly on November 12. The episode is covered in Martin Evans, *Algeria: France's Undeclared War* (New York: Oxford University Press, 2012), 124.

22. Matthew James Connelly, *A Diplomatic Revolution: Algeria's Fight for Independence and the Origins of the Post–Cold War Era* (Oxford: Oxford University Press, 2002); Christopher Harrison, "French Attitudes to Empire and the Algerian War," *African Affairs* 82, no. 326 (1983): 75–95.

23. Four thousand Algerians (immigrants and French nationals) were killed and ten thousand wounded in metropolitan France between 1956 and 1962. Fighting took place in Paris, Lyon, the east, and the north. Benjamin Stora, "La gauche et les minorités anticoloniales françaises devant les divisions du nationalisme Algérien (1954–1958)," in *La guerre d'Algérie et les français: Colloque de L'Institut d'Histoire du temps present*, ed. Jean-Pierre Rioux (Paris: Fayard, 1990), 63.

24. See Charles-Robert Ageron, "L'opinion française à travers les sondages," in Rioux, *La guerre d'Algérie et les français*, 25–44. Ageron argues that opinion polls showed strong attachment to the empire and all that it signified, but attachment was modulated by pessimism about the future of any "union" of France and Algeria and by widespread confusion about the conditions under which the war might end. The upshot was a "presumptive resignation," in Ageron's words. "The public was skeptical, but accepted without illusions or a collective drama of conscience, that Algeria would no longer be a province of France" (31, 41–42).

25. In January 1957, in the midst of the Battle of Algiers, the FLN demonstrated its hold over civilian populations by calling for a general strike to start on January 28. The French military offensive included nighttime arrests and surveillance and control of the Algerian population.

26. General Jacques Massu on "nouvelles formules," cited in Raphaëlle Branche, *La torture et l'armée pendant la guerre d'Algérie (1954–1962)* (Paris: Gallimard, 2001), 105–6, 116. See also Cole, "Unspeakable Acts"; and Neil Macmaster, "The Torture Controversy (1998–2002): Towards a 'New History' of the Algerian War?" *Modern & Contemporary France* 10, no. 4 (2002): 449–59.

27. Pierre-Henri Simon, *Contre la torture* (Paris: Seuil, 1957), 12.

28. Sylvie Thénault, "Défendre les nationalistes algériens en lutte pour l'indépendance: La 'défense de rupture' en question," *Le Mouvement Social* 3, no. 240 (2012): 121–35, 10.

29. Vergès would later defend Klaus Barbie, the "butcher of Lyon," as well as the Khmer Rouge and the Holocaust denier Roger Garaudy. Publicity about the case was saturated with nationalist imagery: wives or daughters sacrificing themselves for their husbands, fathers, and brothers, and appeals to masculine protectiveness. Natalya Vince, *Our Fighting Sisters: Nation, Memory, and Gender in Algeria, 1954–2012* (Manchester: Manchester University Press, 2015), 83–85. See also Malika El Korso, "La mémoire des militantes de la Guerre de libération nationale," *Mémoire et Histoire* 3 (1998): 25–51; and Surkis, "Ethics and Violence." Drif wrote her own account in *La mort de mes frères* (1960) and, later, a memoir, Zohra Drif-Bitat, *Mémoires d'une combattante de l'ALN: Zone* autonome d'Alger (Algiers: Chihab Editions, 2013), translated into English as *Inside the Battle of Algiers* (2017).

30. Gisèle Sapiro, *La responsabilité de l'écrivain* (Paris: Seuil, 2011), 700–702; Pierre Vidal-Naquet, *L'affaire Audin* (Paris: Éditions de Minuit, 1958). Among many accounts are *Les Temps Modernes* 135 (May 1957); the "Dossier Jean Muller," *Temoignage Chrétien* (February 1957); *Les rappelés témoignent* (Clichy: Comité Résistance Spirituelle, 1957); and Stora, *La gangrène* (1959), which recounted the ordeals of Algerians arrested and tortured in Paris—after de Gaulle had come to power in 1958 pledging to change tactics.

31. Beauvoir, Lettres reçues de lecteurs, April 12, 1957.

32. Kuby, *Political Survivors*; Ageron, "L'opinion française," 25–44.

33. Civil servants who signed the petition were prosecuted; the intellectuals were not. As de Gaulle said, you don't arrest Sartre. Sapiro, *La responsabilité de l'écrivain*, 702–3.

34. Frantz Fanon, *A Dying Colonialism*, trans. Haakon Chavalier (New York: Grove Press, 1967), 27.

35. There were other cases, the best known being those of Djamila Bouharid and Jacqueline Guerroudj. See Michael Bruguier, "Plaidoyer pour les Guerroudj," *Esprit* 259, no. 3

(1958): 495–506; Ní Bhriain, "Public Opinion and Passive Complicity during the Algerian War," 97; Vince, *Our Fighting Sisters*; and Malika El Korso, "La mémoire des militantes de la Guerre de libération nationale," *Mémoire et Histoire* 3 (1998): 25–51.

36. On "anaesthetized opinion" and the serial scandal of torture, see Surkis, "Ethics and Violence"; and Branche, *La torture*.

37. The trial was originally scheduled for May 18, 1960; the government would authorize Halimi to be in Algiers only from the sixteenth to the nineteenth.

38. "Pour Djamila Boupacha," *Le Monde*, June 2, 1960. The front page of that same paper reported that Alleg's case was being heard in Algiers on June 13. Boupacha's arraignment was to be on June 17 but was postponed.

Sartre, Aragon, Gabriel Marcel, Geneviève de Gaulle, and Germaine Tillion were among the others on the committee. Germaine Tillion had intervened earlier in the case of the Algerian nationalist Sadi Yacef, urging the government to spare his life. See Germaine Tillion, "Deux rencontres avec le FLN clandestin," an open letter to *Le Monde*, March 11, 1964. Beauvoir scorned those efforts and accused Tillion of softening the revolutionary's image to make him more sympathetic.

On the feminist dimensions of legal strategies and politics, see the different points of view in Lee Whitfield, "The French Military under Female Fire: The Public Opinion Campaign and Justice in the Case of Djamila Boupacha, 1960–62," *Contemporary French Civilization* 20, no. 1 (1996): 76–90; and Codaccioni, "(Dé)Politisation du genre et des questions sexuelles dans un procès politique en contexte colonial." Codaccioni emphasizes how little rape figured in the case and does not believe the case is an example of feminist lawyering.

39. "Pour Djamila Boupacha," reprinted in *Djamila Boupacha*, ed. Simone de Beauvoir and Gisèle Halimi (Paris: Gallimard, 1962), 220–23. See also Beauvoir, *FC2*, 298–306.

40. Beauvoir and Halimi, *Djamila Boupacha*, 223.

41. To take one example, Françoise Giroud wrote about torture in *L'Express*: "If you have never seen being slowly born on the face of a woman or a man the sensual pleasure that he draws from your humiliation, from your suffering, from your degradation, then you know nothing of torture." Cited in Emma Kuby, "From the Torture Chamber to the Bedchamber: French Soldiers, Anti-War Activists, and the Discourse of Sexual Deviancy in the Algerian War (1954–1962)," *Contemporary French Civilization* 38, no. 2 (Summer 2013): 144–45, 141. See Dagmar Herzog, *Sex after Fascism: Memory and Morality in Twentieth-Century Germany* (Princeton: Princeton University Press, 2005).

42. On scandalous banality, see Surkis, "Ethics and Violence."

43. Beauvoir, Lettres reçues de lecteurs, July 16, 1960, Paris.

44. Ibid., June 3, 1960, Dakar, Senegal. See Frederick Cooper, *Citizenship between Empire and Nation: Remaking France and French Africa, 1945–1960* (Princeton: Princeton University Press, 2014); Clifford May, "In Post-Coup Guinea, a Jail Is Thrown Open," *New York Times* April 12, 1984.

45. Name withheld by request, letter to Hubert Beuve-Méry, editor of *Le Monde*, June 4, 1960, Paris, Archives d'Histoire Contemporaine, Paris, Beuve-Méry Papers, BM 140, subfolder Beauvoir/Boupacha." Thanks to Emma Kuby for sharing this material with me.

46. Name withheld by request, June 1960, Paris, Robert Gautier papers/RGl /Affaires de sévices, 1957–1962/Djamila Boupacha.

47. Ibid.

48. Beauvoir, Lettres reçues de lecteurs, August 15, 1965, Seine-Maritime, France.

49. *L'Express*, January 15, 1955.

50. Beauvoir, Lettres reçues de lecteurs, November 21, 1961.

51. Mauriac, "Bloc Notes," *L'Express*, May 26, 1960, cited in Simone de Beauvoir and Gisèle Halimi, *Djamila Boupacha: The Story of the Torture of a Young Algerian Girl Which Shocked Liberal French Opinion*, trans. Peter Green (New York: Macmillan, 1962), 63.

52. Charlotte Delbo's *Les Belles lettres* (Paris: Éditions de Minuit,1961) frames the moral indignation expressed through letters published during the Algerian war. For more, see Amy E. Vidor, "Repurposing *l'art épistolaire*: Letter-writing as Civil Disobedience in Charlotte Delbo's *Les Belles lettres*," *Women in French Studies* vol. 8 (Special Issue 2019): 236–46.

53. Beauvoir, Lettres reçues de lecteurs, June 11, 1960 (158 in 286).

54. The literature on the topic emphasized how many of the women seeking abortions already had several children. Report of Madame Dourlin Grollier to the first Congres de la Prophylaxie Criminelle, September 27, 1960, UNESCO. See Marcelle Auclair, *Le livre noir de l'avortement* (Paris: Fayard, 1962), 13.

55. Boupacha had no desire to be brought into this battle. As she wrote in her own letter to Beauvoir, "This war has taught me many things," including to be wary of European reformers. She was by her own account close to Halimi, but they had no contact after the war.

56. Beauvoir, Lettres reçues de lecteurs, undated, 1960 (163f), responding to an article on Boupacha; July 21, 1960; December 24, 1960, Paris (6 of 113f).

57. Ibid. Notes from the civil suit itself, filed December 4, 1960, are in the 1960 box.

58. The *juge d'instruction*, or examining magistrate, Phillippe Chausserie-Laprée, was less invested in the cover-up. Surkis, "Ethics and Violence," 48–49.

59. The League for the Rights of Man filed a supporting brief.

60. In 1960 the French military was losing ground, and in a January 1961 referendum, 75 percent of votes cast supported Algerian *autodétermination*. In April 1961 a "Generals' Putsch" aimed to overthrow de Gaulle and block any such eventuality; it failed but marked the OAS's emergence. Negotiations with the FLN opened at Évian but broke down in the summer of 1961, though the government continued to make overtures in secret.

61. The numbers are disputed; these are from the chapter weighing evidence in Jim House and Neil MacMaster, *Paris, 1961: Algerians, State Terror, and Memory* (Oxford: Oxford University Press, 2006) 167. See Stora, *La gangrène*, 92–96, and on press reaction, 96–100. The Paris police force was commanded by Maurice Papon, whose role in this violence and earlier participation in deporting Jews from Bordeaux under Vichy would come to light later. See the 2005 documentary *Nuit noire*, directed by Alain Tasma, about the October 17, 1961, massacre.

62. Beauvoir, Lettres reçues de lecteurs, November 25, 1961, Fresnes, France.

63. The OAS attacks centered on Paris but were not confined to the capital. Stora, *La gangrène*, 90.

64. *L'Express*, February 8, 1962, the day of the demonstration that would end in the Charonne massacre.

65. Alain Dewerpe, *Charonne, 8 février 1962: Anthropologie historique d'un massacre d'État*, (Paris: Gallimard, 2006).

66. Beauvoir, Lettres reçues de lecteurs, February 10, 1962, Stockholm; March 1, 1962. See also letters from February 9, 13, and 16, 1962.

67. *L'Express*, January 11, 1962. In the same issue, *L'Express* pointedly ran historical stories about battles between rival factions of Nazis in 1934.

68. Beauvoir and Halimi, *Boupacha*, 1, 12. Halimi found Beauvoir a brilliant publicist for the cause but aloof toward both her and her client. Beauvoir never met Boupacha. She was following her own path, returning to the issues she had raised in *The Second Sex*: rape and its relationship to the more quotidian violence of intimacy; the sadistic cruelty of laws that humiliated women; the complicit silence of the public that refused to acknowledge that cruelty; and the meeting of racial, colonial, and gender domination, though that last theme was treated at a high level of existential abstraction.

69. Beauvoir, Lettres reçues de lecteurs, April 8, 1962, Amiens, France; March 22, 1962. See also April 15 and May 6, 1962.

70. The Évian accords were signed March 18, 1962, and ratified by French voters in May; the vote on *autodétermination* was passed in July 1962.

71. Beauvoir, Lettres reçues de lecteurs, March 21, 1962, Saint-Mandé, France.

72. Stora, *La gangrène*, 115–16.

73. Beauvoir, Lettres reçues de lecteurs, June 29, 1964.

74. Ibid.; February 23, 1962.

75. Branche, *La torture*, 426.

5. Shame as Political Feeling

1. Simone de Beauvoir, *La force des choses*, 2 vols. (Paris: Gallimard, 1963), 1: 398–99, hereafter *FC1* and *FC2* for volumes 1 and 2, respectively.

2. One reviewer called it "le plus beau, et le plus périlleux" of the autobiographical series. *Libération,* November 12, 1963, cited in *Simone de Beauvoir*, ed. Jean-Louis Jeannelle and Éliane Lecarme-Tabone (Paris: Éditions de L'Herne, 2012), 226–27.

3. Beauvoir, *FC1*, 102. Toril Moi analyses these lapses in relation to Beauvoir's love life in *Simone de Beauvoir: The Making of an Intellectual Woman* (Oxford: Oxford University Press, 2008); Susan Rubin Suleiman considers them in relation to the war, in "Memory Troubles: Remembering the Occupation in Simone de Beauvoir's *Les Mandarins,*" *French Politics, Culture & Society* 28, no. 2 (Summer 2010): 4–17.

4. Beauvoir, *FC2*, 212, 248.

5. Maxim Silverman, *Palimpsestic Memory: The Holocaust and Colonialism in French and Francophone Fiction and Film* (New York: Berghahn Books, 2013).

6. Simone de Beauvoir, Lettres reçues, subheading Lettres reçues de lecteurs, Manuscrits, Occident, Bibliothèque Nationale de France. N.A.F. 28501, February 25, 1962; undated but early September 1960; same person wrote again on September 29, 1960; undated, 1960, Rio de Janeiro; undated, 1960, Saint-Dié-des-Vosges, France. See also October 8, 1961, from Uruguay.

7. Beauvoir, *FC2*, 228, 146, 166.

8. Beauvoir, *FC1*, 23, reprising *La force de l'âge* (Paris: Gallimard, 1960), 405–7, 389, hereafter *FA*.

9. Beauvoir, *FC2*, 124–25.

10. Beauvoir, *FC2*, 125.

11. Jean-Paul Sartre, *Being and Nothingness*, trans. Hazel Barnes (New York: Simon and Schuster, 1956), 302.

12. Beauvoir, *FC2*, 177, 45, 125; Joseph Fell, *Emotion of Thought in Sartre* (New York: Columbia University Press, 1965), 20.

13. Beauvoir, *FC2*, 229, 237.

14. A shop on rue Saint-Guillaume, four blocks away, was also blown up just before the second attack on Sartre. That attempt turned out to be directed against a recalcitrant member of the OAS. Beauvoir, *FC2*, 445–46. Beauvoir received a flurry of sympathetically anxious notes and a telegram asking for an interview on the subject of "writers at a time of political crisis." Beauvoir, Lettres reçues de lecteurs, January 9 and 11, 1962.

15. Beauvoir, *FC2*, 446.

16. Beauvoir, *FC1*, 408–9. See Claude Lanzmann, *The Patagonian Hare*, trans. Frank Wynne (New York: Farrar, Straus and Giroux, 2013); and David Macey, *Frantz Fanon* (London: Picador, 2000).

17. See Macey, *Fanon*, chap. 7. This was material Fanon had just written up in *The Wretched of the Earth* (Paris: Cahiers Libre, 1961). Francis Jeanson described equally disconcerting reports from Fanon about the Blida, a "hospital from hell," where he worked with the many victims of colonialism's psychological violence. Francis Jeanson, postface (1965) to Frantz Fanon, *Peau noire, masques blancs* (1952; Paris: Seuil, 1965), 214. The 1965 edition was published posthumously. On Blida, see Camille Robcis, *Disalienation: Politics,*

Philosophy, and Radical Psychiatry in France (Chicago: University of Chicago Press, forthcoming), chap. 2.

18. Beauvoir, *FC2*, 422, 424–25, 455, 425–26.

19. Ibid., 427.

20. Ibid., 421. In another version of this meeting, Fanon made clear that Sartre's preface mattered enormously to him and that he wished they had been able to meet and talk alone, without Beauvoir. Alice Cherki, *Frantz Fanon: A Portrait*, trans. Nadia Benabid (Ithaca: Cornell University Press, 2000), 162–63.

21. Jean-Paul Sartre, preface to Frantz Fanon, *Les damnés de la terre* (Paris: Maspero, 1961), 31.

22. Beauvoir, Lettres reçues de lecteurs, undated (November/December 1963), Saint-Brieuc, France, July 23, 1964.

23. Ibid., June 11, 1960, Besançon, France.

24. Ibid., November 16, 1963; November 21, 1963, Paris.

25. Ibid., undated (November/December 1963), Saint-Brieuc, France; see also January 17, 1963 (34 in 91f, though it must have been written in 1964); November 14, 1963, Saint-Germain-en-Laye, France; January 10, 1964 (box 1).

26. Ibid., January 21, 1964, Paris.

27. Ibid. For more on Jewish experience, recounted apologetically, see December 1, 1963.

28. Jean-Marie Domenach, "Une politique de la certitude," *Esprit* 32, no. 3 (March 1964): 504. *Esprit*, which Domenach edited, was at loggerheads with *Les Temps Modernes*. Reviewing *The Force of Circumstance* allowed Domenach to reprise his critique of Sartre's radicalism.

29. Jean-Louis Jeannelle, *Écrire ses mémoires au XXe siècle* (Paris: Gallimard, 2008), 177–78; Beauvoir, *FA*, 532. On Beauvoir's wartime diaries, see Susan Rubin Suleiman, *Crises of Memory and the Second World War* (Cambridge: Harvard University Press, 2006), 220–24; Sonia Kruks, *Beauvoir and the Politics of Ambiguity* (Oxford: Oxford University Press, 2012), 156; and Ingrid Galster, "Simone de Beauvoir face à l'occupation allemande: Essai provisoire d'un réexamen à partir des écrits posthumes," *Contemporary French Civilization* 20, no. 2 (1996): 288.

30. Jeannelle, *Écrire ses mémoires au XXe siècle*, 178; Michael Rothberg, *Multidirectional Memory: Remembering the Holocaust in the Age of Decolonization* (Stanford: Stanford University Press, 2009); Ursula Tidd, "Simone de Beauvoir et les usages de la mémoire," in Jeannelle and Lecarme-Tabone, *Simone de Beauvoir*, 241–46 develops Rothberg's interpretation. Emma Kuby thoroughly examines how different groups of World War II survivors tried to generalize their experience and the very complicated political ethics involved, implicitly testing Rothberg's thesis. Kuby, *Political Survivors: The Resistance, the Cold War, and the Fight Against Concentration Camps after 1945* (Ithaca: Cornell University Press, 2019).

31. Henry Rousso, *The Vichy Syndrome: History and Memory in France since 1944* (Cambridge: Harvard University Press, 1991). Rousso's theory, following a very loosely Freudian schema, anchors the Vichy syndrome in "incomplete" or "aborted" mourning for hundreds of thousands of lives and a certain idea of France. For critiques, see Dominick LaCapra, *History in Transit: Experience, Identity, Critical Theory* (Ithaca: Cornell University Press, 2004), 94–95; and Alon Confino, "Collective Memory and Cultural History: Problems of Method," *American Historical Review* 102, no. 5 (December 1997): 1394.

32. Beauvoir, *FC2*, 499, 504, 506–7.

33. Otto Hahn, "Simone de Beauvoir: Qu'ai-je fait de ma liberté?," *L'Express*, November 7, 1963, 39.

34. "Cet ensemble unique, mon expérience à moi, avec son ordre et ses hasards . . . Nulle part cela ne ressuscitera." Beauvoir, *FC1*, epilogue.

35. "Cependant, tournant un regard incrédule vers cette crédule adolescente, je mesure avec stupeur à quel point j'ai été flouée." Beauvoir, *FC2*, 508.

36. José Cabanis ends his review with the phrase "Jamais plus un homme." "Le Bilan de Simone de Beauvoir," *La Table Ronde* 192 (January 1964): 10.

37. Pierre-Henri Simon, *Contre la torture* (Paris: Seuil, 1957), 115.

38. Beauvoir, Lettres reçues de lecteurs, December 26, 1963, Strasbourg, France. See also December 8, 1963, a letter sent to *France Observateur* and copied to Beauvoir.

39. Ibid., December 21, 1963, Nice, France. See the similar letter of January 23, 1964.

40. Ibid., November 20, 1963 (the woman was from a working-class family; she had taught for fourteen years and was now at home taking care of a three-and-a-half-year-old son, married to an Egyptian former diplomat); undated (November/December 1963), Saint-Brieuc, France; November 29, 1963, Bamako, Mali (33 in 36f); June 3, 1964; undated, Paris; and many others.

41. Ibid., June, 1964.

42. Ibid., November 17, 1963; June 28, 1964; January 6, 1964; January 17, 1964. See also November 14, 1963.

43. He replied, "Madame, With a kindness I did not expect you let me know that like everyone else, I understood nothing in the famous last pages of your book." Ibid., April 8, 1964 (box 2). See Simone de Beauvoir, *Tout compte fait* (Paris: Gallimard, 1972), 162–68, hereafter *TCF*.

44. Interview with Francis Jeanson, *Simone de Beauvoir ou l'entreprise de vivre (suivi de deux entretiens avec Simone de Beauvoir)* (Paris: Seuil, 1966), 270–71. In her last autobiographical volume, Beauvoir tried to explain what she meant: "Bourgeois culture is a promise. It promises a harmonious universe where one can enjoy the goods of the earth; it offers values that become part of our existence and give our existence the splendor of an Idea. I did not easily tear myself away from such great hopes." *TCF*, 166.

45. Madeleine Gobeil, "Interview: Simone de Beauvoir," trans. Bernard Frechtman, *Paris Review* 34 (Spring–Summer 1965), reprinted in *Simone de Beauvoir Studies* 22 (2005–2006), 86–91.

46. Edgar Morin's *Chronique d'un été* (1961), which films a series of conversations among a range of French individuals and groups about the state of France in 1960, shows that virtually everything of political importance, especially the Algerian war, is censored, repressed, or ducked. The central question, repeated in something of a parody of TV journalism's hot pursuit of a non-event, is "Are you happy?" and the answers reveal either disturbing obliviousness to the miseries and dramas of the world (let alone France and the Maghreb) or an unspecified malaise, tied over several hours and many scenes, as they are in the Beauvoir memoir and many letters, to repression and denial of the past.

47. Hahn, "Simone de Beauvoir," 39.

48. Beauvoir, Lettres reçues de lecteurs, January 4, 1964, Cannes, France (13–18 in 72f); November 11, 1963; January 17, 1963 (34 in 91f, but it must have been written in 1964). On the inability to forget, see also May 5, 1965: "I suffered with you and as much as you the dishonor of being French during the tortures of the Algerian war. I hate the army and France. I have not forgotten because one can't forget the things that mark a people and an era."

49. Jean-Paul Sartre, *Emotions: Outline of a Theory*, trans. Bernard Frechtman (New York: Philosophical Library, 1948), 91.

50. Jean-Paul Sartre, *Being and Nothingness*, trans. Hazel Barnes (New York: Philosophical Library, 1943), 302.

51. Jean-Paul Sartre, *Black Orpheus* (Paris: Gallimard, 1963), 5. See also Jean-Pierre Martin, *Le livre des hontes: Essai* (Paris: Seuil, 2006), 24, and Xavier Martin, *La France*

abîmée: Essai historique sur un sentiment révolutionnaire (Rouen: Dominique Martin Morin, 1991).

52. Frantz Fanon, *Black Skin, White Masks*, trans. Charles Markmann (New York: Grove Press, 1967), 112, 116, 115.

53. Jean-Paul Sartre, preface to Frantz Fanon, *The Wretched of the Earth*, trans. Constance Farrington (New York: Grove Weidenfeld, 1963), 14.

Domenach also argued that shame was "a political feeling, in the best sense of the word," a testament to conscience, sympathy, and engagement. He believed it was an alternative to the dominant cynicism and detachment from public life in the aftermath of the Algerian war. Domenach, "Une politique," 505.

54. Karl Marx to Arnold Ruge, March 18, 1843, first published in the *Deutsch-Französische Jahrbücher* in 1844, in *Marx and Engels: Collected Works* (London: Lawrence & Wishart, 2010), 3: 133.

55. "So different is the perception of these emotional states that it is not possible to use these names with any confidence that another person knows precisely what we mean." Donald L. Nathanson, *The Many Faces of Shame* (New York: Guilford Press, 1987), 4.

56. Compare these four texts: (1) Beauvoir, writing about 1958, of de Gaulle's rise to power and the public's acquiescence: "Something hideous was being unmasked" (*FC 2*, 166); (2) Sartre, in his preface to *Wretched of the Earth*, "We must face that unexpected revelation, the strip-tease of our humanism"; (3) Sartre's editorial in *Les Temps Modernes* on the OAS: "Née du régime, liée à ses hommes, a ses rouages, utilisée par lui-même s'il affecte de la combattre pour en limiter l'influence, elle est le fantôme qui le hante, la vérité hideuse de la guerre qu'il poursuit en Algérie," cited in *L'Express*, February 2, 1962; and (4) Marx: "The glorious robes of liberalism have fallen away and the most repulsive despotism stands revealed for all the world to see." Marx to Ruge, in *Marx and Engels Collected Works*, 3: 133.

On how Sartre and Beauvoir borrow from each other while writing, see Beauvoir, *FC2*, 489.

57. Beauvoir, *FC2*, 429. See Joseph Fell, *Emotion in the Thought of Sartre* (New York: Columbia University Press, 1965), 17.

58. Moi, *Simone de Beauvoir*, 208.

59. Cited in Surkis, "Ethics and Violence," 40. Alleg, too, had written that he was proud as a European to be saluted as a "brother" by Algerian prisoners with whom he was incarcerated. See Beauvoir, *FC*, 159–60, on Sartre's *Morts sans sépulture* (1947) as a reflection on torture.

60. Beauvoir, Lettres reçues de lecteurs, April 12, 1957.

61. For Fanon on the end of the spiritual adventure of the West, see the conclusion of *Wretched of the Earth*.

62. See, e.g., Frantz Fanon, *A Dying Colonialism*, trans. Haakon Chevalier (New York: Grove Press, 1965), 149. Jeanson was stung by Fanon's scorn for his French allies and their efforts: "Fanon manifeste en effet le plus entier dédain à l'égard de ce qui se passait en France, de ce que nous tentions d'y faire et de l'organisation même qui le prenait en charge pour lui faciliter son passage." Francis Jeanson, postface to Frantz Fanon, *Peau noire, masques blancs* (Paris: Seuil, 1965), 209–38, 214, 222 (the edition includes his 1952 preface as well).

63. "Matrices of race, class, gender, etc. figure some subjectivities as more embodied, more self-destructive than others." Jill Locke, "Shame and the Future of Feminism," *Hypatia* 22, no. 4 (Autumn 2007): 158.

64. Eve Kosofsky Sedgwick, *Touching Feeling: Affect, Pedagogy, Performativity* (Durham: Duke University Press, 2003), 37; Eve Kosofsky Sedgwick, Adam Frank, and Irving E. Alexander, eds., *Shame and Its Sisters: A Silvan Tomkins Reader* (Durham: Duke University

Press, 1995). As Norbert Elias puts it: "The anxiety that we call shame is heavily veiled to the sight of others . . . [R]eactions to it are never expressed directly, in noisy gestures." Norbert Elias, *The Civilizing Process*, vol. 1 (Oxford: Oxford University Press, 1969); 492, and see 492–98 more generally.

65. "Une mort très douce," first published in *Les Temps Modernes* 19, no. 216 (May 1964): 1921–85. For condolence letters, see Beauvoir, Lettres reçues de lecteurs, December 8 and 12, 1963, and others without dates.

On *A Very Easy Death*, see the essay by Nancy K. Miller, who is reliably brilliant about autobiography, "Autobiographical Deaths," *Massachusetts Review* 33, no. 1 (1992): 19–47; Susan Bainbrigge, Writings against Death: The Autobiographies of Simone de Beauvoir (Amsterdam: Brill Academic Publishers, 2005), and her extensive references; Christie McDonald, "The Death of Maternity? Simone de Beauvoir's *A Very Easy Death*," *French Politics, Culture & Society* 28, no. 2 (2010): 56–65; Catherine R. Montfort, " 'La Vieille Née': Simone de Beauvoir, *Une Mort Très Douce*, and Annie Ernaux, *Une Femme*," *French Forum* 21, no. 3 (1996): 349–64; Doris Kadish, "Simone de Beauvoir's *Une Mort Très Douce*: Existential and Feminist Perspectives on Old Age," *French Review* 62, no. 4 (1989): 631–39; and Claire Etcherelli, "Un récit sans artifice," in Lecarme-Tabone and Jeannelle, *Simone de Beauvoir*, 247–49.

66. Beauvoir, Lettres reçues de lecteurs, November 22, 1963.

67. Ibid., April 11, 1964; June 19, 1964.

68. Beauvoir, *FC1*, 52–53.

69. Beauvoir, Lettres reçues de lecteurs, January 30, 1964–February 22, 1964.

70. Ibid., December 19, 1963.

71. Ibid., June 23, 1964.

72. Ibid., June 16, 1964 (box 1). Her earlier letter does not seem to be in the archive.

73. Ibid., March 3, 1964.

74. Domenach, "Une politique," 502.

75. Jeannelle, *Écrire ses mémoirs au XXe siècle*, 150–55.

76. Beauvoir, *FC2*, 57, echoing her comments in *FA*, 416. See also *FC2*, 148, 266–70, and 299.

77. Beauvoir, *TCF*, 187–88.

78. Beauvoir, Lettres reçues de lecteurs, November 25, 1963.

6. Second Takes on *The Second Sex*

1. "Ces fortes femmes," *France Observateur* 11, no. 513 (March 3, 1960): 17.

2. "Simone de Beauvoir répond à notre enquête," *France Observateur* 11, no. 514 (March 10, 1960): 14–15. Marie Craipeau's comments on the survey, predictably, highlighted women who succeeded in their careers but "failed" in their love lives.

3. Simone de Beauvoir, *The Second Sex*, trans. H. M. Parshley (New York: Knopf, 1953), xxv, hereafter *TSS* 1953; translated as "[W]omen do not use 'we' " in Constance Borde and Sheila Malovany-Chevallier (New York: Vintage Books, 2009), 8, hereafter *TSS* 2009.

4. Letter to the editor of *France Observateur*, forwarded to Beauvoir. Simone de Beauvoir, Lettres reçues, subheading Lettres reçues de lecteurs, Manuscrits, Occident, Bibliothèque Nationale de France, N.A.F. 28501, March 17, 1960.

5. Simone de Beauvoir, introduction to *Le deuxième sexe*, vols. 1 and 2 (Paris: Gallimard, 1949), 21, 13, hereafter *DS1* and *DS2* for volumes 1 and 2, respectively.

6. Beauvoir, *La force des choses*, vol. 1 (Paris: Gallimard, 1963), 267.

7. Geneviève Fraisse, *Le privilège de Simone de Beauvoir* (Arles: Actes Sud, 2008), 109.

8. Simone de Beauvoir, preface to *Majorité sexuelle de la femme* by Phyllis Kronhausen and Eberhard Kronhausen (Paris: Buchet/Chastel, 1966), 7. Beauvoir's preface was very short. Her contribution, however, was announced on the cover in bright red ink: "Preface by Simone de Beauvoir."

9. Beauvoir, Lettres reçues de lecteurs, May 2, 1966, Ferney, France.

10. Anne Zelensky-Tristan, *Histoire de vivre: Mémoires d'une féministe* (Paris: Calmann-Lévy, 2005); Jacqueline Feldman, "De FMA au MLF: Un témoignage sur les débuts du mouvement de libération des femmes," *Clio: Histoire, Femmes et Société* 29 (2009): 193–203.

11. Sylvie Chaperon, *Les années Beauvoir* (Paris: Fayard, 2000), offers a particularly good account of all these developments.

12. She also claimed that students were better informed and shrewder about politics than the left-wing press made them out to be. "Problems that face students cannot be separated from the problems that face the nation." Beauvoir, Lettres reçues de lecteurs, January 2, 1963.

13. Beauvoir, Lettres reçues de lecteurs, October 28, 1961; January 9, 1960. See the interesting series of letters on January 4, 9, 12, and 31 and February 16, 1960. A reader argued that Catholic women were a "powerful majority" whose anticlericalism needed to be developed lest they become a "dead weight on progress in France." That mean attending to the strand of Catholic women's thought that refused the "monarchist, totalitarian, and phallic" church. January 12, 1960. See also letters of December 3 and 19, 1961; November 6, 1964.

14. Marie Vogel, "Andrée Michel, sociologue sans frontières," *Travail, genre et sociétés* 2, no. 22 (2009): 5–7. On the continuities between antiwar and feminist activity, see Philippe Artières and Michelle Zancarini-Fournel, *68: Une histoire collective, 1962–1981* (Paris: La Découverte, 2008), 18.

15. De Gaulle's government short-circuited the requirement that the National Assembly and the Senate approve constitutional reform *before* it went to referendum. For a good account of the hasty reorganization of Republican institutions in 1962, see Todd Shepard, *The Invention of Decolonization: The Algerian War and the Remaking of France* (Ithaca: Cornell University Press, 2008), 262–68.

16. Andrée Michel, "Les Françaises et la politique," *Les Temps Modernes* 21, no. 230 (April 1965): 61–91. See also Andrée Michel and Geneviève Texier, *La condition de la Française d'aujourd'hui*, vol. 1 (Geneva: Gonthier, 1964), 133–35.

17. Michel, "Les Françaises," 67. Feminist declarations of political independence did not sit well with the left. In two long interviews after de Gaulle's victory in November 1965, Francis Jeanson asked Beauvoir for her opinion on women in politics. Beauvoir replied that she was happy to support *radical* feminism. Jeanson, skeptical, would not leave it at that: "What I mean is this: don't you think that there is sometimes a confusion between what happens at a personal level—the level of everyday life—and the level of struggle? Some women act toward men—whom they live with—as adversaries." Beauvoir replied: "I find this kind of 'challenge' [in English] absurd. It is not a real struggle, because a struggle presupposes something is at stake. This [attitude] is very much that of an 'American woman' and it is extremely irritating." Francis Jeanson, *Simone de Beauvoir ou l'entreprise de vivre (suivi de deux entretiens avec Simone de Beauvoir)* (Paris: Seuil, 1966), 262–64. Jeanson had picked up on Beauvoir's comments about an "attitude of challenge" in *FC2*, 674. See Geneviève Fraisse, *Le privilège de Simone de Beauvoir: Suivi de "Une mort douce"* (Arles: Actes Sud, 2008), 81.

18. Such as Executive Order 11063, prohibiting racial discrimination in federally owned or financed housing, issued by President John F. Kennedy on November 20, 1962. Michel and Texier, *La condition*, 63–64.

19. Shepard, *The Invention of Decolonization*, 5.

20. Jean Foyer, cited by Camille Robcis, *The Law of Kinship* (Ithaca: Cornell University Press, 2008), 162.

21. Beauvoir, Lettres reçues de lecteurs, February 14, 1958.

22. For different views of the discursive politics of decolonization, compare Shepard, *Invention of Decolonization,* and Yoav Di-Capua, *No Exit: Arab Existentialism, Jean-Paul Sartre, and Decolonization* (Chicago: University of Chicago Press, 2018).

23. Beauvoir, Lettres reçues de lecteurs, August 22, 1964; November 25, 1965, Saint-Étienne, France.

24. Edgar Morin, *L'esprit du temps,* vol. 1 (Paris: Grasset, 1962), 13. On Henri Lefebvre as a cultural critic, see Kristin Ross, *Fast Cars, Clean Bodies: Decolonization and the Reordering of French Culture* (Cambridge: MIT Press, 1995).

25. Simone de Beauvoir, *Tout compte fait* (Paris: Gallimard, 1972), 503, hereafter *TCF.*

26. Evelyne Sullerot, *La presse féminine* (Paris: Armand Colin, 1963), 58, 73–74.

27. Beauvoir, Lettres reçues de lecteurs, February 1, 1960, London.

28. Michel and Texier, *La condition,* 33.

29. Betty Friedan, *The Feminine Mystique* (New York: W. W. Norton & Co., 1963), 57, 101, 27.

30. Daniel Horowitz, *Betty Friedan and the Making of "The Feminine Mystique": The American Left, the Cold War, and Modern Feminism* (Amherst: University of Massachusetts Press, 1998). Friedan's politics *were* complicated: she had been a Popular Front labor journalist in the 1940s and organized domestic workers at Smith College. Between 1942 and 1952 she wrote for two radical labor union publications, the Federated Press and the United Electrical, Radio, and Machine Workers' newspaper. The exploitation of women workers was a frequent subject of her labor journalism.

31. Friedan, *The Feminine Mystique,* 249.

32. Horowitz, *Betty Friedan,* 207; especially 200–223. See also Stephanie Coontz, *A Strange Stirring: "The Feminine Mystique" and American Women at the Dawn of the 1960s* (New York: Basic Books, 2010); Louis Menand, "Books and Bombs," *The New Yorker,* January 24, 2011, 76–79; Sandra Dijkstra, "Simone de Beauvoir and Betty Friedan: The Politics of Omission," *Feminist Studies* 6, no. 2 (Summer, 1980): 290–303; and Rupa Mitra, "Simone de Beauvoir et Betty Friedan: Écho transatlantique," in *Cinquantenaire du "Deuxième sexe,"* ed. Christine Delphy and Sylvie Chaperon (Paris: Éditions Syllepse, 2002), 440–46. Friedan borrowed from many others. What's more, as Horowitz points out, Friedan's was one of many American books in the same vein about existential unease and the unfulfilling lives of middle-class women. It had to fight its way through a crowded thicket of similar arguments.

33. Friedan, *Feminine Mystique,* 14.

34. Beauvoir, Lettres reçues de lecteurs, June 19, 1973. See also Beauvoir, *TCF,* 502.

35. "Sex, Society and the Female Dilemma: A Dialogue between Simone de Beauvoir and Betty Friedan," *Saturday Review,* June 14, 1975, 13–20. See Betty Friedan's "No Gods, No Goddesses" in the same issue, 16–17.

36. Ti-Grace Atkinson Papers, 1938–2013, MC 785, Schlesinger Library, Radcliffe Institute, Harvard University, 35.12.

37. Beauvoir, Lettres reçues de lecteurs, June 1, 1963, Rome. *La Stampa* was a daily newspaper with a circulation of 500,000.

38. Jean Fourastié, *Les trente glorieuses, ou la Révolution invisible de 1946 à 1975* (Paris: Fayard, 1979).

39. Beauvoir, Lettres reçues de lecteurs, March 19, 1963.

40. In the United States, Bantam bought the rights to the paperback and published it in 1965. An enthusiastic American reader reported, "I was so happy when the price was reduced

from $10 to 99 cents I sent dozens of the paperbacks out to my friends for Christmas." Beauvoir, Lettres reçues de lecteurs, February 15, 1965, Boston. *The Second Sex* came out in a *livre de poche* three years later.

41. Beauvoir, Lettres reçues de lecteurs, May 24, 1962.

42. Ibid., November 16, 1963.

43. Ibid., November 8, 1960; June 24, 1968; January 27, 1961, Montreal.

44. Ibid., July 14, 1960, London.

45. Ibid., July 17, 1964. See also December 4, 1963.

46. Hincker, "Pour Simone de Beauvoir," 123–31.

47. Beauvoir, Lettres reçues de lecteurs, January 8, 1965.

48. Ibid., July 8, 1964. See also November 11, 1964; August 25, 1966; November 19, 1963.

49. Ibid., January 3, 1960, Strasbourg, France. See Beauvoir, *La force de l'âge* (Paris: Gallimard, 1960), 654, hereafter *FA*. See also September 13, 1963.

50. Ibid., April 8, 1962, Le Vésinet, France; October 8, 1963.

51. Ibid., February 1961.

52. Ibid., January 9, 1960.

53. Ibid., March 29, 1960, Montreal; April 2, 1967, Veyrier, Switzerland (citing Beauvoir, *DS2*, 545; *TSS* 2009, 740–41; Parshley gets this wrong in his translation [New York: Knopf, 1953], 661);

54. Ibid., February 15, 1965. See also March 29, 1960.

55. Beauvoir, Lettres reçues de lecteurs, November 16, 1963, Besançon, France.

56. Beauvoir sets out this dilemma in the introduction to *The Second Sex*. "[I]f I wish to define myself, I first have to say: "I am a woman"; all other assertions will arise from this basic truth." [*TSS* 2009, 5]. On the one hand, the moniker is irritating, a constant reminder of one's status as Other; on the other hand, you can't walk away from being a woman. On this problem, see Linda Zerilli's excellent discussions in "Feminist Theory without Solace," *Theory & Event* 15, no. 2 (2012); and "Politics," in *The Oxford Handbook of Feminist Theory*, ed. Lisa Disch and Mary Hawkesworth (New York: Oxford University Press, 2016), 632–50.

57. Beauvoir, Lettres reçues de lecteurs, April 16, 1967, Zaandam, Holland.

58. Ibid., November 17, 1963. For a particularly good discussion of how Beauvoir reappropriates the Cartesian tradition, see Nancy Bauer, *Simone de Beauvoir, Philosophy, and Feminism* (New York: Columbia University Press, 2001).

59. Beauvoir, Lettres reçues de lecteurs, November 17, 1963.

60. Ibid., January 21, 1961.

61. Annie Ernaux, *La femme gélee* (Paris: Gallimard, 1981), 93.

62. Beauvoir, Lettres reçues de lecteurs, July 8, 1964; April 8, 1962; August 15, 1965; March 9, 1966.

63. Ibid., July 12, 1966, Oslo.

64. Ibid., December 14, 1963.

65. Ibid., Paris; June 24, 1968. See also August 22, 1967; May 2, 1967; July 16, 1964; August 2, 1966; March 3, 1964; and November 22, 1960.

66. "While there is indeed a phenomenology of inhabiting a sex," Riley writes, "the swaying in and out of it is more like ventures among descriptions than like returns to a founding sexed condition." Denise Riley, *"Am I That Name?": Feminism and the Category of "Women" in History* (London: Palgrave Macmillan, 1988), 97–98.

67. Jacqueline Feldman, "Une experience de féminisme: Verité personnelle, vérités sociales, verités sociologiques," 12th World Congress of Sociology, Madrid, 1990, Bibliothèque Marguerite Durand, 13ROC MF570 typescript, 1–14.

7. Couple Troubles

1. Simone de Beauvoir, Lettres reçues, subheading Lettres reçues de lecteurs, Manuscrits, Occident, Bibliothèque Nationale de France, N.A.F. 28501, December 15, 1967, Vienna, with reference to Simone de Beauvoir, *Das andere Geschlecht*, trans. Fritz Montfort (Leipzig: Rowohlt Verlag, 1951).

2. "Marriage has designated the ways both sexes act in the world and the reciprocal relation between them. It has done so probably more emphatically than any other single institution or social force. The unmarried as well as the married bear the ideological, ethical, and practical impress of the marital institution, which is difficult or impossible to escape." Nancy Cott, *Public Vows: A History of Marriage and the Nation* (Cambridge: Harvard University Press, 2000), 3. On the power of conjugal love as a "metaphor for and source of social integration," see Judith Surkis's compelling analysis in *Sexing the Citizen: Morality and Masculinity In France, 1870–1920* (Ithaca: Cornell University Press, 2006), introduction and 51–58.

3. Beginning with Elizabeth Fallaize, "Resisting Romance: Simone de Beauvoir, 'The Woman Destroyed' and the Romance Script," in *Contemporary French Fiction by Women: Feminist Perspectives*, ed. Margaret Atack and Phil Powrie (Manchester: Manchester University Press, 1990), 15–25; and continuing in a volume paying tribute to Fallaize, Margaret Atack et al., eds., *Women, Genre and Circumstance: Essays in Memory of Elizabeth Fallaize* (London: Legenda, 2012).

4. Lauren Berlant, *The Female Complaint: The Unfinished Business of Sentimentality in American Culture* (Durham: Duke University Press, 2008), viii, x.

5. See Kristin Ross, *Fast Cars, Clean Bodies* (Cambridge: MIT Press, 1994).

6. Colin Dyer, *Population and Society in Twentieth Century France* (London: Hodder and Stoughton, 1978), 135. During the postwar decades, the population of France grew faster than in any previous time in history. Fertility rose. Antibiotics, better and better-provisioned medicine, and legislation promoting health care also helped people live longer; the expanded population included a significant number of people in their sixties. Immigration accounted for at least 35 percent of France's total population growth; see ibid., 136–41; and on the reversal of these trends, especially child-bearing, in the mid-1970s, ibid., 187–90. For a more detailed analysis of how these developments varied by class, see Jacques Dupâquier, *Histoire de la population française*, vol. 4 (Paris: Quadrige/Presses Universitaires de France, 1995), 302–9.

In 1935, the average age at marriage was 26 for men and 23 for women; in 1955, the averages were 26 and 24, respectively; in 1965, 25 and 23. Dupâquier, *Histoire de la population*, 528. See also Rebecca Pulju, "Finding a *Grand Amour* in Marriage," in *Domestic Tensions, National Anxieties: Global Perspectives on Modern Marriage Crises*, ed. Kristin Celello and Hanan Kholoussy (Oxford: Oxford University Press, 2016), 126–46.

7. Pulju, "*Grand Amour*." See also Rebecca Pulju, *Women and Mass Consumer Society* (Cambridge: Cambridge University Press), chap. 3.

8. Geneviève Gennari, *Simone de Beauvoir* (Paris: Éditions Universitaires, 1958), 107.

9. Edgar Morin, *L'esprit du temps: Essai sur la culture de masse*, 2 vols. (Paris: Grasset, 1962), vol. 1: 208. Surkis, *Sexing the Citizen,* is a sustained feminist analysis of Morin's observation.

10. Evelyn Sullerot, "Mariage et famille," in *Société et culture de la France contemporaine*, ed. George Santoni (Albany: SUNY Press, 1981), 93.

11. Dagmar Herzog, *Sexuality in Europe: A Twentieth-Century History* (Cambridge: Cambridge University Press), 17–18.

12. Ibid.

13. Pulju, *Women and Mass Consumer Society*, 209.

14. Beauvoir, Lettres reçues de lecteurs, January 9, 1960; February 25, 1965; Ross, *Fast Cars, Clean Bodies,* chap. 3.

15. Jean-Paul Sartre, *Lettres à Castor* (Paris: Gallimard, 1983); Simone de Beauvoir, *Lettres à Sartre* (Paris: Gallimard, 1990).

16. Cited in Ingrid Galster, *Beauvoir dans tous ses états* (Paris: Tallandier, 2007), 67. Galster offers a good short account of the Sartre-Beauvoir relationship (65–67). For more, see Marie-Josèphe Bonnet, *Simone de Beauvoir et les femmes* (Paris, Albin Michel, 2015), 48–92.

17. Toril Moi, *Simone de Beauvoir: The Making of Intellectual Woman* (Oxford: Oxford University Press, 2009), 248.

18. Bienenfeld would vent her anger in a memoir, *Mémoires d'une jeune fille dérangée* (Les Plans-sur-Bex: Balland, 1993).

19. Simone de Beauvoir, *Transatlantic Love Affair: Letters to Nelson Algren* (New York: New Press, 1997), September 23, 1960, 534–36.

20. One of the best accounts is Anne McClintock, "Simone (Lucie Ernestine Marie Bertrand) de Beauvoir," in *European Writers: The Twentieth Century,* vol. 12, ed. George Stade (New York: Charles Scribner's Sons, 1990), https://dept.english.wisc.edu/amcclintock/beauvoir.htm; see also Annabelle Martin Golay, *Beauvoir intime et politique: La fabrique des Mémoires* (Villeneuve-d'Ascq, France: Septentrion, 2013), 151–57.

Galster, *Beauvoir dans tous ses états,* 65–67; Bonnet, *Simone de Beauvoir et les femmes,* 48–92; Louis Menand, "Stand by Your Man: The Strange Liaison of Sartre and Beauvoir," *The New Yorker,* September 26, 2005; Hazel Rowley, *Tête-à-Tête: Simone de Beauvoir and Jean-Paul Sartre* (New York: Harper, 2005); Deirdre Bair, *Simone de Beauvoir: A Biography* (New York: Summit, 1990); Margaret Simons, "Lesbian Connections," *Signs* 18, no. 1 (Autumn 1992): 131–61; and Bienenfeld, *Mémoires d'une jeune fille.* Arlette Elkaim, who was Jewish and born in Algeria, met Sartre when she was nineteen and studying philosophy. After an apparently short sexual relationship, Sartre adopted her. She became executor of his estate when he died. Ronald Hayman, *Sartre: A Life* (New York: Simon & Schuster, 1987), 323. See also Annie Cohen-Solal, *Sartre: A Life* (New York: Pantheon, 1988), 452; and for Francis Jeanson's partisan defense of the Sartre-Beauvoir couple, *Simone de Beauvoir* (Paris: Éditions du Seuil, 1966), 216.

21. Beauvoir, Lettres reçues de lecteurs, July 31, 1964. Her response to him is in his private papers.

22. Sharon Marcus, *The Drama of Celebrity* (Princeton: Princeton University Press, 2019), 151.

23. Cited in Simone de Beauvoir, *Mémoires,* vol. 1, ed. Jean-Louis Jeannelle and Éliane Lecarme-Tabone (Paris: Gallimard, 2018), 1300.

24. John Weightman, "Beauvoir the Beaver," *The Observer Weekend Review,* February 17, 1963.

25. Simone de Beauvoir, *La force de l'âge* (Paris: Gallimard, 1960), 30–31, 74, 85–89, hereafter *FA.*

26. Ibid., 191, 277; on Olga, 189–92; on the trio, 276–78; on its disintegration, 291–99; on the foursome, 323–25. Beauvoir admitted that story was incomplete and apologized for the pain it caused others: "The need for discretion compromised the accuracy of my account in *The Prime of Life.*" Simone de Beauvoir, *La force des choses,* vols. 1 and 2 (Paris: Gallimard, 1963), 1:177, hereafter *FC1* and *FC2* for volumes 1 and 2, respectively; Simon, "Lesbian Connections," 188–96. For an incisive critique of Beauvoir in all these episodes, see Bonnet, *Simone de Beauvoir,* 48–92. The most complete account is in the notes that accompany Jeannelle and Lecarme-Tabone, *Simone de Beauvoir: Mémoires,* 1:1304–9.

27. Beauvoir, *FC1,* 1, 176–77.

28. Beauvoir, *FC1*, 1, 176; Simone de Beauvoir, *Tout compte fait* (Paris: Gallimard, 1972), 211, hereafter *TCF*.

29. Simone de Beauvoir, "Brigitte Bardot and the Lolita Syndrome," *Esquire*, August 1959, 32–38; Simone de Beauvoir, "The Chemistry of Love," *Daily Express*, August 11, 1959; BNF, N.A.F. 28501, Beauvoir: Coupures de presse.

30. Beauvoir insisted she was not George Sand and rejected Sand's "virtuous mask," adding: "To have lovers, deceive them, lie to them—why not? But she can't trumpet her love of the truth, protest that she has been slandered and give herself saintly airs . . . What I cannot forgive her is the systematic falsifying of her interior language, which transforms all her actions into edifying examples." *TCF*, 211–12. Beauvoir protests too much. She found it impossible to avoid the Sand model of writer, intellectual, iconoclast, and expert on love, marriage, and relationships.

31. Germaine Bree, "The Dutiful Daughter in the Corner-Seat: Review of *The Prime of Life*," *New York Times*, June 3, 1962.

32. Beauvoir, *FC2*, 263–64.

33. Beauvoir, Lettres reçues de lecteurs, August 25, 1966.

34. Cott, *Public Vows*; Susan Moller Okin, *Justice, Gender, and the Family* (New York: Basic Books, 1989), 138; Nancy Fraser, "Feminism's Two Legacies: A Tale of Ambivalence," *South Atlantic Quarterly* 114, no. 4 (October 2015): 710.

35. Beauvoir, Lettres reçues de lecteurs, January 17, 1966, London; undated, 1963; October 24, 1964. On Beauvoir as an expert on love and the couple, see Monique Hincker, "Pour Simone de Beauvoir," *La Nouvelle Critique* (February 1965): 127–28.

36. Beauvoir, Lettres reçues de lecteurs, December 1, 1964, Sherman Oaks, Calif.

37. Ibid., August 3, 1966.

38. Ibid., undated, 1964; May 8, 1961; 1968, Aix-en-Provence.

39. Ibid., April 26, 1968, Rabat, Morocco. Another correspondent underscored that she had plenty of sexual and sensual satisfaction, she "flirted," and her life was not "pathetic." May 14, 1962.

40. Ibid., November, 1960, Le Raincy, France. In a 1976 interview with Alice Schwarzer, well after the last volume of her autobiography was published, Beauvoir acknowledged her sexual relationships with women: "Today, I would like to tell women how I lived my sexuality because it is a political, not individual, issue. At the time . . . I hadn't understood the magnitude and importance of this issue, nor the necessity for individual honesty." Cited by Stella Sandford, *How to Read Beauvoir* (New York: W. W. Norton, 2006), 88.

41. Simone de Beauvoir, *The Second Sex*, trans. H. M. Parshley (New York: Knopf, 1953), 425–26, hereafter *TSS* 1953; *The Second Sex*, trans. Constance Borde and Sheila Malovany-Chevallier (New York: Knopf, 2009), 439–40, 458, hereafter *TSS* 2009; *Le deuxième sexe*, vols. 1 and 2 (Paris: Gallimard, 1949), 2:220, hereafter *DS1* and *DS2* for volumes 1 and 2, respectively.

42. Beauvoir, *TSS* 1953, 451, 456; *TSS* 2009, 474, 484.

43. Pulju, *Women and Mass Consumer Society*, 13.

44. Beauvoir, *TSS* 1953, 447; *TSS* 2009, 468.

45. Beauvoir, *TSS* 1953, 463–65, 465–67, 468; *TSS* 2009, 497–500, 499, 504.

46. Beauvoir, *TSS* 1953, 717–18; *TSS* 2009, 754–55; *DS1*, 636.

47. Beauvoir, *TSS* 1953, 717–18; *TSS* 2009, 754–55; *DS1*, 636.

48. Beauvoir, Lettres reçues de lecteurs, May 24, 1962.

49. Beauvoir, Lettres reçues de lecteurs, December 6 and December 15, 1967; April 6, 1967, Madrid.

50. Ibid., November 23, 1960, Paris.

51. Ibid., March 4, 1967 (in English).

52. Ibid., June 2, 1961, Bogotá.

53. Ibid., July 23, 1961. She had also read about French Family Planning and Dr. Marie Andrée Lagroua Weill-Hallé in *Time*, July 21, 1961.

54. *Population* (Institut national d'études démographiques), no. 2 (1960), no. 4 (1963), and no. 2 (1966), cited in Dyer, *Population and Society*, 143.

55. Beauvoir, Lettres reçues de lecteurs, undated, 1962 (no. 57).

56. Ibid., January 27, 1961, Lyon; October 1968, Elma, Calif. Beauvoir answered both of these letters.

57. Ibid., October 18, 1961, Levallois-Perret, France. See also June 18, 1964; and undated, October 1961.

58. Ibid., July 19, 1960; July 10, 1960.

59. Ibid., July 1960; July 19, 1960; July 10, 1960; February 2, 1961; November 7, 1963, Angers, France; June 18, 1964, Aixe-sur-Vienne, France. See also April 16, 1966, London; November 23, 1960.

60. Ibid., December 7, 1963, Paris (53 in 109f).

61. Beauvoir, *TCF*, 175, 177. See Suzanne Dow, "Madness and (Self-)Deception in Simone de Beauvoir's 'La Femme Rompue' " in *Madness in Twentieth-Century French Women's Writing* (Bern: Peter Lang, 2009), 85–112.

62. Simone de Beauvoir, *La femme rompue* (Paris: Gallimard, 1967), 138–39, 149.

63. Elizabeth Fallaize, "Resisting Romance: Simone de Beauvoir, 'The Woman Destroyed' and the Romance Script," in *Contemporary French Fiction by Women: Feminist Perspectives*, ed. Margaret Atack and Phil Powrie (Manchester: Manchester University Press, 1990), 15–25. See also Fallaize's excellent analysis of Beauvoir's fiction, *The Novels of Simone de Beauvoir* (London: Croom Helm, 1998), 43–175.

64. Jacqueline Piatier, "Le démon du bien: 'La femme rompue,' " *Le Monde des Livres*, January 24, 1968, 1–2; François Nourissier, "La femme rompue," *Les Nouvelles Littéraires*, February 1. 1968. On the story's reception, see Beauvoir, *TCF*, 175–79; Bernard Pivot, "Simone de Beauvoir: Une vraie femme de lettres (pour le courrier du cœur)," *Le Figaro Littéraire*, October 30, 1967, 29, cited in Toril Moi, *Feminist Theory and Simone de Beauvoir* (Cambridge: Basil Blackwell, 1990), 88.

65. Beauvoir, *TCF*, 177–78.

66. In Toril Moi's analysis of the story, Beauvoir subverts the conventions of romantic fiction, sowing doubts as the story proceeds about the narrator's veracity. Beauvoir expects her readers to read between the lines, as they might read a case study, identifying with her as the knowing observer and seeing Monique's confusions and incoherence as an analyst would. Moi also underscores the power play in this author-reader dynamic: "There is in *The Woman Destroyed* more than a superficial similarity between Beauvoir's position in relation to her character, and that of Freud vis-à-vis Dora. In both cases, what is at stake in the narrative struggle is the right to claim one's own knowledge as truth, and as a corollary, the right to proclaim the guilt of one's defeated opponent." If Beauvoir fails, that is largely because of the intensity of feeling she pours into her character. Toril Moi, *What Is a Woman? and Other Essays* (Oxford: Oxford University Press, 1999), 470–71, and *Feminist Theory and Simone de Beauvoir* (Cambridge: Basil Blackwell, 1990), 61–93. Indeed, there is considerably more of Beauvoir in Monique than the author was willing to acknowledge. While the diary does sound like some of the readers' letters, it also echoes Beauvoir's own diary, especially in the outbursts of despair in facing the difficulties of writing.

Elizabeth Fallaize's analysis takes a different tack, contending that whatever Beauvoir's *intentions*, they are subverted by the ways in which the story meshes with the genre of romantic fiction, which, combined with the framing in *Elle*, summons the reader to iden-tify with Monique ("Resisting Romance," 15–25). In a third contribution to this debate, Suzanne Dow argues that playing tricks on one's readers is bound to leave an author disap-pointed in their reactions: "To write is always to render oneself vulnerable to the indeter-minacy of reception." Dow, "Madness and Self-Deception," 112. As Dow also points out, Beauvoir tried to correct the tone she struck in the story. She asked Gallimard to include an insert in the book that underscored her interest in individuals who had not managed to take control of their lives (88). One of the letter writers copied out that insert. Beauvoir wrote that her solidarity with women who resist domination did not prevent her from being interested in those who could not, or in the "failure that is in every existence." Beauvoir, Lettres reçues de lecteurs, August 3, 1969. Moi and Dow have returned to these questions in a collection of essays honoring Fallaize's contributions to literary criticism. See Atack et al., *Women, Genre and Circumstance.*

67. Beauvoir, Lettres reçues de lecteurs, undated, January 15, 1968, Marseille.

68. Ibid., April 20, 1961; undated, 1968, Issy-les-Moulineaux, France; May 4, 1968. See also November 1, 1967.

69. Beauvoir, *FA*, 73.

70. Beauvoir, Lettres reçues de lecteurs, November 20, 1968.

71. Ibid., November 13, 1967; October 18, 1967; November 2, 1968 (an Italian liv-ing in Israel); December 2, 1968; November 13, 1967; October 18, 1967; January 23, 1968; March 7, 1968.

72. Ibid., January 29, 1968, in response to Piatier's critique in *Le Monde.*

73. Ibid., December 2, 1968; March 17, 1968, Maisons Alfort, France.

74. Ibid., 1961, Geneva; December 16, 1967 (in English); January 27, 1965.

75. Ibid., January 24, 1968, Boulogne-sur-Seine, France.

76. This longtime acquaintance and her friends saw Beauvoir and Sartre as the incarna-tion of their hopes. Ibid., September 7, 1960 (286f). See also September 28, 1960; Novem-ber 1967, Sercy-en-Brie, France; November 1, 1967; January 1, 1968.

77. Berlant, *Female Complaint*, 233, emphasis added. Berlant argues that the "intimate public" thrives "in *proximity* to the political," providing relief from the values and relation-ships of the political world. It is neither inherently oppositional nor escapist. Ibid., preface, x, 3, 10. See Victoria Heresford, *Feeling Women's Liberation* (Durham: Duke University Press, 2013); and Annamarie Jagose, "Counterfeit Pleasures: Fake Orgasm and Queer Agency," *Textual Practice* 24, no. 3 (2010): 533.

78. Surkis, *Sexing the Citizen*; Cott, *Public Vows*; Camille Robcis, *The Law of Kinship: Anthropology, Psychoanalysis, and the Family in France* (Ithaca: Cornell University Press).

79. Morin, *L'esprit*, 2:215.

80. Quoted in Robcis, *The Law of Kinship*, 162; see 158–67 on these reforms.

81. Marriage, even when overhauled and more egalitarian, was "boycotted" by many in the younger generations. Conseil Économique et Social, *Le statut matrimonial et ses con-séquences juridiques, fiscales et sociales* (1984), 6, cited by Françoise Picq, *Libération des femmes: Les années mouvement* (Paris: Seuil, 1993), 80. See also Evelyne Sullerot, *Pour le meilleur et sans le pire* (Paris: Fayard, 1984), 28–31.

82. Paul Ricœur, "Introduction," *Esprit*, special issue on sexuality (November 1960): 1670.

8. Sexual Politics and Feminism

1. Simone de Beauvoir, Lettres reçues, subheading Lettres reçues de lecteurs, Manu-scrits, Occident, Bibliothèque Nationale de France, N.A.F. 28501, October 1971. Argentina was under a military dictatorship from 1966 to 1973. This regime was less brutal than its

successor, which carried out the massive disappearances of the "Dirty War" from 1976 to 1983, but it was marked by crackdowns on students and labor and by morality campaigns aimed at curbing the countercultural politics of the younger generation.

2. Annie Ernaux, *Les années* (Paris: Gallimard, 2008), 82.

3. The best analysis of these issues is Bibia Pavard, *Si je veux, quand je veux: Contraception et avortement dans la société française (1956–1979)* (Rennes: Presses Universitaires de Rennes, 2012). Several generations of scholars have considered the international dimensions of 1968: Arthur Marwick, *The Sixties: Cultural Revolution in Britain, France, Italy, and the United States* (Oxford: Oxford University Press, 1998); Jeremi Suri, *Power and Protest: Global Revolution and the Rise of Détente* (Cambridge: Harvard University Press, 2005); and Vladimir Tismaneanu, ed., *Promises of 1968: Crisis, Illusion, and Utopia* (Budapest: Central European Press, 2011), especially the conclusion by Charles Maier. More recent work, however, has put women's and gay liberation at the center of culture and politics: Timothy Scott Brown, *West Germany in the Global Sixties: The Anti-Authoritarian Revolt, 1962–1978* (Cambridge: Cambridge University Press, 2013); Tamara Chaplin and Jadwiga E. Pieper-Mooney, eds., *The Global Sixties: Conventions, Contests, and Countercultures* (London: Routledge, 2017); and Tamara Chaplin, *Cabarets to Counterpublics: Female Same-Sex Intimacy and the French Public Sphere, 1930-2013* (Chicago: University of Chicago Press, forthcoming, 2021).

4. Beauvoir, Lettres reçues de lecteurs, January 9, 1956.

5. Simone de Beauvoir, *The Second Sex*, trans. H. M. Parshley (New York: Knopf, 1953), 484, hereafter *TSS 1953*; *The Second Sex*, trans. Constance Borde and Sheila Malovany-Chevallier (New York: Knopf, 2009), 524, hereafter *TSS 2009*; *Le deuxième sexe*, vols. 1 and 2 (Paris: Gallimard, 1949), 2:326–27, hereafter *DS1* and *DS2* for volumes 1 and 2, respectively.

6. See the particularly harrowing autobiographical account in Gisèle Halimi, *The Right to Choose* (Brisbane: University of Queensland Press, 1977). D&Cs are used to diagnose uterine problems, to remove fibroids, or to remove fragments of placental or fetal tissue after a miscarriage and, sometimes, childbirth, for those tissues if retained can produce dangerously heavy bleeding and infection.

7. Lisa Greenwald, *Daughters of 1968* (Lincoln: University of Nebraska Press, 2019), 196. See also Sarah Fishman, *From Vichy to the Sexual Revolution* (Oxford: Oxford University Press, 2017).

8. Jacques Derogy, *Des enfants malgré nous* (Paris: Éditions de Minuit, 1956); Greenwald, *Daughters of 1968*, 197–200.

9. Luc Boltanski, *The Foetal Condition: A Sociology of Engendering and Abortion* (Cambridge: Cambridge University Press, 2013), 160. "Among the set of practices associated with the feminine pole, abortion is probably one of those most forcefully kept out of the public space; it takes place in the shadows, exclusively among women." Ibid., 15–17.

10. Simone de Beauvoir, preface to Marie Andrée Lagroua Weill-Hallé, *La grand peur d'aimer* (Geneva: Gonthier, 1960), 8, 11, 15.

11. Simone de Beauvoir, "Pour Djamila Boupacha," *Le Monde*, June 2, 1960.

12. Beauvoir, *TSS 1953*, 486, 489; *DS2*, 329, 335.

13. Beauvoir, Lettres reçues de lecteurs, June 11, 1960.

14. Beauvoir, *La force des choses*, vols. 1 and 2 (Paris: Gallimard, 1963), 2:297–98, hereafter *FC1* and *FC2* for volumes 1 and 2, respectively. Other feminists associated with Planning shared this image of Weill-Hallé as a slightly clueless figurehead. Author interview with Dr. Cecile Goldet.

15. Weill-Hallé, *Grand peur*, 142. The literature on the topic emphasized how many of the women seeking abortions already had several children. "Rapport de Mme. Dourlin Grollier au Premier Congrès International de Prophylaxie Criminelle (Paris, 27–30 septembre 1959)," cited in Marcelle Auclair, *Le livre noir de l'avortement* (Paris: Fayard, 1962), 13.

16. Weill-Hallé, *Grand peur*, 29–30.

17. Kristen Stromberg Childers, *Seeking Imperialism's Embrace: National Identity, Decolonization, and Assimilation in the French Caribbean* (Oxford: Oxford University Press, 2016), 156–57; Felix Germain, "Jezebels and Victims: Antillean Women in Postwar France, 1946–1974," *French Historical Studies* 33, no. 3 (Summer 2010): 475-495.

18. On the turnaround in public opinion, see Sylvie Chaperon, "La radicalisation des mouvements féminins français de 1960 à 1970," *Vingtième Siècle Revue d'histoire* 48 (1995): 61–74; Michelle Zancarini-Fournel and Philippe Artières, *68: Une histoire collective, 1962–1981* (Paris: La Découverte, 2008); and Martine Sevegrand, *Les enfants du bon Dieu: Les catholiques français et la procréation au XXe siècle* (Paris: Albin Michel, 1995), 230–33.

19. The law did not provide for sex education or for doctors to be trained in how to prescribe for family planning, pharmacists had to keep track of patients who bought the pill, and parental consent was required for minors. Pharmaceutical companies could not get authorization to bring birth control pills to market, and many did not want to be associated with contraception. The Thalidomide scandal was still fresh, and it was difficult to disentangle those fears from opposition to contraception. "In the autumn of 1970, still no oral contraceptive or IUD has been authorized for sale"—and that was three years after the Neuwirth Law was passed. Sophie Chaveau, "Les espoirs déçus de la loi Neuwirth," *Clio: Histoire, femmes et sociétés* 18 (2003): 223–39, 8. In 1972 Lucien Neuwirth, the legislator who proposed the law, and for whom it was named, accused the administration of deliberately sabotaging it.

20. Reich's (1897–1957) iconoclastic life inspired many radicals, but it is a melancholy story. He was an Austrian Jewish radical, thrown out of both the Austrian Socialist Party and the German Communist Party; he studied with Freud but got sideways with Freud's other followers; after moving between Austria, Germany, Great Britain, Denmark, Sweden, and Norway, he ended up in exile in the United States. His radical experiments with therapeutic "orgone accumulators," meant to harness biological energies, got him indicted for scientific fraud. When he refused to appear at his hearing, he was imprisoned for contempt of court and died after one year, in 1957.

On Reich, see Scott Brown, *West Germany in the Global Sixties*, 307–9; Dagmar Herzog, *Sex after Fascism: Memory and Morality in Twentieth-Century Germany* (Princeton: Princeton University Press, 2005), 156–62; and Juliet Mitchell, *Psychoanalysis and Feminism* (New York: Pantheon, 1974), 137–226. Reich's *Die Sexualität im Kulturkampf* (1936) was translated into French as *La révolution sexuelle* in 1968, and *Der Sexuelle Kampf der Jungend* (1932) as *La lutte sexuelle des jeunes* in 1972 in the Maspéro collection of small paperbacks beloved by student intellectuals. Daniel Guérin, *Essai sur la révolution sexuelle après Reich et Kinsey* (Paris: Belfond, 1969).

21. Cited in Ludivine Bantigny, *1968: De grands soirs en petits matins* (Paris: Seuil, 2018), 217–18. This is one of the best recent histories of May 1968 in France.

22. Cathy Bernheim, *Perturbation, ma sœur: Naissance d'un mouvement de femmes, 1970–1972* (Paris: Seuil, 1983), 82–83.

23. "De la misère en milieu étudiant" (On the Poverty of Student Life) http://library. nothingness.org/articles/4/fr/display/12. See Bantigny, *1968*, 203.

24. *Le Torchon Brûlé*, no. 3, cited in Françoise Picq's excellent collection *Libération des femmes: Les années mouvement* (Paris: Seuil, 1993), 62.

25. Pavard, *Si je veux*, 135.

26. Edgar Morin, *L'esprit du temps: Essai sur la culture de masse*, vol. 2 (Paris: Grasset, 1962), 219, 217.

27. *Le Nouvel Observateur* 334 (April 5, 1971), cited in *Mouvement de Libération des Femmes: Textes premiers*, ed. Cathy Bernheim, Liliane Kandel, Francoise Picq, and Nadja Ringart (Paris: Stock, 2009), 179, hereafter *MLF Textes*.

28. Wittig became one of the central figures of the early MLF. She would go on to become one of the most influential theorists of the need to dismantle the scaffolding of binary sexual difference. Her "One Is Not Born a Woman," first presented at a conference on Simone de Beauvoir in 1979, was a declaration of lesbian independence from feminism and an argument that feminism had to thoroughly rethink its premises. Monique Wittig, "One Is Not Born a Woman," in *Feminist Theory Reader: Local and Global Perspectives*, ed. Carole R. McCann and Seung-Kyung Kim (New York: Routledge, 2013), 147. Wittig's book *The Lesbian Body* (Boston: Beacon Press, 1973) developed these arguments, showing how the body's erotic codes and pleasures are written and can thus be rewritten. See Judith Butler, "Variations on Sex and Gender: Beauvoir, Wittig, and Foucault," *Praxis International 5*, no. 4 (January 1986): 505–16.

29. Jacqueline Feldman, "De FMA au MLF: Un témoignage sur les débuts du mouvement de libération des femmes," *Clio: Histoire, femmes et société* 29 (2009): 202. The meeting took place in the spring of 1970. At the time, Feldman still belonged to FMA (formerly Féminin, Masculin, Avenir, renamed Féminisme, Marxisme, Action). See also the account in Anne Zelensky, *Mémoires d'une féministe* (Paris: Calmann-Lévy, 2005), 48, 197.

30. The idea of a public manifesto came from progressive journalists at the *Nouvel Observateur*, people with a keen eye for the media and spectacular politics. Pavard, *Si je veux*, 139–41; "Matière pour une réflexion politique sur l'avortement," *Partisans*, "La libération des femmes: Année zéro," no. 54–55 (1970). French articles were published separately, some of them shortened, by Maspéro as "Petite Collection Maspéro," no. 106 (1972).

31. See Guy Sitbon's cover story "Avortement: La France hors la loi," *Nouvel Observateur*, November 20, 1972, 54–58.

32. Rochefort, "L'idiot liberté," *Le Torchon Brûle*, cited in Bernheim et al., *MLF Textes*, 171–72. "*Boulot, Omo, Marmots, y'en a marre! Contraception pour toutes et tous; avortement libre et gratuit*" ("Work, Washing, Kids—we've had enough. Contraception for all, legal and free abortion." Omo is a laundry detergent, *marmots* is slang for kids; the phrase played on the left critique of *metro-boulot-dodo*, an expression that literally translates as *commute-work-sleep*, but is more akin to the English phrase "rat race.") Bernheim et al., *MLF Textes*, 99, 101. See Greenwald, *Daughters of 1968*, 120–23, for a good discussion of the press. *Le Torchon Brûle* is also online at http://archivesautonomies.org/IMG/pdf/feminisme/torchonbrule.

33. Beauvoir, Lettres reçues de lecteurs, undated, 1971–72, Paris; March 10, 1972; November 23, 1972; September 30, 1972; April 9, 1971. Only a few opponents of legalizing abortion wrote to Beauvoir. See May 5, 1971; and June 30, 1972.

34. Ibid., February 24, 1972. 3,000 francs in 1972 is roughly equivalent to 3,500 dollars in 2019.

35. Ibid., February 24, 1972. See also February 22, 1972, and May 3, 1971.

36. Tony Judt, *Postwar: A History of Europe since 1945* (New York: Penguin Books, 2006), 489. This statistic comes from research conducted by the French Institute for Demographic Studies (INED). Chantal Blayo, "L'enregistrement des avortements en Angleterre, au Pays de Galles et au Danemark," *Population* 29e année, no. 2 (1974): 333.

37. Beauvoir, Lettres reçues de lecteurs, November 4, 1972. See Nancy K. Miller's account of nearly compulsory casual sex, the terror of pregnancy, traveling from Paris to London to get a diaphragm, getting hormone shots from a doctor to bring on her period, and so on. Nancy K. Miller, *Breathless: An American Girl in Paris* (Berkeley: Seal Press, 2013), 46.

38. Grégoire's papers are at the departmental archives of the Indre-et-Loire: Archives Contemporaines, Tours, France, Fonds Menie Grégoire, 1948–2005, FR AD37, ser. J 66, cartons 35–63, Lettres passées à l'antenne"; cartons 176–282, Lettres classées par thème, esp. 228, "*avortements.*" On shifting opinion, see Sevegrand, *Les enfants*, 183–85. The overlapping

audiences are mentioned in Beauvoir, Lettres reçues de lecteurs, February 13, 1970; and undated, 1972, Paris.

39. Fonds Grégoire, J 66, 228, November 30, 1971, Rochefort, Charente Maritime, France.

40. Ibid., May 8, 1971, Créteil, Val de Marne, France. See also May 6, 1971, Seine et Marne, France.

41. Ibid., June 16, 1971, Saône et Loire.

42. Beauvoir, Lettres reçues de lecteurs, January 19, 1972, Saint-Cloud, France.

43. Fonds Grégoire, J 66, 228, February 10, 1970.

44. Beauvoir, Lettres reçues de lecteurs, December 21, 1973, L'Haÿ-les-Roses, France.

45. Fonds Grégoire, J 66, 228, July 5, 1971, Rémilly, France.

46. Pavard, Si je veux, 145. See Le livre blanc de l'avortement, published by the Club de l'OBS, no. 2 (1971): 89–185. Some of the letters are signed; many are from doctors.

47. The protest continued against a public roundtable broadcast from the Salle Pleyel on "the painful problem of homosexuality" in March 1971. Michael Sibalis, "Gay Liberation Comes to France: The Front Homosexuel d'Action Révolutionnaire (FHAR)," French History and Civilization 1 (2005): 265–76.

48. Tout!, no. 12 (April 1971), cited in Sébastien Chauvin, "Les aventures d'une 'alliance objective': Quelques moments de la relation entre mouvements homosexuels et mouvements féministes au xxe siècle," L'Homme et la Société 158 (2005): 117; Todd Shepard, Sex, France, and Arab Men: 1962–1979 (Chicago: University of Chicago Press, 2017).

49. Frédéric Martel, Le rose et le noir: Les homosexuels en France depuis 1968 (Paris: Seuil, 2000), 58. On the relationship between women's liberation and the FHAR in 1971–72, see Chauvin, "Les aventures d'une 'alliance objective,'" 111–30; and Julian Jackson, Living in Arcadia (Chicago: University of Chicago Press, 2009). For a less cheerful interpretation, see Marie-Josèphe Bonnet, "Gay Mimesis and Misogyny: Two Aspects of the Same Refusal of the Other," in Homosexuality in French History and Culture, ed. Jeffrey Merrick and Michael Sibalis (New York: Harrington Park Press, 2001), 265–80.

50. Bernheim, Perturbation, 87. See also the interview with Cathy Bernheim, "Les féministes sont-elles des femmes?," Le Nouvel Observateur, July 4, 2012, http://feministesentous genres.blogs.nouvelobs.com/cathy-bernheim/.

51. Zelensky, Mémoires, 58; Françoise d'Eaubonne, "Le FHAR, origines et illustrations," Revue h, no. 2 (1996): 24.

52. "Le mythe de la frigidité féminine," Partisans, no. 54–55 (1970), 61; Rochefort, cited in Picq, Libération des femmes, 34–35.

53. See Elinor Accampo, Blessed Motherhood, Bitter Fruit: Nelly Roussel and the Politics of Female Pain in Third Republic France (Baltimore: Johns Hopkins University Press, 2006).

54. Beauvoir, Lettres reçues de lecteurs, November 5, 1972.

55. Simone de Beauvoir, Tout compte fait (Paris: Gallimard, 1972), 626–27, hereafter TCF.

56. Gérard Zwang was a French urologist, surgeon, and clinical sexologist, author of Le sexe de la femme and the illustrated Atlas du sexe de la femme (both published in 1967). Beauvoir cites Zwang in TCF, 627.

57. Beauvoir, Lettres reçues de lecteurs, August 1, 1973, Luxembourg.

58. Anne Koedt, "The Myth of the Vaginal Orgasm" (1968), reprinted in "La libération des femmes: Année zéro," Partisans, no. 54–55 (1970): 54–60. See Jane Gerhard, "Revisiting 'The Myth of the Vaginal Orgasm': The Female Orgasm in American Sexual Thought and Second Wave Feminism," Feminist Studies 26, no. 2 (Summer 2000): 449–76.

59. Beauvoir, Lettres reçues de lecteurs, October 24, 1972.

60. Marie-Josèphe Bonnet, Simone de Beauvoir et les femmes (Paris: Albin Michel, 2015), 158–62; Margaret A. Simons, "Lesbian Connections: Simone de Beauvoir and Feminism,"

Signs 18, no. 1 (Autumn 1992): 136–61; Ursula Tidd, "'Le deuxième sexe,' la conscience noire et la conscience lesbienne," *Cinquantenaire du "Deuxième sexe,"* ed. Christine Delphy and Sylvie Chaperon (Paris: Syllepse, 2002), 72–80. Michael Lucey's careful analysis of Beauvoir's "complicatedly dissociative sexuality"—how, for instance, *She Came to Stay* could be read—is much more appreciative of what letter writers plainly saw as Beauvoir's queer-friendliness. Michael Lucey, *Someone: The Pragmatics of Misfit Sexualities, from Colette to Hervé Guibert* (Chicago: University of Chicago Press, 2019), 108–38.

61. Beauvoir, Lettres reçues de lecteurs, November 21, 1956 (see also January 1, 1957); November 21 and April 3, 1956; September 11, 1962, Cornwall, England. On how Christine Jorgensen's story made international headlines in 1952, see Joanne Meyerowitz, *How Sex Changed* (Cambridge: Harvard University Press, 1980).

62. Beauvoir, *TSS* 1953, 407.

63. Beauvoir, Lettres reçues de lecteurs, August 6, 1963, Paris; undated, 1968.

64. Beauvoir, *TSS* 1953, 406.

65. Lucey, *Someone*, 136.

66. Ibid., chap. 6 on Leduc.

67. Beauvoir, Lettres reçues de lecteurs, February 2, 1965; December 28, 1965; April 19, 1968.

68. Ibid., November 9, 1972 (see also February 9, 1972); October 24, 1972; undated, 1970.

69. Ibid., December 11, 1972. See also August 27, 1968.

70. Ibid., undated, 1968, Le Bouscat, France.

71. Ibid., February 11, 1973. This is part of series of letters: January 3, 5, 7, and 25; February 6, 8, and 11; and December 15, 1973.

72. Ibid., May 26, 1968, Paris.

73. Ibid., October 18, 1971, Nice, France.

74. For Marie-Claire Chevalier's testimony, see *Avortement, une loi en procès: L'Affaire de Bobigny* (Paris: Gallimard, 1973), 39–46.

75. The medical profession surveyed its members and found the profession divided. There was a strong current of opinion in favor of liberalizing the law, however, and very few doctors were willing to condemn women who had abortions, let alone prosecute them. Catherine Valenti, *Bobigny: Le procès de l'avortement* (Paris: Broché, 2010), 90–91.

76. For a good, crisp analysis of the movement and Beauvoir's position, see Sylvie Chaperon, "The MLF and the Bobigny Affair," in *Simone de Beauvoir, Feminist Writings,* ed. Margaret A. Simons and Marybeth Timmerman (Urbana: University of Illinois Press, 2015), 181–89. In the second trial, the trial of the older women, Halimi defended Michèle Chevalier and her friends Renée Sausset and Lucette Duboucheix. Micheline Bambuck, the abortionist, chose not to be defended by Choisir. *Avortement*, 39.

77. Halimi, *Right to Choose*, 53; Zelensky, *Mémoires*, 61.

78. Bambuck's testimony, *Avortement*, 39.

79. Witness testimony, *Avortement*, 87, 121.

80. Beauvoir, Lettres reçues de lecteurs, November 18, 1972.

81. Ibid., March 6, 1972; followed up March 11, 1972.

82. On disagreements about courtroom strategy, see Halimi, *Right to Choose*, 46–47, 50–57; and Chaperon, "The MLF and the Bobigny Affair," 188.

83. Valenti, *Bobigny*, 95–98; Halimi, *Right to Choose*, 55.

84. Beauvoir, Lettres reçues de lecteurs, November 5 and 11, 1972. Conservatives were particularly shocked to hear women testify without the requisite somber and traumatized demeanor. Ibid., December 29, 1972. For Choisir's position, see *Le Torchon Brûle*, no. 5 (1972).

85. Beauvoir, Lettres reçues de lecteurs, December 11, 1972.

86. Manicom speaking at Mutualité in 1972, quoted in Patrick Siry, "Bobigny: Entre l'absurde et la honte," *Le Nouvel Observateur,* November 27–December 3, 1972, 59. Jacqueline Manicom (1935–1976) was writing her partly autobiographical *Mon examen de blanc* (Paris: Sarrazin, 1972). She was also compiling case studies of her own patients and fellow workers of color in *La graine: Journal d'une sage femme* (Paris: Éditions France Loisirs, 1974). Her testimony at Bobigny is in *Avortements,* 89–90.

87. "La femme revoltée," *Le Nouvel Observateur,* February 14, 1972, 47–53.

88. The *Nouvel Observateur* had just published an important interview with Guy Hocquenghem by François Paul Concour, "La révolution des homosexuels," *Le Nouvel Observateur*, January 10, 1972, 32–35.

89. Beauvoir, Lettres reçues de lecteurs, February 14, 1972; January 19, 1972; April 19, 1972.

90. Ibid., February 24, 1972; February 22, 1972; March 9, 1972. Beauvoir responded to her critics; see "Débat: Réponse à quelques femmes et à un homme," *Le Nouvel Observateur,* March 6, 1972, 40. That brought her yet more letters. See Lettres reçues de lecteurs, March 5, 1972; March 8, 1972; March 9, 1972; March 15, 1972.

91. Beauvoir's account is in *TCF*, 497.

92. Joan Wallach Scott, *The Fantasy of Feminist History* (Durham: Duke University Press, 2011), 19, 30–31.

93. Picq, *Libération*, 14; Claire Duchene, *Feminism in France from May '68 to Mitterand* (London: Routledge, 2013), 19–21; Nelcya Delanoë, "Quelques réflexions," *Partisans*, no. 54–55 (1970): 101–4.

94. Beauvoir, Lettres reçues de lecteurs, undated (1968), Marseille.

95. Rochefort, "La Politique, c'est la vie même," in *Le Torchon Brûle*, cited in *MLF: textes*, 125–26.

96. See Margaretta Jolly, *In Love and Struggle: Letters in Contemporary Feminism* (New York: Columbia University Press, 2010), 13.

97. Dagmar Herzog, *Sexuality in Europe: A Twentieth-Century History* (Cambridge: Cambridge University Press, 2012), 5; Camille Robcis, "Catholics, the 'Theory of Gender,' and the Turn to the Human in France: A New Dreyfus Affair?," *Journal of Modern History* 87, no. 4 (December 2015): 892–99; "Liberté, Égalité, Hétérosexualité: Race and Reproduction in the French Gay Marriage Debates," *Constellations* 22, no. 3 (September 2015): 447–61.

Conclusion

1. Shulamith Firestone to Laya Firestone Seghi, July 1, 1968. Thanks to Susan Faludi.

2. Simone de Beauvoir, *Tout compte fait* (Paris: Gallimard, 1972), 576–82, hereafter *TCF*.

3. *Les Temps Modernes*, June 4, 1967, with Claude Lanzmann as chief editor. See Beauvoir, *TCF*, 548; and Yoav Di-Capua, *No Exit: Arab Existentialism, Jean Paul Sartre, and Decolonization* (New York: Columbia University Press, 2017).

In 1966 Beauvoir made a brief and awkward foray into the discussion of the Holocaust, writing the preface to Jean-François Steiner, *Treblinka: La révolte d'un camp d'extermination* (Paris: Fayard, 1966). Steiner's critics were outraged by his cold discussion of the absence of resistance in the camps and his suggestion that the *Sonderkommandos* had been complicit in genocide before they revolted. Beauvoir, characteristically, applauded Steiner's confrontation with shameful facts as part of the path to revived resistance. She had little to say about the specific character of anti-Semitism and the Shoah. That is not to say she fits the portrait of a clueless Sartrean in Samuel Moyn's book on the Treblinka controversy, *A Holocaust Controversy: The Treblinka Affair in Postwar France* (Waltham, Mass.: Brandeis University

Press, 2005), 49–50, 69–70. The preface generated a few letters; see Simone de Beauvoir, Lettres reçues, subheading Lettres reçues de lecteurs, Manuscrits, Occident, Bibliothèque Nationale de France, N.A.F. 28501, April 24, 1966; undated, 1971, Le Havre. Many letter writers wanted to talk to Beauvoir about deportations and the camps, but usually by recounting their own memories or family stories.

4. Deirdre Bair, *Simone de Beauvoir: A Biography* (New York: Summit Books, 1990), 522.

5. Beauvoir, Lettres reçues de lecteurs, January 19, 1970.

6. Susan Faludi, "Death of a Revolutionary," *The New Yorker*, April 15, 2013. For a nicely complex version of Beauvoir's role as icon for a new generation of feminists, see Geneviève Fraisse, *Le privilège de Simone de Beauvoir: Suivi de "Une mort douce"* (Arles: Actes Sud, 2008), 55–57, and Fraisse's writing in *Les Revoltes Logiques* (Paris: Éditions Solin, 1975–1981), a journal she created with Jacques Rancière.

7. See Elaine Marks and Isabelle de Courtivron, eds., *New French Feminisms: An Anthology* (Amherst: University of Massachusetts Press, 1980); and Catherine Rodgers, "Contemporary French Feminism and *Le Deuxième Sexe*," *Simone de Beauvoir Studies* 13 (1996): 78–88. Michèle Le Dœuff's very different and appreciative analysis of Beauvoir captured less attention in the United States, but Le Doeuff has proved a major figure in French feminism. See her "Simone de Beauvoir and Existentialism," *Feminist Studies* 6, no. 2 (Summer 1980): 277–89, and *Hipparchia's Choice: An Essay Concerning Women, Philosophy, Etc.* (Oxford: Blackwell, 1991). On the American side of things, Judith Butler reread Beauvoir to upend the distinction between sex and gender, and Toril Moi reread her as an alternative to Butler and the poststructuralist thinking on sex and gender. Judith Butler, "Sex and Gender in Simone de Beauvoir's *Second Sex*," *Yale French Studies*, no. 72, "Simone de Beauvoir: Witness to a Century" (1986): 35–49, *Gender Trouble* (New York: Routledge, 1990), and *Bodies That Matter: On the Discursive Limits of "Sex"* (New York: Routledge, 1993); Toril Moi, *What Is a Woman? And Other Essays* (New York: Oxford University Press, 1999). See also Nancy Bauer, *Simone de Beauvoir, Philosophy, and Feminism* (New York: Columbia University Press, 2001).

On the bitter sectarian disputes within French feminism as a movement, see Lisa Greenwald, *Daughters of 1968* (Lincoln: University of Nebraska Press, 2019), chap. 6.

8. On *La vieillesse* and *The Second Sex*, see Beauvoir, *TCF*, 183–87. Two reports from the Inspection Générale des Affaires Sociales came out at the same time: *Les problèmes sociaux des personnes âgées: Rapport annuel, 1968–1969*; and Marie-Madeleine Deinesch's *Consultation sur les problèmes d'action sociale en faveur des personnes agées* (Paris: IGAS, 1969). Christophe Capuano, *Que faire de nos vieux: Une histoire de la protection sociale de 1880 à nos jours* (Paris: Presses de Sciences Po., 2018). The English-language edition, *Old Age*, was reviewed in the *New York Times Magazine*, March 26, 1972; and by Rebecca West in the *Sunday Telegraph*, "Books of the Week: Meet France's Mrs. Gummidge," March 1972.

9. Beauvoir, Lettres reçues de lecteurs, May 19, 1970; August 14, 1970 (a Jewish woman from Woodmere, N.Y.); March 16, 1970 (a Catholic woman from France); November 12, 1970; November 30, 1970; March 23, 1970; January 25, 1970; April 20, 1970; August 19, 1970.

10. Ibid., June 25, 1970; January 8, 1970; October 20, 1970; January 26, 1970; January 17, 1970; June 12, 1970.

11. Ibid., March 19, 1970.

12. Ibid., May 27, 1970; undated, 1970 (3f).

13. Ibid., undated, 1970 (3f).

14. Monique Wittig, "La pensée straight," *Questions Féministes* 7 (February 1980): 45–53; Frédéric Martel, *The Pink and the Black*, trans. Jane Marie Todd (Stanford: Stanford University Press, 1999), 117; Greenwald, *Daughters of 1968*, 201–5.

15. Simone de Beauvoir, "Littérature et métaphysique," *Les Temps Modernes* 1, no. 7 (April 1946): 1153–63, reprinted in *L'existentialisme et la sagesse des nations* (Paris: Gallimard, 2008), 71–84; Toril Moi, "The Adventure of Reading: Literature and Philosophy, Cavell and Beauvoir," *Literature & Theology* 25, no. 2 (June 2011): 133.

16. Simone de Beauvoir et al., *Que peut la littérature?* (Paris: L'Herne, 1965), 82–83. Translation from Toril Moi, "What Can Literature Do? Simone de Beauvoir as a Literary Theorist," *PMLA* 124, no. 1 (2009): 189–98.

17. She wrote to Nelson Algren while working on *The Second Sex*, "When I see other women around me, I think they have very peculiar problems and it would be interesting to look at what is peculiar in them." Simone de Beauvoir, *A Transatlantic Love Affair: Letters to Nelson Algren*, trans. Sylvie Le Bon (New York: New Press, 1998), 135.

18. Marie-Josèphe Bonnet, *Simone de Beauvoir et les femmes* (Paris: Broché, 2015), 17. For the argument that Beauvoir was sympathetic, see Manon Garcia, *On ne naît pas soumise, on le devient* (Paris: Climats, 2018), chap. 5.

19. See Dominique Aury and Jane Albert-Hesse's reviews at the time of publication, in *"Le deuxième sexe" de Simone de Beauvoir: Textes réunis et présentés,* ed. Ingrid Galster (Paris: Presses de l'Université Paris-Sorbonne, 2004), 203–6 and 266–271.

20. Beauvoir, Lettres reçues de lecteurs, February 9, 1972.

21. Thanks to Indrani Chatterjee for this formulation.

22. Daniel Fabre, *Écritures ordinaires* (Paris: Éditions POL, Centre Georges Pompidou, 1993), 63. Fabre uses Pierre Nora's term loosely, as do I.

23. Kathryn T. Gines, "Simone de Beauvoir and the Race/Gender Analogy in *The Second Sex Revisited*"; Shannon Sullivan, "Race after Beauvoir"; and Diane Perpich, "Beauvoir's Legacy to the Quartiers: The Changing Face of French Feminism," all in *A Companion to Simone de Beauvoir*, ed. Laura Hengehold and Nancy Bauer (New York: John Wiley & Sons, 2017), 47–58, 449–62 489–99.

24. See Margaretta Jolly's particularly good discussion of the affective dynamics of "the feminist world of love and ritual" in *In Love and Struggle* (New York: Columbia University Press, 2009), 13.

25. Many authors get letters from readers. One of the most compelling evocations of that more general phenomenon or cultural practice comes from Belgian writer Amélie Nothomb. Nothomb describes herself as an avid letter writer, enthralled by and nearly compulsively attentive to letters from her readers. Her short novel, *Life Form* (2010), starts with an invented correspondence between her and one of her followers, a man who presents himself as a lonely, bored, and obese American soldier stationed in Iraq. Their epistolary exchange becomes increasingly fraught, riddled with power plays, provocations, intrigue, and deceptions, and the novel becomes an occasion for Nothomb to talk about letters she receives from readers. Her observations on the intensity of the reader-author relationship are wry and wonderful; we see that the dynamics in the Beauvoir correspondence are far from unique. Nothomb's readers boldly conjure up the excitement of discovered connection. Reader meets author "like Robinson Crusoe and Friday on the beach on the island!" They play with recognizing themselves or their opposites in the author: "[T]hat's just like me! That's just the opposite of me!" Nothomb muses on the perils of becoming entangled in this intimacy or infatuated with this apparent communion of souls. As an author, she writes, "you are so intoxicated that you cannot see the danger that lies just ahead. Suddenly the other is there, at your door. Others [the readers] have so many ways of moving in and imposing themselves." Beauvoir's readers moved into her work and have stayed there, and the letters in this archive create a rich novel of their own. Amélie Nothomb, *Life Form*, trans. Alison Anderson (New York: Europa Editions, 2012), 55–56. Nothomb is interviewed at https://www.youtube.com/watch?v=tNYyvqtcaE4.

Archival Sources

Archives Départementales d'Indre-et-Loire: Archives Contemporaines, Tours, France
  Fonds Ménie Grégoire, 1948–2005, FR AD37

Bibliothèque Marguerite Durand, Paris
  Dossiers: Avortement, contraception, MLF, *Le Torchon Brûle*, féminisme

Bibliothèque Nationale de France, Paris
  Simone de Beauvoir, 1908–1986, Lettres reçues, subheading Lettres reçues de lecteurs,
  Manuscrits, Occident, N.A.F. 28501

The Harry Ransom Center, University of Texas at Austin
  Alfred A. Knopf, Inc. Records, Series III, Blanche W. Knopf, 1918–1966, box 689,
  folders 12–13, Simone de Beauvoir
      ——. Series VII, Other Department Files, 1916–96, Bulk 1943–68
      ——. Subseries A, Publicity Dept., 1916–96, Bulk 1943–68
      ——. Sub-subseries 1, Publicity Files, 1916–1967, Bulk 1943–58, box 1177,
  folders 21–22; box 1300, folder 7

The Schlesinger Library, Radcliffe Institute for Advanced Study, Cambridge, Massachusetts
  Papers of Betty Friedan, 1933–1985, MC 575–577
  Papers of Ti-Grace Atkinson, 1938–2013, MC 785

INDEX